THE FOURTH FORCE

THE FOURTH FORCE

The Untold Story of the
Royal Fleet Auxiliary since 1945

Geoff Puddefoot

Seaforth
PUBLISHING

First published in Great Britain in 2009 by
Seaforth Publishing
An imprint of Pen & Sword Books Ltd
47 Church Street, Barnsley
S Yorkshire S70 2AS

www.seaforthpublishing.com
Email info@seaforthpublishing.com

British Library Cataloguing in Publication Data
A CIP data record for this book is available from the British Library

ISBN 978-1-84832-046-8

Designed and typeset by M.A.T.S Typesetters, Leigh-on-Sea, Essex

Printed and bound by MPG Books Group

Contents

List of Illustrations

A fine view of *Tidespring* showing the layout of the 'Later Tide' class. (*George Mortimore*)

PLATE 9
Royal Navy Wessex engaged in vertical replenishment. The squadron badge is just behind the cockpit. (*Gordon Wilson*)

Regent, one of the two R class ammunition ships that had a permanent Royal Navy flight embarked. (*George Mortimore*)

PLATE 10
Grey Rover off Nordenschold Glacier, South Georgia. (*Chris Locke*)

Grey Rover, Trafalgar Day, Falkland Islands. (*Chris Locke*)

PLATE 11
Grey Rover in heavy seas in the South Atlantic. (*Chris Locke*)

Grey Rover in a snow storm off South Georgia. (*Chris Locke*)

PLATE 12
Grey Rover: preparing to RAS HMS *Southampton*. (*Chris Locke*)

HMS *Southampton* seen through the gantries of *Grey Rover*. (*Chris Locke*)

RAS complete, HMS *Southampton* steams away. (*Chris Locke*)

PLATE 13
Sir Bedivere showing her new lines after a Service Life Extension Programme (SLEP). (*Shaun Jones*)

Cardigan Bay, one of the new LSD(A) – a monster compared to the Round Table class. (*Shaun Jones*)

PLATE 14
The replenishment tanker *Orangeleaf* at the 2005 Fleet Review. (*John Allix*)

Wave Ruler, one of two Wave class tankers built to replace the ageing Ol class fast fleet tankers. (*Shaun Jones*)

PLATE 15
Argus, helicopter training and primary casualty receiving ship, at the 2007 Fleet Review. (*John Allix*)

A Vulcan Phalanx rotary cannon, one of the RFA's most potent close-in weapons. (*John Allix*)

PLATE 16
Fort Victoria, dressed overall and with a Merlin helicopter on her flight deck, at the 2007 Fleet Review. (*John Allix*)

A Merlin helicopter embarked on *Fort Victoria*. (*John Allix*)

Acknowledgements and Preface

The author would like to acknowledge the help and advice of Captain Shane Redmond OBE RFA (Retd), Gordon Wilson, Martyn Hobbs, Captain C Puxley RFA (Rtd), David Soden, George Mortimore, and all of the serving and former members of the RFA, too numerous to name individually, who took the time to supply information, anecdotes and photographs, without which this book would not have been possible. Grateful thanks are also due to Commodore R C Thornton, CBE, RFA (Retd), for his contributions on pages 80–85 and 175–176 and for which he retains the copyright.

Especial thanks are due to Roger Jordan, who provided much essential, additional information about the various ship classes. Vice-Admiral Sir Jeremy Blackstone, RN (rtd), Editor of *The Naval Review*, also kindly allowed extracts from that publication to be used.

I would also like to acknowledge the help of both Bexley Library Services and Dartford Library Services staff and the staff at the National Archive and the National Maritime Museum.

In any book on as extensive a subject as the Royal Fleet Auxiliary, the problem is not so much what to include as what to leave out from the vast amount of material the subject encompasses.

I have therefore chosen to include predominantly material, information and personal accounts that reflect the character and development of the service, rather than introducing strictly technical matters that have been dealt with exhaustively elsewhere.

This probably means that some areas are less well and fully documented than would otherwise have been the case. It is, however, my hope that the extensive reference section will serve as an adequate guide to those whose researches require more depth of knowledge than they find available here.

Introduction

Logistic supply has always presented the Royal Navy with one of its major problems and the way in which solutions were developed in the years before the Second World War and during that conflict marked the beginnings of an 'afloat' replenishment service for the Royal Navy.

Postwar changes, however, although in many ways more subtle, were just as significant, and were concerned, among other things, with the loss or change of status of most of Britain's overseas holdings and the contraction of the Royal Navy, both in terms of ships and personnel.

Although naval vessels were tending to become smaller, these were much more complex, with increasingly powerful weapon systems. These changes were particularly reflected in areas such as detection systems and communications as well as, with a serious cold war situation developing, the need to deploy nuclear weapons aboard both surface ships and submarines.

Alongside this naval evolution, changes, of necessity, occurred in the way that logistic support had to be delivered, resulting in the appearance of RFA ships equipped in ways which could never have been imagined, even as late as the 1930s. And with improved ships came improved training and an RFA whose personnel are well able to take care of the Royal Navy's demands, no matter what they are, anywhere, any time and in any weather.

Because one thing did not and has not changed:

R F A still means

Ready For Anything.

Chapter 1

Postwar Changes and the First Tide Class: 1950–9

The service that emerged from the devastation of the Second World War was almost unrecognisable from that which had entered the conflict.

Fundamental technological changes, such as replenishing both fuel and stores while at sea had taken place, changing what had been predominantly a freighting service into a much more professional organisation, beginning to be capable of supplying all the Navy's requirements in an 'afloat' capacity.

Technological change was to become one of the main characteristics of the RFA post war, along with a clear realisation of the demands that such changes made on personnel. Royal Navy thinking in some quarters had even begun to consider a service based on the US plan, whose auxiliaries in the Pacific Fleet train, for example, had been commissioned into the United States Navy, thus achieving a parity of command, pay and conditions for all men serving in the Pacific war zone (see, *eg*, *Naval Review 1950*).

The first real signs of this new style RFA were the addition, in 1954, of the early Tide class replenishment tankers to the fleet.

Admiralty designed, these were large, fast ships, built to remain at sea for long periods in all conditions. Construction was of a standard more reminiscent of a warship than a commercial tanker, with, for example, three boilers and engine room remote controls, constructed of stainless steel, for use in the event of a nuclear attack. This innovative design also owed much to Royal Navy experiments with HMS *Bulawayo*, which was a captured German fleet oiler.

Furnace fuel oil (FFO), aviation spirit (AVCAT), aviation gasoline (AVGAS) and diesel (DIESO) were carried in separate tanks, with their own dedicated pumps and sufficient power to allow all these pumps to be used while steaming at fifteen knots. Three of the new jackstay systems with steam driven, self-tensioning winches were fitted, along with five large derrick rigs. They also had the capability of streaming three hoses astern, specifically for use with aircraft carriers. These new developments meant that the Tide class vessels could easily replenish three vessels at once, even if one of them was an aircraft carrier.

Acquisition of these new Tide class vessels marked a turning point for the service which was, in some ways, as significant as the changes which were implemented after the Falklands. They were far in advance of any vessel the RFA was using up to that time, in terms of both technology and performance but what is not generally known is that they were nearly never built at all because the Admiralty, despite a well-publicised stance on modernisation, could not, or perhaps rather, declined to find enough money from the Navy Vote to pay for them!

The story of the search for a fast fleet replenishment tanker began in August 1950, when a meeting took place in the Admiralty between representatives of the Royal Navy and the Department of Transport to discuss a proposal that had been brought to them by Simpson, Spence & Young, a firm of London shipbrokers.

In simple terms, its proposal was that four ship owners, that the brokers represented, would each undertake to build a fast fleet replenishment tanker to Admiralty specification. It would have a total deadweight of 17,500 tons, later increased to 20,000, a speed with clean bottom in still water in excess of eighteen knots and carry all the necessary gear to conduct extensive replenishment activities. These ships would be chartered like normal tankers in peacetime, but in the event of war, they would be returned to the Admiralty and operated as fast fleet replenishment tankers.

Such a tanker, however, would probably not show a profit when operated at normal freight rates so there was, of course, a catch. In order to build the vessels, the ship-owners wanted a loan for the total cost at an interest rate of 2 per cent, repayable over ten years and they wanted long-term charters for the vessels to have been arranged ... before building began.

The Royal Navy was enthusiastic. There had been several embarrassing experiences with the Pacific Fleet Train, when the older RFAs, some only capable of eight knots while conducting a replenishment operation, could have proved a liability. There was clearly a need for fast replenishment tankers, capable of keeping up with the fleet while refuelling, to minimise the danger from attack by enemy surface forces and, more especially, submarines.

They were not so enthusiastic about the cost of such a vessel, though, which was estimated at £1.9 million,

Although it was very quickly agreed that Simpson, Spence & Young's proposal was, in the succinct appreciation of one civil servant, 'a non-starter', discussion did proceed around the possibility of the government itself building such a vessel, as the meeting put it 'in times of depression in the industry so as to stimulate investment in shipbuilding'.

It was further proposed that such tankers, when not in use by the Royal Navy, could be put out to charter, presumably thereby reducing their running expenses. Prewar RFA experiences of trying to run even a freighting service in this way seem to have been completely ignored. Perhaps the idea was to ask the Soviet Union to wait before declaring war until the ships could be returned from charter, defects made good, the crews trained for RAS, after which, the RFAs could then be sent scurrying after the warships!

There was no RFA representative at this or any of the subsequent meetings, which was unfortunate, because perhaps then several of these flaws, in what must have seemed an eminently sensible idea to land-locked Whitehall civil servants, could have been pointed out to them – probably in unprintable words of one syllable.

As might be expected, the whole idea eventually died from lack of interest on the part of the tanker companies but, by now, a fleet tanker especially built for replenishment at speeds in excess of eighteen knots was becoming, in naval circles at least, of increasing, if not vital, importance.

As a result of this increased naval interest, the first of what came to be known as the early Tide class, *Tide Austral* was laid down in late 1952, with *Tiderace*, *Tiderange* and *Tidereach* started in the following year.

RFA fleet list 1950

Fast replenishment tanker
Olna
Freighting tankers modified for fuelling at sea
Wave Baron, Wave Chief, Wave Knight, Wave Master, Wave Prince, Wave Ruler, Wave Sovereign, Wave Victor
Freighting tankers
Wave Commander, Wave Conqueror, Wave Duke, Wave Emperor, Wave Governor, Wave King, Wave Laird, Wave Liberator, Wave Monarch, Wave Premier, Wave Protector, Wave Regent
Abbeydale, Arndale, Bishopdale, Broomdale, Cedardale, Denbydale, Derwentdale, Dewdale, Dingledale, Eaglesdale, Easedale, Echodale, Ennerdale
War Afridi, War Brahmin, War Hindoo
Olcades
Fleet attendant tankers
Black Ranger, Blue Ranger, Brown Ranger, Gold Ranger, Green Ranger
2,000 ton class
Belgol, Celerol, Serbol, Fortol, Prestol, Serbol
1,000 ton Class
Boxol, Elmol, Elderol, Larchol, Limol, Philol
1,500 ton class
Birchol, Rowanol, Oakol, Teakol
Miscellaneous
Airsprite, Nasprite, Spabeck, Spaburn, Petrobus
Store ships and issuing ships
Bacchus, Fort Beauharnois, Fort Charlotte, Fort Constantine, Fort Duquesne, Fort Rosalie, Fort Sandusky
Robert Dundas, Robert Middleton
Salvage vessels
Dispenser, Kinbrace, Succour, Swin
King Salvor, Ocean Salvor, Prince Salvor, Salvestor, Salvictor, Salviola, Sea Salvor
Tugs
Allegiance, Antic, Cautious, Destiny, Earner, Empire Demon, Empire Netta, Empire Plane, Empire Rita, Empire Rosa, Empire Zona, Enforcer, Envoy, Jaunty, Prosperous, Regard, Saucy, Sparkler, Turmoil
Royal research ships
Discovery II, William Scoresby
Hospital ship
Maine

Total: 106 vessels

These vessels were operated by crews on a variety of agreements, with many ships having been laid up or hulked for a number of years.

Several reforms were discussed in connection with these ships. Of particular interest, was the suggestion that the vessels might be wholly manned by naval ratings. Although naval staffing at that time was rejected, principally on the grounds of cost, the Royal Navy requiring two watches to do what the RFA did with one, the spectre of naval manning for RFAs has never really disappeared, as is clear from several of the developments in today's service.

Another suggestion involved the training of a specialist third engineer officer, to be wholly responsible for the new, complex, auto-tensioning winches. This seems never to have materialised, either, as an ex-RFA officer recalls:

> As I remember, on RFA *Tidereach* (1957) and *Tide Austral* (1960), an engine room PO and a Third Engineer Officer (designated 'deck third') were responsible for all deck machinery. During RAS it was usual for the Second Engineer (2E/O) to remain on deck, with the Chief Engineer Officer (CEO) in the Machinery Control Room (MCR).
>
> With the introduction into service of the 'O' Class the CEO – 2E/O roles during RAS reversed and the CEO usually stationed himself in the Replenishment Control Room (RASCO) with the Chief Officer and the 2EO in the MCR.

None of these Tides were used exclusively for fleet replenishment, since on a number of occasions they transported Admiralty oil from the United States (Baton Rouge in one instance) to the UK. They did not, however, ever appear to have been put out to commercial charter!

Incidentally, a scheme similar to that suggested for tankers was presented to the Admiralty by Watts Shipping, in 1956, to build store ships, using Canadian government money. This Canadian loan would be guaranteed by the Treasury and once again, government assurances not being forthcoming, the scheme was abandoned.

Two of the three new Tide class fast fleet tankers, *Tidereach* and *Tiderange* joined the Fleet in 1955, along with their sister ship *Tide Austral*, which was intended for the Commonwealth of Australia, Department of the Navy. RFA *Tiderace* was completed a year later, in 1956. The Admiralty, in fact, used *Tide Austral* for some years before it was delivered to Australia. In 1958, both *Tiderace* and *Tiderange* underwent a name change because it was found there was some confusion with other ships of the class, *Tiderace* being changed to *Tideflow* and *Tiderange* to *Tidesurge*, after a signal was sent to one of the ships to return to harbour, and the wrong one turned up!

As well as the early Tides, the Eddy class of Admiralty-designed fleet attendant tankers was also introduced during this decade, along with several vessels in the Surf, Fort and Leaf classes. The first of the Eddy class, *Eddybeach*, was completed in December 1951.

A new RFA hospital ship was laid down at Barclay, Curle & Co Ltd, at Whiteinch, Glasgow, on 20 February 1952, and this was intended to replace the elderly *Maine*, which was sold for breaking up in 1954. The order was cancelled in July of the same year, leaving the Royal Navy with no purpose-built hospital ship until *Argus* was re-equipped in 2007, although the Royal Yacht *Britannia* was designed to serve as a hospital ship in wartime.

The RRS *Discovery II* was transferred to the DoS for RFA manning in 1950, while *Retainer* and *Resurgent*, formerly the commercially owned sisterships *Chungking* and *Chungchow* were acquired by the Admiralty in 1952 for conversion to armament support ships. Several tugs, and 'C' (coaling) and yard craft also came into service during this period, and these were manned by RFA crews under Yard Craft, Home Trade and Dockyard D606 agreements.

Finally, in an unusually far-sighted move, the motor vessel *Somersby* was purchased in 1957 for conversion to an air stores support ship, subsequently being renamed *Reliant*. An ex-RFA master remembers the circumstances of *Somersby*'s purchase:

> *Somersby* was originally purchased from the Ropner Shipping Company, initially to run stores to Christmas Island and on the return voyage collect the remaining redundant stores and equipment from Trincomalee as that nbase closed down. On completion of discharge at Rosyth in February 1958 she went for conversion.

Deaths in service with the RFA are sometimes unavoidable and, unfortunately, one such instance occurred in 1950 aboard *Wave Commander*.

Tank cleaning was in progress after dinner when the bosun entered No 6 centre tank, against the orders of the chief officer, to finish cleaning. He was overcome by gas and AB Morris Ellis descended the tank ladder and secured the bosun to it.

Unfortunately, Ellis himself was affected by the fumes and fell from the ladder, hitting one of the frames at the bottom of the tank, fracturing his neck and skull in the process. Death was instantaneous. Morris Richard Ellis was later posthumously awarded one of only two Albert medals awarded to RFA personnel.

Royal Fleet Auxiliary losses are not just confined to personnel and 1951 saw the tragic loss of the former RFA *Bedenham*, then commissioned as a naval armaments vessel, which exploded while unloading her cargo of depth charges into a lighter, having previously tied up to Gun Wharf in Gibraltar Dockyard. One of the depth charges ignited in the lighter, causing a fire, which spread rapidly to *Bedenham*.

Although abandoned by most of her crew when the fire started, her captain and the naval armament stores officer remained on board, only to be blown into the water when the ship subsequently exploded. Both officers were rescued, having sustained no serious injury, although thirteen other people were killed, including George Campbell Henderson, a sub officer in the Gibraltar Dockyard Fire Service. Hundreds were also injured and many of Gibraltar's buildings, including much of the newly constructed postwar housing, were badly damaged, for which the Admiralty paid a massive £250,000 in damages. Henderson was posthumously awarded the George Cross.

Although the RFA's accident record at sea is exemplary, there were also several incidents of this sort during the 1950s.

Wave Ruler was disabled off Oporto on 19 September 1953, while on passage from the Persian Gulf to Swansea with a cargo of oil. She signalled Devonport that she had lost all steam and was drifting south at about one knot. Devonport immediately dispatched the destroyer HMS *Zephyr* from Portland and the tug *Careful* from Plymouth to assist. Late on the night of 28 September, however, *Wave Ruler* ran aground on a sandbank outside Swansea. She could not be refloated with the contents of her tanks still aboard, so, on 30 September, *Wave Monarch* began pumping over her cargo of crude oil. By Monday 3 October, she had been lightened sufficiently to be refloated and subsequently entered Swansea dry dock for repair.

Wave Victor was also unlucky. On 18 January 1952, when an engine room fuel unit caught fire, while she was on voyage in ballast from Swansea to Fawley, near Southhampton. So fierce was the blaze that, within minutes of reporting the fire, a radio message was received reporting that the crew was preparing to abandon ship, although fortunately, she was only nine miles off Bull Point, near Ilfracombe, at the time. The ship was so close to the shore that people walking on the cliff path actually saw the smoke pouring from her and her distress flares.

Several ships came to her aid including the frigate HMS *Carisbrooke Castle*, tugs from Swansea, Milford Haven, Pembroke, Falmouth and Plymouth as well as the Appledore, Minehead and Ilfracombe lifeboats. There were even six members of the Swansea Fire Brigade embarked aboard the tug *Nirumand*!

Captain F C Holt, master of the tanker, and several crew members wanted to remain aboard but the danger of explosion made this impossible, so Captain Holt, seven officers and sixteen crew members transferred to the Appledore lifeboat. The lifeboat then stood by to warn other shipping and await the arrival of firefighting vessels from Swansea. Within hours, the fire had been extinguished and Captain Holt and his men reboarded and secured a tow from *Nirumand*, subsequently arriving in Swansea docks, later that evening.

In line with the new RAS technology now being introduced were changes in personnel recruitment. This chiefly entailed an increasing use of company service contracts when employing officers (contracts originally introduced in 1936) and petty officers (contracts introduced in 1947), so as to try and retain in the service a permanent corps of individuals with the necessary training and experience to ensure the RFA fleet operated efficiently.

Ratings joined the RFA either at age eighteen as ordinary seaman or, if older, as deckhand uncertificated (DHU). In either case, after eighteen months at sea, they sat a Board of Trade examination to be rated as efficient deck hand (EDH). Having returned to sea and subsequently passed his lifeboat certificate, a man was then rated able seaman (AB). Petty officers were promoted from able seaman from within the service.

Deck and engineering officers trained for their certificates of competence or 'tickets' in the same way as ordinary Merchant Navy officers, while also being able to participate in specialist Merchant Navy courses in, for example, firefighting. No provision was made during this period, however, for training either officers or ratings specifically for service in RFAs.

Chief Officer Chris Puxley studied for his certificates in the late 1960s:

I paid off from *Oleander* in Portsmouth (August 1966: apprenticeship begun in January 1964 age 17), having finally got enough sea-time to be able to sit for my 2nd Mate (Foreign Going) examination, the first real academic hurdle of my sea-going career.

Normally, a three month period of 'paid study leave' was granted by reputable shipping companies to their deck cadets, which became a period of intense cramming at one of the few colleges of maritime studies located around the UK. At that time there were six written examination papers and an oral examination to pass in order to obtain a 2nd Mate (Foreign Going) ticket.

The written papers were on the following subjects: 'General Ship Knowledge', including questions on cargo work and ship construction (three hours. There was no minimum pass mark on this subject but marks counted towards overall average percentage); 'Chart Work' (two hours plus oral questions, min. 70 per cent to pass); 'Practical Navigation' (three hours, min. 70 per cent to pass); 'Mathematics' (two hours, min 50 per cent to pass); 'Principles of Navigation' (two hours, 50 per cent to pass); and 'English' (1.5 hours, 50 per cent to pass).

Each subject covered a broad spectrum of possible questions and any weakness detected in the written answers was pounced on later by the 'oral' examiner. Usually it was only those who had really put the work in who later attained the required pass-mark.

Similarly, for his First Mate's (Foreign Going) certificate:

Two years later, I paid off the *Resource* at Plymouth (March 1968), having by now gained enough sea time to go to college and study for all the examinations which, if I passed, would gain me a Board of Trade 'First Mate (Foreign Going)' Certificate.

The subjects covered to obtain this qualification were: 'Navigation' (three hours, minimum 70 per cent to pass); 'Chart Work' (two hours, 70 per cent to pass); 'Ship Construction & Stability' (three hours, 50 per cent to pass); 'Meteorology' (two hours, no minimum pass mark but marks counted towards overall average percentage); 'Ship Maintenance, Routine and Cargo Work' (three hours, 50 per cent to pass); and 'Elementary Magnetism, Electricity and the Gyro Compass' (two hours, no minimum pass mark but marks counted towards overall average percentage).

As with 2nd Mates, the written exams were followed by an oral examination and a 'Signals' examination.

Later, he studied for his Master's certifcate:

Having paid off from *Engadine*, I now looked forward to a long spell ashore again but with some apprehension about the amount of work I would need to cover at the Plymouth College of Maritime Studies, in order to be ready to sit for my Master's ticket (June 1971).

Once again there were a series of written examinations to be passed, accompanied by the dreaded oral examination, which for 'Master's' included a session on compass adjustment. Ship's magnetic compasses are naturally affected by the steel of the ship on which they are mounted. Compensatory magnets need to be strategically placed around the compass to counter and eliminate the ship's own magnetic effect. This then allows the Earth's magnetic field alone to influence the compass. A rudimentary ship model called a 'deviascope' is used to teach and examine students on the 'black art' of compass adjustment! Lumps of iron are hidden underneath and around the 'deviascope' compass by the examiner. The student then, following a recognised procedure, has to compensate for their effect. This varies as the model is swung through 360 degrees or tilted from side to side. Any small residual compass error is called 'deviation' and is recorded in graph form on a 'deviation card'. Survivors of this ordeal then underwent the 'Signals' examination, which included a working knowledge of the 'International Code of Signals', as well as reading and sending semaphore and Morse code blocks of random letters/numbers and messages.

The written papers for Master's were: 'Navigation' (three hours, minimum 70 per cent to pass); 'Magnetic and Gyro Compass' (three hours, 50 per cent to pass); 'Ship Construction and Stability' (three hours, 50 per cent to pass); 'Ship Master's Business' (two hours, 50 per cent to pass); 'Engineering and Radio Aids' (three hours, no minimum pass mark but marks counted towards overall average); and 'Meteorology' (two hours, again no minimum pass mark but marks counted towards overall average). An overall average of 70 per cent had to be attained in order to pass the examination.

Officers, petty officers and ratings alike were still employed by the master of the RFA that they joined, just like any ordinary merchant vessel, although the master himself was invariably a permanent employee under contract. This entailed the men concerned simply signing a form of the usual Board of Trade (BoT) Articles of Agreement, without which no man could sail or serve on a British merchant ship.

Several different types of BoT Articles were in use by the RFA during this period, designed to meet specific needs:

- *Foreign Going Articles* covered voyages to a foreign port outside home trade limits unless specified otherwise. Broadly speaking, this meant outside 12 degrees West and near Europe, with a maximum duration of two years.
- *Home Trade Articles* were for use within those limits and covered multiple short voyages with an overall time limit – for example *Rowanol*, when Clyde Tanker, had a six-month home trade agreement as did *Eddyfirth* and other UK coastal runners. They were also used in *Black Ranger* at Portland, prior to 1962.
- *Running Agreements*, which came into use in the early 1960s, were for a specified length of time regardless of area; *Black Ranger*, for example, when operating as Portland tanker used a Running Agreement, after 1962, as did most RFAs. Agreements ended upon return to home port regardless of the time left to elapse.
- *Company Service Contract*. If, however, along with his Articles, an individual had a Company Service Contract (CSC), with the RFA or any other shipping company for that matter, the company employing him could send him to any ship as and when they felt it to be necessary, where he had to remain, which was, of course, an arrangement much to the employer's advantage.

To make up for this, men on CSCs were paid slightly more than their non-contracted colleagues as well as having a pension scheme, although during the 1950s at least, not much notice seems to have been taken of the contracts' terms and conditions. As one retired RFA master put it:

If he felt like it, a contract man could still give a 48 [48 hours notice] and leave the ship. When he was ready to come back, unless there was some disciplinary reason for not doing so, he was usually taken on again, with what amounted to a gentle slap on the wrist.

The same officer also had a story about one of his early experiences with RFA employment practices:

As a young 3rd Officer I joined RFA *Olna* and sailed Westabout for Xmas Island and The Far East. On the way home I was told to transfer at Aden to *Tide Austral* then on passage to Singapore.

Having by then completed 11 months and with my time in for my next Certificate of Competency (Mates), I was not happy with the position I found myself in. Mutiny loomed before me and I thought that if I was signed off *Olna*, I could refuse to sign on *Tide Austral* and they would have to get me home!

However, the Shipping Master in Aden made it quite clear that he did not see things quite as I did and that I would remain there until my money ran out and then he would ship me home as a Distressed British Seaman (DBS). Not being too worldly wise at age 21, I believed he could do just that. Needless to say I signed on PDQ and spent another 5 months away!

Although the RFA was now providing a replenishment-at-sea service for the Royal

Navy on a routine basis, its crewing arrangements were clearly far from perfect, despite a gradual increase in contract officers, petty officers and ratings. A large number of ratings were still employed from the Merchant Navy Pool, often for only a single voyage, although there were many who were 'if not continually employed as non contract personnel, were certainly very regular visitors to RFAs'.

As one senior ex-RFA officer succinctly put it:

> Many, however, did not have even rudimentary knowledge of RAS techniques and much of the training was, of necessity, undertaken by the more experienced officers and especially POs, 'on the job' or during the ship's initial 'work-up.

A naval (?) correspondent in the *Naval Review* (January 1958), just back from detached service aboard an RFA, was, however, clearly impressed almost despite himself:

> I would challenge any Merchant Navy captain to take on with equanimity the responsibility of fuelling at night, with their ships darkened, a Fleet carrier on one side, a destroyer on the other and a frigate astern simultaneously in the Arctic, knowing that about 75% of his crew, he himself, his Chief Officer and Boatswain had joined only a week previously. Most of the crew had no previous replenishment experience whatsoever, yet this was achieved, completely successfully and without fuss. ...
>
> The quality of seamanship must be extremely high; a deck full of winch wires and cordage and a cluster of heavy hoses swinging overhead in the dark, calls for qualities displayed by our seagoing forefathers in sail. ...
>
> Are the casual leavings of a Merchant Navy Pool the best we can offer to RFA Captains with which to undertake duties such as these?

His comments about a lack of specialised and experienced ratings are enlightening, too:

> The consequent lack of specialised replenishment experience reflects back to the officers, and this is aggravated by shorthandedness at replenishment periods (in spite of additional hands being allowed). Officers are forced to do the crew's jobs and have to be here, there and everywhere at critical periods. One would not expect the Chief Engineer to be operating the hose discharge valves and blowing through hoses himself, yet he does. Nor should the Chief Officer be dipping tanks, testing for water or connecting up hoses; he does because with a crew recruited at the last port and mostly leaving at the next he often has to do these duties – there is no one else. If none of the crew fancy firing a Coston gun to pass the first line, there is nothing that can be done – an officer must do it! Small wonder that many of the junior officers themselves elect to leave.

One former RFA master who read this extract had *slightly* different memories of those times:

> My experience from this period (1957 to the late 1960s) is that all RAS rigs were controlled by an Officer or Cadet with the Chief Officer (ChOff) in overall charge on deck. A rating in the RAS rig gang would be told to open or close gate and air valves.
>
> Dipping tanks on completion of RAS was down to a cadet or rig officer who passed the measurements to the ChOff who worked out the issued figure. Water dips, done daily again, by a cadet or on the very very rare occasions where a RAS capable RFA had no cadets, the Third Officer. Certainly I never saw the ChOff or CEO do any of this at

sea or when loading in port. Must have been a weird ship!!!!!! As for a ChOff connecting up a hose, I don't think so. As ChOff of *Olna* in 1970, I had a 'Fuel King' rating to look after dips and samples and PO's were certainly running rigs by the late '60s.

He suggested that perhaps the RFA's well-known sense of humour, especially at the Navy's expense, accounted for the discrepancy!

The *Naval Review* correspondent had something further to say on administration as well:

> ... Can we not offer *responsible* posts at managerial level to senior RFA officers, and perhaps a few lower down to up and coming deck officers and engineers (with a limited tenure of office before going to sea again)?

And concerning the future of the RFA:

> ... Somehow the freighting side must be entirely divorced from the sea replenishment side [as, by then, was the case in the USN: author's note] and solid and liquid replenishment ships regarded as units of the Fleet, not available for freighting. The personnel of these replenishment ships must be made to feel they are part of the Navy, with good career prospects, which will enable them to contribute their invaluable professional experience at the highest level. The belated granting of the honorary rank of Commodore to the Senior Master alters little – he still has his ship to run. Could he not be the Director of Sea Replenishment? [Perhaps implying that this should be a shore appointment; as the Commodore (RFA) became as late as 1993?, author's note].

Clearly, 'navalisation' of the RFA was still considered a desirable option by many in the Royal Navy, despite the decision not to introduce it with the Tide class. In perhaps a foretaste of this preoccupation, on 7 October 1951, another innovation was introduced when, at noon, Captain S G Kent OBE hoisted his Broad Pennant as the first Commodore, RFA. Headquarters appointments also included a senior captain as Chief Marine Superintendent, effectively 'uniform head of the RFA' in 1951. A senior uniformed marine engineer had been appointed as Chief Technical Superintendent some years before, in 1948.

Despite its specialised working environment, the RFA's pay and conditions were still set and negotiated by the National Maritime Board (NMB), although RFA personnel did now receive both a Far East Bonus and a Mediterranean Station Allowance of 25 per cent and 15 per cent respectively as well as a War Bonus of 150 per cent on their standard pay, well above the NMB contract figure. Pension provision was also improved with changes implemented for most RFA officers from 1950.

However, these improvements did not prevent the Pakistani crew of *Wave Governor* from mutinying in November 1957.

The vessel was on its way to Brazil but after several of the crew refused to carry out their duties, it was diverted to Port of Spain, Trinidad. The men alleged they had been badly treated while aboard and after a court case, which also involved the Master, Captain Holton, all charges were dropped and the vessel proceeded to its original destination with a new crew.

Mutiny aside, the international situation meant that the ships and crews of the RFA had plenty to do, with atomic bomb tests and the Far East involvement just part of the agenda.

Chapter 2

Korea, 'Grapple' and the Cod Wars

Launching of the new Tide class, unfortunately, came too late for deployment in Korea (1950–3), the Navy being supplied here by tankers of the older Ol, Ranger and Wave classes, along with several of the original Fort class store ships. *Maine*, the Royal Navy's only hospital ship, also saw service and received the Presidential Unit Citation of the Republic of Korea for meritorious services in the Korean War theatre from February 1951 to July 1952.

Unfortunately, in a less than far sighted move, at the beginning of the year, all RFAs had been ordered to land their guns and mountings at their home port, and as a result some of those involved in the Korean deployment went without any armament at all.

It had always been the intention of the Allied powers that, with the end of the Second World War, Korea would assume the status of an independent state. Postwar tension between East and West, however, resulted in the country being divided, along the 38th parallel, into Communist North Korea and the southern, Western-orientated Republic of Korea (ROK).

Inevitably, relations between the two new states were far from harmonious and, in June 1950, North Korea invaded its neighbour, sweeping over the 38th parallel in force, while diversionary landings were made on the Republic's east coast. Seoul, the South Korean capital, was overrun within three days by the main attacking force of seven infantry divisions and one, highly mobile armoured division, equipped with Russian built T-34 tanks.

Having captured the capital, this force then crossed the Han River and raced towards Taejon where it was opposed by UN forces, predominantly Americans commanded by General Douglas MacArthur, who had been airlifted in to try to stem the North Koreans helter-skelter advance. By mid-July, the UN forces in Taejon had been pushed back to within forty miles of Pusan, South Korea's only remaining good harbour and the war seemed to have settled down to a stalemate.

This, of course, did not satisfy MacArthur, and on 15 September, against the advice of his subordinates, he launched an amphibious invasion at Inchon, on the west coast. Six battalions of US marines swiftly captured the town and having quickly received infantry reinforcements, these troops moved on Seoul. Simultaneously, the American 8th Army began a counter offensive out of the Pusan pocket. So successful was this operation that by October, ROK troops had reached Chosan on the Yalu River, which forms the border between China and Korea.

Presumably feeling this US offensive to be a threat, China intervened and after a series of offensives and counter offensives, spring 1951 found the Americans, having quickly defeated a last, massive Chinese attack, in good defensive positions, north of the 38th parallel. The war now settled down to a series of sporadic, local engagements although UN air and sea strikes against North Korea continued.

Royal Navy involvement in Korea and the RFA's parallel logistics role were usually confined to the west coast, although Royal Navy ships were occasionally deployed with the Americans in the east.

Operations consisted predominantly of bombardment of enemy positions, while Sea Furies and Fireflies from the light fleet carriers HMS *Triumph, Theseus, Glory* and *Ocean* carried out anything up to fifty sorties a day against enemy targets.

Destroyers kept up a day and night bombardment, often firing over a thousand rounds from their main armament and this together with the fuel requirements of both ships and aircraft meant the RFA's supply role was crucial.

Two RFAs were usually deployed to supply the fleet – a tanker fitted for RAS and a Fort class store ship. They operated on 'one-month about', that is, one month on operations with the following month in port, usually Sasebo, Japan.

Captain Roy Matthews RFA (Rtd), then a cadet aboard a Wave class tanker recalled this period:

> I transferred from RFA *Wave Monarch* in Hong Kong to RFA *Wave Knight* in Sasebo, Japan, during February 1953 and stayed with her until August of that year, the war actually finishing in June. This transfer was in order to increase the Deck Officer complement from three to five.
>
> British and Commonwealth ships with the odd American frigate covered the west coast of Korea, supported by two tankers [I think RFA *Wave Knight* and *Wave Prince* during this period] as well as a Fort class stores ship, the Fort usually being based in Sasebo or Kure, Japan.
>
> One Wave was stationed off the west coast, at anchor off the islands of Haiju or Te Chong Do, if it was safe to do so. If the ship couldn't anchor, we patrolled the waters in this area.
>
> Replenishment-at-sea [RAS] of all the ships in the area took place most days and at night as required. Fuel and fresh water were the main commodities, but lubricating oil, a limited supply of fresh vegetable (potatoes, carrots and cabbage) along with the odd case of stores were all transferred by light jackstay.
>
> When it was safe to stay at anchor, small ships would fuel alongside. Cruisers, on the other hand, would always fuel using the stern rig, picking up the end of the hose and a mooring rope, before moving astern and securing both rope and hose. This method was only carried out if there was sufficient tidal flow to keep the ships apart. Aircraft carriers, because of their size, were always fuelled at sea. Whilst at anchor, the South Korean commandos used the ship as a halfway stopover on night raids to the mainland and were given any supplies or assistance they needed. A few Script dollars were sometimes exchanged for the odd bottle of Scotch to ease the pains of the wounded on their return from a night raid.
>
> At the end of a patrol, ships would rendezvous and formally hand over. The relieved ship would then sail back to Japan, either with or without escort, depending upon how the Navy perceived the threat.
>
> On arrival, usually at Sasebo, the ship went alongside the oil fuel jetty and loaded fuel and stores. Once loaded, she was moved off the berth, anchored at the outer end of the harbour and placed on 12 hours standby for sea. This anchorage was about eight miles from the landing jetty, which entailed an hour's ride in one of the ship's lifeboats, since RFAs in those days didn't carry a liberty boat. These lifeboats were smelly, dirty, painfully slow and to add insult to injury, frequently broke down so

that when going ashore you were never quite certain that you'd make it.

Once ashore, however, the American PX made up for the trip. This was just like our NAAFI except 100 times better. Cheap, tax-free shopping and food, ice cream, thick steaks and orange juice, the like of which of which had never been seen before by a young, UK, ration-fed youth. Not to mention the delights once outside the base in downtown Sasebo!

Curfew was at 2300hrs. It was best not to be late getting back, either, since if you weren't out of the bars and off the streets in time, the American Special patrols hit you hard with their night sticks and threw you into the Hurry Up Wagons. No questions asked, either.

Having survived the R&R period of approximately two weeks, with all the crew exhausted and broke, the ship weighed anchor and proceeded through the boom defence of Sasebo harbour at a heightened state of alert.

Once in the open sea, the DEMS gunners would check and fire off all weapons, watches would be set and the ship darkened. Incidentally, a War Bonus of 150% was paid as soon as we cleared the Sasebo minefield, along with our usual East of Suez bonus of 25%. After rendezvousing with our escort, both ships would proceed up the west coast, a trip usually lasting 2–3 days, with the ship zigzagging all the way. If you were lucky, you weren't shaken out of your bunk when the escort let fly a depth charge at an elusive submarine.

On arrival in the patrol area, hand over took place and the received ship returned to the security of Japan.

Replenishment at sea was still a fairly new procedure to many RFA crews and Captain Matthews has also provided a description of a stern RAS aboard a Wave class RFA. It should be noted, however, that, in Korea, RAS was predominantly abeam and that both Wave and Ranger classes were equipped for this procedure:

The stern RAS gear was on the starboard side of the Wave class, on a catwalk 4–5 feet wide, running the whole length of vessel from poop, over bridge deck and onto the focs'le. A set of rollers ran the full length of this deck, with the rubber RAS hose joined and laid out on it.

On the focs'le there were a number of windlasses, one of which contained a wire rope as long as the ship, connected to the inboard end of the main hose. The other end of the hose was connected to a second wire rope with a marker buoy at the other (outboard) end. This marker buoy was so constructed that it produced a chute of water, which could be clearly seen when in the water.

At the beginning of the RAS, the first bridge marker buoy was streamed. This was on a wire of the same length as the hose with another marker buoy attached, so that the warship could use it for station keeping.

The marker buoy on the hose was then launched. This marker buoy pulled its own rope taut, (approximately 300 feet) then usually pulled the hose out, over the rollers, its speed being controlled by the focs'le winch. When this hose was almost fully out, *ie* upon having reached the poop, it was clamped ten feet from the end and the wire rope detached. The hose was then connected to its outlet point on the poop, the strain being taken by the clamp.

Having by now positioned itself on the bridge marker buoy, the warship then grappled the hose marker buoy and hauled the hose in through the focs'le via a set of rollers (two 3" vertical, one 6" horizontal). The warship then clamped and connected its own ends of this hose in the same way as the RFA, except the clamp on a warship was usually 15 feet from hose end.

When all was correct, the warship waved a green flag, which they then dropped, in a hole in deck so as to leave it flying. The RFA then replied with a green flag, also dropping it into a hole in deck so it remained flying, before opening the poop valve and turning on the pump. Oil now flowed until the warship was full, when she waved a red flag. The RFA acknowledged with a red flag and both red flags were left flying.

The RFA then closed its oil valve on the poop and flew a white flag to show it was ready to blow through the hose. The warship acknowledged with a white flag and compressed air was turned on aboard the RFA, to blow the remaining oil through, this oil in the hose going into the warship's fuel tanks. Fifteen minutes was usually allowed for this operation. When the warship had only compressed air coming through the hose, it capped the end, released the hose and should have allowed the marker buoy and rope to run out cleanly so that if another ship wanted to RAS, she had only to take station on the bridge marker buoy, grapple the marker and repeat the process. In practice, the Navy were usually careless and the rope and marker buoy often needed untangling before the operation could be repeated.

Aboard the RFA, the wire was attached to the hose and the clamp cast off. Then the focs'le winch was started, the empty hose drawn aboard, while simultaneously being re-laid on the deck rollers. The vessel was then ready to begin another RAS.

Warships were also RAS'd in harbour. The procedure was similar except the receiving ship was on a hawser and the hose was simply passed along this.

Rates of between 127 and 230 tons per hour (tph) were achieved for fuel transfers to Royal Navy vessels by RFAs using these methods. Transfer rates to destroyers did rise to 300 tph, however, when two hoses became normal practice during RAS. Transfers to US Navy destroyers were slightly higher, 350tph, despite the fact that they still refuelled using only one hose.

A Canadian destroyer actually set the record for connecting up for replenishment during this period when HMCS *Athabaskan*, in a RAS with *Wave Knight*, managed it in one minute and forty seconds, from the line hitting the deck to coupling of fuel hoses. Their captain was so anxious to win that he brought his ship within yards of the tanker so that the line could be heaved, instead of fired, across thereby saving valuable time.

Store and ammunition ships also saw action in Korea. Frank Evans, then Second Mate aboard *Fort Rosalie*, remembers how she nearly never made it:

'Rosie' was being loaded for Korea, in the summer of 1950, with a variety of ammunition in Portsmouth harbour. With 4000–5000 tons of explosives already aboard, about half her load, the remaining 5000 tons, in a depot nearby, blew up.

Sabotage must have been suspected, because the authorities sent an armed guard aboard, followed by civilian experts, who began looking for timing devices in the cargo. They concentrated their searches particularly in the cavities behind the filling openings in the depth charges. Was this because the depth charges ashore had initiated the explosions and so were the first suspects?

All this time we were being towed resolutely out to sea by two naval tugs. Throughout the night the search went on, as our threat to Portsmouth diminished with our distance from it.

Luckily, nothing was found and, soon after, the ship sailed uneventfully for the Far East.

By 1953, the stalemate, which the Korean War had become, was resolved, with a new demarcation line established on the existing front line and a settlement about POWs, thus permitting a general ceasefire to be signed on 27 July 1953. The UN forces suffered nearly half a million casualties, 7000 from the British Commonwealth while Chinese and North Korean deaths totalled three million, one million of which were civilians.

Fortunately, no RFA personnel were killed in Korea.

RFA vessels deployed to Korea

Tankers
Birchol stationed in Hong Kong for some years
Oakol stationed in Singapore
Brown Ranger limited underway capability
Green Ranger limited underway capability
Echodale freighting tanker only
Wave Chief fitted for underway replenishment
Wave Conqueror
Wave Knight intermediate modification
Wave Laird intermediate modification
Wave Premier intermediate modification
Wave Prince fitted for underway replenishment
Wave Regent freighting only
Wave Sovereign fitted for underway replenishment
Store/ammunition ships
Fort Charlotte at Sasebo as stores depot
Choysang (MFA) 1,500 ton temp/ASIS; at Sasebo and freighting from Hong Kong
Fort Rosalie at Sasebo September 1950 to June 1952
Fort Sandusky from June 1952 onward
Fort Langley (MFA) transferred to RFA in 1954
Hospital ship
HMHS *Maine*

Some months later, in January 1954, *Sea Salvor* and several of the Fort class were involved in the search for a BOAC de Havilland Comet airliner (Flight 781), which, on 10 January 1954, suffered an explosive decompression at altitude and crashed into the sea near the island of Elba. Tragically, everyone on board was killed.

Sea Salvor was instrumental in discovering the cause of the crash, recovering three of the Comet's four engines as well as substantial amounts of other wreckage, including pieces of fuselage. This enabled investigators at the Royal Aircraft Establishment at Farnborough to partially reconstruct the aircraft and discover the cause of the crash to be metal fatigue, brought on by, of all things, poor window design.

Sea Salvor remained in RFA service until 1973 and she was kept hard at work most of the time, as Eugenio Teuma, one of her long-serving engine room staff explains:

One of the longest serving naval ships serving in Malta naval base was without doubt, RFA Sea Salvor.

This fine vessel served as a boom defence vessel in Malta port as well as being involved in different kinds of salvage work, which after the Second World War was plentiful around the Maltese Islands. There were a number of jobs done by the hard working crew of this vessel, which was manned by Maltese seamen under the RFA flag. At the time there were several RFA ships that were manned by Maltese crews, serving under British Board of Trade Regulations. It was a must that once you joined an RFA ship, you had to be a National Union of Seamen Member, which at the time was one of the strongest British unions.

I joined the ship way back in 1965 after I had finished my time on RFA *Resurgent*. At the time *Sea Salvor* was still a salvage ship, and was also serving as a stores and maintenance ship with the Royal Navy minesweepers, who used to do NATO exercises in the Mediterranean during the six year period that I spent onboard the ship.

We visited Gibraltar and ports in France, Italy, Turkey, Greece, Cyprus, Rhodes, St Torino and Libya; we also visited other Arab ports which I cannot recall the names of.

The crew consisted of a British Captain, Chief Officer, a 2nd Officer, a 3rd Officer and a Radio Officer. The Deck crew consisted of the Bosun and five deck hands and the Engine Room had a Chief Engineer, 2nd, 3rd and 4th Engineers, an Electrical Officer as well as 6 Greasers, a Fireman, 2 Mechanics, and in the Galley were a Catering Chief Steward, Assistant Chef, Assistant Cook and a Catering Boy, all of whom were Maltese, making a crew of 29 in total.

On several occasions we used to carry naval divers for special jobs, sometimes we also had a doctor with the naval divers.

An episode I remember clearly is when our Salvage Ship was salvaged. It was about 04:30 in the morning and we were on exercise around the Greek Islands. I was on watch in the boiler room and because it was so hot I had to come up for a breather. Now, *Sea Salvor* had a door on both the port and starboard side of the boiler room, and we used to keep the doors open for fresh air. I had come up on deck for a few moments when I noticed that the engines were still running on full speed, but we were not moving. I phoned up the engine room, informed them what was happening and the engineer of the watch quickly informed the Bridge what was happening and all engines were stopped. All of a sudden, the hustle started when it was found that we were grounded on a sandbank. Thank God, the sand was soft; otherwise the engines would have stopped straight away.

The whole crew turned out and with help from other ships in the fleet that was forming, they managed to pull us off the sandbank. After hours of very hard work all was quickly forgotten and we got back to what we were supposed to do.

Another episode I remember well was the salvage of the *Christine Pace* a Maltese cargo ship which had suffered a fire onboard. We towed her from outside the entrance of Grand Harbour to Pinto Wharf, where we stayed for several days, working day and night. The fire had gutted her engine room, boiler room, crew accommodation and one of the holds and she was later sold for scrap.

On another occasion we were told that *Sea Salvor* was going to Libya.

On board for the voyage was a crew of specialist navy divers and their doctor. For this trip we were accompanied by two Minesweepers. We visited two ports in Libya, one was Tripoli. I cannot recall the other port, but it was a small place and we arrived during the night. In the morning we could see that it was a very nice port, but not very busy. Not far from the port was a Palace and we asked who the Palace belonged to. We were told later that it belonged to King Idris, that evening some of the Officers from *Sea Salvor* and the minesweepers were invited to the Palace.

We never knew what our divers' mission was in Libya. We stayed there for four days and when we left we sailed into one of the roughest sea storms we had ever come across. As a matter of fact, we had to assist a yacht which was being badly battered by the rough weather. We stayed with her all night. She had a red ensign and belonged to a British family living in Malta. When the sea calmed down a couple of engineers went aboard and fixed the engines so that she could return safely to Malta.

One day a delegation from the Ministry of Defence arrived in Malta for a special purpose, which was to change the role of *Sea Salvor* from an RFA to a Royal Navy Auxiliary Service [RNAS] vessel. My service with the RFA terminated when *Sea Salvor* finished. We were told by the delegation from the MOD that the vessel was being changed to RNAS. The crew did not like this and elected three representatives to meet these men from the Ministry, and I was one of the representatives for the engine room. The talks came to total disagreement and stopped, then the National Union of Seamen took over the case and the ship was impounded and was without a crew for over a year, and if I remember only the Captain and Chief Officer were aboard. Then the decision was made by the MOD to terminate the service of *Sea Salvor* from Malta. This fine vessel was taken to Plymouth and she left behind a lot of very sad men.

Another salvage vessel, *Kinbrace* was also heavily worked during this period, as one of her crew, Ted Morton, remembers:

I joined the Admiralty Salvage Ship, RFA on the 6th May 1955 as a deck boy, when she was based at Dover employed on clearing the Western Docks entrance, which had been blocked in 1941 to stop enemy submarines getting into the harbour. One of the ships used to block the Western entrance, the *Minnie de Larrinaga*, is still there.

In 1947, the first steps were taken to remove the hulks, but delays occurred due to adverse currents, bad weather and the difficulties of the task faced by the divers. It was part of my job on the *Kinbrace* to assist the divers when they had to dive.

A survey of the hulks by Admiralty frogmen took until 1950. That summer the actual work of removing the obstructions began. RFA *War Sepoy* was buried under the hull of the First World War block ship *Spanish Prince*, so the divers concentrated on removing her stern portion first as well as working on the ballasted *Minnie de Larrinaga*. Most of the stern of *War Sepoy* was cut up by 1952, it was hoped to have the remains of the *Minnie de Larrinaga* up by 1953, but it took nearly ten more years before the Western entrance was safe again for navigation. In August 1960 the first really large sections were lifted. In September a section even larger than the other weighing about 300 tons was lifted.

The last big piece of *War Sepoy*, nearly 300 tons in weight was lifted in July 1962 and the final portion in August of that year. On April 26 1963, the Golden Arrow vessel *Invicta* left Dover through the reopened gap. Captain William Waters, senior master of the Southern Fleet gave a great blast from his siren to celebrate the event.

Other salvage work we were involved with was a Greek merchant ship outside the harbour. I received the sum of £20, which was my share of the salvage money.

Then there was a terrible tragedy of the S class submarine HMS *Sidon* on the 16th June 1955: HMS *Sidon* was moored alongside the depot ship HMS *Maidstone* in Portland Harbour. Two experimental torpedoes, code name 'Fancy, had been loaded aboard for testing, with fifty six officers and men were aboard. At 0825 hrs, an explosion in one of the 'Fancy' torpedoes (but not the warhead) burst the number three torpedo tube it was loaded into and ruptured the most forward watertight bulkheads. Fire and toxic gases plus smoke accompanied the blast. Twelve men in the forward compartment died quickly and seven others were seriously injured. The submarine started to settle by the bows with a list to the starboard side. Her commanding officer, Lt Commander Verry, was still on board the ship. Evacuation of the remaining seamen was through the engine room and escape hatches, thanks to the rescue parties from HMS *Maidstone*. The medical Officer from *Maidstone*, Surgeon Lieutenant C E Rhodes, was killed during the rescue and he was awarded the Albert Medal for putting his life in danger to help others. At about 0850hrs HMS *Sidon* sank.

One week later the wreck was raised, with the involvement of RFA *Kinbrace*, amongst other vessels. She towed the wreck into a causeway on Chesil Beach, the bodies of 13 casualties were removed and buried with full military honours in Portland Naval Cemetery on top of the cliffs, overlooking the Naval Base. A court of inquiry cleared anyone aboard *Sidon* for the loss of the vessel and the direct cause of the accident was determined to have been a malfunction of the 'Fancy' torpedo. Following this incident, the use of this type of torpedo was terminated.

It transpired that a torpedo readied for the morning test shot had begun a 'Hot-run', its engine had started while it was still inside the submarine and was over speeding, creating very high pressure in its fuel system. The 'Fancy' torpedo used High Test Peroxide (HTP) as an oxidizer, so when the oxidizer line burst, HTP sprayed on to copper fittings inside the torpedo, decomposing into oxygen and steam. The torpedo warhead did not detonate, but its hull burst, violently rupturing the torpedo tube and causing the flooding that destroyed Sidon.

HMS *Sidon* was refloated and then sunk as an ASDIC target on 14 June 1957.

On the 31st July 1947 the remains of HMS *Codrington* which was on the beach in Dover, in front of Waterloo Crescent, was being lifted after two months of preliminary work and previous attempts to move the wreck by the Admiralty salvage ship RFA *Kinbrace*. I remember this, as I lived in Dover throughout the war. I do not know if this was the same ship as I served on, but have been told that it was.

In January 1955, a vessel in the early Fort class, *Fort Rosalie* was deployed to dispose of some 1500 tons of nuclear waste in the sea off Land's End. The material, enclosed in steel or steel and concrete containers was destined to end up in 1200 fathoms of water, safe from recovery and in a location where the currents were unlikely to wash them ashore.

Unfortunately, as *The Times* recorded, things did not go quite as planned.

First, two drums, which had been fastened together, came apart, although there was no leakage of radioactive material. In a second, more serious, incident, the outer concrete casing of another container actually broke, allowing some of the packing to leak out. Again, no radioactive material escaped but both the ship and members of the crew were examined: '... more for reassurance than because there was any risk'.

As one official put it:

Incidentally, this deployment added another record to the RFA's collection, being the biggest dumping operation ever carried out, up to that time. RFAs were involved in many operations of this sort, some as late as the 1970s, in which obsolete or dangerous military stores were dumped in deep water well off the Continental shelf. Such operations are covered by the thirty year rule, so full details are not available.

Still on the subject of atomic technology, prior to the introduction of vessels using nuclear fuel, the Navy experimented with high test peroxide (HTP), as a fuel for both submarines and torpedoes, for a short period during 1955.

Spabeck, based at Vickers Armstrongs, Barrow-in-Furness, was used to transport this fuel to the submarines HMS *Explorer* and *Excalibur*, which were then undergoing trials. High test peroxide is dangerous and highly unstable, as the tragedy aboard HMS *Sidon* demonstrated all too clearly, so *Spabeck* was exactingly modified for her role. Special, pure aluminium tanks were built into her existing cargo tanks, along with cargo pumps of the same material, allowing the carriage of 111 tons of special fuel and 17 tons of aviation spirit (Avcat).

Although they now had an increasingly specialised role, or perhaps because of it, working and even living conditions aboard RFAs were still left pretty much up to the discretion of the master. Captain Shane Redmond OBE, RFA (Rtd) remembers his first ship, an elderly Fort class store ship and a master with decided views on his officer's conduct:

I joined my first ship, *Fort Dunvegan* at Chatham, on my birthday, 25th November, 1955. This ship was run on very autocratic lines. At dinner, for example, the door of the dining salon was locked until the Captain, Hennin, I believe, the Supply Officer, the Chief Officer and the Chief Engineer came down stairs to be greeted by the 2nd Steward, who opened up. We all filed in, every officer in full mess uniform, sat down and waited for the top table to be served. The typical call was for 'Captain's Steak'. In harbour, Mess (undress) was the order of the day after 17:30, which, for cadets and junior officers, was day uniform with a bow tie substituted for a tie.

Food was not that bad, though, as this menu for Christmas 1958, aboard *Tideflow*, clearly demonstrates:

Xmas Dinner
Hors D'Oeuvres
Cream of tomato soup
Fried fillets of halibut. Egg sauce
Roast turkey and ham and stuffing
Saratoga chips and duchess potatoes
Brussels sprouts and green peas
Xmas pudding and brandy sauce
Fruit salad and cream
Assorted nuts
Fresh fruit
Cheese biscuits
Coffee

A very complete menu, and with no mention of alcohol, except in the brandy sauce. A very considerable improvement on the old timer's boiled salt pork and currant duff, too!

More changes were afoot in 1956, with decisions being made at the Commonwealth Prime Ministers' Conference in London which allowed the Admiralty to begin the build up of a force of modern auxiliaries, in conjunction with the new commando carrier, HMS *Bulwark* and its more flexible amphibious role. These new RFAs would incorporate the latest RAS and aviation technology, this latter including the projected use of RFAs in an early force multiplier role, with anti-submarine warfare (ASW) helicopters eventually using the larger, more stable RFA vessels as landing points.

Experiments with helicopters had begun in 1950, just after the start of the Korean War, with helicopters operating from a makeshift platform supplied and fitted by the Malta dockyard on *Fort Duquesne*. Once the Fort's conversion was complete trials were conducted in the English Channel, using Westland Dragonflies operating from Gosport and RNAS Culdrose.

It was not, however, until the mid-1960s, that the first permanent flights would be assigned to *Regent* and *Resource* in the form of Wessex HU5s from Naval Air Squadron (NAS) 829, so that this essential technology could became a normal part of RFA replenishment operations.

Alongside the Service's more fundamental, internal changes, RFA vessels were involved during this period in the Suez Crisis (Operation 'Musketeer') and several of the first A-bomb tests, Operations 'Hurricane', 'Mosaic' and 'Grapple'. By August 1959, RFA vessels were also supplying the Royal Navy during their involvement in the first of the Icelandic Cod wars.

Royal Fleet Auxiliary ships were involved at all stages of the Suez Crisis (1956), replenishing ships of the invasion force and remaining in the area, after the ceasefire, while the salvage and Canal clearing operations went forward. Among the RFAs involved in 'Musketeer' were members of the Ranger, Ol, Tide, Wave, Spa, Eddy, Dale and Fort classes, while *Kinbrace*, *Succour* and *Sea Salvor* served in Suez with the recovery teams removing wrecks from the main shipping assembly area.

Since earliest times, the passage to India, China and the Spice Islands has been long and arduous for European travellers, involving, as it did, the dangerous and exhausting voyage around the Cape of Good Hope.

The building of the Suez Canal in 1869, connecting the Mediterranean with the Red Sea brought immediate benefits to world trade, and soon boosted by the discovery of oil in the countries bordering the Canal.

British involvement in Egypt dated back to the early nineteenth century and she quickly bought stock in the new canal, soon becoming a major shareholder. Increasing dependence upon oil further ensured Britain's stake in the region.

With the end of the Second World War, and the establishment of the embryo state of Israel, however, racial and religious tensions in the area looked set to reach flashpoint.

Trouble flared intermittently almost from the date of Israel's founding but the first move in what came to be known as the Suez Crisis was made by the Egyptian premier, Nasser, who, having been refused military aid along with the financial package he had negotiated for building the Aswan Dam, turned to the Russians for support, from whom he quickly received enormous amounts of Czechoslovakian military equipment.

Great Britain and France then withdrew aid for the Aswan project and Nasser responded by nationalising the Canal.

Meeting in secret three months after nationalisation, Great Britain, France and Israel formulated what came to be known as the Sèvres Protocol.

Under this agreement, Israel would invade Sinai, on the pretext that they were preventing Nasser closing the Canal, whereupon England and France would occupy the Canal Zone, to prevent either belligerent damaging the Canal.

From the military point of view the plan went smoothly.

Israel began hostilities on 29 October 1956, with the French and British sending an ultimatum to Egypt on the 30th and then beginning hostilities on the 31st with a bombing campaign using aircraft of Bomber Command based in Cyprus and Malta, along with several French Navy Corsairs, which attacked Cairo aerodrome on 3 November. In response, Nasser ordered the sinking of all the ships in the canal, forty in total, resulting in its closure until early 1957.

Two days later, on 5 November, British and French forces captured Port Said, on the Egyptian side of the Canal. Among the invaders were members of 45 Commando, participating in the world's first helicopter-borne assault.

Commodore R Thorn CBE, RFA (Rtd), was aboard *Olna*, as Third Officer:

> RFA *Olna* was a fast fleet tanker, Captain F A Shaw, RFA, in command. *Olna* was the fastest fleet oiler in the Med Task Force and rendezvoused with the fleet 60 miles north of Suez on the night of the attack, making her possibly the first ship in the area!
>
> She was escorted off the North African coast by a New Zealand cruiser HMZS *Royalist*, who had asked to join in and had been told she could only fire in self-defence! *Olna* did a fast run back to Malta – mid operation to top up with fuel oil – running darkened ship through the US Fleet – not unchallenged!
>
> Captain Shaw [Olna] and the captain of HMS *Jamaica*, with hand signals from the bridge, did a 180-degree course alteration, in 10-degree steps, while refuelling underway – this was possibly the forerunner of the now commonly practised 'Corpen November'. We were awarded the Naval General Service Medal.

Captain Shane Redmond, then an eighteen-year-old cadet, also saw action ... of a sort:

> Keith Millan and myself were both deck cadets on RFA *Tidereach*, then moored inside the outer harbour. We joined the boat pool after the invasion and spent most of our time running around Port Said harbour transporting, amongst others, General Stockwell, the Allied Commander, and also the Israeli GOC whom I took from the east bank to GHQ based in the old canal building.
>
> On one particular trip up the harbour a grenade thrown from the roof of Simon Arts, the large water front department store, narrowly missed the 25' cutter I was coxing at the time. Though an air burst, no one was hurt.
>
> On a more career damaging occasion, returning Commodore Elder to his ship, I made a closer than advisable approach to the gangway passing under one of the starboard side discharges at the wrong moment. The Commodore's remarks concerning my boat handling left nothing to the imagination. An exciting adventure at 18 and they were kind enough to give us a medal (NGS) as well!

But it was all for nothing. Bringing financial and UN pressure to bear, the US forced Britain and France to declare a ceasefire. Without offering any further guarantees, the Anglo-French task force had to finish withdrawing by 22 December, to be replaced by members of what was later to become the United Nations Peacekeeping Force (UNPF). In the long term, both British and French influence in the region had been severely damaged and in many ways has never fully recovered.

After the ceasefire, several British ships remained to help with the salvage work. These included *Sea Salvor, Salveda, Blue Rover, Fort Duquesne, Spapool, Kingarth, Kinbrace, Uplifter, Succour* and *Dispenser*.

Even after the ceasefire, things seem to have stayed interesting, according to an unnamed sailor aboard *Blue Ranger*:

> RFA *Blue Ranger* stayed in Port Said after the Fleet withdrew on Christmas Eve 1956. Many of the Maltese crew aboard the salvage and supply ships requested to be relieved and their places were taken by Royal Navy personnel, mostly from the seaman branch.
>
> On Boxing Day 1956 after the Fleet was rushing back to have Christmas in Malta, the ships left behind were entertained with a fly-over by Russian MIGs.
>
> These Naval crew members were not allowed to wear Naval uniforms and the 'civvies' we were given were overalls and a boot-neck's beret (with no badges). At first, the Egyptian police tried to board the ships to get our names and addresses, but were turned away by the UN soldier assigned to each ship and power hoses. Later, we were allowed untampered mail and fresh water.
>
> On New Year's Eve, several large barges were set adrift to foul our moorings but were diverted to the entrance to the canal and left to float into the Med.
>
> *Blue Ranger* left Port Said at the end of February 1957and towed a 'Z' craft on to Tobruk and then on to Malta. Not long after this, the rest of the salvage craft finished their work in Port Said and made their way back to Malta and Gib.

These recollections neatly illustrate another point about RFA crewing in that, while officers were obliged to possess British Merchant Navy tickets, it was often found expedient to recruit ratings locally. Maltese, Singapore Chinese, Lascar (Pakistani and/or Indian) and Seychellois crews were common while the Landing Ships Logistic, commonly known as the 'Sir' boats (*eg, Sir Galahad, Sir Tristram*) invariably had Hong Kong Chinese crews, because of these vessels' long association with the Far East and the British India Steam Navigation Co Ltd, which managed the vessels.

RFA vessels deployed to Suez (Operation 'Musketeer)'

Tankers
Blue Ranger, Brown Ranger, Dewdale, Eaglesdale, Echodale, Eddybeach, Gold Ranger, Olna, Spalake, Spapool, Surf Pioneer, Tiderace, Tiderange, Tidereach, Wave Conqueror, Wave Laird, Wave Master, Wave Premier, Wave Protector, Wave Sovereign, Wave Victor
Store ships
Amherst, Bacchus, Fort Charlotte, Fort Constantine, Fort Dunvegan, Fort Duquesne, Fort Rosalie, Fort Sandusky, Retainer
Salvage vessels
Dispenser, Kinbrace, Kingarth, Salvida, Sea Salvor, Succour, Uplifter

Chief Officer Chris Puxley RFA (Rtd) remembered a trip through the Canal he made as a deck apprentice in 1964, when things were a lot more peaceful:

Aden was my first real experience of Arab culture and as a 'first tripper' it hit me like a cloth in the face! The intense heat and brilliant sunlight reflecting off the calm waters of the harbour, the stark and barren hills surrounding this seething mass of waterborne activity, the noise and shouting coming from every direction, including the bumboats lying alongside, where traders were frantically trying to persuade you to buy their goods; everything from binoculars and radios, to alarm clocks and stuffed camels. As newcomers to this environment, we apprentices were told to make sure that anything of value was locked away, portholes closed securely and cabins locked, otherwise things would probably go missing very quickly.

The visit to Aden was quite short, with just time to load our cargo and fresh water from the refinery at Little Aden, located across the bay from the main town. We were glad to get away to sea again and open up our accommodation areas and cabins. *Wave Knight* had no air-conditioning so we tried to keep our cabins cool at sea by fixing an air scoop through the porthole. This device was useless in port or in a following wind and was supplemented by a rickety portable fan, whirring away day and night. We seemed to get used to the heat after a while, taking a daily ration of salt tablets with our meals.

After a passage up the Red Sea our next landfall was at Suez, to be followed by the canal transit. It was at anchor here that the local barterers were so persistent that my colleague and I were ordered to keep them away from the ship with fire hoses and the threat of dropping a heavy shackle into the bottom of their flimsy boats. It was all quite exciting and great fun! The canal transit of about 100 miles through the desert was very interesting. Ships went through in a daily convoy, pausing at the Bitter Lakes to let a southbound convoy pass in the other direction. Every so often along the canal there appeared a signal station surrounded by a small oasis of vegetation and palm trees, beyond which there was nothing to see but sand and more sand. A road and railway ran alongside the canal, linking the signal stations and the north to the south. Occasionally a lorry or train would thunder past kicking up a minor sandstorm. On long straight sections of the canal I noticed that it was possible to detect the gentle curvature of the Earth's surface.

At Port Said, the northern end of the Suez Canal, we dropped off our pilot, as well as the two Arab mooring boats which had been suspended on either side of the ship. They had to be carried in the event of us having to stop and moor to the canal bank for any reason. We also had to carry a special searchlight mounted on the bow during the transit. (The searchlight had a split beam, in order to see both banks of the canal ahead whilst moving at night). Now released into the Mediterranean Sea, we steamed for the island and British military base of Malta. We sailed into the Grand Harbour to much excitement from our Maltese crew. This was my first opportunity to see other RFA ships and I recall seeing another 'Wave' boat, the *Wave Baron* as well as the old *Olna*, which was sitting in a large floating dock. Our berth was at the 'dolphins' by Corradino Hill, where we discharged our entire cargo and commenced tank washing. This operation took a few days and the off-duty crew were happy to get a few nights at home. Time was running out for this old ship and we started to dismantle the replenishment rigs, laying the derricks out horizontally prior to the vessel being laid up for disposal when she got home.

Nuclear weapon tests (1952–60)

Although given separate operational names, Operations 'Mosaic', 'Hurricane' and 'Grapple' were really a continuing series in the same programme. Royal Fleet Auxiliary ships of Wave, Rover and Fort classes took part in all of these deployments.

Operation 'Hurricane', in 1952, was the first. Based around the remote Pacific islands of Monto Bello and Christmas Island, the actual test was conducted with an atomic device, exploded in the River class frigate HMS *Plym* (launched 1943). The test concluded successfully resulting in, as one eyewitness put it: '... the complete vaporisation of HMS *Plym*'.

Similarly, Operation 'Mosaic' was another operation designed to test an A bomb, also on Monto Bello Island.

Operation 'Grapple', however, was much more serious. In this operation, the intention was to test the performance of Britain's first hydrogen bomb, dropped from an RAF bomber, and exploded in the air above an area of sea some distance from Christmas Island. The operation was based on Christmas Island and its near neighbour, Malden.

Several RFA ships were tasked to provide logistic support throughout the period of the operation, both to personnel based on Christmas and Malden islands and the fleet of Royal Navy ships, deployed to provide what were loosely termed technical and operational control facilities.

The operation began with the arrival of the Deputy Task Force Commander and his team by RAF Shackleton on 19 June. They were closely followed three days later by the stores issuing ship *Fort Beauharnois*, which was to be used as a temporary headquarters ship as well as for logistic support.

Other RFAs, of the Wave, Fort and Ranger classes soon joined these new arrivals, along with Royal Navy ships and specially chartered merchant vessels. The Wave class vessels were especially important, being capable of transporting aircraft fuel in bulk for the RAF bombers, as well as replenishing the warships.

In total, the fleet transported over 20,000 tons of cargo, including 600 vehicles and cranes, tractors, bulldozers, cement mixers to the area prior to the test, which took place successfully on 15 May 1957.

The fleet's job was not finished, however, because with the test concluded, all the equipment and scientific personnel, including the spare atomic devices had to be transported back to the UK, a job which was also assigned to the specialist RFAs. The RFAs deployment finally ended early in 1960.

Martyn Hobbs was Third Officer aboard *Fort Constantine* during this period and has memories of the trip to Christmas Island and their role in ship berthing:

> Storing in Singapore took two or three weeks which, added to the same sort of period spent de-storing, gave the officers and naval stores staff attached to the ship plenty of time to relax and form social relationships with the large ex pat community of Singapore. When we finally sailed for a 'secret' destination – nobody was supposed to know that we were going back to Christmas Island – we left a lot of friends and some families waving goodbye on the dockside. I wondered whether security might have been prejudiced as we moved off the quay to the strains of Bing Crosby 'Dreaming of a White Christmas' playing on the SRE which had been hooked up to the Loud Hailer!

Our passage to Christmas Island was due east as the crow flies but there were many islands between here and there. It was the most fascinating voyage I had experienced up to that time and one that I will never forget. Threading our way through narrow passages between green tropical islands beneath cotton wool skies brought sharp reality to some of the tales of Joseph Conrad that I had read in my school days.

Fresh water was a highly valued commodity in Christmas which accounted for Fort Constantine's double bottom tanks having been modified so that she carried considerably more fresh water but at the expense of oil fuel bunkers. It is a long haul from Singapore to Christmas so we had to call at Manus, a port in the Admiralty Islands north of New Guinea to replenish bunkers. This was where I first witnessed the skills of the old man in berthing the ship without the aid of tugs or thrusters (thrusters had not been invented anyway!) no mean feat for a single screw ship with limited power.

We stayed only long enough to get fully fuelled before setting off again for Christmas passing many more islands on the way. Upon our arrival at Christmas Island we moored on 'Charlie' buoy in the anchorage off Cook Island which became our 'home' for the rest of the year apart from a number of trips to other islands.

All of the non perishable bulk stores for the Task Force came out from UK in commercial ships chartered by the Ministry of Supply. Ships that I remember included the Ben Line *Ben Wyvis* [*Benwyvis*], a Bank Line ship and Ropner's very smart cargo liner *Somersby* which later became RFA *Reliant*.

As the resident 'experts' in berthing ships in the anchorage off Cook Island, Fort Constantine was called upon to look after each new arrival. Captain Edwards would be taken over to the arriving chartered cargo ship to provide a pilotage service and his 'pilot boat', either one of our NST's or our 32ft cutter before its loss, would become the mooring boat and the coxswain and crew would turn into buoy jumpers. For this exercise the coxswain would be either Chris Brunt or the Third Officer (me!).

Buoy jumping is not a sport to be undertaken lightly! Fortunately for us jumpers Franklyn George Edwards was a highly skilled ship handler and made our job that much easier. Looking back at what we did in those days I wonder what Health and Safety would have to say about it now?

As soon as the supply ship was secured to her buoy the offloading of her cargo would commence. The main lighterage task fell to the squadron of LCMs crewed by the Royal Marines detachment. They would move the bulk of the stores delivering either to Port Camp or to Fort Constantine. If the weather was really calm and set fair we would sometimes have the supply ship alongside Fort Constantine which remained on Charlie Buoy. This was the faster way to transfer NAAFI stores and dry provisions etc which were stored and issued from *Fort Constantine*.

On a lighter note, he also remembered a barracuda curry that might have had serious side effects:

With the ship moored for days on end, many of the off duty crewmen were to be seen dangling fishing lines over the side or off the stern and using all sorts of baits and lures. The water was so clear that shoals of parrot fish and what looked like mackerel could be seen and were frequently caught. We had already been warned not to eat the parrot fish as they were toxic and didn't taste good anyway. The mackerel-like fish did not appeal as they appeared to feed frenziedly on the overside discharge from every toilet flush! Logically they became known as 'shitfish'. However they proved ideal as a live bait for bigger fish.

This brings me to the tale of the big barracuda. A group of the sailors had lines out over the stern, at least one of which was baited with a live mackerel doing its best to get off a large hook. The catch from this method was usually Wahoo or Grouper both of which were very good eating when fresh although they tended to lose taste after being frozen down. On this occasion, amid great excitement, the sailors landed a 70lb Barracuda which seriously objected to being hauled out of the water and nearly took off one of the Sailors' legs before being despatched with a hand spike. It was a weekend and in no time the Indian Crew galley in the poop deck house was busy converting the Barracuda into a huge curry. Occasionally individual officers were invited to sample the curries from the crew galley and I can truthfully say they were always delicious – but it was best not to observe the preparation if you had anything other than a strong stomach! On this occasion we had our own Officers galley amidships preparing meals for our regular Sunday 'curry tiffin' so the Barracuda curry was only eaten by the deck and engine room ratings. The Officers' cooks and stewards also fed from the midships galley.

Within hours there was a queue of very sorry looking sailors and engine room crew pleading for medicine from the ship's doctor. It did not take long to work out that they were suffering from food poisoning and some were becoming very ill with it. We ended up with virtually the entire deck and engine room complement laid up with vomiting and diarrhoea for several days and about half a dozen of the seriously ill having to be taken ashore to be treated in the Island's hospital facility.

Today, some 50 years after the event, I discovered from an article in 'Seaways', the journal of the Nautical Institute, that it is dangerous to eat so called 'tropical reef fish', particularly Great Barracuda (Sphyraera barracuda), because they frequently contain the non bacterial form of poison Ciguatoxin and especially those of about 40lbs or more. On *Fort Constantine* we called it Barracuda's Revenge! The article recounted the recent sad experience of a ship trading in the Caribbean which had to land 23 sick men out of their total crew of 35 after eating a barracuda caught on a fishing trip!

I don't suppose we were the first to learn of the hazards of dining on Barracuda and evidently we were not the last!

RFA vessels deployed on nuclear tests

Tankers
Eddyrock, Gold Ranger, Green Ranger, Olna, Tiderange, Wave Baron, Wave Chief, Wave Knight, Wave Master, Wave Prince, Wave Ruler, Wave Sovereign, Wave Victor
Store ships
Fort Beauharnois, Fort Constantine, Fort Rosalie, Reliant, Somersby
Salvage craft
Salvictor

Late in that year, 1957, following Operation 'Grapple' and in line with the prevailing spirit of innovation, the Admiralty ordered a study on the possibility of a nuclear powered installation for a fleet replenishment tanker. By 1961, the study had been shelved, supposedly on the grounds of economy, although by then, the anti-nuclear movement was beginning to gain momentum, at least in Britain. Also, in March 1957, the Geneva Conference – a meeting between the United States, the Soviet Union and the United Kingdom to discuss discontinuing the testing of nuclear weapons – had begun.

Although usually designated a 'war' by Britain's media, the first Cod War was really a policing action, which was brought about by Iceland's extension of its fishing limits from four to twelve miles.

British fishermen reacted angrily, refusing to accept the new delineation of what they considered their rightful fishing grounds and the Royal Navy was quickly deployed to ensure the fishermen continued to enjoy their rights.

There followed a period of net cutting and similar harassment until talks began in Reykjavik, on 2 October 1960, resulting in a settlement, although this did not prove to be permanent.

Ships belonging to Wave, Ranger, Ol and Tide classes were deployed at various times during this operation.

The Royal Navy returned to Icelandic waters on 1 September, 1972, when Iceland expanded its fishery limits to fifty nautical miles. Events took a similar turn to those of the previous decade, although sense prevailed in a shorter period of time and after British warships were recalled on 3 October, a new agreement came into force, allowing British fishing activities within the fifty nautical miles limit but limiting their catch to 130,000 tons annually. This agreement expired in November 1975, when the third and last Cod War began, after Iceland had imposed a 200 nautical miles exclusion limit.

In many ways this war was the worst of the lot, with many trawlers having their nets cut by the Icelandic Coast Guard and several incidents of ramming between the Icelandic ships and British trawlers, civilian tugboats and Royal Navy warships. Twenty two Royal Navy frigates, along with a number of supply ships, tugs and support ships were involved in these operations although only six to nine vessels were on station at any one time.

Britain effectively capitulated in June 1976, when Iceland threatened to close the NATO base at Keflavik and British fishermen were forced to remain outside the limit without any further discussion. This, along with other factors, has severely affected the economies of Britain's northern fishing ports such as Grimsby, Hull and Fleetwood, decimating jobs and industry in these once thriving ports.

RFA tankers deployed during the Cod Wars

First Cod War 1958–60
Black Ranger, Olna, Tideflow, Tidesurge, Wave Baron, Wave Chief, Wave Laird, Wave Master, Wave Prince, Wave Ruler, Wave Sovereign, Wave Victor
Second and third Cod Wars 1972 and 1975–6
Blue Rover, Green Rover, Olwen, Tidepool, Tidereach

Although the RFA took part in several highly dangerous operations during this period, there were lighter moments, such as the service's involvement with the British film industry.

Olna played the part of *Altmark*, with *Fort Duquesne* playing *Tacoma* in the 1956 film *The Battle of the River Plate*, which starred Peter Finch and John Gregson. In a later film, *Silent Enemy*, made in 1958, *War Brahmin* played the Italian vessel *Olterra*.

Big changes had occurred in the RFA since 1950, both in the job its ships were required to do and the equipment their crews were operating.

Unfortunately, employment, recruitment and especially training provision, although showing signs of gradual improvement, had not really kept pace with these technological and administrative advances and it still remained to be seen how quickly the Service could improve these aspects of its operation to meet the increasingly complex tasks which afloat provision for the Royal Navy would impose upon it.

Chapter 3

A Fleet Within a Fleet: 1960–9

After their experiences in the Pacific and Korea, the Royal Navy had become very well aware that properly organised, smoothly delivered fleet logistic support needed to become a major, integrated part of both their tactical thinking and budgetary commitments.

Consequently, by about 1962, the RFA had become part of what was collectively termed 'afloat support', according to *Naval Review* January 1962, designated as 'Those ships maintained by the Royal Navy which are designed to supply the Fleet at sea and to provide it with mobile repair and maintenance services.'

An arbitrary division of the RFA's vessels had also been made, their ships now being described, by the Royal Navy (*Naval Review*, January 1961) at least, as either:

(1) Front line support: Being those ships, which transferred fuel, ammunition and stores to fighting ships while under way. These included the early Tide, modified Wave and Ol classes of fast fleet replenishment tanker and the early R class fleet replenishment ships.
(2) Freighting support: In this group the Navy included vessels in the unmodified Wave, Surf, Leaf and early Fort classes.

According to Adams and Smit (2005), front line support was further divided into:

(1) Fleet replenishment ships: Fully fitted and manned for RAS: permanently manned with full RAS crew complement (about twice that required for a freighting run) even if temporarily on freighting duties.
(2) Stand-by fleet replenishment ships: fully fitted for RAS, but with only a normal freighting crew and a nucleus of RAS-competent officers and petty officers. In reality, there was little difference between these ships and the previous group.
(3) Transfer-at-sea ships: capable of limited RAS with a freight crew.

This ship designation does not appear to have been reflected in a similar division of personnel, although as one ex-RFA officer put it:

... people did tend to get sent to the ships which most suited them! One also quite often heard certain officers referred to as 'front line men', a term specifically used to me by an RFA Appointer as late as 1968/70.

Pay scales also reflected this. Masters of Tide class ships, for example, were paid significantly more than their home trade counterparts, although the situation, especially as regards leave, was far more complicated than this. Captain Shane Redmond has described the arrangements briefly:

All personnel serving on Foreign Going Agreements, the vast majority of the fleet, were paid at the appropriate scale (RFA Contract, or MNB). The few on Home Trade agreements, generally small Eddy, Robert and Ol classes scattered around the UK coast and bases, were lower paid. Leave rates were less also.

Leave rates were also extremely complex and subject to an enormous number of variations: Contract, non-contract, station ship leave, Home coast, Sundays at sea, Sundays worked in port etc!

Alongside this naval reclassification and despite the RFA's improving efficiency, yet another committee was established in 1960, designated the 'The Way Ahead sub-working party', which had been, once again, assigned to investigate, among other things, the possibilities of White Ensign manning of RFA vessels. And once again, nothing significant appears to have come from the committee's deliberations.

Apart from its preoccupation with naval manning, another major concern of the Admiralty, soon to be integrated into the Ministry of Defence as the Navy Department, centred on the age of much of the RFA fleet, with particular regard to the speeds at which RAS had to be performed with these vessels.

In some of the Second World War-built ships this could be less than ten knots, so, in line with the service's changing and increasingly important role, several of these ships were laid up or disposed of. At the same time, several new classes were ordered, making for some interesting and diverse additions, thus increasing the service's operational flexibility. Along with these changes to its fleet, in 1962, the RFA's administrative staff moved into a new headquarters, Empress State Building, known 'affectionately (?)' as the 'Mad House'. Gordon Wilson, RFA Fleet Manager during the Falklands campaign, has clear memories of his early days there, when he moved in, in 1963:

> The Thames froze over in 1963. John Kennedy was assassinated. Valentina Tereshkova became the first woman into space. The John Profumo (then Minister for War) scandal broke. And I exchanged working in the dusty but historic Queen Anne's Mansions in St James' for the shiny new Empress State Building in Earl's Court.
>
> Living in Notting Hill Gate at the time, I had got used to the grubby, impersonal travel on London Underground. As an occasional treat, I would walk to work through the pleasant Kensington Gardens, followed by Hyde Park, Green Park and St James' Park. An hour's walk through leafy parks in central London was as unexpected as it was enjoyable. The shops, transport, sight-seeing, pageantry and evening theatres surrounding Queen Anne's Mansions were all left behind, but on moving to Empire State Building my cramped, creaking Dickensian office became a light, modern, open plan environment, full of new furniture, making it easy to communicate and socialise with others.
>
> We were among the first in, so had lots of choice in things like layouts, though we had to endure a few practice fire drills, including full evacuations. Being allocated to the 13th floor, the office also had superb views over London (made even better if you took the fast lifts to the 26th floor and on to the observatory), and over the Earls Court Exhibition car park. This latter view sounds strange, but in fact gave an aerial picture (with sound) of the horses, bands and regiments parading and practising for such events as the Royal Tournament. And all for free. In addition, plenty of exercise was always available simply by walking up the endless flights of stairs from time to time.
>
> There was (there always is) a downside. Fulham was not in those days the finest quarter of London (though things have changed a bit since then). It was easy to stock up on fruit and vegetables from the open air North End Road market and the pubs were proper old fashioned London hostelries, but St James' or Knightsbridge it wasn't.

For me, however, there were other plus points. It was a shorter journey (by Underground or on foot), and it was much closer to the flat where my girlfriend (now my wife) lived in Parson's Green.

In the Ministry, as in life, there are always pros as well as cons. The trick is to gear up the pluses!

Among the first of the new vessels to join the fleet, in 1963, were two new Tide class fast fleet replenishment tankers, *Tidespring* and *Tidepool*, eventual replacements for the early Tide class.

These new Tides were not built to the same exacting specification as the older class. Only two boilers were fitted instead of three, for example, and the ships were built of lower grade steel, more properly merchant ship hulls in every way than the previous class, which had been warships in all but name. Despite their less demanding specification, they cost very significantly more, £4.2 million each as opposed to the £1.9 million for the old class.

One very significant and reassuring improvement they did show, however, was in their nuclear, chemical and biological warfare defence equipment. This was to warship standard with, among other features, trunked air to boilers and diesel auxiliaries, remote control of machinery, gastight citadels (when refits were carried out properly) and sophisticated cleaning and pre-wetting arrangements. Both *Tidepool* and *Tidespring* gave good service for twenty years, serving right through the Falklands campaign, although *Tidepool* had been sold to the Chilean Navy, some months before the Argentinian invasion.

Chief Officer Chris Puxley RFA (rtd), who served aboard the new Tide class, remembers *Tidepool*'s excellent accommodation very well:

Officers and crews living conditions were comparatively luxurious compared to those on warships at that time, although possibly rather less spacious and more functional than on many merchant ships, especially commercial super-tankers.

The officers' accommodation was reasonably comfortable, where each officer had his own air-conditioned cabin with porthole. Cadets were berthed two to a cabin. Cabin spaces, which increased in size with seniority, were furnished with a bunk-bed, seating, a wardrobe and drawer spaces for clothing and personal belongings, a bookshelf, bureau desk with a radio antenna socket, a carpet runner and a wash basin. Senior officers had wider bunks and en-suite facilities, whilst junior officers had community toilet and shower spaces located throughout the accommodation block. Masters and Chief Engineers usually had a suite of rooms. Bedding, towels and soap were provided for officers and crew, changed on a weekly basis. The Catering Department provided a steward service for officers' cabins. Cadets and crew cleaned their own facilities.

UK crewmen usually had their own cabin space, whilst non-UK crews berthed two to a cabin, except the Petty Officers, *ie* the Bosun, Carpenter, Store-Keeper, Yeoman and Donkeyman. 'Captain's Rounds', a weekly inspection of the officer's and crew's accommodation and the catering areas, usually ensured that a high degree of cleanliness and tidiness was maintained throughout.

Most ships had a small laundry of sorts, with a washing machine and ironing board. Larger RFAs had a more sophisticated laundry and carried a couple of Chinese laundrymen to cope with bed and table linen. They would also launder personal items for a small payment. Officers' dining saloon was usually spacious, with table service provided by the catering department stewards. Three cooked meals a day were available, with a choice of hot or cold dishes. The dining saloon was usually located close to the galley for convenience. Larger ships had a small coffee annex attached to the dining area.

The officers' lounge area usually included a small bar area for liquid refreshments, with drinks served by a steward on the larger ships. Furniture in officers' public rooms and cabins was fitted with loose linen covers.

All ships were provided with a selection of library books, courtesy of the Seafarers Education Service, which were changed from time to time. Larger ships often had their own quiet library/reading area.

Outgoing personal and business mail from the ship was collected by the purser/ship's clerk, bagged and dispatched on arrival in port via the ship's local agent by air to the UK. Incoming mail to the ship was initially addressed to the UK British Forces Post Office in London, and then bagged and dispatched by air to the ships next predicted port of call. Occasionally, the predictions were thwarted by operational diversions, much to the dismay of the ship's personnel. The mail then had to be returned to the UK and re-dispatched to the next anticipated destination. When in company with warships, the services were somewhat better, with regular deliveries to the task group. This was particularly enhanced if there was an aircraft carrier in the group, which could fly off a fixed wing aircraft, usually a 'Gannet', to a pre-determined airport to collect the mail. The mail was then distributed around the group, either by helicopter or during the frequent replenishments, when ships were able to exchange such items.

Of course, the early Tide class were also still in service, including RFA *Tideflow*. One of her crew recalled a couple of her more hair raising RASs:

On *Tideflow*, in 1960, we were doing a RAS with the carrier HMS Albion off the Portuguese coast on our way from UK to the Med. There was thick fog, visibility only about 50 yards. We were in the middle of the RAS and barely 100 feet apart, when a small boat passed down between our two ships. As you can imagine, the two fishermen's faces were a sight before they were lost into the fog astern. It seemed comical at the time but could have been a nasty (not to say messy) disaster.

In another, hilarious incident, we were refueling an Indian frigate, INS Kukhri (Type 14) from memory. They had requested 100 tons FFO so we knew how many minutes that would take. As the time approached we eased down as usual and waited for the 'Stop pumping' signal ... none came. Suddenly, oil came gushing out of a gooseneck overflow pipe abaft the funnel and flowing freely along the upper deck towards the stern!

We did a crash stop but by this time she had a lot of black deck cargo ! I was manning the phone line at the time and a voice said:

'This is Indian ship *Kukhri*, please to be telling me why you have stopped pumping?'

I replied:

'Because you are full up!'

He came back:

'We are not full up, please continue pumping.'

I suggested he took a look aft, at which point several officers came onto the bridge wing, looked aft and lots of yelling started! The voice on the phone line then said:

'Tideflow, please to be stopping pumping.'

That creased me up. The Chief Officer reacted similarly when I reported it to him.

These tales show clearly how difficult a RAS could be. It is certainly a complex and potentially dangerous procedure, and the RFA's method of operating is worth describing in more detail.

In a normal replenishment operation, the RFA is stationed within a specified RAS box, a designated area of sea within which it must conduct replenishment. When the receiving ship signals that she needs fuel, a rendezvous is arranged within that area. Warships never wait until they are virtually 'empty', because a safe reserve of stability is dependent upon retaining a certain amount of fuel in their tanks to serve as ballast. Once this critical point is reached it, the ship has to refuel either from a nearby port or an RFA.

As the warship approaches, the RFA will call her crew to RAS stations and the deck crew will prepare the rigs. With the rigs in place and the RFA on a steady course and speed, she then hoists flag 'R' (or Romeo) to the top of the signal mast to indicate that she is ready. The receiving ship will also raise the same flag to the same position when she too is prepared and commencing her final approach.

With the receiving ship alongside, a member of the deck crew of the RFA gives three short blasts on a whistle, signals a warning with a red hand held bat and the gunline is then fired across using a normal military rifle with a special adaptor on the muzzle and blank ammunition. At the base of the sausage shaped projectile is attached a thin line made of Polypropylene, leading a messenger, with distance and telephone lines clipped to it, which in turn leads into the hose line or the jackstay messenger depending on the type of rig being used. The distance line is rigged where it can be seen from the receiving ship's bridge as a guide to maintaining a safe distance between the ships, and communication is established via the telephone cable.

When everything is coupled up the receiving ship will then signal the RFA to commence transfer, at which point the RFA begins pumping at rates up to 400 tons or 80,000 gallons an hour per hose. Large ships, like aircraft carriers, often deploy two hoses at a time, but a complete RAS might still require two or three hours. Transferring other liquids like lubricating oil, aviation fuel or fresh water can extend the period alongside to as much as eight hours. On the other hand, the more capable RFAs can refuel three ships at once – one on each side and one astern.

When the receiving ship is nearly full, the 'prep' flag is hoisted at the dip to signal '15 minutes to the end of the RAS', and when replenishment is complete, the 'prep' flag is raised to the top of the signal mast. The issuing ship acknowledges the signals, the hose is detached and hauled back aboard the RFA and the whole sequence is ready to begin again.

Although difficult and dangerous, such operations are regularly carried out in sea states up to force 7, and during the Falklands campaign working in force 9 conditions was a regular occurrence.

There was still little love lost between some senior naval officers and the RFA during this period and one of *Tideflow*'s crew described an interesting experience they had:

In 1960, RFA *Tideflow* was alongside in Stores Basin, Sembawang. On the opposite side of the basin was HMS *Belfast*, flagship of Flag Officer 2 FES, a certain Vice admiral who was a bit of a b*******. Both ships were painting their ship's sides. We received a very terse rebuke:

'Your sailors are painting over rust.'

We had been watching their sailors doing the same thing, so our Captain replied:

'Just following the motions of the senior officer's ship.'

All hell broke loose on *Belfast*, so we went off to smoko!

Another of these early Tides, *Tide Austral*, was finally handed over to the Royal Australian Navy in 1962 and commissioned as HMAS *Supply* at Portsmouth.

Leading Cook Ray Clausen (R53268) has some vivid memories of that period:

On the 16 August 1962, 40 members of the RFA *Tide Austral* assembled at the Sydney office of Qantas for the flight to London. All dressed in suits wearing ties, we were transported to Mascot. Stops of one hour at Darwin, Singapore, Karachi, Athens, Cairo and then London followed.

One hour into the flight to Darwin we were informed that there would be no more beer served because they had run out. So our stop over in Darwin required this beverage to be restocked and for the remainder of the trip the demand for beer was limited. I recall the stop in Athens where several of us went to the lounge for a beer. I handed over a pound note and my change was all in 3 and 6 pence coins much to the amusement of the blokes with me. I had the last laugh because when I counted the change I found that I had 19 shillings and I know those four beers was not that cheap.

Arriving in London tired and a little dishevelled we were transported to Southampton where we joined the ship. We all mustered in the cafe and were addressed by the Executive Officer CDR Noble. He informed us of his expectations and he made strong and particular reference to behaviour and bad language.

After several weeks in Southampton, we sailed to Portsmouth where the major ship's husbandry took place. It did not matter which branch you belonged to; all at some stage pitch in. The crewmembers that were detailed to clean tanks really suffered and this did not endear them to the RN Auxiliary. Emerging back onto the RAS deck, eyes stinging with perspiration and swearing, which soon came to the attention of Cdr Noble.

Nelson's ship, HMS *Victory* is a feature in the Dockyard at Portsmouth. I noticed that after several days that patrol activity was stepped up around the ship when we were in port. I think this was an over reaction because I did not hear of anything that happened to cause this response. Our nickname for the *Victory* was the woodpecker's lunch box.

Generally the ship was in bad shape, though it was mostly cosmetic, but the crew accepted the challenge. The main motivation was to show the RN that the colonials could present a ship in pristine lines.

Experiencing the mess system in destroyer-style accommodation in Supply was bliss. Two-berth cabins fitted out with wardrobes, drawers and writing desk. The first and only time I had this luxury. The cabin experience at weekends was a bonus. It was left to each individual if he wished to arise at wakie-wakie.

Professionally, the galley was a pleasure to work in. Large with good ventilation and all the cooking equipment allowed a varied and full menu to be produced. The Argentine steaks (boot leather) and English style sausages (10% meat 90% bread) were not of our liking. The separate bakery was a bonus, which allowed the bread, various buns and cakes to be baked and eaten fresh daily.

Sea trials took place in the English Channel and most weekends we were in port to allow the crew to travel.

Sailing from England in company with the minesweepers, it was not long before we experienced the very bad weather, which the Atlantic is noted for. The crews on the minesweepers had a very hard time: Gibraltar was a welcome port.

Gibraltar allowed us access to southern Spain and the ferry to Tangier, Morocco.

The entry from Gibraltar to La Linea was casual walk across the causeway to experience the Spanish way of life. Spain in these days was still very much under the dominant rule of Franco. Happy alcohol induced behaviour certainly attracted the attention of the Spanish police who were a law unto themselves. A few of the crew experienced the Spanish gaol hospitality and the subsequent follow up at Captain Gladstone's table.

The trip by small craft supplied by the RN to Tangiers lasted about an hour and about half way there and about 1000 metres ahead we observed very turbulent waters and it was not very long before the still waters of the Med became rough. I recall our trusty medic staying outboard taking photos and in the process taking a good soaking. This water pattern was caused by the Med merging with the Atlantic.

On transit from Gibraltar to Malta refuelling of the minesweepers occurred and one of the sweepers received the wrong fuel, which caused no end of trouble. I would recommend Malta, interesting culture and history and the climate equal to the Greek Isles.

Then we moved via Malta, through the Suez, to Singapore. While in Singapore the ship was completely repainted. Prior to our arrival back in Sydney we anchored in the Whitsundays for 24 hours to again repaint the ship in RAN Grey. The mind boggles on reflection.

Shortly after the arrival in Sydney I was posted to *Vendetta*. Unfortunately, I was never given the opportunity again to serve on HMAS *Supply*, a ship that has very fond memories for me.

Along with the new Tide class, the first of the Army's Landing Ship (Logistic) (LSLs), *Sir Lancelot*, was also introduced in 1963, replacing, as a class, the ageing and expensive Landing Ships Tank (LST). These LSLs were administered (managed), until 1970, by the British India Steam Navigation Co Ltd, London, a member of the P&O group. As mentioned earlier, because of this association, as well as several other factors, their crews were always Hong Kong Chinese, although from 1970, officers were RFA.

Although they were popular ships, the LSLs had flaws, mostly associated with the flat bottomed design and bow doors, which made them 'interesting' to sail in. Richard Fearnley, a former radio officer in *Sir Lancelot*, clearly remembers one incident during a China Sea hurricane:

The 'Sir Boats' as they were referred to, were a series of War Office designed LSLs (Landing Ships Logistic), a sort of naval version of a Ro-Ro Ferry.

The ship I served on twice, joining the first time in Liverpool 1972, and then again at Southampton in 1974, was RFA *Sir Lancelot*.

Sir Lancelot was the first of the class, being slightly smaller and having 4 cranes forward rather than the 3 the other five of her class carried. L3029, like all her class, was a very bad sea boat, and she rolled like a pony on wet grass. She did actually move in dry dock once, which only added to the stories about her sea-keeping qualities.

The ships were initially run by the British India Steam Navigation Co (BI) and had the traditional white hull and blue band of a troopship (This often became visible after rough weather when the Admiralty gray paint wore off!). That all changed when the RFA took over management of the ships in 1970, and they were painted gray and manned by 68 RFA Officers and Chinese crew.

The reason the ships were awful sea boats is that they were virtually 'flat' bottomed, to enable them to conduct beach landings, but this meant that they rode high in the water and were 'lively' to sail in!

Because of the stability problem the hull was steel, but the superstructure was aluminium, a totally new concept, which reduced the 'top heavy' weight of the vessel considerably; otherwise, they would have been even worse.

On one occasion on passage to Hong Kong from Singapore, *Sir Lancelot* hit some very heavy weather in the South China Sea, and not only did we lose some paint, but the bridge and superstructure went one way and the hull went another! A huge gap rose between the base of the superstructure and the deck, where the steel and aluminium met!

The ship went into dry dock at Hong Kong for immediate repairs, which proved difficult as aluminium cannot be welded. 'L' plates were made and welded to the steel and the other side the 'L' was clamped and riveted to the superstructure. Once repaired, we continued on our way.

The other problem encountered in bad weather was that the 'bottle screws' holding the bow doors together used to give way. The *Herald of Free Enterprise* disaster was the result of its bow doors opening and, whilst at sea, if the bow doors had gone, then we would have been one of the largest submarines in the Navy! I can remember the Bosun and the Bosun's Mate standing by to replace these door bolts whilst actually under way.

Mr D Preston RFA (rtd), served aboard *Sir Lancelot* during his first voyage to the Far East. He remembered it distinctly ... including a spot of shore leave:

My first trip to sea in the RFA was on RFA Sir Lancelot. I must have been the most Junior Junior Engineer in the Far East Fleet. Most of the time, I didn't know what was going on, only that we were to sail to, for instance, Penang with supplies and stores for the Army base there. The trip took four days from Singapore and the day we arrived it was pouring down with rain. We had had a breakdown of some kind and I was on the twelve to four watch with Ron Bell (Third Engineer). I had taken over from Nick Lowe, the Junior on the eight to twelve watch, and was informed that I was to make a square plate of given dimensions with holes of the size and position noted on the drawing.

Well, by morning, I had buggered it up. I think that we must have been doing extra hours as well because I remember going into the duty mess and Brian Hall, the Second Engineer was there, already in his boiler suit. Second Engineer Hall's eyes tended to look like they were bulging out of their sockets anyway, but on this occasion, well ... 'One square plate, four holes, two juniors, eight hours ... I don't know why some people bother coming to sea, I really don't. So, as you can imagine, the weather matched my mood on that day.

Sailing up to Penang, was my first trip to sea and I think that the above incident occurred on that trip. For the four days sailing there, I was sea sick, heat sick, home sick and pig sick. Sailing back, I stopped trying to get over it and sat in the Wardroom having an extra beer before going to my bunk. This would be after eight o'clock and

I was on duty at twelve. The junior Deck Officer remarked that I would only puke the beer up again when I went on watch, I replied that if I was going to be sick, I would be sick, so I may as well enjoy the beer while I could. After that, I was not sea sick again and even got to grips with the heat in the engine room, from the engines and Ron Bell's ire.

When we went ashore in Singapore, we used the Peter Bar in Sembawang Village, for those who have been there you will recall, once a hostess struck up a friendship with you, then she would always sit with you when you were in the bar. She would not sit, or accompany, any of your shipmates. Of course, during the evening, you would see her over on the other side of the bar sitting with some Jack from the RN, but then that was their job.

The girl that always sat with me in the Peter Bar called herself Lillia. Lucia sat with my mate, Hughie Lyons. I think it was Lucia who told us how the hostesses conducted themselves and that it was to 'Avoid discord' amongst shipmates. In those days, I have to admit I was rather naïve. It was my mate, Les Smiles who joined the ship later on in 1971 that put me wise to the 'other' business of the hostesses. He also wised me up to the fact that the 'Ruby Wine' (Four Singapore dollars a glass) was in fact cold tea. Two dollars went to the bar and two dollars to the hostess (OK Bar Girl).

In Hong Kong, whenever Jack attempted to put Hong Kong Dollar coins into the juke box, the Mama San would start rattling away, 'You no put them in there, Johnny!' She would then rush over with a stack of old pennies. 'You put these. Save dollars and give them to me'. This was true of any of the bars in Hong Kong we frequented. I would think that it was Jack that got the bad name for stuffing pennies into the juke box and obviously Mama San that got the dough.

Empire Gull was not quite what her RFA crews expected either, as Chief Officer Chris Puxley remembers:

This old tub turned out to be one of my most interesting appointments. She was so totally different to all the other ships that I had been on so far. She was operated by, and to the requirements of, the Ministry of Defence (Army). The cargoes were to be all sorts of military and engineering vehicles, as well as munitions and general freight. The RFA had just taken over this last remaining LST (Landing Ship Tank), as well as six recently built LSLs (Landing Ship Logistic), which were named after 'Knights of the Round Table'. All these ships had previously been crewed by a commercial shipping company, but I think the tendency now was to integrate these vessels more into naval and military operating procedures. This was a technique that was common practice with the RFA.

She looked very different to the normal RFAs we were all familiar with. This rather squat vessel had a black hull, white superstructure and a buff coloured funnel. The accommodation inside was very basic, painted pale green and the fittings were fabricated in thin steel plate, rather than the wood or Formica type materials that we were used to. She had two engines and propellers, which made her quite manoeuvrable. Her cargo space consisted of a large rectangular shaped tank deck, with doors at the bow, above which was the vehicle deck which had a ramp that could be lowered to the deck below and a cargo hatch served by derricks mounted on a pair of samson posts. Troop dormitories ran along either side of the tank deck. A stern anchor enabled the ship to haul herself off a beach or away from a landing stage after having discharged or loaded her cargo.

There were more important introductions to the Fleet, between 1964 and 1967, including the MoD-designed *Olynthus* or Ol class of fast fleet tankers, *Oleander, Olna* and *Olynthus*. Along with these, three new Dale and several Leaf class tankers were taken up, the two latter classes having been taken up on what is known as bareboat charter.

Incidentally, the *Olynthus* class was redesignated *Olwen* in 1967, with two of the ships, *Olynthus* and *Oleander* also being renamed *Olwen* and *Olmeda* respectively. This was done to prevent confusion with two Royal Navy ships with similar names, HMS *Olympus* and HMS *Leander*.

According to one of her crew, *Oleander*'s first RAS was not wholly straightforward:

> In 1966, when RFA *Oleander* went to the Persian Gulf to load her first cargo of Dieso and FFO she also undertook her first ever RAS. This was with HMS *Eskimo* and on completion of the RAS, the signal was sent by VS (lamp);
>   'Thanks, you were our first RAS – it took an Eskimo to break the ice.'
>   Almost immediately the reply came;
>   'OK but do you require a tow?'
>   This caused some confusion on the bridge until 'Bunts', the signalman, came in and said to Captain Ditchburn;
>   'Sorry Sir, forgot to take down the NUC (Not under command).'
>   This signal, which was displayed when RAS-ing was two black balls, hoisted one above the other.
>   The signal was flashed back to *Eskimo*;
>   'Sorry for the balls-up.'
>   and we proceeded on our way out of the Gulf.

Rivalling these new additions were some of the older RFA ships, which were showing real improvements in efficiency as well.

In 1960, for example, a new record was established, when, in a replenishment-at-sea operation between *Fort Charlotte* and HMS *Bulwark*, 75.5 tons of victualling stores and thirteen tons of naval stores were transferred in 103 minutes, an average of 51.55 tons an hour. *Fort Charlotte*'s crew had shown everyone concerned that 'navalisation' was not the only route to improved RFA efficiency.

Despite their crew's proven abilities, these Second World War-built, Fort class ships were among the vessels whose performance was giving the Navy cause for concern, so several new store ships were brought into service to replace them. *Bacchus* and *Hebe* were launched in 1962, and, after completion, immediately taken over from the British India Navigation Company on bareboat charter. Further additions to the fleet's victualling and ammunition ships appeared between 1965 and 1967, with the launch of *Stromness, Lyness* and *Tarbatness*, the three much-loved, MoD-designed Ness boats.

Several more specialised and very sophisticated vessels also entered service during this period, in the shape of *Engadine*, the helicopter training ship, and *Regent* and *Resource*, the two big R class stores and specialist ammunition ships with dedicated nuclear storage. These R class ships also had a specialist rig for handling Seaslug missiles, then in use on County class destroyers. The R class had a number of revolutionary features that were explained to her crew on occasion by the designer himself. Captain Shane Redmond was aboard when it happened:

While RFA *Regent* was anchored at Portland during her initial sea trials, she had a visit from Mr Chislett, who was at that time responsible for the design and build of *Regent* and her sister ship, *Resource*.

During the course of discussions, one officer asked a question regarding the absence of watertight arrangements in the holds below the upper deck. Mr Chislett responded by saying 'The R class are designed to sink in the upright position'.

While the rest of us were thinking about this, Captain Henry (Henry L'Strange) flashed back, 'Mr Chislett, I thought ships were designed to stay afloat'.

Of course, this was a play on words as the answer was technically correct, since the ship's design allowed any water that entered the hull to automatically flow down thereby preventing the R class developing a dangerous list and the risk of capsize. This exchange brought a peal of laughter and lighter tone to the rest of the evening!

Chief Officer Chris Puxley also served aboard *Resource* when she first entered service. He had less than fond memories of her accommodation:

I travelled north to join this new ship at Greenock, on the Clyde, where she had been built and had just completed her sea trials. The *Resource*, along with her sister-ship the *Regent*, had been designed by the Ministry of Defence at Bath. Consequently, both were functional but not the prettiest or most comfortable of ships. They had the appearance of a tanker from a distance, with a large accommodation block amidships and another at the stern to cater for the large complement of personnel. These two accommodation areas were linked by a pair of long alleyways which ran along each side of the ship, immediately beneath the main deck. The alleyway on the port side, with crew cabins, was known as 'Union Street', after a thoroughfare well known to seafarers in Plymouth, and the starboard side alleyway with civilian stores personnel cabins was known as the 'Burma Road'. Deck Officer cabins were in the midships island, along with the radio officers, pursers, the helicopter pilot and the senior armament stores officers. The after accommodation held cabins for the ship's engineers, petty officers, junior armament stores officers and the RN helicopter maintenance detachment. The officers' lounge and dining saloon were aft, below the flight deck.

In addition to the normal manning requirement of RFA officers and crew for a vessel of this size, these ships also carried a large contingent of armament stores personnel. Their responsibility was to manage the vast amount of naval and aircraft munitions held on board. She also carried a wide range of ordinary naval stores and victualling supplies for transfer to warships at sea. *Resource* was, however, principally an armament supply ship, with her dangerous cargo carried in deep holds, with decks interconnected by large electric lifts. When not in use, the lift platforms were stowed at the main deck position and the deck sealed pneumatically, to prevent the ingress of water. Any item of stores held below decks had to be readily accessible, therefore each hold compartment was fitted out like a warehouse and serviced by mini forklift trucks and other specialised handling equipment.

For security reasons, much of the hold space was 'out of bounds' to RFA personnel. That was unless they had been 'positively vetted'. Less painful than it sounds, this meant that the individuals background and character was researched in depth by the Ministry of Defence. This procedure was usually reserved for armament staff and senior RFA officers (first officer and above).

These R class vessels were also equipped with nuclear containment facilities, which may explain the high levels of security.

On a slightly more mundane note, *Green Rover* was launched in 1968, the first of the Rover class of small fleet replenishment tankers, intended as a replacement for the elderly Rangers.

Despite the efficiency and excellent training of all parties, accidents happen at sea and, in November 1960, the crew of *Black Ranger* were involved in such an incident with a Royal Navy submarine, HMS *Thule*. Due to some oversight, the submarine actually surfaced under the RFA and in response, the sub's captain sent the following message: 'Thules rush in where Rangers fear to tread.' The RFA's response is not recorded!

Black Ranger seems to have had a run of bad luck during her time as the Flag Officer Sea Training (FOST) tanker, as one of her officers recounts here:

> I was Third Officer in *Black Ranger* (Portland Tanker) from 29 Feb to 13 Oct 1960 after which she went to refit. Captain Sam Dunlop in command. I have no recollection of the incident with the *Thule* described above during my time. But I do remember working-up an Israeli submarine, I believe named *Rahiv*.
>
> During a CASEX (combined anti sub exercise) with *Black Ranger* as the screened (protected) vessel and having worked out his firing solution undetected, *Rahiv* prepared to fire a single practice torpedo. Concurrent with the firing I believe he had some sort of problem with his stability/ballasting and the boat partly surfaced. The result was a surface runner at fairly close range travelling at over 35 knots (practice torpedoes were set pass well under the hull of *Black Ranger*).
>
> There was no time to get out of the way, although the ship did manage a partial turn to port. The aim was pretty good and we were hit on the port side adjacent to the engine room – luckily on a heavy web frame. Apart from the E/R watch keeper's comments, I don't recall Captain Sam saying very much on this occasion … which came as something of a surprise to us all, 'Black' Sam not being known for keeping his opinions to himself ! Incidentally, guess who the Officer of the Watch (OOW) was at the time!

Less amusing was the loss of *Green Ranger*, driven ashore a few miles south of Hartland Point, North Devon late on 17 November 1962, stranding her crew of seven. She had been under tow by the tug *Caswell*, on passage from Plymouth to Cardiff for a refit, when the tow parted in a northwesterly gale.

Lifeboats from Appledore and Clovelly were launched and went to the aid of the tanker, but, after being swamped in the ferocious seas, the Clovelly boat was forced to put back. The Appledore boat stood by, but during the night of Saturday 17 November, the seas were too rough to safely remove the crew of seven.

By Sunday morning, conditions had moderated and all the crew was taken off the badly damaged RFA by breeches buoy. She remained aground until 8 December, when her hull broke in two and she was declared a total loss.

Along with its fleet expansion and consolidation, RFA training provision was also seeing some significant improvements.

An RFA second officer attended the lieutenants' course at the RN Staff College, Greenwich, for the first time in 1961 and courses for flight deck officer (FDO) (Portland Naval Base), helicopter controller (HC) (also at Portland) and unit security officer (USO) (RN run) were also introduced. During the same period, headquarters appointments included both a catering and electronics superintendent. Captain Redmond also remembers how quickly poor cadet recruitment was addressed, some years later:

> The first RFA (Snr. 2/O) Recruiting Officer was appointed as Careers and Training Officer in September 1969. The appointment was suggested by Captain Sam Dunlop, then serving as a Marine Superintendent in HQ, following the disastrous low Cadet in-take in both the previous and current recruiting year – a failure to recruit more than 20 cadets when the target figure was 60+.
>
> With a small team of two fairly junior Civil Servants, we revised the recruitment process and the outcome of this was that by the end of that year we had established:
>
> (1) An effective series of careers booklets and general literature.
> (2) Productively targeted advertising.
> (3) A policy of localized preliminary interviews.
> (4) Formalised HQ selection boards and, last but by no means least
> (5) Cadet Training Units at sea.
>
> The local interviews resulted in some 200+ pre vetted applicants being called to London for final interview. 69/70 targets were met in full (as a matter of interest, Commodore Bob Thornton was one of those Cadets that I interviewed).

Once recruited, officer training also included some very specific courses, as one retired officer explained:

> My first specialist course was an Admiralty Gyro course at The Admiralty Compass Lab at Ditton Park Slough Feb 1963, followed by the Lieutenant course at Greenwich in 1964. I believe both courses were up and running the year before.

Although improvements in training were taking place, some provision, such as the introduction of helicopters to RFA ships, was not being implemented quite as smoothly as the senior management would perhaps have liked. This hair-raising story from a newly qualified flight deck officer, was not, hopefully, the usual situation:

> Apart from the experimental landings on *Fort Duquesne*, I think the following may have been a first, if not day, then night landing on an RFA without naval personnel in support … unless of course someone knows otherwise!.
>
> I was serving in *Olynthus* (Capt I B Roberts) as Snr 2nd Officer (Navigator) during her first period in service (1965–6). Though fitted for helo opps in the material sense, we were under the impression that this would be a 'hostilities only' activity.
>
> Consequently, we had no helo controller or properly trained RFA personnel competent to undertake onboard helo operations and certainly, not at night in adverse conditions. However, while carrying out night operating on the northern coast of Ireland in generally unpleasant weather we had a call from an ASW (anti sub) Wessex helicopter who simply said he needed to land on. With no trained controller I got the job of sitting in front of the chart room radar screen talking to the pilot and following the recently published procedure laid down in Admiralty Fleet Orders (AFOS). Part of the process to recover a helo is to provide location information and direction until visual contact is made with the (FDO) Flight Deck Officer, at which time, the pilot takes direction from the FDO. Not being a trained Helicopter Controller and reading from a pamphlet on my lap, my advice was

somewhat slower than the aircraft. I think I had got about three quarters of the way through the list of approach procedures when the pilot called 'OK, I am on your deck!'

On a more serious note, this was not good thinking on the part of our administration as it must have been blatantly obvious to anyone with a grain of sense what an asset a large deck, hangar, fuel and a stable platform must be to any force commander and not just in time of war. But then the Service has always done the job first and asked the pointed question afterwards.

Chief Officer Chris Puxley had a less hair-raising time as helicopter control officer aboard *Tidepool*:

The fact that this ship was fitted with a flight deck meant that another of my duties was as the 'Helicopter Control Officer' (HCO). This was a new task for me and I had recently been on an HCO course at HMS *Dryad*, a shore establishment near Portsmouth. This aspect of my job, which I really enjoyed, was very similar in many ways to that of an Air Traffic Controller at an airport. It entailed operating a radar set coupled with UHF radio communications to keep track of, and ensure the safe transit of, airborne helicopters to and from and in the vicinity of your own ship. As well as keeping in contact with the helicopter pilots, you were advising both the bridge and flight deck teams onboard your ship of local aircraft activity. It also involved talking the pilot on to and down a pre-determined glide-path to your flight-deck, so that he could land safely in the event of poor visibility. If I recall correctly, the glide path was angled at red 165 degrees relative to the ship's head. Although the ship did not have to steer directly into the wind to recover the aircraft there were pre-calculated limits of relative wind speed and direction for each class of ship, within which the aircraft could actually land on the flight deck. The helicopter having previously been positively identified by a special radar signal, was directed by course alterations to a position about two miles astern of the ship. Having attained the glide path at a normal operating height of about 400 feet, the aircraft speed was reduced and it was ordered to gradually descend on a course that would bring it along the glide-path towards the ship and flight-deck. At certain distances from the ship the aircraft height was checked with the pilot to ensure that he was descending at the correct rate. In limited visibility the pilot would have been using only his instruments to keep the aircraft on the appropriate compass course and at the right height, until at a distance from the flight-deck of a quarter of a mile when he was asked by the HCO to look up for sight of the deck. Confirming in sight he would then be handed over to the ship's Flight Deck Officer. If not in sight he was told to overshoot and try again. The ship of course could be stationary or proceeding at anything up to maximum speed during these evolutions. The various aircraft that I worked with included Royal Naval Sea Kings, Wessex and Wasps'.

Meanwhile, headquarters had a suggestion of its own to make about helicopters. In August 1964, Armament Supply HQ in Bath circulated a memo to, among others, Flag Officer, Naval Air Command, suggesting that contract manning might be introduced for the Air Department of RFA ships. Main advantages listed involved saving manpower and money (surprise, surprise), but unusually enough, the official concerned also had something to say about the disadvantages of his scheme. His objections are added here:

Possible disadvantages of contract manning:
(a) Would it be difficult to find a charter firm ready to undertake the task at a competitive price observing that sea service for the personnel of such a firm may not be popular in relation to service ashore.
(b) The need for civilian pilots (unless ex-service) to acquire service background and communications procedure.
(c) Would a charter firm:
    (i) Be able to replace personnel in an emergency (ie sickness)
    (ii) Satisfy security arrangements.
Would accommodation problems be involved (for example, would maintenance personnel require to be afforded wardroom status).

The Flag Officer, Naval Air Command's reply to the memo has unfortunately been lost but, perhaps, not surprisingly, helicopters on RFA ships continued and continue to be manned by the Royal Navy!

Changes in employment conditions and training were not confined to the bridge. Company service contracts (CSCs) for POs and ratings in foreign going (FG) tankers and store ships were improved in 1961 and the first training course for RFA petty officers was introduced in 1963.

These CSCs (foreign going) were quite comprehensive, being of two years duration with National Maritime Board (NMB) standard pay rates. On top of this were included efficiency pay and several RFA allowances such as contract allowance, signalling allowance, RAS proficiency bonus, station allowances, and Eastern bonus.

Part of the package included extra leave entitlement on RAS ships, pension and other gratuities. RFA ratings on these contracts could, however, be transferred between ships, without consultation, and petty officers were responsible for providing their own uniform.

Pay was also showing signs of improvement in other areas. The RAS proficiency bonus was introduced for non-contract deck and engine room ratings in 1960 and, in an undoubtedly welcome change, officers' salaries were paid monthly for the first time from 1967, instead of at the end of each voyage, with regular 'prompts' in between.

Increasing use of helicopters on RFA ships had brought about the introduction of both the FDO and HC courses. Replenishment, both liquid and solid, was also becoming more demanding, however, especially when it involved weapon's transfer and this had, in turn also necessitated changes to the deck officer complement in both the new classes of ship and certain of the older vessels.

Aboard both the Wave and early Tide classes, ships which had no aviation facilities but were equipped for routine 'front-line' replenishment (*ie*, ships that RAS-ed warships while underway), the deck officers carried were *roughly* as follows:

Acting Third Officer (3/O)(when present):
Cadet studying for his second mate's (FG) certificate (8–12 watch keeper). Officers holding this rank were widely used in the Wave, Dale and Surf classes on freighting or commercial charter. RAS capable units almost invariably had a certificated third officer in complement. RFA ships were either complemented with a 3/O or an acting 3/O, never both.

Third Officer (3/O):

Watch-keeping officer promoted on gaining his second mate's (FG) certificate (8–12 watch keeper)

Junior Second Officer (2/O):

Watch-keeping officer with either second mate's (FG) or mate's (FG) certificate (12–4 watch keeper).

Intermediate Second Officer (2/O):

A watch keeping officer, with either a mate's (4–8 watch keeper) or master's certificate. Usually only on the early Tides, if the ship was committed to a heavy RAS program to allow senior second officer to work in daytime as navigating officer. Later, on the Ol and R classes, there were usually three 2/Os, the senior being a non-watch-keeping navigator.

Senior Second Officer (S2/O):

Navigating and operations officer with master's certificate, if intermediate second officer aboard. If no intermediate, then he kept a watch as well as his other duties.

Chief Officer (C/Off):

Second in command and head of deck department and as such occupying a place roughly analogous to the first lieutenant in the Royal Navy. He was responsible for operational aspects of RAS, discipline, aviation and maintenance and upkeep of the ship, excluding machinery and catering areas.

Discipline was a touchy area aboard RFA ships during this period because although the chief officer was responsible for overall discipline, departmental discipline was referred to the head of a man's department.

As an ex-RFA master explained it:

> If a man came back off leave drunk and p****d in the corner of the bridge, it was the Chief Officer's job to discipline him. If he was drunk on watch, however, it was down to his Head of Department.
>
> During the sixties, discipline was laxer than it should have been and I estimate I saw perhaps one assault a week, usually on Saturday nights. Drunk on watch was not unknown either and if I saw it, when serving as Chief Officer, I usually sent the man below and dug out another officer to stand his watch, leaving him to be dealt with in the morning by the Captain.

He added, 'Any man drunk on watch or guilty of assault when I was Master went home on the next plane, and no arguments about it! It never had to happen more than once, though, I have to say.' Incidentally, drunkenness and assaults were not an RFA Master's only problems.

In 1962, an RFA rating was arrested aboard *Reliant*, while in Singapore, after the discovery of ten pounds of opium. Later the same week, more opium was found aboard *Fort Dunvegan*, resulting in the prosecution of three Chinese crewmen. Whether this was the beginnings of an organised gang is unclear, although the media did suggest this, but the arrests seem to have put an end to the matter, at least for that time.

Another ex-RFA officer had something further to add to the newspaper story:

> While serving as Chief Officer in RFA *Regent* (Capt McWilliams) in early 1970 the

Senior Supply Officer contacted me to say that one of his stewards had failed to report for work.

At the time, we were operating in the central Med and following a visit to Gibraltar; it became apparent that drugs were being used by some elements of the Catering Department. Though the suspected supplier, a steward, was no longer with us, we knew that some stocks of cannabis remained in private hands.

I went to the steward's cabin with the Supply Officer, opened up the cabin door and found him apparently asleep on his bunk. As we approached he jumped up, catching us somewhat by surprise, punched the Supply Officer and, as he turned towards me, I hit him on the side of the head. He was duly cuffed and then later released pending a visit to the Captain. However, with a rather sore left hand I paid a call on the Ship's Surgeon, a charming gentleman who, I think, was 72 at the time.

It was quite obvious that I had damaged my left hand and so, a couple of days later I was referred to the bone specialist at RNH Bighi (Malta). Within a second or two it became quite obvious that a Saturday consultation was not his favourite way of spending a part of his weekend – this became more obvious as he read the referral letter and I detected an annoyed note creeping into his voice. Having told me he had no time for brawling RFA types (at this time I should say that intending to go into town afterwards I was dressed in casual civilian clothes), enough was enough, I thought, and insisted on seeing the note. Doc had written 'This seafarer was involved in fisty cuffs onboard …'. There was no indication of how I received my injury! We parted on much better terms though I spent a week in hospital having two bones in my hand reset. On return to the ship the Bosun (Don Seaton) and the sailors met me at the head of the Gangway with a cake the cooks had made in the shape of a boxing glove. The steward was held onboard until my return, found wanting by the Captain and discharged.

This was by no means an isolated incident and throughout my period as Chief Officer in UK crewed RFAs (late1960s to early 70s) drugs were always a concern. But by far the most serious and unpleasant was having to be regularly called out late at night to deal with weekend drink related assaults.

Disciplinary considerations aside, with the advent of the newer ships, such as the Ol class with their aviation facilities and particularly the new R ships with their permanently embarked helicopter flight (serviced by RN personnel) and dedicated nuclear storage, it was felt another officer, with more specialised training, was needed.

So, for these two classes, and several later ones, the post of first officer (1/O) was established, between senior second officer and chief officer in rank.

A first officer almost always held a master's certificate and was borne in ships of the early Tide class and certain other units committed to heavy fleet work, usually in lieu of the senior second officer, where he also acted as navigator. They were also carried in all aviation-capable RFA ships.

As well as assisting the chief officer, his duties included acting as flight deck officer, unit security officer, nuclear, bacteriological and chemical defence (NBCD) officer and public relations officer (PRO). A further small number of first officers were introduced into the fleet from 1969 onwards to run cadet training units embarked in certain RFA ships (these officers were designated chief training officers or CTO).

In the later R class (*Regent* and *Resource*), he was unit security officer, responsible to the chief officer for all aspects of ship security, both physical and documentary. This included arranging clearance to normal vetting (NV) levels of all personnel onboard, security (offices, holds, etc.) and safety (fire) patrols.

These patrols or rounds as they were known, were crucial to the safety and internal security of the ship, particularly once the magazines were loaded with their allocated holding of shells, bombs and missiles. High on the list of the patrol's priorities was the security of the nuclear containment facility, the R class being the first RFAs purpose built for the carriage and storage of nuclear weapons. First officers were, incidentally, required to have passed the requisite Royal Navy training courses before they could be promoted to this rank.

A 1/O's security job aboard ship was not quite that simple, though, as another ex-RFA first officer explains:

In practice security clearance wasn't quite as cut and dried as it should have been.

With our system of non contract ratings being directly employed from the Merchant Navy 'Pool', it was quite usual for a man to join, report his details to the First Officer, who then forwarded them to Director of Naval Security (DNSY) and waited for a clearance to arrive, at best some two weeks later! Meanwhile, the man remained employed onboard; not a very clever arrangement. On occasions, we were instructed to discharge a man or transfer him to another non-R Class RFA. No explanation was to be given for this action on our part though the individual usually realized what the reason was from the sudden termination of his employment.

As a matter of interest, during my time as First Officer aboard RFA *Regent* (from build and throughout the ship's first year) I can recall three specific attempts to penetrate the ship's security. One by a member of the ship's company and two from external sources.

Chief Officer Chris Puxley was studying for his tickets during this period and remembers his duties as third officer aboard *Bacchus* very well:

The 3rd Officer at sea was the 8–12 watchkeeper. I was usually called at about 0700 by the steward, in time to take a shower and then have breakfast at 0730 before going up to the bridge and taking over the navigation duties from the Chief Officer at 0800. This involved keeping a good lookout for shipping or other hazards and taking the appropriate avoiding action. Also, keeping the ship as near as possible to the planned track, allowing for the effect of wind and tide or ocean currents.

During the morning watch, if within detectable range of land or electronic 'Decca' signals, the ship's position would be fixed at regular intervals and plotted on the chart. If we were well away from the land and were not covered with cloud, a couple of sun sights would be obtained with a sextant. These gave position lines that could then be moved forward by the amount of the ship's estimated course and speed and crossed with a noon-time sun altitude reading. This would then give the ship's position at noon. At 1200 I would be relieved on the bridge by the 2nd Officer. He and I would take and compare 'noon' sextant readings (the sun's highest altitude for that day). This usually occurred sometime between 1130 and 1230, depending on how 'ship's time' compared with 'real time' at that position on the Earth.

There was normally time for a quick and refreshing drink in the bar before lunch was served at 1230. The afternoon was usually spent catching up on a bit of work or my paperwork duties. These included lifeboat and firefighting gear maintenance, updating various navigational publications, amending the lifeboat and firefighting watch bill, keeping records of lifeboat and firefighting equipment maintenance, recreational film returns and numerous other bits and pieces.

If the workload permitted I would try to catch up on a bit of sleep or enjoy a bit of 'bronzying' (sunbathing). At 1530 there was a break for afternoon 'smoko', when the stewards served tea and 'tabnabs' (biscuits or cake), to the officers. At 1730, the 3rd Officer relieved the Chief Officer on the bridge for half an hour, whilst he went below and got his dinner. The bar would open again at about that time for those off watch who wanted a drink before their dinner. Then at 1800, all the off-watch officers and the Captain had the evening meal together in the saloon. There was then a short period of relaxation before it was time to go up to the bridge again for the evening 8–12 watch. At midnight the 2nd Officer took over the navigation duties and it was time to go below and get 'turned in' before the next call at 0700.

Brambleleaf was refitting when he was promoted to second officer:

After a couple of freighting trips to Trinidad and to Augusta in Sicily, bringing oil cargoes back to the UK, the ship was programmed to go to dry-dock at 'Cammell Laird's' in Birkenhead for a refit.

It was always interesting to see a ship being brought into dry-dock and lined up with the keel blocks. Cranes then lifted the side timbers into position as ship settled down when the water was pumped out of the dock. As the water level continued to fall, the yard workers got started on cleaning the weed and growth off the ship's side and eventually moving under the hull as the dock dried out. Overboard discharges would be plugged or piped away from the ship and the anchors and cables laid out on the dock bottom for inspection. On going down into the dock yourself and walking under the hull, you really got to appreciate the enormous mass of your vessel.

Meanwhile, up on deck, the recently smart and orderly ship was turned into what seemed like an absolute shambles of ladders, skips, power cables, scaffolding and all sorts of repair equipment.

Usually, most of the ship's personnel were paid off for the refit duration of two to three weeks. Those remaining had to move ashore as there was unlikely to be any heating, power or fresh water supplied for the ships normal facilities. Everything that could be moved had to be kept under lock and key and carefully watched, otherwise it disappeared! All valuable and attractive items were put into locked containers, delivered to the ship for that purpose

I stayed with *Brambleleaf* throughout the refit, during which time I was promoted to 2nd Officer. My new responsibilities meant that I was now the ship's navigator and operations officer, understudying the Chief Officer as required.

During my time at sea, I think that being the navigator was the job on all ships that I enjoyed the most. You were at the hub of all the operational information and knew all about what was going in all departments, and of the outside influences that would affect your ship, now and for the foreseeable future. Primarily, you were responsible to the Captain for the safe navigation of the ship and its timely arrival wherever it was meant to be.

At sea I now kept the 12–4, or 'graveyard' watch, possibly so called because it was generally quiet on board the ship during that time as others slept. The day started with a call and a cuppa at about 0900. If the call didn't wake you the crew with their chipping hammers did! After a slice of toast or similar, (breakfast had long been cleared), there was possibly an operational meeting with the captain, or a bit of day-work to do such as chart correcting, or maintenance to the gyro compass and repeaters. There may even be a bit of work to do on the Chernekeef log that was playing up again. This important piece of equipment, which projected from the hull under water, indicated the ship's speed. It was probably located in some place that was almost inaccessible, down in the bowels of one of the pumprooms.

Lunch would be early, at 1130, before taking over the watch on the bridge at 1200. Quite soon into the watch there would be the noon position to ascertain by measuring the sun's altitude with the sextant. This gave you your latitude, which was then crossed with transferred position lines of the earlier sights taken by the 3rd Officer, to give you the ship's noon position. All this business was not of course necessary if you were within detectable range of land. The 'day's run' would then be recorded and various reports written. The navigation watch was handed over to the Chief Officer as he arrived on the bridge at 1600. Time for a period of relaxation and maybe a movie, before a drink at the bar at 1730 and dinner at 1800. After dinner there was time to see the end of the movie, or relax, before turning in at around 2100 and sleeping until going on watch again at midnight. At 0400, the sleepy smiling face of the Chief Officer appeared in the dim lighting of the chartroom. He took over the watch again as you either went below to have a chat and a beer with the 3rd engineer who had also just come off watch, or you went straight to bed.

Training, personnel and ship development were clearly improving during this period and that was just as well, considering some of the challenges the RFA faced during the 1960s.

Chapter 4

Aden and the RNSTS

Instability was still a hall mark of the world political scene and consequently, between 1960 and 1965, the RFA found itself involved in supporting the Royal Navy during its operations in Kuwait, Brunei and Zanzibar as well as the long-drawn-out Indonesian campaign (1962–6).

Due to swift action by the Royal Navy, operations in Kuwait during 1960 ended up as a simple policing action, rather than the full-scale war with Iraq, which might have developed. Several RFAs were deployed in support of the Fleet, including ships of the Wave, Ranger, Tide, Ol, Leaf, early Fort and early R classes.

Kuwait supplied over 40 per cent of Britain's oil during this period and, in order to safeguard these vital stocks, the British government had signed a defence agreement with the country's ruler. Soon after, Kuwait announced its intention to apply for UN membership, which provoked General Kassem, then ruler of Iraq, into announcing his intention to annex his tiny neighbour.

By 30 June 1960, the situation had become so worrying that Kuwait's ruler asked for British assistance. Before twenty-four hours had elapsed, HMS *Bulwark* had disembarked 42 Commando in Kuwait, with 45 Commando flying in from Aden the following day. Air cover was provided by the carrier HMS *Victorious*, controlling her own aircraft and a number of Hawker Hunters operating from Kuwait airfield. Over 5000 British troops were deployed within nine days and consequently, the planned invasion never happened.

The RFA ships *Tidereach*, *Reliant* and *Resurgent* between them provided over 600 tons of fuel, stores and provisions during each day of the operation.

RFA ships deployed to Kuwait

Tankers
Gold Ranger, Olna, Orangeleaf, Pearleaf, Tidereach, Wave Master, Wave Ruler
Supply ships
Fort Charlotte, Fort Dunvegan, Fort Sandusky, Reliant, Resurgent, Retainer

---

In Brunei, one of the four states into which the island of Borneo is divided, fighting broke out in 1962 between British troops stationed there and rebel forces, calling themselves the North Borneo National Army, and which were intent upon destroying the country's oil installations. Troops were quickly deployed by air to reinforce 42 Commando, a battalion of the Gurkha Rifles and the 1st Battalion Queen's Own Highlanders who were already present.

A small naval force consisting of HMS *Tiger* and HMS *Alert* as well as two minesweepers and two tank landing craft, was also dispatched. *Gold Ranger* was deployed to replenish the naval vessels.

Control of the capital was quickly established, although, because of the presence of hostages, it took longer to regain possession of the oil fields. This was eventually achieved, however, and British troops were able to return to their peacetime duties.

Brunei had been a short, relatively straightforward operation, but the Indonesia confrontation (1962–6), which followed soon after, was much more complex and was to take far longer to resolve.

Borneo, in 1961, was divided into four separate states; Indonesia-controlled Kalimantan, the kingdom of Brunei, and the two British colonies of Sarawak and North Borneo.

In line with its decolonisation policy, Britain was planning a withdrawal from its southeast Asia colonies. With that end in view, the UK was moving to combine its Borneo colonies with Malaya, to form a new federation known as Malaysia.

Indonesia's President Sukarno opposed the idea, claiming it would increase British influence in the region and after an abortive referendum, President Sukarno opted for a campaign of guerrilla warfare, which lasted four years.

Both British and Commonwealth troops and naval units were deployed to deal with the threat, including two units of Royal Marines and the Brigade of Gurkhas.

The conflict ended in May 1966, after an Indonesian coup, led by General Suharto, displaced President Sukarno from office.

Ron Robins was RFA agent in Singapore at the time and has vivid memories of those times:

> There was a certain nervousness generated in the Naval Base at Singapore during 1962 as we watched the events unfolding in Borneo, supported by Indonesia. British Naval patrols were increased around the coast of Borneo and in the Straits, while the RAF at Changi and Seletar increased their 'over-flying' of the areas, and the Sunderland Flying Boat Squadron (resplendent in gloss white) from New Zealand were much in evidence, based at Seletar.
>
> In the Naval Base, meetings between the Stores Organisations and Navy HQ were increased for 'briefings', particularly from the Fleet Logistics Officer (FLOGO). These Stores Organisations were the Naval Stores headed by Lew Cooper (SNSO) and the Armament Org (SASO) headed by Jack Walton, and Victualling Org (SVSO). Measures were triggered to ensure that the Naval Stores Fuel Depot was replenished on a regular basis with fuel delivered from the UK by stepped-up visits from Leaf class tankers. Stores deliveries by *Bacchus* and *Hebe* were accelerated on a regular basis and the normally 'tranquil' Naval Stores Basin saw traffic and alongside activity growing every day.
>
> By January 1963, when Confrontation was declared by Indonesia, the Navy was already very much on a 'War Footing', visits to the Naval Base by Commando (I think 41 and 42) from Nee Soon Barracks, with a 'run' on operational stores, like RIBs etc. Eventually deployment to Borneo littoral areas required amphibious reconnaissance, which meant, in turn, that the relevant vessels and stores were in very short supply, so all Naval Stores tenders were withdrawn from the 'Fort' class and handed over to the Royal Marines.
>
> The peaceful role of *Eddyrock* and *Gold Ranger* was transformed as they became 'front-line' tankers deployed off Johore Shoal Buoy, and beyond, offering fuel and

dry stores, including a worrying cargo of petrol stored forward on deck. Aircraft carrier patrols in the Straits were intensified, which kept RFA Fleet tankers permanently escorting them, particularly *Tideflow* and the Wave class. RFA *Reliant* was at sea on a shuttle basis offering Naval Stores and Air Stores support to the Carriers, while *Resurgent* and *Retainer* were offering full armament and dry stores support. The Fort class RFAs, also offered 'at sea' back-up which was exhausting for these 'old ladies'. The Naval Stores Officers in all ships were kept extremely busy, what with the exhausting work ashore consolidating the demands rendered by the Fleet through FLOGO, and then, sailing with their ships to organise and provide for the under-way replenishment of their stores. Jack Crosswell is a well remembered and respected member of that team of Officers, he served in *Fort Dunvegan* and *Fort Charlotte*, as combined STO(N) for BOTH!

The RN Fleet increased exponentially and Naval Stores Basin and the 'Carrier Berth' were jammed full with ships alongside three deep at times.

Threats of underwater sabotage by Indonesian supported divers was a very real concern and required continuous vigilance to protect all ships in the Base. RFAs at JSB were under threat from sea-borne attack from fast sampans operated by Indonesians. Added to this, the civilian staff Naval Base residences were under threat of attack from Barisan Socialist elements from Singapore and all civilian officers in the Base were enlisted in 'night-time vigilante' patrols, armed with baseball bats!

Gordon Wilson RNSTS (Rtd) began his career in the Far East, just after the Indonesian deployment, and remembers very well his difficulties as a supply officer:

Singapore was a strange place in the Sixties. I arrived there in July 1964 less than four weeks after getting married in Scotland, and within a fortnight was caught up in serious local unrest over the State of Singapore joining up with Malaya. My new wife and I were in the city having dinner with friends when rioting caused an immediate curfew to be imposed. Instead of just dinner, we stayed with our friends for 10 days. A weird introduction to life in the Far East.

Within six months I was appointed Assistant Victualling Stores Officer on board RFA *Fort Charlotte*, second in charge of sufficient fresh, frozen and dry food to feed 15,000 sailors for a month, at the tender age of 23. Now I had to rely heavily on my earlier experience in depots and HQ, and all the food training courses I had done. We were the station ship (with the 'stop me and buy one' flag), meeting warships out from UK, replenishing station ships, and feeding numerous visiting naval ships from Australia and the USA. The ship (Victory class, similar to the Liberty class) was said to be capable of 10½ knots clean from refit. In practice, 6–7 knots was more normal, and replenishing an aircraft carrier (of which there up to six on station – happy days!) was a navigating officer's nightmare because, at our full speed, the carrier could only just maintain steerage. This made station keeping incredibly difficult, which was brought home to us, on one occasion, when the carrier we were storing accidentally veered away. The manual tensioning of the steel hawser joining the two ships could not cope and the hawser instantly parted with an almighty crack, dropping the stores into the sea and injuring several sailors on the carrier.

This speed difference may have been one reason (though it would also reduce military vulnerability) for trialling the use of helicopters, then in their early days and carried only on aircraft carriers, using a 'Dragonfly'. We had a rudimentary flight deck constructed on the stern over the accommodation, with access only by ladder. All stores to or from helo transfer had to be manhandled (and without 'through decks' also had to be manhandled through the ship using different levels). Everything needed to be pre-arranged and prepared, but still was dreadfully slow. I recall our Chief Officer being highly sceptical of this method of transfer. 'Too slow, too expensive, too complex' was his view. 'It will never catch on'.

Fort Charlotte was fitted with steam derricks on both sides, and with an experienced Chinese crew load transfers (up to a ton each) every 40 secs or so were commonplace. Stores had to be set up on the correct side of the ship as moving them from one side to the other could only be done laboriously by hand, there being no open deck access across the ship. Thus, if the receiving ship appeared on the wrong side it could be quicker to tell them to go round to the other side than to move everything over.

After some months I transferred to *Fort Dunvegan*, a sister ship, as acting Victualling Stores Officer (still only 24). Almost immediately we stored up fully and went off on a SEATO (the South East Asia Treaty Organisation) exercise with the whole Far Eastern fleet, supplemented by ships from the Philippines and USA, some 47 in total.

On one memorable day the Flag Officer in command got all the ships into seagoing formation, a truly formidable sight now unlikely to be repeated.

Many other new experiences came my way. I recall being ferried into Manila to stock up with large quantities of fresh produce from the local market. I engaged an interpreter, selected many large wicker baskets of tomatoes, lettuce, fruit and vegetables, and tried to haggle prices. To gauge value for money I needed the aid of an old exercise book to convert prices in pesos per kati into US$ (the cash currency I had with me) per pound weight. Oh for a calculator! Then in a hired 'jeepney' – a brightly coloured and religiously adorned pick up truck – we got all the stuff back to the harbour and thence to the ship. Office job this wasn't!

At one stage we were off the coast of Saigon, and at night we heard and saw the flashes from the US fleet's naval gunfire support for the Vietnam troops ashore. We came across some of these ships in Olongapo, a coastal port north of Manila used by US troops from Vietnam for rest and recuperation. We saw the unusual sight of naval guns burned red from prolonged use. Seeing the US troops letting themselves go there was also an eye opener. All streets off the main road in the port were out of bounds, and even the bouncers at the door of the many clubs and bars carried guns. At that time Indonesian Confrontation was nearing its end, though there were still many very unpleasant naval skirmishes. Near the end of my time on *Fort Dunvegan* we transited Indonesian waters – the first British ship to do so after Confrontation – sailing through narrow passages and past idyllic islands en route to Labuan, in Borneo.

Little did I know when I accepted an appointment to Singapore ('ashore and afloat'), at Earls Court in London, what an insight I would have into the old days of the British Empire.

Chief Officer Chris Puxley was aboard *Tidereach* during her Indonesia deployment, which included a trip to the RAF base at Gan:

Gan is a small flat island, part of Addu Atoll, at the southern end of the Maldive chain of islands and located just forty one nautical miles south of the Equator. This island was used as an important RAF air staging base, with the runway taking up virtually all of the available land space. I believe that there was only one woman on this island at the time, a formidable female civil servant connected to the Air Force who stood no nonsense from the hundred or so airmen! We had called in there to top up the RAF diesel and avcat reserves in the old *Wave Victor*, which was then leased to the Air Ministry as a fuel storage hulk and anchored within the atoll reef.

After just a few hours alongside the hulk and with no shore leave, we sailed again, this time to join a group in support of Special Forces that were operating in the jungle of North Borneo. At this time there was quite a high state of tension, a 'confrontation', between Indonesia and Great Britain. On board *Tidereach* we were all issued with gas masks and steel helmets. Our involvement took us into the Sulu Sea to support British warships there. I remember that on one occasion we moved close inshore to Darvel Bay, to pick up some soldiers who had been fighting terrorists in that region. As an eighteen year old apprentice this seemed quite exciting stuff!

We later sailed for Singapore and I recall standing watches with the engineers down below in the engine and boiler rooms, as we approached the island and manoeuvred up the Jahore Strait. I was stunned by the stiflingly hot conditions that they regularly worked in. The heat in these spaces was intense, especially so in the tropics. The only relief was to stand beneath one of the ventilator trunkings for a while before moving off again into the maze of pipe-work and deafening machinery.

In the boiler-room of this inferno, the firemen controlled the steam pressure by lighting or extinguishing a series of oil burners. These were high-pressure jet nozzles, which atomised the oil spurting into the boiler furnace area. Protected by a steel wall with a small glass window, the firemen lit the burners by opening a small door and thrusting in a lighted rag on a stick!

Incidentally, it was suggested at the time that several Royal Navy vessels had nuclear weapons embarked while deployed during the confrontation and that both R class vessels were also carrying them.

While it is certainly possible that both *Retainer* and *Resurgent* had such devices aboard, no hard evidence exists to suggest that they did.

RFAs deployed to Indonesia

Tankers
Appleleaf, Brambleleaf, Eddyrock, Gold Ranger, Orangeleaf, Rowanol (?), *Tideflow, Tidepool, Tidereach, Tidespring* (1965–6), *Tidesurge, Wave Ruler, Wave Sovereign.*
Stores and ammunition ships
Bacchus, Hebe, Fort Charlotte, Fort Constantine, Fort Dunvegan, Fort Duquesne, Fort Langley, Fort Rosalie, Fort Sandusky, Resurgent, Retainer
Tug
Typhoon

Zanzibar is a small island off the coast of East Africa. In 1963, it experienced a period of unrest, culminating in the overthrow of the elected government.

As a precaution, one hundred and fifty-six British nationals were evacuated on HMS *Owen*, a Royal Navy survey ship (113 passengers) and the *Hebe* (forty-three passengers). The crews of both vessels gave up their cabins for these temporary guests and those left over were housed on camp beds, under deck awnings. Except, that is, for a number of teenagers and twelve evicted journalists who choose to rough it under the stars. Writing for a living does tend to toughen one, of course!

The operation was entirely successful, all passengers being supplied with, as the captain of *Owen* put it: '... four course dinners and ample breakfasts in the dining halls whilst hamburgers and soup were available to a late hour'.

This treatment was to continue until their arrival and final disembarkation at Mombasa.

The RNSTS

Brought into existence to replace the previous unwieldy fuel and stores departments with a single, streamlined organisation, the Royal Navy Supply & Transport Service (RNSTS) was formed on 1 January 1965, becoming responsible for the supply of everything a Royal Navy ship required to remain at sea, from a new Olympus turbine to the supply officer's paper clips. As well as this immense task, the Service also organised the food supply for the whole of Britain's armed forces.

Government organisations responsible for supplying the Royal Navy had been in existence since the sixteenth century, but prior to 1965, naval supplies had come to be the responsibility of four separate, predominantly independent Directorates, supervised by their own heads of department, namely the Director of Stores, who was responsible for, among much else, the day to day operation of the RFA, Director of Armament Supply, Director of Victualling and Director of Fuel, Movements and Transport.

By the early 1960s, however, the need for rationalisation and integrated Afloat Support was becoming clear and so a new Service came into being, headed by a senior Civil Servant, the Director General of Supplies & Transport (Naval), who was directly responsible to the Chief of Fleet Support (Fourth Sea Lord on the Board of Admiralty).

The Headquarters branch of the Service was divided into four separate administrative Directorates, each headed by a Director of Supplies & Transport. Their responsibilities were: Armament Supply and Management Services (DST (AS)), Fuel, Movements and Victualling (DST (FMV)), Naval Stores (DST (NS)) and Finance (DST (FIN)).

Complementing the Headquarters organisation was an integrated stores organisation in the main dockyards and several specialist inland depots for stores like ammunition and electronics. Additionally, there were also various ammunition and fuel depots run by the new Service on behalf of NATO.

The RFA functioned as RNSTS means of delivery at sea and was the direct responsibility of the Fleet Manager RFA, under the DST (FMV).

Introduced in 1966, the Fleet Manager was attached to headquarters staff of DST (FMV) and ranked as Assistant Director, responsible for management of the whole RFA fleet. Later, the post was split, first into Fleet Manager (Tankers) and Fleet Manager (Dry Cargo and LSLs), then finally into (Materiel) and (Personnel and Operations).

This newly reorganised Service soon had its hands full because, with Ian Smith's 1966 unilateral declaration of Rhodesian independence, the RFA found itself assigned to what came to be known as the Beira Patrol, replenishing Royal Navy warships employed in blockading access ports to Rhodesia, to prevent the import of crude oil.

Chief Officer Richard Walker, who served on several of the LSLs during this period, has briefly described the background to the Beira deployment:

> In 1964 Nyasaland and Malawi were granted independence from Great Britain but Ian Smith's Southern Rhodesia made an illegal Unilateral Declaration of Independence on the 11th of November 1965, so as well as sanctions Great Britain was forced to blockade Beira, the principal port of Portuguese Mozambique from March of 1966. Ships of the Royal Navy manned the blockade and were supported throughout by ships of the RFA.

Unfortunately for the Wilson government, South Africa and Portuguese Mozambique circumvented the blockade. South Africans freely donated petrol to their Rhodesian neighbours while Mozambique opened the railway line from Lourenço Marques to Rhodesia, thus totally negating any effect the blockade might have had.

Finally, in 1976, to the consternation of his white supporters, Ian Smith, leader of the Rhodesian government, announced a two-year plan for the introduction of black majority rule.

This resulted in the country being renamed Zimbabwe and the eventual election of one Robert Mugabe, a former terrorist, as president, in 1980. The appalling history of that unfortunate country, after the Unilateral Declaration of Independence (UDI) and under Mugabe's rule, is too well known to need any reiteration here.

The Beira Patrol lasted from 1967 to 1975 and RFA ships on this assignment spent long periods at sea, along with their naval colleagues. It turned out to be more a test of patience than fortitude, with sixteen tankers and ten store ships supplying the Royal Navy at various times.

Air cover was provided by Royal Navy carriers to begin with but these were soon replaced by RAF Shackletons and the normal Royal Navy deployment was two frigates with an RFA tanker for replenishment. Warships usually did a spell of four weeks on the patrol on their way out to the Far East and another four weeks on their way home. The RFA ships were not so lucky.

The record for endurance was set by *Tidespring* during 1967. She spent ninety days continuously on the patrol, steamed 33,000 nautical miles and replenished ships at an average of six per week.

George Mortimore remembers an amusing dichotomy during the Beira supply run:

> In early 1973 RFA *Tarbatness* called at Durban to load fresh meat and veg. This we supplied by RAS to the HM Ships blockading Beira (and Rhodesia). So, this meant that the South Africans were feeding the ships that were blockading the Smith regime who were, we understood, their friends. Funny old world.
>
> Also while on Beira, we discovered that the HM Ships were lending Royal Navy Film Corporation movies to the resident Portuguese frigate in exchange for Port wine. I believe Harold Wilson found out about this and told them to stop it. We were also told by the same chap not to listen to Radio Rhodesia.

The NATO Standing Naval Force Atlantic (STANAVFORLANT) came into existence in 1967, as a permanent multinational peacetime naval squadron. The Royal Navy still contributes ships periodically, although the RFA participation only amounts to an occasional tanker.

The Army's last two LSLs, *Sir Percivale* and *Sir Geraint* were also launched in 1967 and they soon joined a number of RFAs allocated to the Aden Task Force, covering the withdrawal of British troops from the region.

Aden lies on the Gulf of Aden, nearly at the point where Yemen butts into the ocean at the junction of the Red Sea and the Gulf. The town itself encloses the eastern side of a vast natural harbour that comprises the modern port, while the western peninsula of little Aden is the site of the oil refinery and tanker port.

It has always been an important port on the sea routes between Europe and India and in 1839, having been ceded some seventy-five square miles of the area by its ruler, the British East India Company landed Royal Marines at Aden to occupy the territory and prevent pirates using the area to attack the shipping routes to India.

Roughly equidistant from the Suez Canal, Bombay and Zanzibar, all important British possessions, Aden developed extensive replenishment facilities. Steamer Point, one of several sub-districts, was the site of a coaling station and there were also arrangements for supplying boiler water.

After Indian independence, and the loss of the Suez Canal in 1956, Aden became the main British base in the region.

Little Aden, in particular, was well known to seafarers, including RFA crews, for its tanker port and an excellent seamen's mission, situated near the BP Aden tug jetty, complete with swimming pool and an air-conditioned bar.

Trouble began when, in an attempt to stabilise the region politically, the British incorporated the colony of Aden into the Federation of Arab Emirates of the South, as the State of Aden; the Federation itself was then renamed Federation of South Arabia (FSA).

This incorporation, officially having taken place in January 1963 and very unpopular with many of the city's inhabitants, was directly responsible for what has come to be known as the Aden Emergency.

Sporadic fighting, especially in the hills, went on for the rest of that year until 10 December, when a grenade attack on the British High Commissioner, planned and carried out by the National Liberation Front (NLF), killed one person and injured another fifty, including the Commissioner himself.

A 'state of emergency' was declared after this attack but in 1964 the end of the fighting appeared to be in sight, with Britain announcing its intention to grant independence to the FSA in 1968, with the proviso that the British military would remain.

Unfortunately, this announcement brought no cessation of the violence and January 1967 saw mass riots between the NLF and their rivals, the Front for the Liberation of South Yemen (FLOSY) and a wholesale escalation of terrorist attacks on troops.

Up to 1963, the RFA had had considerable involvement with Aden. Both BP and Shell had chartered tankers from the service to transport crude oil from ports in both the Red Sea and Persian Gulf. Both companies also sold furnace fuel oil (FFO) to the Royal Navy and, of course, it was RFA tankers, which were used to transport the FFO from the companies' nominated refineries to naval depots such as Malta.

By 2 November 1967, Foreign Secretary George Brown had set end of November as the date for British withdrawal and both the army and Navy began to plan accordingly.

Unable to determine whether their military colleagues would be forced to make a fighting withdrawal, the Royal Navy provided a Task Force, designated Task Force 318, formed specifically to cover the military withdrawal from Aden and consisting of four aircraft carriers, two assault landing ships, a guided missile destroyer, a submarine and five landing ships sank (LSTs). They were accompanied by a number of RFA ships, including *Tidespring, Stromness* and several of the Leaf class. *Retainer* also spent some time anchored in the harbour although her stay was far from uneventful.

After only a few hours at anchor, the big armament support ship was forced to move quickly out to sea when it was discovered that the FLN had established a missile launching site overlooking her anchorage.

After this close shave, the RFA ships found themselves condemned to sailing box courses, out of missile range of the coast, in between replenishing the ships of the task force.

Captain Phil Roberts, then navigating officer aboard *Tidespring*, remembered it well:

> Although the military were concerned about an imminent collapse of law and order, in the end, the withdrawal went extremely smoothly, with troops being shuttled out by Hercules transport aircraft. Nearly 4000 troops were moved to Bahrain in the Gulf, for eventual transport to the UK.

The final evacuation of Government House and the other military strong points was covered by 1 Para, along with 42 and 45 Commando, and these left by helicopter for the troopships, fortunately without sustaining a single casualty.

Aden was left to the Nationalist government, and now designated the People's Republic of Southern Yemen.

Bacchus was deployed to Aden during this emergency as her then Third Officer, Chris Puxley, remembers:

> During a homeward passage in June 1967, having recently sailed from Aden, we were part way up the Red Sea and heading for the Suez Canal when the Arab-Israeli Six Day War broke out. Had we been two or three days further ahead, we would have been trapped in the Canal Zone. Less fortunate ships than us were caught up in the conflict and were held in the Great Bitter Lakes for a couple of years until the political situation became stable again. As it was, we turned about and proceeded south around Africa via the Cape of Good Hope. We were also fortunate in having a 'Worldwide' folio of Admiralty charts on board. Many commercial ships normally only carry and correct the charts that they are expecting to need. We heard that many had to navigate for a while using atlases, when the sudden rush for African coastal charts exhausted all available supplies! Our subsequent voyages to and from the Far East were all routed around the Cape of Good Hope, calling at Cape Town briefly for mail and fresh supplies. It was due to this little diversion that I acquired a taste for that lovely South African orange liqueur called 'Van der Humm'.
>
> During 1967, the simmering Aden situation developed into a crisis, amounting to a local war. The Yemeni rebels wanted the British out of their land. *Bacchus* was sent there, along with several other RFAs and warships, to standby to withdraw the British Forces and all their equipment. Many of the soldiers in the surrounding hills were having a tough time of it, with awful atrocities inflicted on any who were captured by the rebels. A Colonel nick-named 'Mad Mich' led the British troops who were hanging on by their teeth. We loaded a lot of their equipment to prevent it falling

into rebel hands and could hear the sound of battle even from the harbour. The ships provided a temporary rest centre for exhausted troops, where they could unwind for a brief period before rejoining the fray. Having loaded as much of their surplus gear as possible we sailed via the Cape and back to the UK.

On one homeward voyage we called in at Gan, in the Maldives, to replenish the RAF base with stocks of bagged cement and beer. On arrival and seeing our deck cargo of old buses, one RAF wag said 'Blimey, you don't see a bus here for months, then four come along at once!'

The airmen stevedores, having manhandled the cement bags into cargo nets, barges and ashore, must have worked up a rare thirst in the equatorial heat and probably drank all the beer before we were even over the horizon.

Chief Officer Richard Walker also has some clear memories of Aden at that time and the subsequent fate of the LSLs:

At about the time of the Beira Patrol deployment, Britain was trying to extract itself from a terrorist led insurrection in South Yemen, centred on the port of Aden. The two main groups of terrorists were the Front for the Liberation of South Yemen and the National Liberation Front. Both groups were to commit atrocities before our Forces pulled out and it's fair to say that we perhaps gave more grief than we took onboard but pull out we did on the 27th of November 1967 with sovereignty being granted on the 30th. I had joined the BI managed ship *Sir Bedivere* at Marchwood and we sailed rather hurriedly from Southampton and headed for Aden calling in at Gibraltar for repairs on our way. *Bedivere* was a new ship and there were lots of problems, especially with SW (sea water) cooling pipes fracturing. We arrived in Aden in the October and the Fleet, the largest since Spithead divided into two groups, one in the inner harbour and one outside. Our station was the inner and we all remained on Stand By till the day we finally left.

Within our group were another two Landing Ships (LSLs), a collection of smaller LSTs and some of the RFA ships with which we fraternised at every opportunity. Our orders were that should our forces have to beat a hasty retreat we were to beach and take them off. In the event our last forces, which I believe were 1 Para, marched out of Camp Radfan on the 27th with weapons loaded and boarded our ships in a more conventional manner. We had also taken onboard Marines and a number of logistical troops. As well as the personnel, our tank deck and upper deck had been loaded from the mexi floats with all manner of colonial paraphernalia plus ammunition and other ordinance.

All the ships left the inner harbour without incident and we formed up with the outer ships into one group to await the last defiant gesture which was a fly past of helicopters led by a single Sea King carrying our last High Commissioner, Sir Humphrey Trevelyan. After a bitter inter-terrorist struggle and 128 years of British control, Sir Trevelyan signed over Aden to the NLF, which had beaten the Egyptian backed FLOSY.

With that completed, the Fleet sailed for various destinations, some to the Beira Patrol, while others returned to the UK. We were ordered to Singapore but not before stopping mid-Indian Ocean and dumping into the sea most of that which we had refused to leave the new authorities in Aden.

RFAs deployed to Aden

Tankers
Appleleaf, Dewdale, Olna, Tideflow, Tidespring
Ammunition and store ships
Bacchus, Fort Sandusky, Reliant, Resurgent, Retainer, Stromness

---

January 1968 marked a major turning point for both the Royal Navy and RFA when the Wilson government's annual Defence Review signalled the loss of the Royal Navy's aircraft carriers and a rundown in the Middle East and Far East bases, probably with a proportionate reduction in RFA ships. Slightly better news arrived in December, however, when Whitehall announced that from 1970, manning and management of the Round Table class LSLs would become the responsibility of the RFA.

Richard Walker was serving aboard *Sir Geraint* at the time of the changeover and remembers it clearly:

> In 1968 I joined *Sir Geraint* and after completing nearly a year out on the Singapore station, we returned to the UK for refit and it was at this time that the RFA's involvement with the LSLs began.
>
> Shortly after our arrival, we were informed that the RFA were to take over the running of the Logistic ships which comprised *Sir Lancelot, Sir Bedivere, Sir Geraint, Sir Percivale, Sir Tristram* and *Sir Galahad*. British India's (BIs) personnel department had agreed with the RFA that we could transfer over if all parties concurred.
>
> Prior to this, BI had also taken over the running of the smaller Landing Ship Tanks (LST) from Atlantic Steam Navigation (ASN), commencing a scrapping programme of that fleet, some sixteen ships altogether being lost during the sixties. As the programme progressed more and more ASN Officers crossed over to the LSLs, replacing the BI Officers, thus allowing them to return to their more familiar vessels. By the time that RFA took over the management from BI only one of the LSTs remained, *Empire Gull*.

The transfer itself was not exactly unopposed, as one retired RFA officer remembers:

> There seemed to be a feeling of not quite belonging as far as the LSL Officers were concerned Though not fully supported at the time, a number of senior RFA officers were against employing any British India LSL personnel. The main reason given was that, although they knew LSLs, they had no experience in the broader context of the RFA and therefore could not be incorporated on a rank for rank basis. Classified as a consolidation and not a takeover, the argument failed.

Aden's peace talks and Suez were still both providing complications during 1968, with RFA vessels tasked to support the Royal Navy in both areas. The talks had only required Royal Navy presence off the old port for the duration of the discussions but with the Suez Canal still closed, it had been forced to establish a refuelling point off St Helena.

Known as the Guinea Gulf Patrol, this deployment consisted of RFA ships of the Wave and Rover classes maintaining a replenishment service, usually in the region of

St Helena, while using Freetown to load fuel supplies and the Simonstown naval base for both loading and repairs.

Much had changed for the RFA during the preceding decade, with improvements in training enabling the service to be much better able to meet the increasingly technological requirements of the Royal Navy, particularly in areas such as the transfer and storage of both conventional and nuclear weapons and in communications. Side by side with this new training programme, larger and better equipped ships, particularly the recently introduced R class, were also providing the equipment needed to meet the challenges, some new and many all too familiar, which the 1970s held in store.

Such improvements meant that the Royal Navy had begun to see replenishment at sea as their preferred option. This enabled them to be all but independent of their traditional bases, whose availability was starting to become problematical anyway, given the political and economic situation in many of the countries where they were situated.

Finally and perhaps most importantly, the RFA itself was beginning to develop an autonomy all its own, turning it from a collection of converted cargo tramps and tankers into a specialised fleet crewed by highly trained individuals, well fitted to take its place within the Royal Navy's logistic organisation and appropriately described by one of its staff as 'A fleet within a fleet'.

Chapter 5

The Doldrum Years: 1970–9

Despite the wholesale cutbacks to the Royal Navy occasioned by the Wilson government's 1968 Defence Review, the RFA initially seemed to have emerged relatively unscathed.

In 1958, the fleet had consisted of 109 ships, with a total workforce of 3,400 men, and operating costs of £7,050,000. By 1970, after the loss of several vessels in the Eddy, Surf, early Fort and Wave classes, among others, these numbers had decreased to less than eighty, although personnel numbers had remained relatively constant. These ship losses reflected, to a certain extent, the very real change in the RFA's role. As a result of the loss of many Royal Navy overseas bases, freighting fuel was now of much less importance, the naval emphasis being placed far more on the RFA capacity for replenishment at sea.

Although the fleet was shrinking, the decade began with the service actually acquiring a whole new class of ships, when, in 1970, transfer of the LSLs was effected, with Marchwood Military Port becoming the base port.

Originally, the 'Knights of the Round Table' or Sir class, as the LSLs are more correctly known, had been designed by the Ministry of Defence (Army Department) for the secure, rapid movement of troops and their equipment. Building and management of these vessels was the responsibility of the British India Steam Navigation Co Ltd (BI), a member of the P&O group, and operating on behalf of the Board of Trade Sea Transport Division.

British India had a long tradition of liaison with the British Army, dating back to 1856, when the newly formed company (then the Calcutta & Burma Steam Navigation Co) chartered its first two ships to the government for trooping service. As time went on and the company grew larger, the government chartered more and more of its ships for service in campaigns such as Abyssinia, Egypt, Sudan, Burma, China and the two Boer wars. British India ships were also involved in both World Wars but with the move to air transport for troops that took place during the 1950s, BI took over management of the Army's LSLs and LSTs, until the sale or scrapping of most of the latter during the 1960s and the transfer of the LSLs to RFA control in 1969.

In addition to their almost unique flat bottom design, LSLs can also carry what are known in the RFA as Mexeflotes (this name is derived from *M*ilitary *Ex*periment *E*quipment). Technically, they are called 'Class 60 load carrying pontoon equipment' and consist a single 120-foot, ninety-ton pontoon, powered by two Hydromaster six-cylinder seventy-five horsepower outboard diesels. These motors are stowed separately and lowered into their housings once the pontoons are in the water. Mexeflotes may be disassembled and transported as deck cargo or, more usually, they are winched vertically and carried flat on the side of the LSL. In use, they may then be dropped or lowered into the water, the engines fitted and the raft is then available to transport men and equipment ashore or joined together, form a bridge between the ship and the

RFA fleet list 1970

Fast replenishment tankers
Tidereach, Tiderace, Tiderange
Tidepool, Tidespring
Olmeda, Olna, Olwen
Replenishment tankers
Blue Rover, Grey Rover
Wave Baron, Wave Chief, Wave Laird, Wave Prince, Wave Ruler, Wave Victor
Mobile reserve tankers
Derwentdale, Dewdale, Ennerdale
Freighting tankers
Bishopdale,
Appleleaf, Bayleaf, Brambleleaf, Orangeleaf, Pearleaf, Plumleaf
Fleet attendant tankers
Black Ranger, Blue Ranger, Gold Ranger, Brown Ranger
Eddy class
Eddyfirth, Eddyness
1,500 ton class
Rowanol
Miscellaneous
Spaburn
Store ships and issuing ships
Fort Langley, Fort Rosalie, Fort Sandusky
Retainer, Resurgent
Bacchus, Hebe
Lyness, Stromness, Tarbatness
Regent, Resource
Robert Dundas, Robert Middleton
Landing ships (LST and LSLs)
Empire Gull
Sir Bedivere, Sir Galahad, Sir Geraint, Sir Lancelot, Sir Percivale, Sir Tristram
Specialist ship
Engadine
Salvage vessels
Sea Salvor, Succour
Tugs
Bustler, Cyclone, Empire Fred, Empire Rosa, Reward, Samsonia, Typhoon

Total: 65 vessels (all in service; tugs alone on yard craft agreement)

In 1970, the proportion of replenishment tankers had increased, such that they now considerably outnumbered the older, slower freighting tankers. New R class store ships had also been introduced, these being the first RFAs with purpose-built nuclear containment facilities.

A number of vessels in the Surf and Eddy classes came and went during 1950–70. Hence, although their names appear elsewhere, they will not appear in either the 1950 or 1970 lists.

shore if conditions do not allow the vessel to beach. When used as transport, they can carry about one ton per foot of length.

Mexeflotes are not crewed by the RFA, but by specially trained personnel from 17 Port Regiment, Royal Logistics Corps (RLC), based at Marchwood Military Port (renamed Marchwood Sea Mounting Centre in 2000), home port to the LSLs.

Marchwood Military Port (MMP), lies on the western side of Southampton water, opposite the docks. Established in 1942, it has extensive ammunition and explosive handling facilities, of necessity, because it is the only strictly military port in the country.

In 1948, a permanent 'Port' regiment was organised, responsible for dealing with all matters of administration and cargo handling involving any vessel, civilian or military, using the port and named 17 Port & Training Regiment, Royal Engineers. Later, it became 17 Port Regiment, Royal Corps of Transport before receiving its present designation, 17 Port Regiment, Royal Logistics Corps.

The port itself consists of a series of jetties, with extensive roll-on-roll-off (ro-ro) facilities and railway access, capable of handling vessels with a number of different ramp configurations and up to 16,000 deadweight tons. There are extensive, heavy duty cargo handling arrangements and the largest jetty, which is 220 metres long, is equipped with a thirty-five-tonne rail-mounted crane. The year 1986 saw further improvements, when the port was extensively rebuilt to improve the jetties.

Colonel Mike Bowles, who served with the Port Regiment during the Falklands War and later commanded it, knows Marchwood intimately and has offered a few observations of his own about the port and the LSLs:

When I think of Marchwood and particularly my early days in the Regiment there, I think automatically of LSLs. The 6 Landing Ships Logistic of the *Sir Lancelot* class were such a part of the Marchwood scene that it was hard to think of one without the other. Marchwood was, of course, the home port of these ships and close relationships were inevitably forged between the crews and the personnel in the Regiment. RFA officers used to enjoy visits to the Mess in Byam's House and vice versa for military officers going on board the ships. I can remember one particular party aboard one of the LSLs alongside in the port but probably best I don't go there!

My first posting to Marchwood was in 1973 when the operation in Northern Ireland was in full swing. A regular commitment for the Regiment was to provide a Port Operating detachment with a young officer in charge to go with the LSLs running between Seaforth Container terminal in Liverpool and Belfast. We would carry roulement Battalions over for their tour of duty in the Province and then back again on the return journey at the end.

The LSLs were crewed in those days by Chinese seamen which had a number of advantages. Not least of these advantages was the ready supply of blue movies that they held and which they were happy to show to embarked personnel for a 'small consideration'! The Marchwood guys got in free, needless to say!

Another part of Regimental life that I remember from the 70s was the routine dumping of ammunition. This was ammo that had gone past its 'use by' date and was loaded on to ships at Marchwood and then taken out to a suitable part of the ocean (*ie* where there was a big hole!) and pushed over the side. I'm not sure King Neptune approved but it was around the time that one of the ships coming back from a Norway deployment had her bow doors caved in by a wave in a storm in the North

Sea! Perhaps Neptune was not happy. I am not sure that Greenpeace would be content these days either!

We were also heavily committed in the export of Chieftain tanks to Iran. Seems funny to look back on now! I don't think this involved the RFA except that they would have been aware of the movement of the tanks through the port. It was in the days before a decent approach road to Marchwood Military Port existed and the huge tank transporters had to negotiate their way carefully down tiny lanes to get to the port area. Once there the tanks were loaded to either LCTs or to Mexeflote for the trip down to Cowes Roads were they were transshipped to a Heavy Lift ship for the journey to the Gulf.

I mentioned the Chinese before. There was nothing to beat the very authentic curry lunches they produced. I have a long abiding memory of an LSL in the port in the 70s, before there was a second jetty, and there was seemingly always, at least one Chinaman on the RoRo fishing in the murky depths of Southampton Water. I used to do a bit of windsurfing in those days and seeing the colour and content of the water was always a great encouragement not to fall off my board! I remember seeing a dead seagull floating past on its back, feet in the air one day and resolving more than ever to stay out of the water. I am sure the fish thrived on it though and after all, what the eye doesn't see, the heart doesn't … etc!

Yet another LSL deployment for me was going on an exercise to the southern flank of NATO, ie Turkey and Greece. On this occasion we were to load the ship (Sir Percivale) in Milford Haven and we were to take the Blues and Royals to the exercise. They were equipped with light armoured vehicles of the Scimitar series which came to Milford Haven by train. In good military fashion, the crews traveled on a different train from the vehicles and the almost inevitable happened that one of the trains was delayed – the one with the personnel on board! Not a problem to the ever ingenious stevedores of the Port Regiment.

My Senior NCO in charge of the Port Op detachment assured me that the stevedores were all trained to drive the Scimitar vehicles and so we could commence the loading process without the actual vehicle drivers being there. This appeared to be a reasonable and pragmatic solution in the circumstances, particularly as there was little time to spare between the arrival of the cargo and the vessel sailing time. One thing I did not know was that all the vehicles were locked for the rail journey and so the ingenious stevedores needed to knock the padlocks off in order to gain access to said vehicles! The Scimitars were duly offloaded and driven to the port and loaded in to the LSL. There were a few interested parties around watching the loading, in particular the daughter of the Chief Engineer of the ship who just happened to be a very glamorous looking teenager wearing a very short skirt! The inevitable happened and one of my stevedores asked the daughter if she would like a ride in one of the Scimitars coming on board. Having helped her very gallantly (can't you just picture it!) into the driver's seat he then sat on the top of the vehicle and instructed her as she manoeuvred the vehicle in the tank deck. I was on the upper deck, observing proceedings below through the open after hatch. Just as the Scimitar being driven by the aforementioned Chief's daughter hove into my view, so at my elbow, arrived the Adjutant of the Blues and Royals. The timing was perfect. As the Adjutant and I peered over into the deck below, the Scimitar in question being driven (aimed might be a better word) by the said daughter, careered totally out of control into the side of the tank deck causing fairly severe damage to the vehicle – thankfully there were no people injured. This was an inauspicious start to my 6 weeks embarked with the Blues and Royals although I have to say that they did recover their calm fairly quickly. I spent many happy hours on the flight deck with them clay pigeon shooting once we were under way.

A subsequent tour of duty took me to the USA as an Exchange Officer for a couple of years in the mid 80s. I was stationed in Fort Eustis, Virginia, and teaching officer courses at the US Army Transportation School. We had a lot of contact with Military Sealift Command (MSC), a close equivalent of the RFA. One day I was in Norfolk Naval Base which was close to us and spied a familiar looking ship. She was in MSC colours but on investigation turned out to be the former RFA *Stromness*. I think that all three of the Ness class were bought by MSC after the Falklands Conflict.

I had the honour of Commanding the Regiment at Marchwood between 1992 and 1994 and very much valued my further contact with the RFA. One memorable occasion was an exercise with our equivalent French Regiment, 519 Regiment du Train at La Rochelle. For the exercise we took a large element of the Regiment embarked in an LSL to the La Rochelle area for about a week. I had invited a Brigadier in our chain of command to accompany us on the exercise. As so often happens he was too busy to come for the whole exercise and so I arranged that he would join us by helo transfer on route. The time arrived and it was a pig of a day. In the Bay of Biscay, low cloud, raining, about 50 knots of wind and the Captain of the LSL cheerfully told me there would be no way he would be conducting flying operations that day! Imagine his surprise therefore when a call came from an Army Air Lynx inbound to the ship. Panic – not even a Navy Lynx but an Army one with skids and not wheels! Was the chap mad?! The LSL duly turned on a flying course and with the weather worsening, lashing rain and the instruments showing gusts of 55 knots across the deck it seemed inconceivable that he was going to attempt a landing. However, in he came, successfully dropped off his passenger and was gone again. A pretty neat piece of flying I thought. The Captain of the ship was highly impressed (once the guy was safely gone!). The Brigadier, having felt very queasy during the flight, was happy to get out of the aircraft but half an hour later was throwing up from sea sickness! I think he might have been regretting his decision to visit the exercise at this stage! The weather improved and the exercise went well. I have to say the French compo rations are interesting with their small bottle of wine for each man each day! The highlight of the exercise for me was the beaching of the LSL. It was the first time I had experienced it and the evolution was a total success.

I was posted back to the Falklands in the mid 90s immediately after having completed my tour of duty in command at Marchwood. I had previously taken a Squadron from the Regiment on Op Corporate in 82. My new post was on the staff of HQ British Forces Falkland Islands. Here was to be one of the funniest coincidences of my career. Frequently on station in the Islands in those days was the RFA *Diligence*, purchased from Stena by the MoD after the '82 Conflict. On board was a chap by the name of Lee Upton as Chief Officer who I had last encountered some 30 years before when he was the Lt Cdr TASO and midshipmen's training officer aboard a Tribal Class Frigate, HMS *Mohawk*, and I was a midshipman in the ship! We had a beer or two for old times' sake – as you do.

Seeing the new Bay Class Landing ships of today's RFA, I have to wonder how they will substitute for the LSLs. Certainly they are larger by quite a degree and I understand with correspondingly greater draft. How far off shore will they therefore be sitting when mexeflote is launched? This of course will depend on the location but the LSLs were a wonderful asset with their ability in the extreme to beach themselves – but always to be close in to shore with their shallow draft.

Before 'Corporate' came along and interrupted everyone's Spring of 1982, I had been busy arranging a Squadron exercise for my Port Sqn in Cyprus for June of 1982. I did a recce in February and whilst there met a Battery Commander from the Royal Artillery who was going to be doing the same sort of exercise with his men and overlapping with us. We therefore agreed that we would have some inter-unit sports and social events. The Argentine invasion changed all those sort of plans but imagine my surprise on arriving at Ascension en route south to find the same Battery Commander and his men waiting to board the self same ship that I was embarked in! We had planned to meet on an Island – just a different Island in the end!

Two of the new Rover class, *Grey Rover* and *Blue Rover*, were completed in 1970, and sisterships *Gold Rover* and *Black Rover* joined the fleet in 1974. Ships in this class of small fleet replenishment tanker are among the RFA's most useful types, with conformation and equipment making these suitable for a wide range of duties, which included, in 1976 and 1977, an experimental RAS with two tankers of the BP British River class.

Although experience gained during these trials allowed commercial tankers of this type to be quickly deployed in 1982 during Operation 'Corporate', the RAS equipment was primitive in the extreme and they suffered several problems, including some equipment failure, during their time in the South Atlantic.

A vessel of the Rover class was also involved in another incident that was later to prove of crucial importance when, in 1971, a vertical short take-off and landing (VSTOL) Harrier jump jet landed on *Green Rover*, while the latter was anchored in the Thames.

Seen at the time as no more than a good publicity stunt, the landing foreshadowed the extensive use that had to be made, again during the Falklands campaign of 1982, of the aviation facilities of both RFAs and converted merchant ships, in particular the ill-fated *Atlantic Conveyor*. Later, in 1975, *Engadine*, the Royal Navy's helicopter training ship, also conducted trials with the Hawker Siddeley VSTOL Harrier, as did *Stromness* in 1978.

Two more important new additions to the RFA fleet were launched much later in this decade. Both were ammunition and stores ships, the first, *Fort Grange*, completing at Scott Lithgow's Cartsburn yard, Greenock in 1978 and her sistership, *Fort Austin*, joining the service a year later. Equipped with modern navigation and com-munications equipment as well as having two permanently embarked Sea King helicopters (they have room for five), both these vessels have proved an essential part of the RFA's increasing military commitments.

Fort Austin, then commanded by Commodore S C Dunlop CBE, was, in fact, the first British surface ship ordered south at the start of the 1982 Falklands War, her master receiving his orders in Gibraltar on 26 March, 1982, just as the ship and crew were preparing to leave for the UK, after six months on the Armilla patrol.

Several RAS-capable Leaf and Dale class tankers also came into service during the 1970s, although many of the service's older ships were laid up or sold during this period, so that by the beginning of 1980, the fleet had been reduced to twenty-seven vessels and approximately 3000 officers and ratings. Although the fleet was much smaller, its character had continued to undergo a marked change, with every vessel now RAS capable, an improvement of which the Royal Navy took full advantage.

Incidentally, all these ships would have been involved in work-ups, as an essential part of a new ship's preparation, giving the crews a chance to exercise and become familiar with their new vessel's equipment before joining the operational fleet. They were organised during this period by the Commander Sea Training, based at Portland.

Tragically, one of the more recent additions to the fleet, *Ennerdale*, was lost at sea in 1970, happily without any casualties.

Ennerdale left Mahe, in the Seychelles, at around 7.00 am local time. She had cleared the harbour and arrived opposite Victoria when she struck a pair of uncharted granite pinnacles. Mr R Hollis, then a Third Officer (Engineer) remembered that morning vividly:

> I was on watch in the engine room that day (Engineer (3rd)). We had left Mahe earlier at around 7.00 am to refuel HMS *Andromeda*, but didn't make it after hitting the pinnacle at about 0737hrs local.
>
> All of the ship's centre tanks from No 1 to No 9, the pumproom and the engine room were holed, sea water was pouring out of the crankcase explosion doors and very quickly reached the generators. The lights soon went out!
>
> We all managed to get into the life boats but it was a few hours before we were all picked up as there was some doubt about the seriousness of the situation, by those ashore. I recall staying in a beautiful house for a week, before the whole crew boarded RFA *Hebe* and were taken to Gan for the flight home.

A further tragedy occurred in 1978, when *Hebe* was severely damaged by fire while at Main Wharf, in Gibraltar's Admiralty Dockyard. Much of the bridge and accommodation was destroyed, with one rating killed. Subsequent investigation showed the cause of the fire to be arson and later, a crew member was charged with arson and convicted. This case became a quite drawn-out affair because the deck hand that started the fire later confessed and was finally imprisoned for life, after being convicted of the manslaughter of a fellow crewman, Leslie Mason.

Another of the Dale class was involved in a slightly less dangerous incident in 1972, when *Derwentdale* was deployed as part of Operation 'Testudo giganticus'.

The population of giant tortoises on St Helena had, for a number of reasons, become reduced to a solitary 150 year old male named Jonathan. This was potentially very serious because tradition said that if ever the giant tortoises disappeared from the island ... so would the British. So it was the RFA to the rescue. *Derwentdale* was tasked for the operation, collecting a young female giant tortoise called Myrtle, en route, and depositing her on St Helena where hopefully the happy couple settled down to domestic bliss ... or at least what passes for domestic bliss if you are one hundred and fifty and lugging your house around on your back!

Helicopters have become essential equipment on RFAs in recent years and this was emphasised, in 1978, when 824 Naval Air Squadron (NAS) became the parent unit for RFA helicopters.

The RFA has always had a close working relationship with the Fleet Air Arm, stretching back to 1951, and the first helicopter trials involving *Fort Duquesne*. Westland Dragonflies of NAS 705 were used for the trials and these were so successful that many of the older RFAs were fitted with helicopter pads to allow these aircraft to land and refuel, although proper maintenance facilities were not available.

Both were fitted with helicopter pads as part of their standard build, as well as being assigned permanent helicopter flights flying Wessex HU5s from NAS 829, originally based at Yeovilton. Wessex HU5s or 'Wessies', were the usual helicopter aboard RFAs during this period. They were a basic helicopter with a robust airframe and without weapons or sophisticated navigation aids, which kept their maintenance requirements low and made them ideal for their 'workhorse' role aboard the big R classes.

Usually, RFAs transfer dry goods by heavy jackstay, which involves a steel rope that is passed between ships so that palleted loads of about one ton can be literally swung across.

Sometimes, for a variety of reasons, like time, weather, sea conditions or delicacy of the load, this method cannot be used for dry goods and the pallets are then transferred by helicopter in a process termed vertical replenishment (VERTREP). VERTREP has a number of advantages over the jackstay, the main one being that ships in a formation or on screening duties do not have to leave their position and can continue to carry out their allotted tasks. Weapon arcs, sonar and radars are not compromised by being alongside and movement is free so that, for example, ships can zigzag in the event of submarine attack.

Newer RFAs, such as the modern Fort class, carried either Wessex or Sea King helicopters, with RN aircrews and maintenance staff embarked as part of the ship's complement.

Mike Tidd, Commanding Officer of Tidespring's flight during the Falklands War, where he flew a Wessex HU5, explains the procedure for VERTREP:

> Whilst many of the heavy stores that need to be transferred between ships at sea are transferred by good old 'seaman-like' jackstay transfers, if deck space and helicopters are available and/or the weather is rough, vertrep is quicker and safer.
>
> The aim once airborne on a vertrep sortie was to keep the loads moving as quickly and efficiently as possible. To make pickup and drop-offs slick, aircraft would usually fit an 8ft strop to the load-lifting hook. This gave better clearance from obstructions, allowing more rapid manoeuvring above the deck, as well as keeping the underslung load clear of the airframe in transit.
>
> If the load had to be lifted from amongst higher obstructions then a 20ft strop could be used, though this made station-keeping more difficult as the aircrewman conned the pilot into position over a pitching, rolling deck.
>
> The deck crew would be equipped with a 'shepherds crook' with which to catch the hook and earth it to get rid of the static build-up before handling it. In rough weather this static gave quite a kick!

Sea Kings were introduced as the Royal Navy's standard helicopter during the 1970s, gradually replacing the rather basic Wessex. These were reliable, robust and could be easily adapted for any of the roles required by the Royal Navy or Royal Marines. They did, however, have one major disadvantage. They were too heavy to be embarked on frigates or destroyers.

So Sea Kings usually had to be carried on the much larger RFAs, the new Fort class being able to carry up to five of these big helicopters in full battle order, emphasising the Royal Navy's reliance on the RFA even further. It also greatly increased the Service's involvement in military operations, a role for which the RFA had never been intended.

Other technological advances for this period included the fitting of a satellite communications terminal to *Olmeda* and the trialling by *Resource* of the Mk2 RAS rig, which allowed transfer of Seawolf missiles to UK warships, both of which took place in 1979. *Lyness* also had a trials GEC MK II rig fitted in the early 1970s. Incidentally, the rig, which was located at Station 1, apparently failed more times than it worked!

The RNSTS stores personnel had by now become well integrated into their afloat role aboard the big RFA stores and ammunition ships and Mr David Soden, a senior member of the 'STONNERY', as the afloat branch of the RNSTS were known, had a few stories of his own to tell, from the other side of the counter:

The STO(N) (Supply Transport Officer [Naval]) department is a MoD civilian manned organisation employed on RFA solid support vessels providing a floating supermarket for the Royal Navy. It was born some 60 years ago when it was realised that RN ships normally only embarked stores whilst in port which restricted the length of time the ship could remain at sea before running out of certain commodities.

Initially, a small range of items was embarked on an RFA in support of the RN and MoD civilians were asked to sail with the ship as custodians of the cargo. Since those days the department has grown and has been established on solid support ships ever since which have become an integral part of the RFA serving in nearly all operational conflicts around the world including Lebanon, the Gulf, Sierra Leone and the Falklands.

The present department is made of volunteers recruited from MoD depots and establishments and these volunteers are carefully selected for their expertise in the management and handling of the embarked cargo. When these volunteers are selected for service afloat they are subject to a medical examination and undertake both sea survival and fire fighting courses just like those undertaken by their RFA colleagues. Once successfully completed, the volunteer would be appointed to a ship and expected to serve a minimum of between 12 to 15 months on the same ship before returning to his /her parent depot/establishment.

Appointments weren't always been so well organised. During the mid 1970s the STO(N) dept was having to supply staff for *Resurgent*, *Reliant*, *Resource*, *Regent*, *Stromness*, *Tarbatness* and *Lyness*. On some occasions, it was helpful that staff were willing to extend their tour afloat. I met one man who had served continuously on the same ship for 10 years and the only time he went back to his home depot was when the ship went into refit. There were others that were away from home for so long that by the time they finally left the ship their home depots had closed.

The cargo (up to 10,000 different items) carried can range from something as small as a nut or bolt to frozen meats or even to something as big as a guided missile. All solid support ships are likely to carry a standard cargo load which is dictated by the MoD with additional items as required by the accompanying RN vessels. When fully stored and the ship is operational it is the STO(N)'s responsibility to manage and account for all the items under his control, prepare them when required for transfer at sea and ensure that they are received by the customer in a serviceable condition.

If you were appointed to serve aboard the R class solid support ships and had to work in the No 3 hold (victualling hold) you knew that you were going to be subject to a manual working existence whilst on the ship. Unlike the Fort class ships, the R ships' refrigerated compartments had very small entrances with a lip at floor level, so no mechanical lifting equipment could access the compartments so every item had to be manhandled.

Number three hold had 15 refrigerated compartments with 6 of them containing frozen stores. Besides manhandling all the stores into the compartments, life was a little more awkward when stores had to be prepared for transfer at sea. This lack of working space meant all frozen loads for transfer had to assembled on the day of the RAS and on some occasions, when replenishing ships like HMS *Ark Royal* or *Hermes*, the number of frozen loads could be as many as 40. The amount of effort required to prepare the pallet loads and get them to the RAS point on time meant an early start for staff. If the RAS happened to be either postponed or cancelled, the frozen loads would have to be decanted from the pallets and returned to the fridges.

Things were different aboard RFAs in the decade before the Falklands War. As just one example, ship's fire exercises would normally take place on a Friday. As a lot of the crew were non contract on some occasions they actually refused to take part in the fire exercises!

During the 1970/80s, when the ship went to sea and you were not in TV range there was little else to do in your cabin but read, listen to music and maybe watch a video.

Individual messes organised their own entertainment which was usually a quiz on a Saturday or a reel to reel film night shown on a Wednesday and a Sunday night. These were the times when the whole mess would make the effort to socialise. In addition to the organised entertainment, some people were more adventurous and organised games which were a little more dangerous. I can remember challenges being made such as who could dive over the bar counter. Other challenges ranged from drinking a yard of ale, eating cream cracker biscuits at speed without drinking water, bar stool games and an engineer's passion which was to make a mountain of beer cans as their beloved 'magic roundabout.

Sunday lunch at sea in 1970 was always the same routine. After smoko we would get dressed and head for the bar by 1200. At the bar there would be a range of small eats consisting of sausage rolls, curry puffs, crisps and nuts. After a few beers we would enter the saloon for lunch which traditionally consisted of tomato soup, steak and finished with ice cream. After finishing lunch we would return to the bar for a coffee and complement the coffee with a liqueur or two

Several minor but significant improvements to the RFA's operational organisation were introduced during this decade, beginning with the appointment, in 1971, of an RFA officer to act as Operations Room Logistics Officer (later Fleet Logistics Officer). This individual was responsible for organising the deployments of RFAs attached to what was now simply 'the Fleet', after the abolition of the post of Commander Far East Fleet and the amalgamation of both fleets under the control of C-in-C Fleet. In the same year, catering and accounts duties were rationalised and integrated, becoming the responsibility of one officer ranked as 'purser'.

Ashore, 1975 saw the General Council of British Shipping take over as the central organisation representing UK shipowners, with the RFA represented as 'Ministry of Defence' shipowner. Council responsibilities include acting as employers' representative on the National Maritime Board, the Merchant Navy Training Board and the National Sea Training School.

Chapter 6

Apollo, Malta and a Pre-'Corporate' Trip

Royal Navy warships were tasked on an increasingly global scale during the 1970s and so the RFA logistics role also took on a wider scope, beginning with a little job, early in the period, for NASA.

Apollo XIII was launched in April 1970, for what was becoming almost a routine moon landing. This time, however, trouble developed in the service module that contained the main engine and the astronaut's only oxygen supply, turning their routine trip into a space traveller's worse nightmare. Unable to turn the crippled vehicle around, astronauts Lovell, Swigart and Haise were forced to orbit the moon before heading back to Earth. Ninety hours later, they had reached Earth and were ready for re-entry.

The drama was not over yet, though, because the selected landing site was now found to be in the path of a hurricane. Two new sites were quickly designated and Royal Navy ships, along with accompanying RFA ships, got the job of covering them, despite NASA's claim that they needed no help.

Mauritius in the Indian Ocean was considered the most likely alternative and HMS *Nabian*, *Phoebe* and the survey ship *Vidal* were dispatched there, along with *Tideflow*, *Ennerdale* and *Tarbatness*. *Dewdale* stood by in the second area south of Rio, accompanying HMS *Hermione* and *Rothesay*. *Tarbatness* was a particularly good choice since she had lifting gear capable of raising twenty-five tons in a single load. Royal Navy assistance proved unnecessary, however, because the capsule containing the three astronauts made a safe splash down at the Pacific site on 17 April, to the relief of all concerned.

Tarbatness had been involved in something far more controversial earlier in the year, this time for the US military.

British involvement in the Vietnam War (1962–75) has always been an area of military and naval operations shrouded in mystery and denial. Most official sources claim that the British military had no involvement in the war, but after extensive research, one individual has come forward who claimed to remember a trip made by *Tarbatness* into Vietnamese waters. The individual concerned was a NAAFI manager aboard the Ness ship and his account is here reproduced in full:

Having completed a visit to Japan and Hong Kong, during February/March 1971, RFA *Tarbatness* was returning to Singapore, when, under the watchful eyes of US Forces, she was ordered to enter hostile Vietnamese waters, in order to offload stores.

The sky was overcast and the waters grey in colour. American Air Force jets flew above us, at some distance from the low lying, tropical tree lined shore. Closer in, Chinook helicopters patrolled the air space, while stores were offloaded on to pontoons, using the ship's cranes. The whole operation took about six hours, after which *Tarbatness* resumed her passage to Singapore.

Reading the extract, several points stand out. First, to have had so much air cover, they must have been unloading something valuable (*Tarbatness* was a naval stores issuing ship and her cargo could have included both munitions and missiles). Second, there must have been a lot of it, six hours is a long time to spend off-loading any cargo. Third, it must have been a covert operation, because it did not take place anywhere with the convenience of even a jetty. Any conclusions must be conjecture, since the author has been unable to independently corroborate the man's story, but one thing is clear. Unless this account is a complete fabrication, and there is no good reason to suspect this, the RFA seem certainly to have been involved in covert logistics supply to US forces in Vietnam, on *at least* one occasion.

Logistics supply was not the RFA's only Vietnam involvement. Chief Officer George Mortimore (Rtd) remembers a different sort of job entirely off the coast of Vietnam:

In September 1970, RFA *Tideflow* (Capt A M Telfer) was on passage from Hong Kong to Singapore when she received a call from a British Merchant ship of the Hain Steamship Company asking for medical assistance. Both ships were close to the Vietnamese coast and a request had also been sent to the US authorities there who had agreed to send a helicopter to uplift the casualty. It was decided that *Tideflow*'s doctor would treat the patient and prepare him for transfer.

So at about 1900 we launched a lifeboat with myself, the Doctor, 4th engineer, Bosuns Mate John Azzopardi and three Maltese ratings. On arrival alongside the ship, the Doctor went to the casualty who had been badly burned while the BM and I prepared an after hatch for the helo transfer. This involved rigging obstruction lights on derrick heads and clearing FOD.

A USN helo arrived at about 2030 and winched the patient on board for transfer to Da Nang. The *Tideflow* team returned on board, in worsening weather at 2100. A few days after arrival in Singapore we received a signal from Commander Far East Fleet (COMFEF) congratulating us on the handling of the incident. As far as I can remember, we didn't hear from the Hain Co. or the casualty whose fate was unknown.

Trouble of a different sort reared its head two years later, in 1972, involving one of the last British strongholds in the Mediterranean.

Malta had been a British naval base since 1814, when it officially became part of the British Empire, under an edict of the Treaty of Paris. For many years it was used as a shipping way station and fleet headquarters, its position between Gibraltar and the Suez Canal making it ideally suited for such a role.

During the Second World War, its heroic defence earned the island the George Cross but, following the election in June 1971 of a new prime minister, Dom Mintoff, relations began to sour. This culminated in a demand by the Maltese prime minister, on 1 January 1972, for an increase of £11 million in the rent the UK government paid for its bases on the island. Failure to comply with his demands would result in him insisting that Britain pull out the 3500 service personnel then occupying the UK's Maltese bases.

Mintoff's ultimatum was received with a certain amount of coolness and Peter Carrington, then Defence Minister, noted bluntly that Britain had paid its rent until March and if Mr Mintoff felt the same way, Britain would be glad to pull out then.

A pullout looked certain and during the months of fruitless negotiation, *Bayleaf* freighted the Maltese fuel oil to the UK, while *Sir Geraint* moved service equipment and *Lyness* provided stores support.

Final agreement was reached in March, with Malta due to receive a yearly rent for its bases of £14 million, £5.25 million from Britain with NATO contributing the remaining £8.75 million. *Lyness* remained in the area, providing further stores support for the previously denuded service bases.

It was all pointless, however, because by 1979, the Royal Navy had finally withdrawn from Malta, and the dockyard was closed. *Bacchus, Sir Lancelot, Olna* and *Tarbatness* were all deployed during the withdrawal, with *Sir Lancelot*, the last vessel to leave, having previously embarked 41 Commando Royal Marines.

Eugenio Teuma, a Maltese who was a member of the RFA for many years, has recorded his memories of the dockyard and its closure:

> Malta has been a significant maritime power in the Mediterranean since the 18th century, and Vittoriosa ship building yards were one of the finest in that area. The Grand harbour was the safest port, surrounded by strong fortifications, thus offering security to all ships seeking shelter there.
>
> In 1798 the French captured Malta, a call for help was made by the Maltese to the British and in 1800, the British enforced a naval blockade of Grand Harbour. When the British came to Malta, it was with the intention of protecting the Maltese people, but they gradually realised that Malta had strategic potential, so they made Malta a crown colony.
>
> Malta was sanctioned by the Treaty of Paris in 1814; this treaty solemnly declared that the island of Malta and its dependencies belonged in full sovereignty to his Britannic Majesty. From that time Malta became a naval base to the strongest maritime power in the world.
>
> Over the years, the base at Malta provided employment to a considerable number of workers, especially those concentrated around the harbour area, including Vittoriosa, Cospicua and Senglea. The dockyard school was considered to be the best place to train for trades and skills, the most experienced Masters of the various disciplines, including shipbuilding and ship repairing, used to teach at the Naval school, with between 150 to 200 applicants sitting the entrance exam, hoping to be chosen to start apprenticeships of 4 years.
>
> The strongest departments within the dockyard were the Dockyard Captain, Queen's Harbourmaster and the SNSO department (Senior Naval Stores Officer), as well as the ship repair facilities. The Dockyard Captain and the Queens Harbour Master looked after all the ports on Malta, with British pilots, who were Captains of the HM Tugs such as *Expert, Confiance, Sea Giant* and *Robust*, plus some smaller Tugs called Tanacs, some of these pilots became quite well known, such as Mr Jacquest, Mr Rowe and Mr Fairgrieve.
>
> The Naval Stores department was a very busy part of the Naval Base, as, apart from all the various stores, it also incorporated the Royal Fleet Auxiliary Department.
>
> Hundreds of Maltese (British) Seamen used to form the crews of RFAs. They signed Board of Trade Agreements and were all members of the NUS (National Union of Seamen), because no seaman was allowed to work on an RFA unless he was a member of the NUS. The NUS even used to have a branch office on Valletta waterfront. There were several RFA ships which were manned by Maltese seamen, with British officers, for example *Hebe, Bacchus, Blue Ranger, Fort Duquesne, Fort Dunvegan, Tidereach* and *Tidesurge*, plus many others and the RFA department was the last to shut down after the closure of the Naval Base.

The closure of the base started in 1959, when Messrs C H Bailey of South Wales took over the running of the dockyard. The intention of Bailey Malta Limited was, apart from running the docks, to start commercial ship repairing, including naval vessels and other secondary industries.

When Bailey's took over the ship repairing side of things, business was very good. Until, that is, politics invaded the ship repairing business and a strike was called by the unions, which lasted for over seven months and saw the yard descend into a state of misery and shambles.

The official end of the naval base was on the 31st March 1979, when the cities of Vittoriosa, Cospicua and Senglea found themselves in the limelight, as the last British naval vessel, HMS *London*, left Malta. The whole of the Port area and every vantage point was crowded as the people of Malta watched this unfortunate event. Some people were cheering, but most were crying, because they knew what they had lost.

Although the British left Malta with pride, friendship still exists between our two countries and this is getting stronger year by year.

The Suez Canal gave the Royal Navy more employment, in 1974, when ordnance had to be cleared from the canal in the wake of the Yom Kippur war of 1973, *Bacchus* being deployed with the mine hunter squadron. Later that year, the RFA was involved once again in the Mediterranean when British citizens needed to be evacuated from Cyprus during the Turkish invasion. *Gold Rover* and *Olna* were deployed.

Nuclear testing, although much reduced from its heyday in the 1950s and the 1960s, was still being conducted, especially by the French, and RFAs were sometimes tasked to keep an eye on these operations.

Kinterbury had previously had problems with the French authorities back in 1973, when an armed party from a French customs launch had stopped and boarded her in the English Channel.

Nothing had finally come of the incident but this was not the case when George Mortimore was aboard one of the Ranger class, this time *Brown Ranger*, which also found herself caught up in an embarrassing situation with the French navy, during one of these nuclear surveillance operations, early in 1974:

On May 26th 1974 the small fleet replenishment tanker RFA *Brown Ranger* transited the Panama Canal to the Pacific Ocean. She was en route to the area of the Tuamoto Archipelago in French Polynesia where the French government were conducting a series of nuclear bomb tests over the Island of Mururoa.

The object of the exercise was to support RFA *Sir Percivale* with fuel and a small amount of naval stores. *Sir Percivale* sailed from Callao in Peru at the end of May and joined *Brown Ranger* in early June when the first replenishment was carried out. *Sir Percivale* was tasked to covertly observe the French nuclear tests and to measure any fallout she may encounter. For this purpose she was supplied with a barrage balloon from which were suspended monitoring instruments and which she deployed from her flight deck. She also had a team of scientists on board to collate the readings and two RAF NCOs, who were landed at Pitcairn Island to set up a monitoring station there.

Brown Ranger stayed with *Sir Percivale* for the remainder of June and in mid July she detached to Fiji for essential engine repairs. During this period the two RFAs had several times been approached by frigates of the French Navy but without direct contact. The French had continuously broadcast warnings to all ships to stay clear of the area of Mururoa, but the RFAs were well outside the proscribed area.

On the first day of her passage from the area to Fiji, *Brown Ranger* was steaming in a westerly direction at about eleven knots. She was about fifty miles south of Pitcairn Island. At about 0900 hrs on a calm day in July, she was approached by the French frigate *Commandant Bourdais* (F740) and ordered to stop.

After *Brown Ranger* hove to, the French frigate said that the Captain and Chief Officer were to report on board the *Commandant Bourdais*, and that a boat would be sent for them. Both officers duly boarded the French boat and were taken to the frigate. Upon arrival on board, the Captain was taken to the CO's quarters and the Chief Officer to the wardroom.

Both RFA officers were interrogated at length as to what their ship was doing in the area and what information they had gathered concerning the nuclear tests. Both officers insisted that the sole purpose of *Brown Ranger*'s mission was to gather metrological data for transmission to Pitcairn Island. It was clear that the French officers did not believe this and insisted that the ship was only interested in gathering information about the nuclear tests. After several hours' interrogation, the French realised that they were not going to gain the admission that they required and released the two officers back to *Brown Ranger*.

However, on their departure (after a good lunch) the Captain of the frigate enquired of the *Brown Ranger*'s Captain: 'And how were things on RFA *Sir Percivale* when you refuelled her yesterday?' This gave the impression that the French had known all along what the *Brown Ranger* was doing in the area and that the interrogation of the two British officers was an exercise in Gallic superiority and probably to let the British Government know that the area was under strict French control and other ships were not welcome.

No report of the incident was made to MoD (N) as it was not deemed at the time to be of any great importance and very little time had been lost from the voyage to Fiji. But today, thirty years later, some comparison could be made with recent events in the Persian Gulf and although *Brown Ranger*'s officers were 'captured' by a reasonably civilised navy, they were held in a state of considerable uncertainty for several hours and by today's standards, would have been excused if they had 'revealed all' to the French. But they did not and were subsequently to continue their careers with their self respect and integrity intact.

Nuclear involvement for the RFA was not just confined to monitoring the activities of other countries, however. The service was also tasked to carry nuclear weapons, of course, and it was easy enough to get into trouble, especially when another country's 'Press' got involved, as Captain S Redmond OBE (Rtd) remembers from his time as a First Officer:

In 1967 I joined *Regent* as First Officer – duties NBCDO, FDO, Unit Security Officer (USO) and Public Relations Officer (PRO). On our way back from Singapore we called at Cape Town. Captain Henry L'Strange asked me as PRO to give an interview to the female Naval Correspondent from a Cape newspaper (*Die Afrikaaner* or something like that).

She was quite charming but forceful and the interview moved rapidly to the nuclear question, that is, how many on board, where from, where to, could they be transferred at sea, etc. I clearly stated that I could not answer any such questions and moved to less problematic topics but not to be deterred, she returned again and again to her main subject.

On the way down the deck to the gangway she said that regardless of what I said she knew we had the weapons and that, in not answering her questions, we must have them and, that had we had none, I would have said so! I told her it did not work like that, said good bye and she left the ship. Later that day I got an invitation to a party given by her, needless to say I did not attend. The following day the paper reported our arrival complete with a nuclear arsenal! I forgot to mention, the lady was also known by our people to be a member of the South African Intelligence Service!

It was not just nuclear questions that could see RFA personnel in hot water with the Press, either. Captain Redmond again:

While in command of *Black Rover* during the Far East Deployment of 1979 we visited New Caledonia. As is customary during such visits I called on the French Governor and Military Commander (an Admiral normally based in Tahiti) accompanied by the Australian Consul who was acting for us. All went well until we met the Admiral (me no French, him no English) but as the Consul had previously suggested, smile, let him do the talking and answer 'Oui'. We were subjected to a good ten minutes lecture, the main point of which, I later found out, was unlike France, the UK had wantonly abdicated her responsibilities in the Far East.

Well, you can guess the outcome, I smiled said 'Oui' and returned to the ship. Unknown to me a press release reported the meeting and that the visiting 'Senior British Naval Officer' had told the French Military Commander that he agreed all that was said and in particular, it was a disgrace that we had reneged on a moral responsibility for the defence of the Far East. I had some really fast talking to do when the papers hit the street. Backed up by my Australian friend, the Consul, my Admiral and the British High Commission in Canberra gave me the benefit of the doubt!

Mind you, the Press did not always have its own way. George Mortimore again, this time on a trip to New Zealand:

When RFA *Brown Ranger* arrived in Auckland NZ on a Sunday morning, several newspaper reporters were entertained to lunch and a few drinks. One of the questions asked was 'what did she do in the war'. I replied that at one point she was on Russian convoys. The next question was 'Which ones?' and the only convoy I could think of was PQ17 so I said 'PQ17'.

The next morning headlines in the Auckland paper screamed 'Survivor of PQ17 arrives in Auckland!' A couple of days later letters appeared in the paper to the effect 'I was in PQ17 and I don't remember *Brown Ranger*'. This correspondence somehow reached the MoD who sent the ship a tetchy signal asking for an explanation. We replied that if gullible newspaper reporters spent Sunday lunchtime aboard an RFA they must expect whatever is thrown at them. We heard no more!

The RFA deployments do at least have the virtue of variety. *Tidesurge* was involved in one such deployment, when she was assigned to support Lord Shackleton's Falklands survey in 1976. Ownership of these barren lumps of rock in the South Atlantic had been in dispute for many years, with both Britain and Argentina claiming sovereignty.

Shackleton, having toured the islands and met many of its inhabitants, then went home and wrote his report. Basically, he advocated a cash injection of several million pounds to allow the islanders to continue to live independently, which infuriated the Whitehall mandarins, who were desperately trying to get rid of the place, and sent relations with Argentina, never cordial at the best of times, plummeting.

Earlier in the year, Whitehall had deemed the situation so bad that, during the annual negotiations with Buenos Aires, *Tidesurge* and HMS *Eskimo* had been deployed to the South Atlantic, from February to April, in order to discourage any thoughts the Argentines might have had of military adventures against the Falklands.

This was not the RFA's only Falklands involvement during 1976, though. *Orangeleaf* enjoyed a very different deployment between April and June, described here by the wife of her Master, Mrs Gillian Downham:

When an opportunity arises, do you grasp it with both hands? My husband, Marshall, then Captain of the RFA *Orangeleaf*, announced one day, that such an opportunity had arisen. Did I want to travel with him on the *Orangeleaf* to the Falkland Islands, meeting HMS *Chichester* on a certain wave in the South Pacific, on her way home from the Hong Kong station?

The decision was not difficult to make, yes, but the logistics were much more of a problem. Three children, aged 6, 8 and 10 to be looked after, 2 cats, 1 dog and a house and garden. Fortunately, my parents were ready to take on the responsibility and I was nearly on my way.

But another opportunity arose. As a primary school teacher, and with our three children at primary school level, what an opportunity to create a project covering almost every aspect of the National Curriculum for a whole term. Our daughter Kate, was 8 and her teacher, Mrs Chick was thrilled with the idea. So the work started. Each child in the class wrote about themselves, their families and hobbies, had photos taken and all the information was collated and put in a book.

Information about Steyning, West Sussex was also to be included, and then I would take this book to the equivalent class in Stanley's tiny primary school, in the Falkland Islands. Then it was agreed that I would write a day-by-day diary on the journey of the *Orangeleaf*, and send it back to Kate's class at each port of call. The school in Stanley was told of our plans and the children there prepared a book for me to collect to bring back to the children in Steyning.

So seemingly, with everything in place, we left Portsmouth on a cold, foggy, blustery, wet day for Bermuda, Curacao, the Panama Canal, the Falkland Islands and home again to Portsmouth. There were 3 ladies on board, the Chief Engineer's wife, the Purser's wife and myself, the Captain's wife. Just as we were getting our sea legs, the wind reached force 10 or more, and I then realised how high the waves could be and how low the troughs were. My diary to the children contained hair-raising stories of how small the ship seemed in these very heavy seas. We all survived, of course, but were two days late arriving on the sunny island of Bermuda.

Here we had brilliant weather, blue sky, blue sea, golden sand and wonderfully coloured fish. I sent my first epistle back to the children, and received my first batch of questions from them. 'How long was the ship, how wide was the ship, how many sailors on board, what did we have to eat, did we have to drink sea water, could we have a bath, how much beer did the sailors drink and had we seen any whales?'

After a reception at the Naval Base, and a walk over the smallest 'opening' bridge, just wide enough to let the tall masts of the yachts pass through, we left this beautiful island for Curaçao. On this part of the journey, I had to see about answering all the children's questions. I heard later that when the measurements of the ship were received, two classes of children went out on to the playing field to mark out the size of the ship. Apparently it seemed so huge, Mrs Chick had to go indoors and check the measurements!

In Curaçao, we loaded fuel and fresh water and prepared for our trip through the Panama Canal. What an experience! I sat on the monkey island from dawn to dusk. Going up through the locks, out into the Gatun Lakes, seeing the memorial to the men who lost their lives as they created the canal through 'The Cut'. Seeing, and hearing the sounds of the dense tropical jungle, and finally sailing out into the Pacific Ocean under the Trans American Highway at dusk, with a pelican on every post and the lights of Panama City twinkling in the distance on one side, and the blackness of dense jungle on the other. What a magical day!

We were not expecting to make landfall between Curaçao and Port Stanley, so there was time to write the diary and record all the wild life we had seen. The children were intrigued by the flying fish, and I was able to send them a pair of 'wings' of a fish that landed on the deck. Of course we also saw whales, dolphins and porpoises. At one point I saw what I thought was a cardboard box sailing towards us, it turned out to be a turtle!

We also met up with a yacht somewhere north of the Galapagos Islands. We thought they were in trouble as they seemed to be trying to get our attention. After a large detour we managed to get close enough to see what they wanted. They had rigged up a sheet between the masts, and it said 'Where are we?' This caused a certain amount of hilarity as you can imagine, but they were duly informed of their position and we moved on again.

We saw whales and dolphins as we sailed towards the Galapagos Islands, but by now the rain had really set in again and as we sailed through the islands they were just patches of grey land and we did not see any wildlife.

As we were early for our rendezvous with HMS *Chichester,* we sailed towards Easter Island and asked for permission to go ashore. After many messages going back and forth, we were eventually given permission from Chile, and the liberty boat set off with about 15 of us looking forward to hearing about the magnificent statues that make the island so famous. The Captain and I were met by the Governor and taken off for a tour of the island in his Land Rover. We were taken to see the extinct volcano, Rano Kao, and to hear the legend of the 'birdmen'. The story was that if you could fly to the rocks off the coast you would become sacred. Needless to say this never happened, but another version was that you could climb down the rocks, swim to the rocks off the coast, find an egg of the sooty tern and bring it safely back to shore. Then you became a 'manu' or sacred man for a year.

We were also shown the quarries where the huge statues were carved. Again, another legend that the statues were all carved but were not given eyes. They all faced Polynesia and the statues then drew the people of Polynesia towards the island. This did seem to happen as in various times there was quite a large population, but the island could not sustain them and the population died out. Although I can remember being told this, I cannot find it confirmed in my book of Easter Island.

It was an amazing day, seeing the statues, hearing the stories, seeing the birds – they have small hawks that behave like sparrows, and of course, the bartering of items of clothing in return for carved statues. The younger members of our party were prepared to swap blue jeans for carvings and return to the ship in their underwear. The Captain's wife was not prepared to do that but even so, just before dinner that evening, a young islander arrived at our cabin door asking for my jeans. I'm afraid he didn't get them. For the only time on that trip, I was taken down to the Chinese crew's quarters because they had been fishing. All their shower stalls were full of water and swimming around were the most beautiful tropical fish, but I think most of them were destined for the cooking pot rather than the aquarium.

Now we set off in earnest to meet up with HMS *Chichester*. We arrived early, but they were not far behind. Again, dreadful weather – I seem to recall in my diary starting many new days information with 'another grey day'. The RAS was completed without any problems, personnel were transferred by jack-stay and then it was my turn to go over and spend a day on *Chichester*. But the weather really closed in, and as it seemed I might be stuck on *Chichester* with no means of getting back to *Orangeleaf*, the Captain decided I could not go. I was very disappointed, but then we can't always do what we want. At this point, *Chichester* took off at speed for the Falklands and we followed at a more dignified pace! Then, round the Horn.

We ladies on board, well accustomed to being at sea by now, were looking forward to this part of the journey. We did not mind if the sea was very rough, after all, we had had some practice crossing the Atlantic. But would you believe it, we rounded the Horn in a flat calm. Again an amazing experience – calm sea, snow capped scenery and a bright sunny day. Once round the Horn, the weather changed again as we headed for Port Stanley and we were lucky to arrive safely in the outer harbour. *Chichester* was in the inner harbour, but as we were a tanker we had to stay outside. Not a problem until we wanted to go ashore for a cocktail party on *Chichester*. Well, we all made it but the rise and fall of the boat taking us ashore was huge, and you had to judge your step very carefully. The Purser's wife damaged her ankle quite badly at this point. We had a great evening, but by home time the weather was even worse, so most of us stayed ashore. Marshall and I stayed with the agent, Terry Spruce and his wife Joan, with whom we are still in touch. But Second Officer, Chris McKenzie had to be back on board. I believe he went by helicopter but he was certainly back on board for his watch.

The next day we had lunch with the Governor and were taken round the island in the official car, a red London taxi, called The Red Barrouche! We even had our wire basket carried for us as we shopped in 'The West Store', almost the only shop in Stanley. After shopping, we walked along the main street, looked in the Cathedral and I bought stamps in the Post Office to add to my collection of Falkland Island stamps.

I went to the school in the afternoon. The children were delightful. They were thrilled with all the letters from Steyning and proud to give me their work. They made me so welcome it was a real joy. But the weather was still very poor, it was June and their winter, so with snow on the ground and more forecast, my visit was pretty short. My souvenir from the Islands is a smooth oval stone about 14" in length from Joan and Terry's garden. It was carried back on board by the Third Officer, Les Oates and it spends most of its time in my garden, but comes to be very important every year when it is used in my Easter Garden in church, as the stone that is rolled away from the tomb.

Then the homeward journey began. Nothing to look forward to really, just sea and sky and of course, the film evenings and 'tea and tabnabs' on Sunday afternoons. As we left Stanley, we realised we had a passenger on board. A blue footed booby had joined us and travelled with us for several days. We were beginning to get worried about it as we were getting further away from land, but it eventually took off and we hoped all would be well.

At the same time we had a following of albatross. What amazing birds they are. There must have been 30 or 40 of them, just traveling with us, gliding through the air, then flying very close to the water so that their wing tips just skimmed the sea. We also saw schools of dolphin. They have such fun playing around the ship – they really look as if they are enjoying themselves.

By the time we reached Gibraltar the weather was appalling. Marshall was beginning to have very severe pains in all his joints and continuous watch on the bridge because of fog didn't help him at all. By the time he left the ship in Portsmouth he was really ill, but that's another story.

I was able to take the Falkland children's work down to Mrs Chick's class, and of course my own children were pleased to see me home again. The children in school had really enjoyed their term's project, had learnt a huge amount about themselves, about children at the other end of the world, about ships, and all sorts of other aspects of life in general, and about the National Curriculum. They were also a small group of young people who took a huge interest in the Falklands War (they were now 14 years old), who knew where the islands were and could appreciate some of the problems facing the islanders. This was probably the most worthwhile project I have undertaken as a teacher, and certainly the most rewarding. I count myself very lucky to have had the opportunity, and that Marshall and I grasped it with both hands.

A new Commodore was appointed to the Service the following year (1977) in the person of Captain S C Dunlop MBE, and this coincided with the Queen's Silver Jubilee Review of the Fleet, which also involved a number of auxiliaries.

The RFA ships put on a good show, independent observers remarking that the ships and ships' companies had been turned out to Royal Navy standard.

Later in 1977, there was more Falklands involvement, when, following the Argentine occupation of South Thule, a small task force was sent to the area, consisting of a nuclear submarine, two frigates, the tanker *Olwen* and the store ship *Resurgent*. Designated Operation 'Journeyman', the vessels' deployment proved unnecessary and remained a closely guarded secret, until James Callaghan revealed it, just after the Stanley invasion in 1982.

Commodore Thornton has provided an account of his experiences during a voyage aboard another Leaf class ship in the same period, this time RFA *Cherryleaf*, which also paid an early visit to the Falklands:

With an appointment to a shiny new *Rover* boat on the cards and the world returning to normal after the safe delivery of our first born, life was not bad at all. The hessian wallpaper (well it was popular in the 70s!) and the decoration of the lounge was nearing completion in our modest first family home when the phone rang … 'The Navigator of the *Cherryleaf* has just walked off; the ship is berthed in Rosyth and she is due to sail in two days; we must get her away. We don't have anyone else and it is only for a few weeks to do a quick trip to Curaçao and then we can get you to the Rover boat as originally planned'.

I am not entirely sure what it was that caused me to say 'OK. I'll pack my bags, catch the sleeper from Cornwall tomorrow and be on the ship ready to go as soon as I get there. Maybe it was ambition, or perhaps some sense of duty but I had just committed to an extraordinary adventure, on an extraordinary ship. That quick trip to Curaçao became something quite different and it began after a long and uncomfortable journey from Truro on a train that rattled through the night to arrive at Inverkeithing station bright and early the next day. I had travelled on the sleeper train, but at short notice and inevitably a sleeping berth was not to be had for love or money. (Not that love would have been on the cards anyway!)

Tired and bedraggled but determined to do my bit and get the ship away, the reader might imagine my surprise when I was told over breakfast that 'Actually, we are not sailing for another week yet – gives you a bit of time to plan the voyage and get your charts sorted.' Oh well, best get on with it, so I did. The next few days were spent doing what sailors do on a ship that is not familiar to them. Finding out where things are, getting to know the rest of the team and taking the opportunity to walk up the road to enjoy a pint before leaving the familiar shores for foreign parts.

Now, 'The Good Ship *Cherryleaf*' was on charter from London & Overseas Freighters and I knew from family connections and subsequent conversations that the owners could not have wished for a better arrangement; but more of that later.

She was fitted with a 'lay-on-deck' stern rig and apart from the odd 12-inch signal lamp and a very basic UHF fit, that was the extent of her military features. Off we went on our great adventure under the Command of Captain H J C Wheatley whose CV escapes me now, but he had a good sense of humour and a striking grey, slightly pointed beard in an almost cavalier style. He would stroke this beard with one hand in times of angst, giving the end a twist as he did so, before applying both hands to the twist of the moustache. I will refer to him henceforth as HJC. As it turned out he would certainly need the good sense of humour, for our first task was to rendezvous with Her Majesty's Yacht *Britannia*, about half way across the North Atlantic and fuel her with that rather messy stuff we called Furnace Fuel Oil, or FFO for short. Well, 'The Good Ship *Cherryleaf*' was rather utilitarian and had a somewhat used appearance, while *Britannia* was all sparkle, panache and bright work, so one cannot imagine a greater contrast between two ships. I suspect we were regarded as a bit of a necessary evil as we set up the pipelines, warmed through the steam turbine pumps and tested the gear before streaming the snaking black hose that was the stern rig. All was good to go and the Yacht (fortuitously devoid of any members of the Royal family) made her approach, grappled, hauled inboard, connected and signalled 'start pumping'.

Now, perhaps you can tell me why the pin hole in the hose had to be just outboard of the Yacht and just out of reach of all attempts to smother the fine spray of black oil that issued from that wretched puncture. Fuel must be passed, otherwise the Yacht just would not go, so it was grin and bear it as the starboard side of that fine and sparkling ship dulled to a murky brown despite the best efforts of yachtsmen to drop rags over that offending pinhole. I leave the content of the signal from Flag Officer Royal Yacht to the reader's imagination, just as I will leave the reaction of HJC to your mind's eye. His beard and moustache took a pounding that day and I thought I did well to suggest that silence was probably his best course of action.

Never mind – pick yourself up, dust yourself off and start all over again – so it was next stop Curaçao. The task was to load the maximum Dieso (diesel distillate and marine gas turbine fuel) and then shift ship to a berth beneath the battlements of Henry Morgan's Fort, to load maximum FFO (that black stuff) from the Royal Dutch Shell refinery. Cargo work meant 6 hours on and 6 hours off for the likes of me, while the Chief Officer was on call throughout – particularly necessary when topping off the tanks, reconfiguring the pipelines and other critical activity. So with Dieso rushing into the wing tanks and me on watch, I recall the strangled cry of alarm, albeit with a hint of puzzlement, in the voice of the jetty watchman as he shouted that fuel was coming out of the side of the ship! 'Surely not', says I, only to be equally amazed as I peered over the side of the ship to see a steady flow of Dieso issuing from a small crack in the shell plating – observant these refinery operators. The story boils down to loading short of maximum, getting Lloyds to give us the OK and off we went to load the FFO. Yes it had to be me on watch again when, peering down the open tank hatch of 3 Centre preparing to top off and change tanks to 2 Centre, when something akin to an eruption of low temperature, lava like liquid issued forth from a previously loaded and secured 4 Centre. Paddling in black, sticky, smelly, sludgy FFO is an experience denied to many and experienced only by the unfortunate few. Fortunately, the scupper plugs did their work and contained our deck cargo sufficiently well to prevent a diplomatic incident. It transpired that stripping lines could equally well pass liquid in the opposite direction to that for which they were designed. In current jargon this was rich territory for identifying and learning lessons. Never mind, all part of life's rich pattern and on the basis of experience so far, entirely in keeping with life on 'The Good Ship *Cherryleaf*'.

If you recall, it was advertised as 'A quick trip to Curaçao and back' when I joined so it came as a bit of a surprise to learn that next stop would be the Falkland Islands. Now it was several years before the conflict of 1982, so while rather disappointing in terms of a speedy return home and that appointment to a shiny new Rover boat, the adventure of discovering and visiting some far-flung corner of the Empire was a reasonable compensation. A hurried letter home would have to suffice in terms of breaking the news of my prolonged absence to my wife and bouncing baby boy. Such is the life of a sailor!

The voyage hardly tested my navigational skill, as it was simply a case of leave the Caribbean, turn right and keep on until the weather gets wild and cold. The 'skill' that was tested was that of my medical training and knowledge. I found myself attending to a sailor with a sexually transmitted disease – 4 million units of penicillin with a shot of adrenaline to hand in case of allergic reaction (and that is a rather long and strong needle!). I also had the pleasure of removing a lump of glass from a steward's foot and neatly stitching it up on completion. Perhaps most interestingly, a case of suspected TB provoked barrier nursing and some long signals to and from our destination. All turned out well in the end and we got the hospital painted by the poor unfortunate who would otherwise have been jolly bored!

The Falklands and the events of 1982 are now a matter of history, but perhaps less well known was the tension during the year of this tale, 1977. Secret signals were followed by radio silence, which was followed by periscope sightings, and a silent four-day voyage north in the grey and bleak South Atlantic. You can imagine the surprise when a Wessex helicopter appeared from the greyness and hovered alongside the starboard bridge wing. The aircrew waved a cheery greeting and held up a chalkboard with the word 'Hello' on it. I mouthed a reply and they turned the board over to reveal the instruction 'Steer 052' – so we did! An hour or so later, we came upon *Olna* and soon began a lengthy pump-over of FFO. Being clever chaps, we soon put the requirement of lots of black oil with the letters BL on the tail pylon of the Wessex to conclude that we were not alone. In fact, we had become part of a small force hastily assembled to signal our intent to those who had less than honourable intentions towards that lonely windswept outpost of Empire.

After a week or two we were released to proceed downwind to Cape Town and Simonstown to shuffle the remaining Admiralty oil from one to the other. Christmas had passed and New Year was upon us as we made our way eastward. In fact, I seem to recall it was New Year's Eve, when the pumpman popped his head round the mess door to let us know that 'There's water in the forward pumproom!' This brought the inevitable question of clarification from the Chief Officer of 'How much?' The pumpman was surprisingly calm in his reply as he disclosed 'Oh, about 30 feet or so – but it's not all the way across – it's in a fountain!' The phrase 'Wardroom Fire Party' is a good descriptor for what happened next as the canvas bags with bungs and hammers were hurriedly rushed to the scene. The four things that stick in the memory are (a) the South Atlantic is cold; (b) when the first bung goes through the hole, use the next size up; (c) surprising what you can use to bulk up the contents of a cement box; (d) in future, make sure that dripping turbine drains are not left to drip endlessly on the inner face of the shell plating! As the reader has probably deduced, we finally arrived safely in Cape Town to begin the task of shifting the oil around the corner to Simonstown. That done we departed in a bit of a dilemma, for we were not sure where we were bound next. Left or right was the question of the moment when HJC exercised his command prerogative, held out his right arm as if on a bicycle, and ordered 'Starboard 30'.

We were half expecting Freetown in Sierra Leone to be the next stop, but as a result of a jetty survey, Kissi was deemed unsafe for us (at least I think it was that way round!) and quite why we ended up in Gibraltar I cannot bring to mind, but I guess we discharged the remaining cargo to the tanks in the Rock. However, it was a welcome stop and enabled us to take on stores and water for the next bit of the adventure that, much to our surprise, was to take us through the Mediterranean, through the Suez Canal and onward down the Red Sea, round the corner and into the Arabian Gulf as far as Bahrain to load cargo once more. In the days before mobile phones and the expensive convenience of satellite communications from the ship, I remember booking a call and waiting at the post office in Gibraltar, to speak to my wife after many months out of touch, save for the written word. Emotions were stirred and while I felt deeply the distance and the time between us, there was little I could do save to regret my naivety in believing those who offered 'A quick trip to Curaçao'.

So armed with new charts, a calibrated sextant, a rated chronometer and a pretty ropey radar, off we went on the next leg of 'The Voyage of the Good Ship *Cherryleaf*. I can skip the tedium of the sea passage; the frustrations of the Canal transit; the increasing temperatures with a following wind; the lack of effective air conditioning and move on to our arrival at Sitra Deep Water Terminal. If the haze and dust lifted, we should be able to see the refinery in the far distance – but they did not, so we did not! We were all set to load once the surveyor had taken another look at that crack in the shell plating, but to our surprise (we should not have been) Lloyd's insisted that we leave the terminal, go to anchor and have repairs done. It was then the challenges of bursting steam lines, brake failure on the windlass, closely followed by an exploding steam cylinder on that same windlass, stretched our patience somewhat. De-ballasting preceded gas freeing, which preceded ballasting as we made good the repairs, attended to those things that we had not foreseen and finally returned to the terminal and got the full cargo onboard. I was not alone in feeling a marked sense of relief as we left that berth behind us.

The ship turned from the Arabian Gulf into the Gulf of Oman as we turned our thoughts to the voyage and prospect of home. But this was the Good Ship *Cherryleaf* and home was to be some months away yet! Once more the Radio Officer delivered the news that we were to stay put, and what was worse we were to maintain radio silence again. The MoD would let our families know that we were safe and would return in due course!

There followed a spell of supporting both British and American warships in the Gulf of Aden and the Red Sea. In fact it became a routine of fill one up, turn, transit the Strait of Bab el Mendeb, rendezvous with another, fill her up and return through those straits that became so familiar over a six week period. The reason for this presence was the conflict between Ethiopia and Somalia and I suspect we will never know the scale of the horrors that were unfolding in that troubled region. Even now, some 30 years after these events we see dreadful images of the suffering of the displaced and starving. For us at the time, it was just routine and what is more, by now, we were running low on any number of types of food and drink, the latter even included water! So HJC's independence of mind and spirit came to the fore with a decisive flourish that ran something akin to 'Sod it – Sparks, tell their Lordships that I'm off to Mombassa to get some butter and water' and we did! Now from my point of view this was great because I could do with a leg stretch and enjoy a game of Squash at the Mombassa club, followed by a meal beneath the tropical sky and of course, a beer or two. It was warm and a jacket over the shoulder makes an easy target for a pickpocket after a wallet. So the next day was spent at Barclays International, not far from the tusks arched over the main street, stopping the credit card and all that jazz. My dear wife was surprised to receive a phone call shortly thereafter from Barclays in UK, asking where the new card should be sent as I had reported the previous one stolen in Mombassa. Now, the MoD had not quite managed to pass the message regarding our new tasking and associated delayed return home, so my wife was prompted to remark 'So that's where he is', resulting in a moment of uncertain silence and puzzlement at the other end of the phone.

Departure from Mombassa was definitely a step closer to home and while we made the transit of the Strait of Bab el Mendeb for the last time, we were held back to await the arrival of a warship, I cannot recall which, as they made their way homeward from the Far East. It was here, at the southern end of the Red Sea that my medical skills were really tested, for I received a call from the Chief Engineer to attend an Officer who was on the bottom plates and had apparently broken his arm. It was fairly obvious that the poor unfortunate had indeed broken his arm because it seemed to have two elbows in it and rolling back the sleeve of the boiler suit revealed blood and bone … mmmm. Best have a look at the rest of him. Sure enough, his other arm had two elbows … great! The lessons came flooding back as I started at the top and worked slowly downward to assess the extent of any further damage and I came across some more blood and bone where a normal calf should be. Clearly, he would need to be removed from the bottom plates and that was going to be painful, so a couple of shots of morphine seemed appropriate.

After a few moments, the drug took effect and my patient was drifting on a cloud, time to slide the blanket under him and transfer him to the Neil Robertson stretcher for the difficult trip up and out of the machinery space. Let me tell you that the First Aid and medical lectures omit to inform you that, despite splints and drugs, people in severe pain will scream like you have never heard a scream before. It is at this point that you must grit your teeth and tell those helping that you really do know what you are doing and that you know best, so get on with it.

There is a happy ending to this tale, for after a short helicopter ride (winched up in his stretcher) the patient received treatment on the warship, was transferred to hospital and returned home to UK where, after several months, a few pins and a lot of physiotherapy, my patient was able to get back onto his motorbike!

I cannot recall our port of arrival in the UK, but it certainly entailed a cargo discharge, tank cleaning, ballasting and the usual de-store in preparation for refit. The ship was certainly in need of some attention and this was duly delivered on the southern shore of the river Tyne. Although I stayed with the ship for a few weeks, I did manage to get home at some point to find that, during the 'quick trip to Curaçao', that bouncing baby boy had grown, was sitting up and taking notice of the world around him and perhaps most telling – was just a few weeks shy of his first birthday!

It is not beyond the imagination to conceive of the eagerness of my wife to have me home again, for after so long apart her needs were great. That half finished decorating, featuring hessian wallpaper was really getting on her nerves and you can probably guess what my first task was!! (The reader is invited to exercise a little imagination.)

The good ship *Cherryleaf* remained with the RFA service for some time to come and while we rose to the challenges of keeping her going, the family connection was pleased to tell me that the charter arrangement represented a very useful source of income from a ship that otherwise they would not have retained. Something akin to leasing your failing second-hand and unwanted car! We still have a smile about it occasionally.

It is of interest to note, in the light of Commodore Thornton's experiences and those of the RFA in general during the Falklands campaign, the standard of refit *Cherryleaf* seems to have been subject to during her working life. Refits for ships like *Cherryleaf* on bareboat charter, incidentally, were an RNSTS problem and not in any way the responsibility of the owner.

A big part of the RFA's job has always been humanitarian aid. One such operation involved relief to Pakistan in the aftermath of the 1970 cyclone, described here by a senior RNSTS official, now retired:

In 1970, Pakistan was divided into two parts: West Pakistan, the area of the present country; and East Pakistan (now Bangladesh). On the night of 12 November 1970 the southern part of the Ganges delta in East Pakistan was struck by an unusually severe cyclone which caused a tidal wave on the low-lying shallow waters of the delta. The tidal wave was estimated at twelve feet in height and it caused huge devastation to the delta, its people, livestock, agriculture, limited communications, roads and river systems.

The survivors were in desperate trouble, with no means of sustenance or immediate hope of supply. The magnitude of disaster did not become apparent for many days because days of twenty four-hour TV news channels with reporters out-numbering the dead were many years away. When the East Pakistan authorities finally assessed the damage, offers of help poured in from all over the world. Iran and India sent relief stores and the United States sent helicopters.

The United Kingdom Government mounted a relief task force from its Far East Command Base in Singapore. At the time, these forces were engaged in their day-to-day work, which included the planned rundown of the Singapore Base and the Far East Command. The Royal Navy did not have either an aircraft carrier or helicopter carrier (LPH) on station. HMS *Intrepid* was available, together with two landing ships (LSLs) which had only recently been taken into RFA management. Other units in the area included destroyers, frigates, survey ships and some other supporting RFA ships.

However, HMS *Triumph*, a former light fleet carrier converted into a heavy repair ship, was based in Singapore. By chance, in the weeks before mid-November 1970, HMS *Triumph* had been used in her secondary role of helicopter landing platform for commando forces. Along with HMS *Intrepid* and other units of the Far East Fleet, it had deployed to Hong Kong with Royal Marine Commandos and helicopters of the Fleet Air Arm based in Singapore. The exercise off Hong Kong had to be curtailed because of an approaching typhoon but, in the course of the exercise, HMS *Triumph* had carried out over 200 helicopter deck landings, which was far in excess of her normal yearly total.

The fleet units then returned to Singapore Naval Base, but not before a frigate HMS *Llandaff* had been involved in humanitarian work off the South East Philippines when a typhoon had left thousands homeless. The relief operation in East Pakistan (code-named Operation 'Burlap') began to swing into operation on the 18th of November. RAF and Army units were alerted, and detailed planning began in the Far East Command. The members of 40 Commando Royal Marines and 847 Naval Air Squadron, plus additional Royal Engineers and infantry units, including medical teams, were embarked in *Intrepid* and *Triumph*. The ships were loaded with engineering equipment, trucks, tents, bulldozers, water purification, bridge building and medical equipment, together with essential food including substantial quantities of rice. The personnel and families of the Far East Command had collected over four tons of clothing and this was also loaded, along with blankets and other necessities. RFA *Sir Galahad* (LSL) having just returned from Calcutta was also loaded with relief stores and carried additional Army units. The Royal Air Force, especially its versatile Hercules aircraft, also began to mobilise.

The problems faced by the naval task force were awesome. The nature and navigation channels of the Ganges Delta had been changed dramatically by the effect of the tidal wave. HMS *Hydra* (a survey ship) joined the task force and was aided by very recent satellite photography provided by the United States military. *Hydra's* task was to re-chart the delta and find safe channels for the relief ships. Initially, the relief force and its afloat support, consisting of RFAs *Olwen* and *Resource*, had to anchor thirty-five miles offshore, while HMS *Hydra* commenced its survey work to enable the ships to get closer inshore. Significant numbers of helicopters, landing craft and rigid raider craft were available aboard the ships and they were able to begin ferrying the necessary equipment and men ashore.

Once on land, the scenes of devastation were unimaginable, one Royal Marines Captain reporting that on one island in the Delta only 2,000 out of a population of 12,000 survived and that he saw no woman or child below the age of seven. Gradually, despite tremendous obstacles, order was brought to the chaos and the suffering people provided with essential aid. Bases ashore were set up and contact made with the East Pakistan military and civil authorities, using whatever buildings were left as ground headquarters.

After a relatively short time, RFA *Sir Galahad,* was able to sail up the Delta and berth, while, in the meantime, landing craft and helicopters were ferrying the essential relief stores and the men ashore to provide the vital aid needed by the population. RAF Hercules aircraft were soon able to land and airbases were established to provide support to aircraft from other nations now arriving. HMS *Triumph's* heavy maintenance facilities proved invaluable as substantial buildings, bridges and mobile clinics were made and adapted then shipped ashore.

Major fleet units were kept supplied with their own food, fuel and pure water from the two RFAs. With so much debris in the sea, not least dead bodies, ships could not make their own water while at anchor. All the men ashore had to be inoculated against disease and their health had to be constantly monitored. There were more than enough medical problems without the aid personnel being afflicted. Weather was also a constant problem to the fleet, as it was the tropical storm season and the forecast required constant monitoring and updating to ensure that the operation could continue without any more risk to personnel and ships.

Intrepid had recently been fitted with the new Skynet satellite communications equipment and this proved invaluable for keeping in touch with not only Singapore but also London. Close co-operation was established with the Pakistan military and civil authorities and other aid agencies. By 26th November, the UK Minister for Overseas Development was able to visit and see for himself what the British operation was achieving and what further aid might need to be provided.

Sir Galahad was now able to get to and from Chittagong harbour, delivering stores for the operation from the main units still anchored several miles offshore. Additionally, local coasters were drafted in to help, being able to take stores from *Intrepid*, *Triumph* and the RFAs to ports that had been opened by the men on the ground. Medical and aid teams from other countries were arriving with near neighbours being able to provide vehicles and vessels. By the first of December, the fleet units could withdraw together with the men, landing craft and helicopters as other aid agencies and aid came in by road and air.

It was never properly established just how many died or were displaced in the disaster. Some estimates put the death toll at one million. Whatever the statistics, there is no doubt that the aid provided by the UK's Far East Fleet, Army and Royal Air Force had been vital. The UK's aid to the area continued. The RAF continued to supply vital aid for some time with assistance from the RFAs *Hebe* and *Bacchus* (store carriers) which made stops at Chittagong en route between their regular freighting ports of Singapore and Chatham. The British Government and aid agencies chartered ships with aid embarked for many months.

The historical postscript is interesting. East Pakistan had been simmering with political unrest prior to the disaster. The scale of the disaster, and a perceived view that there was little interest from the main seat of Government in Islamabad, led to civil unrest and an uprising in 1971 after elections that resulted in the election of a Bangladesh independence party. India supported the uprising after being inundated with refugees and went to war with Pakistan in late 1971. The war led to the declaration of the independent state of Bangladesh in December 1971. The newly independent country has since undergone many trials and tribulations caused by nature. The people of the Delta lead a precarious existence but have never forgotten the help provided by the British Forces in their worst trial all those years ago.

The British Far East Forces had no sooner returned to their normal role than in February 1971 floods swept Pahang State in mainland Malaysia. RFA *Sir Lancelot* was pressed into action carrying Royal Marine Commandos, emergency stores and equipment and the faithful Wessex helicopters of 847 Naval Air Squadron. Three thousand people of the Temeresh region had been without food or fresh water for over a week until this aid arrived.

Consolidation was the RFA's main priority during the Seventies, with only a few new ships introduced into service. The Tide, R and LSL classes were over fifteen years old by the end of the decade and these had been fifteen hard years, with all the vessels showing distinct signs of wear and tear. In many cases, refits had been of a mediocre standard and some equipment was either working poorly or completely inoperative.

Despite the new initiatives in training and fleet introductions begun in the previous decade, somehow the RFA had, once again, slipped down the Navy Department's list of priorities. Little did anyone realise how serious this period in the Doldrums, with its consequent shortfalls in equipment, would be when the events of April 1982 began to unfold in a group of little islands in the Southern Ocean.

Chapter 7

The Falklands War and the RFA: 1980–3

Royal Navy involvement in the Iran-Iraq conflict, and hence also that of the RFA, began in 1980 with the deployment of a task force to the Persian Gulf to assist the US Navy. RFAs were assigned to this task force, which came to be known as the Armilla Patrol. A single tanker together with an armaments/stores carrier was the usual deployment, beginning with *Olwen* and *Stromness* from October to December 1980.

Earlier that year, the MoD had bareboat chartered the products tanker, *Hudson Deep*, which, after conversion, was renamed *Brambleleaf.*

Unlike the store/armament ships and the Tide, Ol and Rover classes of RFA tanker, the giant Leaf class support tankers (*Brambleleaf* has a displacement of over 40,000 tons) were all under long-term bareboat charter, a form of charter which the Admiralty introduced for RFAs in 1958.

In this arrangement, the ship owner provides only the ship, the charterer being totally responsible for the vessel's operation, *eg*, appointing the crew, repairs, refits, cargo and, most importantly from the RFA's point of view, running the vessel where he wants to within any limits set by the ship owner or Classification society.

The Navy continued its deployment on the Armilla Patrol in 1981, operating in the Red Sea, Gulf of Oman and Persian Gulf, with continuing RFA support.

Fuel, of course, was and is a major part of the RFA's work and by the end of 1981 the fleet consisted of fifteen tankers, equipped for both replenishment and freighting, together with its stores ships and LSLs, making a total of twenty-seven vessels.

RFA fleet (April 1982)

Five fast fleet tankers
Tidespring, Tidepool, Olwen, Olmeda, Olna
Five small fleet tankers
Blue Rover, Gold Rover, Black Rover, Green Rover, Grey Rover
Five freighting tankers
Pearleaf, Bayleaf, Appleleaf, Plumleaf, Brambleleaf
Five armaments and general stores carriers
Fort Austin, Fort Grange, Stromness, Regent, Resource
Six landing ship logistics
Sirs Galahad, Bedivere, Tristram, Percivale, Geraint, Lancelot
One helicopter training ship
Engadine

This situation was not to last, however, because in May 1981, Mr John Nott, then Minister for Defence in the Thatcher government, published his long awaited Defence review.

In brief, Mr Nott's plan was for Trident to become effectively the main UK weapons system. Wars would, in the view of the Thatcher government, now be conducted only by the superpowers, with all their forces concentrated in the North Atlantic. Small wars, so characteristic of nineteenth century military operations, were unlikely to be a consideration. Surface ships could therefore be run down, while numbers of Trident carrying submarines had to be increased. All very logical.

The RFA was hit hard. Immediate losses were *Tidespring*, *Tidepool* and *Stromness*, while by the mid eighties all six LSLs would be sold off as well and replaced with cheaper, slower RO-RO ferries, although the various departments involved were still arguing about this when war broke out.

Graham Ferguson RFA (rtd), then First Officer aboard *Fort Austin* remembered an embarrassing coincidence, which occurred while Her Majesty Queen Elizabeth II was making her first official visit to an RFA in August 1981:

> In 1980, I joined RFA *Fort Austin* as First Officer in Mombasa as part of the Armilla Patrol. The underlying reason for this was to act as Commodore Sam Dunlop's 'gofer' for the then unannounced visit of HM the Queen and the Duke of Edinburgh the following summer.
>
> One interesting point about the visit that many missed was that John Nott chose the very day of Her Majesty's visit to *Fort Austin* in Portland to announce the infamous Navy cuts.
>
> By an amazing coincidence, the majority of the ships, including HMS *Hermes*, which Nott was planning to scrap happened to be in Portland that day. The press who came down and photographed the Queen looking out at her sinking Fleet had only expected a very staid picture of the Queen and Commodore!

Manning levels were to reflect the reduction in fleet numbers, with over 1000 RFA men being made redundant, 420 of those officers, just about a third of the entire workforce.

Most worrying, however, was that it was the future RFA, which was being hit as well. With the loss of six ships between 1977 and 1981 and the further proposed losses under Nott's defence review, there was what the RFA personnel department called a '... serious surplus of RFA Deck and Engineer Officers at junior level'.

One result of this was that in 1981, there was no possibility that the Service could absorb any of their deck or engineering cadets who had qualified that year.

The father of one of these young men wrote to the relevant Government department about, among other things, his concern over Britain's defence capability if the Royal Navy lost the use of the specialist replenishment ships of the RFA. The relevant paragraph of the Parliamentary Under-Secretary of State for Trade's reply is reproduced here in full:

> Mr ... also implies concern about our defence capability in the light of the decline of the fleet. In the event of hostilities, the *merchant fleets of Nato countries* would be pooled and allocated to tasks in the best interests of the alliance. (author's emphasis)

This reply suggests a solution remarkably similar to that involving the early Tide class in the 1950s, when the Navy wanted a fast fleet tanker but did not want to pay for it. And how could an ordinary merchant ship replenish a destroyer, at the speeds (usually 16–18 knots) necessary to reduce the risk of a submarine attack?

Even more interesting was the reply from the Minister of State for the armed forces, in which, after explaining that their priorities had changed due to '... rapidly rising cost of some kinds of equipment', by which he presumably meant Trident, he finished by saying '... we shall retain sufficient auxiliaries to meet all foreseen requirements for essential afloat support'.

Mr John Parry, MN (rtd) was aboard one of the ships which would probably have been one of the 'merchant vessels pooled and allocated to tasks in the best interests of the alliance'.

This was a BP River class tanker *British Esk*, modified for RAS in the 1970s and he found the design of the RAS gear something short of sophisticated:

> MV *British Esk* was one of thirteen 25,000 dwt product carriers operated by BP Shipping Limited. The ships were a little smaller than the industry norm at the time, but were dimensioned to fit the lock at Grangemouth. They were built by four different yards and because *Esk* and *Tamar* were the only ones fitted with bow thrusters, they spent most of their time on short voyages in North Western Europe or the Mediterranean.
>
> In the 1970s, they were both selected for modification for use as Naval support ships in the event of hostilities. Basically, the modifications comprised the installation of a number of tripod supports down the starboard side of the main deck to support a stern refuelling rig and a suitable shoe to carry it over the stern. Some additional cargo piping was fitted, namely high suctions in the two largest centre tanks and a line down the starboard side of the accommodation to a valve on the poop deck to which the refuelling hose could be connected. The hose was paid out and recovered by means of a wire on one of the forward mooring winches.
>
> After testing, the hoses and tripods were removed, the tripods disappearing into a naval store somewhere, from which nobody expected them to emerge.

The stern rig was reinstalled during the ship's hurried refit at Portland but there were problems:

> The refuelling rig had been tested after it was fitted and appeared to work. When we tried it, however, the hose was too long. With it secured by the bridle provided there was too much hose on the poop and no matter how we rigged it, we could not get rid of the kinks. In the end, we modified it by adding a few extra shackles to each of the chains, after which we successfully deployed and recovered it a few times.
>
> We also had a 'beam rig reception point' on the port side which consisted of nothing more than an eye plate which picked up a couple of holding down bolts between our hose crane and its pedestal, to which we could secure an RFA tanker's beam rig. It transpired that our ability to fuel warships was regarded as an *emergency measure*, the plan being for us to transfer most of our cargo to RFA tankers.

Things did not quite go that way:

> We fuelled HMS *Exeter* late one night and *Antelope* a day or two later and, when we recovered the hose, it was found that the couplings were weeping diesel. The Type 21 frigates were not equipped with coalescer filters and could not cope with any water in their fuel, so there was no option but to repair the rig before we refuelled our next customer, HMS *Ambuscade*.
>
> Needless to say, it was an awful night. Gill, our Captain, managed to find a course which gave us a reasonable amount of shelter on the narrow deck at the side of the

accommodation. The reason for the leakage was obvious as soon as we opened the first coupling. They were made of aluminium, with a face-to-face seal, one side of which had an undercut groove for a D-shaped sealing ring. The matelots who had fitted it at Portland had found it was much easier to put the sealing rings in upside down so we had to open every coupling to change the seal, which took most of the night. *Ambuscade* was so low on fuel that her Captain had no option but to heave to and wait for us to return. They must have had a very uncomfortable night.

Given *British Esk*'s experiences, further comment about what might have happened to the Royal Navy if this scenario with its 'pooling the merchant fleets of NATO countries' and 'foreseen requirements' had been in place during the Falklands or later Gulf War seem a little superfluous, to say the least.

Loss of the assault ships HMS *Fearless* and *Intrepid*, both slated for eventual sale, as well as the disappearance of the LSLs from the RFA fleet, also meant the Royal Navy's ability to stage any sort of amphibious operations would have disappeared completely, limiting the options Britain's armed forces had available even further. Perhaps disastrously so.

To his credit, Mr Nott realised this after a visit to HMS *Fearless* in November 1981 and both LPDs were reprieved, although the LSLs were still slated for disposal. Alongside this loss of amphibious capacity, disposal of the two Tide class fast fleet tankers would also have seriously reduced the Navy's ability to remain at sea for extended periods.

The First Sea Lord, Sir Henry Leach, did not need this spelling out and he fought an articulate and inevitably doomed rearguard action on those very grounds.

It looked hopeless.

Then the Argentinians landed on South Georgia.

And on a final, deliciously ironic note, the first redundancy notices were issued to RFA personnel on 2 April, the day Argentina chose to invade Port Stanley.

Despite this, RFA men rushed back to work on receipt of those desperate telephone calls, worked round the clock to restore their elderly ships, often with a complete and total disregard for the loading regulations, and headed south at top speed, without bothering to ask questions about their future. Even ex-RFA men jammed the switchboard at the 'Madhouse' (RFA Headquarters in London), many of them well past seagoing age, demanding to be sent south.

And all this, with redundancy notices still decorating mantelpieces or sitting, disregarded in back pockets.

The Falklands war: Origins and outcome

Logistics support and the build-up to invasion
The Falkland Islands lie in the Southern Ocean (position 52° S, 60° W) and consist of two distinct land masses of roughly equal size, East and West Falklands, separated by a narrow stretch of sea, Falkland Sound. Most of the population, who earn their living farming sheep for the islands' owners, live on East Falklands. In 1982, the Falkland Islands Company (FIC) owned two thirds of the Islands.

Settlements lie mostly on the coast, of necessity, since boats are the usual means of transport, overland travel, even by four-wheel drive, being impossible for much of the year. Climatically, the islands are similar to northern Scotland and the Western Isles, although wind and sea conditions are far less predictable and more turbulent, owing to the shallow nature of most of the seabed. The waters surrounding the islands are, however, very productive, both round fish and shellfish being trawled commercially.

There was a long association between the RFA and Port Stanley, the Falklands capital, since RFA tankers had for many years been responsible for refilling the fuel bunkers at Port Stanley, from which HMS *Endurance* periodically replenished her tanks. *Endurance* was the only ship in the Royal Navy without a RAS capacity and this lack, incidentally, would give *Tidespring* yet another operational headache later on.

The origins of the war itself can be traced as far back in 1833, when Captain Richard Onslow RN, took possession of the islands for Britain, after the US Navy had razed the original Argentine settlement to the ground in a dispute over the trade in fur seal pelts.

This began the long running dispute, with Argentina claiming prior ownership while Britain's claim was eventually based on 150 years of continual possession and, most importantly, the right of the population to self-determination. And to a man (and woman) the Islanders wanted to stay British.

Compromise proved impossible, despite many subtle and potentially advantageous schemes being suggested, particularly by the British government. Whitehall, or rather the mandarins occupying the big offices there, had long regarded the Falklands as not worth the trouble they cost to keep the Argentines out, but with a powerful lobby backing the FIC and enough flag wavers demanding that this last bastion of Empire be retained, the civil servants found themselves forced to find a way to effect at least a peaceful, if not democratic transfer.

Meeting followed meeting and dialogue followed dialogue without much being achieved. Until, that is, 1970, when a senior Foreign Office official, one David Scott, came up with a scheme which looked like it had a chance of working. What Mr Scott did was ignore all the sovereignty issues and broker a deal, the 1971 Memorandum of Agreement, which satisfied both the Islanders and the Argentine government, based solely on economic considerations.

Under the terms of this new deal, Argentina would run an air service from the mainland, if Britain agreed to build and maintain the necessary airstrip, as well as operating a shipping link to the Argentine mainland.

An air service meant Islanders could enjoy the benefits of tourism as well as being able to use Argentine schools and hospitals. Imports would increase, particularly fresh fruit and other 'luxury' items, previously only available via the FIC's vessel *Darwin*, which was losing money and had been earmarked for withdrawal at the end of 1971, anyway.

And Scott's subsequent approach to the islanders was nothing short of masterly, reiterating constantly, as he did that, his major concern was a better standard of living for the islanders, not sovereignty for Argentina or anyone else.

The Agreement, which was signed on 1 July 1971, marked the real high point in the relations between Argentina and the islanders.

At first, things seemed to be going well. The Argentines began the agreed air service with an Albatross flying boat and the younger islanders appear to have been enthusiastic about the prospect offered by more financial and cultural links with the mainland.

It was not to be, however. No permanent airstrip was ever built and Scott's painfully constructed accord was, by 1976, in tatters. Publication of the Shackleton Report, late in 1976, with its suggestion of a massive £13 million to increase the independence of the island community did nothing to help, especially since Whitehall's intention had been that the Report should be a basis for forcing concessions from the, by now, thoroughly disillusioned islanders.

Once again, incident followed incident, including Argentina's attempted occupation of South Thule, in 1977, thwarted when a secret task force was deployed which included two RFAs. An RFA officer, who was aboard *Olwen*, one of the RFAs sent south at that time, recalled that deployment and the lengths the government went to ensure secrecy:

> The totally unexpected highlight of this period was our emergency dash towards the Falklands (with HMS *Dreadnought* and two frigates) as pre-emptive support to the Callaghan government in persuading the Argentines not to invade the Islands over the Christmas '77 period. This was successful but the Labour Government was so terrified that a Left Wing political party would use this example of 'gunboat diplomacy' against them that we were ordered (illegally) to destroy all reference to the operation, codenamed 'Journeyman', including the ship's log and cadet workbooks.
>
> It remained secret until Callaghan himself asked – during the Saturday debate on the Argentine invasion – why Maggie Thatcher had not followed his example!

So the stalemate continued – the British government anxious to unload what was becoming to Whitehall an increasingly burdensome and irrelevant piece of South Atlantic real estate, while neither the Argentine government nor the Islanders seemed willing to budge on any of the issues where some compromise might have meant a way forward.

A new face appeared in the Foreign Office in 1979, however, with the election of Britain's first woman Prime Minister, Margaret Thatcher, and the appointment of Lord Peter Carrington as Foreign Secretary.

Lord Carrington and more especially his junior, Nicholas Ridley, quickly looked into the Falklands dispute and, having examined a number of previous options, Ridley eventually advocated a policy of 'leaseback', whereby Argentina was granted sovereignty of the island, with a British administration in place for an agreed period of time, possibly as long as twenty years.

Problems arose almost immediately when this solution was presented to Parliament, upon Ridley's return from the islands, and he was quite unfairly crucified for what was in essence, a practical solution to a near impossible stalemate.

Matters stood thus, when, in 1981, a new government took power in Argentina. Formed as a military junta, it was headed by a hard drinking ex-cavalry officer called Leopoldo Galtieri.

Galtieri could hardly have chosen a worse time to take office. Argentina was in the middle of yet another financial melt-down, the long running Beagle Channel dispute had just been settled in favour of Chile and with the 150th anniversary of the loss of the Falklands approaching, the population were screaming for some positive move to be made in the Malvinas (as the Islands are known in Argentina) dispute.

It seems that the junta was actually planning a move against the islands, later in 1982, during the southern winter, when weather and sea conditions would have been extremely unfavourable to any attacking force trying to retake the islands against determined opposition. They might well have succeeded in keeping the Royal Navy out if things had gone to plan, but the junta's hand was forced by events precipitated by an Argentine scrap metal merchant, one Constantino Davidoff.

Mr Davidoff was and is often cited as the prime cause of the 1982 Falklands conflict, but, in reality, what one Foreign Office official referred to as his 'lightweight misdemeanours' were really only the spark in a powder keg that had been waiting to explode for generations.

Davidoff had been granted access to South Georgia in order to dismantle and remove the old whaling stations there. He went to have an initial look at the place on an Argentine navy vessel and either forgot or ignored the formalities required for entry to the island.

Britain, of course, protested to Buenos Aires without eliciting any response until 9 March 1982, when Davidoff informed the British embassy in Buenos Aires that he was going to begin his contract by initially transporting forty of his workmen to South Georgia aboard a transport vessel belonging to the Argentine navy.

He landed on the island without clearing his paperwork again with the relevant British authorities and there then began a period of diplomatic wrangling which eventually resulted in the British threatening to use HMS *Endurance*, the Royal Navy ship permanently on station in the island group, and her embarked Marines, to remove the scrap workers. Argentina, or rather the junta, responded by stationing two missile carrying corvettes between the Falklands and South Georgia, with the clear intention of intercepting *Endurance* and removing its Argentinian passengers, if this threat was carried through.

There was a final desperate diplomatic initiative but by 26 March, the junta had committed itself to an invasion of the Falklands and the necessary orders mobilising the fleet had been given.

The first intimation the British had that this might be taking a more serious turn was actually on the 26th, when British intelligence reported suspect preparations in and around the main naval ports, although the considered assessment was that this was in line with a joint Easter exercise taking place with the Uruguayan navy.

By 29 March, the situation had become so bad that a nuclear submarine was dispatched to the area, as reinforcement for *Endurance*, with *Fort Austin* also deployed, to replenish *Endurance*'s rapidly dwindling supplies and remain on station to service any other ships sent to the area. On the same day, Rear Admiral John (later Sir Sandy) Woodward was ordered to prepare to detach a group of ships from the annual Gibraltar exercises, Operation 'Springtrain', ready to proceed south, *Tidespring* and *Appleleaf* being among those selected.

On the 31st, the British Naval Attaché in Buenos Aires signalled the Ministry of Defence that most of the Argentine fleet was at sea, destination unknown, and that this seemed very much in advance of the planned Easter exercises. In the early evening of the same day, Mr Nott was informed by MoD officials that intelligence had been received strongly indicating that the Falkland Islands would be invaded by Argentine armed forces on 2 April. Almost immediately, he was able to meet with the Prime Minister, together with Foreign Office and MoD officials, the latter including the then First Sea Lord, Sir Henry Leach.

When Mrs Thatcher asked Sir Henry what could be done about the situation, the

Second World War veteran did not hesitate. He replied that he could assemble a task force and then use it to retake the Islands.

Sir Henry was ordered to assemble such a task force and, on 1 April, both HMS *Hermes* and HMS *Invincible*, the Royal Navy's only remaining carriers, were put on twenty-four-hours notice for sea. This was awkward, because *Invincible* was being put back together after a major refit and still had scaffolding around her bridge structure. Despite this, twenty-four hours later, she was ready to move.

Argentina invaded the Islands on 2 April 1982. The Royal Marine garrison at Port Stanley was forced to surrender within hours, followed, on the 3rd, by the small detachment of 'Royals' stationed on South Georgia.

Not, however, before the tiny garrison on South Georgia had blown so many holes in one of the Argentine French-built corvettes that she was forced back to the mainland for repairs, and shot down a troop carrying helicopter.

Of course, the government's response was immediate and, to some observers, seemed suspiciously akin to an ill-considered knee jerk. That infamous Saturday meeting of Parliament certainly ensured that any diplomatic solution that did not involve total withdrawal by the Argentinians had little chance of success.

Admiral Woodward's group and the carriers had, by now, been preparing for several days, but in the UK, restoring began immediately, even of those ships, such as *Stromness*, which had been emptied for disposal. *Stromness* was actually restored and converted into a troopship in order to carry 429 members of 45 Commando south, in just five days.

Off Gibraltar, *Tidespring* and *Appleleaf*, as ordered, joined TG 317.8, which consisted of:

HMS *Antrim* and *Glamorgan* (County class destroyers), HMS Coventry, *Glasgow* and *Sheffield* (Type 42 destroyers), HMS Arrow (Type 21 frigate) and HMS Brilliant (Type 22 destroyer). This group spent the day restoring, off Gibraltar, from those RN ships that had also been attached to Operation 'Springtrain' but which, for a variety of reasons, had been ordered back to the UK.

Captain Shane Redmond, Master of *Tidespring*, remembers the Sunday before the order came vividly:

> We'd been to church in Gib, as usual, and in the afternoon, many of us, RFA and naval officers, attended a concert in St Michael's Cave.
>
> Earlier that week, on the 26th, Commodore Dunlop visited me, at which time we discussed the situation in the South Atlantic at some length. We were both of the opinion that there was a very strong possibility ships would be sent south and that *Tidespring* and *Fort Austin* would also deploy for obvious reasons. We both agreed that, *Tidespring* being alongside, the way ahead was to load everything I could get my hands on and, departing a day after everyone else, we did just that. (The delay was due to a minor incident resulting in a six-foot gash on my starboard side – somebody moved the South Breakwater knuckle which got in my way as I was leaving harbour.) *Tidespring* subsequently sailed at 100% plus capacity, our inventory including AS12 missiles in the swimming pool, hundreds of drums of Lub-oil over our normal operational load lashed down on the upper decks and enough food and general stores for six months at normal consumption rates.
>
> Unfortunately not all our RN colleagues were in the same well found position!
>
> Following a general signal to report holdings of essential stores, it became apparent

that some units were in fact well under provisioned. An averaging out then took place which left *Tidespring* below her normal stock level, a situation we were to find particularly discomforting, post S. Georgia, with nearly three times our normal numbers to feed and take care of!

At the Fulham 'Madhouse', the war interrupted rather a good party, as Gordon Wilson, who had then just been appointed as the RFA's new Fleet Manager remembers:

My last day as Assistant Director (Industrial Relations) for the Royal Naval Supply & Transport Service was Friday 2 April, 1982. The invitation list for my farewell drinks was long, and included many colleagues from naval circles in Whitehall. As the morning wore on, the trickle of apologies swelled to a flood as we realised something big was afoot. I saw a copy of a signal ordering many warships to sea, and bringing an impressive list of others to immediate notice. The word 'Exercise' did not appear in the signal: this was for real. My new appointment as RFA Fleet Manager for Personnel & Operations had started with a bang.

Almost immediately, daily meetings were being held of the National Maritime Board (on which I now represented the RFA, one of its largest members). The burning issue was to reach agreement on the boundaries of a War Zone to enable *Canberra* and *Uganda* to be taken up from the trade to sail for the Falkland Is. [British Merchant Navy rules required all members of the crew to be told of the potential danger and given the option to leave the ship prior to sailing. Once in the Zone, very substantial bonus payments were earned.]

I argued that the RFA differed from other shipping companies in that its primary task – its whole reason for being – was to support the Royal Navy anywhere in the world. Bonus payments for doing this were either unnecessary, or should be kept to an absolute minimum. Under terrific pressure from ship owners and naval operational staff to reach agreement and get the first ships away, a deal was finally struck. For all British merchant ships, except the RFA, the War Zone would be the (huge) sea area south of Ascension Is. For the RFA it would be limited to the Naval Exclusion Zone, 200 miles around the Falkland Is.

Whilst these negotiations were ongoing the whole RFA fleet (27 vessels) was gearing up for war. Refits were being hurriedly completed, crews were augmented, full (and often rather unusual) loads were embarked and extra equipment fitted, and the roles of some were changed (*eg* to help carry large numbers of troops south) – all in record time. In all, 22 ships joined the operation, with the remaining 5 deployed on other essential tasks – the first time ever, I believe, that the whole fleet was at sea at the same time.

Having quickly got over the initial shock, every Royal Navy Supply and Transport Service depot in the country, particularly those situated at the major naval dockyards, now began a massive stores, fuel and clothing deployment to the ships going south, desperately trying to second guess the requirements of the sailors and marines whose job it would be to make Operation 'Corporate' succeed.

The RFAs were not being left behind, either.

Sir Tristram (Captain R Green) sailed from Belize on the 2nd with *Brambleleaf* (Captain M Farley) detached from Indian Ocean to join the Task Group (TG) 317.8 (South Georgia Group) by way of Cape of Good Hope on the same day.

By the 4th, *Tidepool*, on her way to her new owners, the Chilean navy, and almost at her destination, had been recalled and was making for the Panama Canal at top speed.

Olmeda (Captain G P Overbury) sailed from Devonport, on the 5th, in company with HMS *Alacrity* and *Antelope*, while *Pearleaf* left Portsmouth on the same day, together with the Carrier Task Group, HMS *Hermes* and *Invincible*. *Pearleaf* was carrying FFO, an important commodity, because it was required to replenish the older HMS *Hermes*. *Sir Percivale* (Captain A F Pitt) also left Marchwood on the 5th.

By the 6th, *Fort Austin* had reached Ascension and begun to embark three Lynx helicopters, complete with Sea Skua missile system. *Resource* (Captain B A Seymour) left Rosyth the same day, equipped with a Sea King for VERTREP, before picking up last of stores at Portsmouth, then rendezvousing with *Olmeda* and her escort. *Sir Geraint* (Captain D E Lawrence) and *Sir Galahad* (Captain P J Roberts), the latter carrying 350 men of 40 Commando, among others, also sailed on the 6th, leaving Devonport at 1500 Zulu, closely followed by *Sir Lancelot* (Captain C A Purcher-Wydenbruck), who left from the LSL's home port of Marchwood.

Captain Phil Roberts remembers the first signal mentioning Operation 'Corporate':

> On 2 April 1982 I received the signal with the magic words 'Operation Corporate'. At first I thought it was some paper exercise that the Radio Officer and I had forgotten about, but no, it was for real (and how).
>
> The Falklands war had begun. We proceeded at best speed to Plymouth, arriving on 3 April. Our cargo, ex-Norwegian exercises was quickly off-loaded and fantastic efforts were made by the Dockyard to back-load with ammunition, rations, rigid raider boats, petrol, land rovers, waterproofing kits and a whole host of ancillary stores. This was completed by the evening of 4 April.
>
> On the morning of 5 April we embarked some 350 Royal Marines of 40 Commando, HQ and Signals, 59 Commando, No. I Raiding Squadron plus three Gazelles and their crews from 3 Commando Brigade Air Squadron. Ten Royal Corps of Transport soldiers were embarked as part of the ship's company to act as stevedores. Three Royal Navy signalmen were also embarked.
>
> My ship's officers were frantically storing up with every conceivable item that we thought we might need over the next ninety days. Every available space was crammed to capacity, as were the main fridges.
>
> *Sir Galahad* proudly set sail from Plymouth at 1500 on 6 April with the Royal Marines lining the ship's side, Gazelles ranged on the flight deck, battle ensign flying. We all felt very honoured to be setting off to do our utmost for Queen and country.

Captain Tony Pitt recalled *Sir Percivale*'s sailing and a slight departure from Board of Trade loading regulations:

> Throughout Sunday and Monday the loading of cargo and stores continued as and when the materiel became available. A lot was accomplished in a short time. The passengers commenced arriving late Monday morning and continued throughout the afternoon. Three Gazelle helicopters of M Flt Brigade Air Squadron were also embarked in the early afternoon.
>
> After consultation with Heads of Departments, it was decided to sail as soon as all passengers, stores and cargo were embarked and secured. This would enable the ship to 'shakedown' the next day, Tuesday, away from the confines of Marchwood, which was becoming more like a 'madhouse' by the minute.

The ship finally sailed from the jetty on Monday the 5th of April at 1820Z, 14 inches over-loaded and in possession of a quite lethal deck cargo. That night the ship anchored in Lyme Bay, well clear of prying eyes.

In mid Channel, the four LSLs and *Pearleaf* (Captain J McCulloch) rendezvoused with *Resource*, *Olmeda* and HMS *Alacrity* and *Antelope*. These ships formed part of the Amphibious Landing Group, which then proceeded to Ascension. HMS *Fearless* (Landing Platform Deck (LPD), *ie* assault ship) also left Portsmouth on the 6th, with Commodore M Clapp aboard, the intent being to use her as Brigade HQ. Arriving off Portland, she took Brigadier Julian Thompson aboard by helicopter, together with three No 846 NAS Sea Kings.

In the UK, the National Maritime Board (NMB) convened and agreed that the NMB death/injuries agreement and 150 per cent bonus should be paid to all Merchant Navy (MN) and RFA personnel who served within 200 miles of Falklands with a second zone west and south of Ascension and south to Antarctica for MN personnel only.

Next day (7 April), *Stromness*, previously scheduled for disposal to the USN, departed from Portsmouth, having completed her rapid refit, restore and conversion, now carrying 45 Cdo RM. The main RNSTS party arrived at Ascension Island on the 7th as well, beginning to set up for the massive logistics operation to be centred there.

Some of the chartered merchant ships were also refitting in record time, although their MN crews had certain reservations about some of the installations, as John Parry, then Chief Engineer of motor tanker *British Esk* which underwent its refit, later in April, at Portland, explains:

Our Naval party soon on board after we reached Portland, consisted of a Chief Officer, Radio Officer, Bosun and two seamen from the RFA, an RN Signals PO and two seamen and two RAF mechanics.

Early on, the stern (RAS) rig was brought out of store and refitted together with two portable radio stations in Chatham Containers (shelved wooden containers known universally as 'Chacons'), which were installed in the swimming pool. None of us thought putting radio equipment into what was effectively an open topped steel tank was a particularly good idea, but the Navy knew better or thought they did.

As well as this radio gear we also had an MoD Telex installed in the radio room, working through our transmitter and receiver. It was a long way inferior to our own, recently installed telex being an ancient Siemens device which tended to stick on upper case. It was plain that this was not unusual, because the two RN signalmen on board could read telexes full of !£**&) (as if they were in clear!

MoD must have thought merchant ships spent a good deal of their time blacked out because they supplied a pair of diesel generators for back up as well, together with a pair of RAF corporals to operate them. We also had an RFA master, who came on board at Portland to help see us through what were assumed to be unfamiliar tasks, although he seemed surprised that we managed to load, bunker, store and change crew in one day,when he assumed we'd take three!

It was not just the RFA who went south either, Dave Soden had some experiences of his own while representing the 'STONNERY' aboard a Cunard banana boat:

In 1982, during the Falklands War, I was appointed to the STUFT ship MV *Saxonia*, which was a Cunard line banana boat.

Within hours of the ship's arrival at Portsmouth Naval Base, STO(N) volunteers arrived ready to commence loading the ship and it came as something of a surprise that no accommodation was available onboard for the STO(N) staff because the Cunard crew (who all occupied single berth cabins) refused to share their cabin space. The whole department was forced to live ashore until bunk beds had been made and located in the Captain's sea cabin, making 12 persons altogether in the same cabin.

Once storing was completed the ship left Portsmouth heading for the South Atlantic. En route, the ship attempted to undertake a fire exercise (RFA style) but this had to be abandoned because, during the ship's loading at Portsmouth Naval Base, the brass ends of the ship's fire hoses had been removed. It was agreed that replacement hoses would have to be found from the recently embarked transit stores!

After a pleasant journey South, the realisation of the conflict became apparent when, upon leaving Ascension Island, the ship was instructed to darken ship at night and no radar was to be used. The Cunard Captain soon appealed to the STO(N) department for extra staff to act as look outs at night because of this darken ship routine and, later in the voyage, the same staff acted as lookouts for sighting icebergs.

Before arrival in South Georgia all of the crew were issued with a standard, once only, orange sea survival suits. It was to our horror that when a demonstration was arranged to show the crew how to use the suits we were to find that the suits allocated to the ship had been partly shredded and should not have been loaded.

Within minutes of arrival in Grytvikan some of the Cunard crew dumped black plastic bags full of gash into the sea. Calls were received from the shore side military to say that the dumped gash should be recovered immediately. It was decided to launch one of the lifeboats to recover the gash and as the lifeboat was about to enter the water, one of the shackles attached to the lifeboat sheered and the boat entered the water at an angle. Needless to say, after recovering the lifeboat a full survey was undertaken by the embarked RFA bosun of all life saving equipment and urgent remedial action commenced. Whilst at Gryvikan the ship proceeded over the following days to transfer its cargo to ships that had been diverted from 'Bomb Alley'.

With the end of the war, the ship was instructed to return to the UK, reload and return to the Falklands. On the homeward voyage, the ship went via Ascension Island. The STO(N) staff at short notice were told to transfer off the ship onto the Ascension Islands and return home, take leave and rejoin the ship upon its arrival back in the UK. After landing on the island we were directed to a rather weather worn tent for an over night stay. The fun really started when we went to the cook house for dinner. We queued in line with all the other military staff and it soon became very apparent that we were not in possession of any cutlery nor a plate and without these we would get no food (it transpired that these utensils had been issued to the military staff before flying to the Ascension Island and there was no way they would share them with us).

We had to quickly improvise to overcome the situation so we tore up the lid of an apple box and presented it to the cooks who obliged with portions of chicken and chips.

By the beginning of April, the main body of RN and RFA vessels had been stored and sent on their way, leaving the way clear for the more involved task of converting, loading and allocating RFA and RN personnel to the fifty-one STUFT merchant vessels which were needed to supplement the activities of the specialised RFAs.

Throughout the rest of the war, the RNSTS worked tirelessly behind the scenes, running, among other things, a STUFT cell, which organised ship charter or requisition, a casualty cell, responsible for dealing with enquiries from families about their men (and women) who were on the ships and believed possibly injured or dead and a personal enquiry cell. A senior RNSTS manager recalls:

> The Officers and Ratings in the RFA reacted magnificently to the challenge of putting the entire RFA Fleet to sea during Corporate and also to manning the STUFTs – but the role of the entirely civilian Appointers, Managers and general support staff, mostly very young and junior in rank, is not so well recognised.
>
> This team sustained 24/7 operations during the entire period of the South Atlantic campaign, often turning up for work at their normal time in the morning, doing a full day's work, then a full night shift in the Ops Cell followed by another day's work before going home to snatch a night's sleep before starting the process again.
>
> A complete generation had passed since the Department had faced the problems of support to large scale combat operations and their commitment and professionalism in facing challenges and difficulties completely outside their experience was extraordinary.

This immensely complex logistics operation, although controlled and organised by those RNSTS personnel, relied on the RFAs and STUFT for smooth delivery of both the liquid and dry goods which the ships and men of Task Force would need. Liquid supplies included fuel, lubricating oil and water while dry goods were mainly food, sundries (such as clothes) and ammunition [bullets, depth charges and missiles]. In addition, the Ammunition, Food and Explosives Stores (AFES) ships, such as *Resource*, carried naval stores and a war outfit.

Royal Fleet Auxiliary and STUFT tankers carried several different types of fuel – furnace fuel oil (FFO), which the older vessels like HMS *Hermes* used, diesel (Dieso), which newer ships like the Type 42s used, aviation fuel [Avcat] for jet aircraft and helicopters and the RFA tankerman's nightmare, petrol [Mogas] used for the soldiers' Land Rovers and Rapier generators.

The RFAs were also responsible for some less well publicised cargoes. Operation 'Corporate' was implemented too quickly for any of the ships carrying nuclear weapons to off load their cargoes so the RFA R and Fort classes, which had special containment facilities for these 'special' weapons, dealt with them as well.

Getting ships to sea and thus being seen to be reacting positively to Argentine aggression was the priority in those early days, although the need to modify many of the STUFT (ships taken up from trade), slowed the logistics effort initially. Chartering these STUFT was, of necessity, a complex business but once achieved, the vessels were swiftly modified in any one of a number of UK dockyards. Every STUFT had RFA personnel aboard, usually including a radio officer, a deck officer, a petty officer and one or two deck ratings (three STUFT also embarked an RFA engineer officer), while some ships also carried RN communications ratings.

Forty RFA radio officers (ROs) were embarked on STUFT and this drastic reassignment of ROs meant that, at one point, with 90 per cent of the RFA's RO complement at sea, there was no RFA 'sparks' available for duty in the UK, except the two at the headquarters building!

Chronology of nuclear weapons transfer during Operation 'Corporate'

RFAs involved:
Fort Austin, *Fort Grange*, *Regent* and *Resource*
Nuclear rounds designation:
600: Bomb Aircraft HE (High Explosive) 600lb MC
600(S): Surveillance round
600(T): Training round

April
13th
Fort Austin RAS(L) from *Tidespring*, the latter on her way to South Georgia as part of *Antrim* group (TG317.8/grp I)
14th
TG 317.8/grp I, including Fort Austin rendezvous HMS *Endurance*. *Endurance* RAS(L) from *Tidespring*, RAS (dry stores) from *Fort Austin*; *Antrim* group and *Endurance* head south, *Fort Austin* goes north to rendezvous *Brilliant* group.
16th
Fort Austin rendezvous *Brilliant* group – transfer one 600 round from HMS *Brilliant* and one 600(S) round from HMS *Sheffield*.
17th
Resource arrives Ascension.
18th
Resource leaves Ascension in company Carrier Battle Group (including HMS *Broadsword*).
19th
Fort Austin arrives Ascension, still carrying one 600 and one 600(S) nuclear rounds, restores and heads south again for rendezvous with Carrier Battle Group.
20th
HMS *Broadsword* transfers one 600 nuclear round to *Resource*, in open sea.
25th
South Georgia recaptured; Carrier Battle Group rendezvous *Brilliant* group, 1500 nautical miles from Stanley; *Resource* (still carrying nuclear round) and *Olmeda* sixty miles astern, escorted by HMS *Yarmouth*.

May
1st
Carrier Battle Group now enters Total Exclusion Zone (TEZ). Attack on Stanley.
3rd
Fort Austin (with 600 round) enters TEZ and rendezvous Carrier Battle Group.
9th
Fort Austin transfers 600 round to HMS *Hermes*.
11th
Regent joins Carrier Battle Group.
14th
Resource transfers 600 rounds to HMS *Invincible*, receiving training rounds in exchange.

15th

Resource transfers one 600 and one 600(T) to *Regent*. This appears to be one more 600 round than she should have.

17th

Fort Austin transfers one 600(S) and one 600(T) to *Regent*. HMS *Coventry* transfers one 600 (S) to *Regent*. *Regent* now has one 600 round, two 600(S) and three 600(T).

25th

Atlantic Conveyor hit by Exocet, while in company with Task Force. *Regent* also in company and carrying 600 round.

26th

Regent transfers one 600 round and two 600(S) rounds to *Resource*.

June

2nd

HMS *Invincible* transfers one 600 round to *Fort Austin*.

3rd

HMS *Brilliant* transfers one 600 round to *Fort Austin*; HMS *Glamorgan* transfers one 600(T) to *Fort Austin*; *Resource* transfers one 600 round, two 600(S), two 600(T) to *Fort Austin*; HMS *Invincible* transfers one 600 round to *Fort Austin*; *Fort Grange* transfers one 600(T) to *Fort Austin*. *Fort Austin* now has three 600 rounds, two 600(S) and four 600(T) in her nuclear containment facility.

7th

Fort Austin leaves, unescorted, for the UK, arriving Devonport 29 June.

26th

HMS *Hermes* transfers one 600 and two 600(T) rounds to *Resource*. *Resource* leaves for the UK, arriving 20 July.

One RFA officer, seconded to *British Wye*, recalls how frantic the preparations for sea were:

I joined the *British Wye* on the 20th April having been called off leave, along with Peter Breeze (First Officer) and an RFA Bosun's Mate. The *Wye* was undergoing modifications in Portsmouth dockyard; most importantly being modified to receive a NATO fuelling rig on her starboard side. It was fairly evident that she had been built with modifications in mind and that the installation kits were ex-stock. The *Wye* was undergoing a crew change at the time, the new crew being a little wary of just where we were going and for how long. There were some tense negotiations regarding wives at sea! We were fortunate in that the new Captain David Rundle realized the importance of what was happening.

Goods kept arriving from Naval Stores without being ordered, RAS hoses, connectors, clothing, ration packs, torch batteries, sound powered phones, Sun-line, etc. I was given two bags of confidential books, two coding machines and a portable UHF set. Having no safe on board I took them home every night for safekeeping.

We left Portsmouth and proceeded to Devonport to load a full cargo at Yonderberry, this included over 200 drums of lub-oil. Space was so tight that we used the bridge wings and swimming pool to store the drums. Once loaded we were sailed south to Ascension.

One of the problems we faced was trying to change the mind-set of the BP crew from being a freighting tanker running a standard routine to having to face the certainty of some fleet work, station keeping and RAS. The BP manning scale was minimalist, and the ship, apart from the bridge, ran a 9–5 routine, the engine room being un-manned at night. The major occupation was carrying out the planned maintenance routines.

Between Peter Breeze and myself we laid down the basics for fleetwork and RAS reception although what Flag Officer Sea Training (FOST) would have made of it is debatable and the BP Health & Safety Manager would certainly have had to re-write his manuals. However it all worked!

Looking back it now seems rather strange that although the Ministry of whatever were involved with the designs of the ships, it seems nobody thought to give some basic, regular training to the Officers and crew. Most of them had no idea of how the Navy was controlled, or how a Task Force operated. Fortunately, you *could* learn the basics in a couple of days … And everyone did!

As soon as ships were loaded, they were sent south, usually stopping at Ascension Island, which the US government had made available, where some rearrangement of stores could be made. This was vitally important, so as to ensure that ships, particularly the vulnerable LSLs, would spend as little time as possible at the beachhead.

Added to their loading difficulties, however, several RFAs were certainly showing their age. *Tidespring*, for example, which had been commissioned in 1963, had a number of worrying defects.

Tidespring defect list (Courtesy Captain S Redmond OBE RFA (rtd))

a. A positive pressure could not be achieved in either the forward or after citadels due to a failure to carry out proper repairs and tests after other work had been completed during refit. Ship's engineers were successful in plugging air leaks and recovering the forward citadel. (Defence against airborne contaminants – gas etc. – a possible threat in the S. Atlantic)

b. The dimmer switches associated with the navigation lights were inoperative having been removed from the refit list of defects. Repairs could not be carried out by ship's staff as no spares were held. (Safety)

c. The Type 182 Sonar was inoperative despite efforts by the Communications and Engineering branches. Again, a failure to carry out maintenance at refit. (Anti torpedo defence – poor but better than nothing)

d. De Gausing was inoperative. Thought to be due to being disconnected and later, damp penetration (mine countermeasures – not relevant in S Atlantic)

e. No Electronic Counter Measure systems were in place though 3-inch rocket launchers (chaff) were later provided and fitted by ship's staff with the assistance of naval personnel. (Anti-missile protection)

f. There is no doubt that the ship's company lacked formal training for operating in a hostile environment. This is hardly surprising given that 40% of the Rating element was drawn from the Merchant Navy Pool and were not RFA personnel.

An appropriate internal organisation covering all aspects of threat and defence had not at this stage been developed for the RFA and counter measures had largely been directed towards the peacetime emergencies of fire and damage control. However, with a nucleus of ex-service ratings and a small number of RFA personnel who had attended formal training courses it was possible to bring the ship's company to a passable level by the time South Georgia was reached. Similarly, a functional though somewhat sketchy defensive organisation was cobbled together that seemed to work surprisingly well!

g. Clothing. While in the strictest sense not material, the climatic conditions in South Georgia and the Falklands Operational areas made the near absence of proper protective clothing a major concern. Bridge lookouts, Flight Deck and RAS personnel work in highly exposed positions where temperatures can have a serious detrimental effect on a ship's overall efficiency. *Tidespring* received twenty outfits of cold weather clothing at Ascension Island. Due to variations in size this provided sufficient outfits for some sixteen personnel – a woefully inadequate allocation. On a lighter note, a flood of gloves, socks and woolly hats were eventually received onboard courtesy of wives, mothers, the WI and numerous other charitable sources at home. These were most gratefully received!

The above list represents a snapshot of a more comprehensive report on defects and other items relating to RFA operations in the South Atlantic contained in my ROP and subsequent papers.

Engineering remained a considerable concern throughout the campaign based on the experience of the previous three months in the Caribbean during which breakdowns were fairly commonplace. It is worth noting that throughout the period in question there were no such occurrences due entirely to the effort of George Norcott the Chief Engineer, his deputy Bob Kirk and the Engineering Department as a whole, a group of men for whom I had the highest regard. Without their sterling efforts there is no doubt that *Tidespring* would have been at considerable risk.

What was in many ways even more worrying was that, according to Captain Redmond's draft Report of Proceedings (ROP), most of these faults were present *after* the 1981 refit.

This business of inadequate refits was a fairly long standing one. As long ago as January 1977, in fact, a meeting had been held at Portland naval base, between the staff of FOST and the RFA Director of Fuel and Movements (DST (FM)), at which the Commodore Sea Training (CST) had expressed concern over the state of RFAs arriving after refit. He found them often cluttered and dirty, with equipment and stores hastily embarked and needing to be properly stowed. Some even appeared to have major corrosion problems, although as the Director pointed out at the time, all RFAs were still subject to periodic Lloyd's Register and DoT inspections, and they would not be allowed to leave refit if there was any doubt about their safety!

Unfortunately, no list is available for any ship other than *Tidespring* but given the general age and work rate of the RFA's fleet, some of the other vessels must have been suffering at least as many faults as her, if not more.

Initially, the first of the small task force groups went south with their own tankers, *Antrim*'s group, Task Group 317.8, for example, which was responsible for retaking South Georgia, had *Tidespring*, while HMS *Fearless* and the LSLs were accompanied by *Pearleaf*.

Later, when the Total Exclusion Zone (TEZ) was established, distribution became more organised, with a system of what was known as 'motorway' tankers. These vessels were stationed anywhere from 1000–2000 miles south of Ascension, sailing a box course and tasked to refuel the warships or supply vessels as they made their way south.

Station tankers were also designated for Ascension Island and Cumberland Bay in South Georgia, these ships being changed on a regular basis. Nearer the TEZ, was the Tug, Repair and Logistics area (TRALA, originally the Logistics and Loitering Area, LOLA) and the Red Cross Box, this latter being designated strictly for the hospital ships, such as *Uganda* and the ambulance ships, HMS *Hecla* and *Hecate*, although on several occasions, *Uganda* anchored in the calmer waters of San Carlos to allow more delicate procedures to be carried out.

The RFAs, including tankers, store ships, LSLs, STUFT troopships such as *Canberra*, and tugs and repair ships, such as the Stenas, were temporarily marshalled in the TRALA, under the command of a Royal Navy frigate. This vessel, designated the TRALA manager, organised the dispatch of vessels and escorts to where they were needed, usually either to Ascension or South Georgia for replenishment or south to San Carlos when the invasion began to gather momentum. Other RFAs remained in company with the Task Force, from where their replenishment activities were controlled.

Once the Task Force was established in the vicinity of the TEZ, the system for replenishment, in general terms, was:

The STUFT ships moved fuel or dry goods (these latter waterproofed and palleted to normal RNSTS specifications) from the UK or Ascension to either the TRALA or, more usually, Cumberland Bay, South Georgia, where they were transferred to RFAs who replenished the warships, either in the war zones, like San Carlos water, or at sea with the Carrier Battle Group. Several fuel replenishments to RN vessels were also carried out by STUFT tankers, notably vessels belonging to the BP River class, which, some years earlier, had been trialled as 'convoy escort oilers', for North Atlantic work.

Troopships were slightly exceptional, in that they usually anchored in Cumberland Bay before moving briefly to the TRALA or Carrier Battle Group, where they picked up an escort, frequently being joined by other vessels inbound to San Carlos, the major concern here being to make the passage from South Georgia to San Carlos in the shortest possible time, thus keeping the troops on board vessels such as *Canberra* or *Stromness* in peak condition.

Ascension Island was the first stop for most of the Task force ships on the weary trek south.

Situated about 8° S, 14° W, Ascension Island enjoys a mild, warm climate whose main feature is the SE trade wind which, blowing almost continually, serves to make the incessant dust and ash an everyday feature of life there.

Named from the date of its discovery, Ascension day, 1501, it is volcanic in nature, the thirty-four square miles of the island consisting predominately of lava, with a covering of fertile soil on places like Green mountain, known locally as 'the peak'.

The British arrived in 1815, garrisoning the place with a detachment of Royal

Marines to prevent Napoleon's rescue from nearby St Helena. By 1982, facilities included a 10,000-foot runway, operated by Pan-Am for the US military at Wideawake and the BBC's high power short wave relay station together with a manual telephone exchange run by Cable & Wireless.

Converting this chunk of dust and lava in mid-Atlantic to a half-way house for the Falklands Task Force fell to the lot of the newly appointed Commander of British Forces, Ascension Island, Captain Bob McQueen CBE RN.

He soon came to be known as Captain One In, One Out because of his firm intention not to allow non-essential personnel to remain and use up the island's sparse resources, particularly accommodation and water, which were to remain in short supply for the whole of the war.

The organisation of which he was in charge was a threefold deployment; RN operations, including helicopters, RAF operations, predominantly the C130 Hercules of Transport Command and the hugely complex RNSTS logistics effort. Despite these complexities and the inevitable clash of personalities, ruthless RN efficiency began to achieve order out of the initial chaos. Fuel, food and accommodation were the main requirements, together with the need to operate both fixed wing aircraft and helicopters safely. Organisation of these vital necessities was quickly achieved, together with training areas and firing ranges for the troops embarked as the invasion force.

Among the first arrivals was *Antrim* Group, comprising HMS *Antrim* and *Plymouth*, and *Tidespring*, stopping off on their way to South Georgia, arriving on the Saturday 10 April. *Tidespring* immediately embarked her two designated Wessex, which had been flown out from England, together with their crews. Preparations complete, the Group followed hard on the heels of *Fort Austin*, tasked to resupply HMS *Endurance* with dry goods, which she achieved on the 12th. *Tidespring*, following with *Antrim* Group, also rendezvoused with *Endurance* and, after much manipulation of fuel lines, finally managed to replenish her fuel on the 14th.

Fort Austin then turned north, moving to rendezvous with the *Brilliant* Group on the 16th in order to carry out what became known to the crew as the 'MEGA RAS'. Beginning on the 16th, this operation lasted until midnight of the following day. In that time, *Fort Austin*'s crew and RNSTS contingent issued 580 loads as well as back-loading things like paint and ceremonial equipment the Royal Navy did not want. Some of *Fort Austin*'s crew went without sleep for forty-six hours continuously, so it is no wonder the operation earned another epithet – Operation 'Insomnia'.

Together with her normal stores, *Fort Austin* also back-loaded the Group's 'special weapons', taking one 600lb L (live) round from *Brilliant* and one 600lb (S) (surveillance) round from *Sheffield*.

Several more of the British task groups arrived at Ascension during the days following *Antrim*'s departure, including, on the 11th, Admiral Woodward's Task Group (TG) 317.8 II, consisting of HMS *Glasgow*, *Sheffield*, *Coventry*, *Arrow*, *Brilliant* and *Glamorgan*, the last carrying Admiral Woodward and having been joined on passage by *Appleleaf*.

Brilliant's group left Ascension on the 14th to act as cover for Gp I (*Antrim*). Commanded by Captain J Howard (CO *Brilliant*), they proceeded at twenty-five knots to a position 1200 miles south of Ascension, acting as a screen for the Carrier Group and cover for *Antrim*'s attack on South Georgia. *Brilliant*'s group was accompanied by *Appleleaf*.

HMS *Glamorgan* followed more sedately, rendezvousing with *Hermes* on the 15th and transferring Admiral Woodward to the elderly carrier, now in company with HMS *Alacrity*, *Broadsword* and *Yarmouth*, the whole group arriving at Ascension on the 16th. Supplemented by the newly arrived *Resource*, the whole group headed south on the 18th, now designated the Carrier Battle Group (TG 317.8).

Next day (19 April), the five LSLs arrived, escorted by HMS *Antelope*, together with the LPD, HMS *Fearless*, to be joined the next day (20th) by *Canberra* and the motor vessel *Elk*.

Troops from, both the LSLs and *Canberra* were speedily disembarked, to begin a period of intensive training.

Captain Phil Roberts remembers *Sir Galahad*'s final visit well:

At Ascension we spent ten days frantically cross-decking Royal Marines and our cargo. By now it had been decided which LSL would be doing what at the landing. This meant considerable reshuffling of the cargo which had been hurriedly loaded at Plymouth and at the other ports where our sister ships had been loaded. We did get a Bofors, 6 GMPGs and a Blowpipe Missile launcher fitted here, together with crews to fire them. We were also allocated sandbags, which after a great deal of hassle we managed to fill and place on the upper bridge deck as protection for the GPMG crews.

In our role as logistic support ship we sailed from Ascension loaded with War Maintenance Reserve and a mixed array of vehicles and with the following embarked: Commando Logistic Regiment, HQ and Sigs, elements of the Field Dressing Station. We knew of the very large Argentinian Air Force yet to be neutralized and also of the many Exocet missiles they were capable of deploying against us.

Captain Tony Pitt, Master of *Sir Percivale* also remembers the frantic activity associated with the LSL's visit:

We anchored in Clarence Bay at first light 19 April, before receiving a visit from Marine Superintendent Captain D Thompson concerning our Chinese crew.

Throughout the period in Ascension, redistribution of cargo took place, interrupted only by a small hiccup on 22 April when, for a short time, it was thought the force might have to sail early. Further delays were experienced from the night of the 26th onwards as all ships had to proceed to sea every night because of the possibility of under water swimmer attack. Each ship was given a sector to patrol and deployed in 'darken ship' routine. During the first night of this dispersal, we had a close quarters situation with the ocean going tug Irishman who seemed to be wandering about aimlessly.

On the ship defence side, the armament was fitted. Standing Orders were produced by CPO Harvey (Gunnery Officer) and, although the system had to be tried, we appeared to be ready to defend ourselves. Due to the fore deck configuration it was only possible to fit one Bofors 40/60. A stern anchor was flown out from the UK to replace one damaged in previous operations. This was duly fitted at the port quarter so enabling an Operational Defect to be cleared.

It had been hoped that the troops would be able to put in some training but due to various circumstances only one exercise was completed. This involved helo transporting 7 Battery and their guns to the airfield by helicopter for a mock assault. From the point of view of ship organisation it seemed to go very well.

On logistics, the lub oil stocks were replenished from RFA *Blue Rover* in the early hours of Tuesday 27th and fresh water was fully topped up from the tanker *Fort Toronto* overnight Thurs/Fri (29th/30th) whilst lying alongside. On completion of watering at 0520 Z Fri 30 April the ship was, in all respects, ready to proceed to the Falkland Island area. *Sir Percivale* steamed to the south west of Ascension and waited until the early hours of Saturday morning for all the other LSLs to be watered. Some passengers had been transferred before departure. We had lost 148 and 8 Batteries and 59 Cdo Sqdn Condor Troop and embarked Cdo Log Reg Main B, total passengers, now 335.

Much restoring and rearrangement of cargo took place at Ascension, especially among the LSLs, who were now to form the main logistics arm of the invasion force.

Given the problems of night attacks and Ascension's less than perfect anchorage it is hardly surprising that the back-load did not all get done, of course.

The Rapier missile systems, for example, had been sensibly loaded in the bottom of the LSL holds, wrapped in plastic so as to minimise the effects of salt corrosion, but the delay entailed in finding and moving such equipment meant they could not be checked at Ascension and this resulted in a long wait before they became fully operational at the beachhead.

The LSLs did, however, receive some welcome means of self-defence in the form of Bofors and a Royal Artillery Blowpipe detachment.

Unfortunately, while this redeployment and cross-decking was going on, the usually reliable Hong Kong Chinese crews of the LSLs began to be uneasy about the role they might be called upon to play and a certain amount of unrest appears to have developed. A senior officer, Captain David Thompson, RFA was despatched from Empress State Building to assess the situation, but by the time he arrived, the men had settled down into normal working. The problems clearly had not been fully resolved, however, because trouble was to develop once again, weeks later, on the San Carlos bridgehead.

Helicopter replenishment (VERTREP) and the landing craft (LCUs) eventually got almost everything were it was needed and this period did prove invaluable, allowing the RFAs and STUFT practice in both damage control and air defence. Troops were able to practice embarkation drills and to zero all their weapons, including the Royal Artillery's 105mm field guns, weapons that proved essential later on.

Other benefits were more nebulous but no less important, best expressed in the words of Commodore Michael Clapp, Commodore Amphibious Warfare (COMAW) who wrote later, that, during the Ascension stopover '... a huge degree of confidence and trust was achieved'.

Which was to make an incalculable difference later, in the hell of San Carlos, better known to the crews who endured it as 'Bomb Alley'.

The LSLs of the Amphibious Task Group finally sailed on 1 May, followed by the *Canberra* Group on the 7th, but the logistics effort slowed not at all, with a tanker designated to replenish the visiting Task Force vessels remaining on station. For much of this period, it was motor tanker *Alvega*, which began duty on 21 May.

Ascension's role was undoubtedly crucial.

Without the 'island base', supply lines from the UK would have been impossibly long, air cover, except by the overworked Harriers, all but nonexistent and there would have been no convenient half-way house to allow troops essential time to train, zero weapons and rest after their sea voyage from the UK. On a more mundane but no less essential note, even mail delivery would have been next to impossible.

All of these factors made Ascension an essential logistic prerequisite to both Operation 'Paraquat', the attack on South Georgia and the vastly more complex Operation 'Sutton', as the Falkland's invasion itself was designated.

Chapter 8

South Georgia, 'Sutton' and Fitzroy

South Georgia (Operation 'Paraquet')

Having successfully replenished HMS *Endeavour*, the *Antrim* Group now continued south, arriving off South Georgia on 21 April, ready to try and retake the island.

The trip south had not been uneventful. There had been several dubious Sonar contacts, at least by those ships with working Sonar, which did not include either of the RFA ships, and although some of these were identified as whales or thermal layers, enough were doubtful to keep most of the crews on edge.

Captain Shane Redmond, Master of *Tidespring* was emphatic about the submarine menace. In his own taped log he recorded on the 20th: 'Several red contacts from the Navy last night. Personally, I am convinced that we have had company since the 17th.' There was something else exercising Shane Redmond's thought processes that freezing autumn day off South Georgia, though.

With a cargo of the 200 Royal Marines of M Company, his own crew and a swimming pool full of AS12 missiles neatly surrounded on all sides by fuel tanks full to the brim, after leaving Gibraltar, he had the grand total of four machine guns for ship defence.

At Gibraltar, just before leaving, Captain Redmond had a conversation with Admiral Woodward, on the subject of arming RFAs, which left him considerable food for thought:

> Immediately before the S Georgia Task Group split from the main body returning to the UK, Admiral Woodward asked if I needed anything. My response was yes, some weapons, to which he responded that we would probably be more of a danger to ourselves than an enemy. In hindsight, how wrong can you be!

The subject of arming RFA ships has always been fraught with problems, mostly concerned with the status of a merchant vessel carrying weapons and it was a subject that was to considerably exercise the minds of RFA management after the war.

For now, there was nothing to do but get on with it so, next day, *Tidespring* was somewhere off South Georgia, waiting for her Wessex to be used to land her embarked SAS men on Fortuna Glacier. *Tidespring*'s two Wessex duly departed with the SAS aboard and Lt Mike Tidd, who as *Tidespring*'s Flight Commander, was piloting the leading aircraft, takes up the story:

> South Georgia, a crescent-shaped island, 105 miles long and 18.5 miles wide, rises sheer out of the sea to a height of between 7500ft and 9500ft at its spine. Over half its land mass is permanently covered by ice in the form of glaciers. It lies in the South Atlantic on the edge of Antarctica at virtually the same latitude as Cape Horn and

bears the full brunt of the wild weather that sweeps around the Cape. Operation Paraquet (or 'Paraquat' as it was unwittingly dubbed by all involved) was the codename given to the operation to retake South Georgia in April 1982, at the start of the Falklands campaign.

We arrived off the North-west tip of South Georgia on the morning of the 21st and, after Ian Stanley had carried out an initial recce in Humphrey, we embarked the troops and then got airborne in a three ship echelon and set off through driving snow showers towards the coast. In accordance with normal Jungly operating procedures, our two Wessex 5s flew with a single pilot and aircrewman, myself in Yankee Alpha with Tug Wilson, and Lt Andy 'Pullthrough' Pulford RAF in Yankee Foxtrot with Jan Lomas.

Our first sight of the coast, as we made landfall at Cape Constance, was pretty awe-inspiring as black cliffs rising 1000ft vertically from the sea appeared through the driving snow. We skirted round through the low ground at the landward end of Cape Constance and emerged into Antarctic Bay, where the foot of the Fortuna Glacier disgorges into the sea. The turbulence was impressive: we would be using full power just to maintain height one moment and then be in full autorotation (no power applied) and still going up the next.

Weather on the glacier was wall-to-wall snow and, after orbiting in Antarctic Bay for some time, Ian Stanley made the decision to return to the ships and refuel.

At 1145 we tried again. This time we were able to make better progress and climb up on to the upper slopes of the glacier, though it was still very murky and there was severe turbulence and a lot of snow being whipped up from the surface by the wind. To add to our deep joy and happiness, we could see that the surface of the glacier was heavily crevassed which meant that, whilst we might gain some visual references from the surface once we got close enough, we would have to be careful about where we put down. Ian Stanley led us up to near the top of the glacier and then turned into wind and made his approach using his Doppler and Automatic AFCS to let himself down onto the surface. As I turned into wind I realised how few visual references were going to be available to me, particularly as the last 200ft of the approach was partially obscured by flying snow, and that the standard snow-landing approach would not be feasible. I overshot and went round again while Tug Wilson, my aircrewman, and I discussed the problem.

On the second approach I kept the aircraft orientated as best I could using the few distant references available, while Tug did a sterling job of talking me down gradually to the surface. It was a challenging approach to say the least. Apart from the lack of visual references, we were on the updraughting slope of the mountain and had to go into virtual full autorotation to persuade the aircraft to descend. Once we got close to the surface we could see that the crevassing was even worse than we had thought. We eventually touched down with a crevasse about 10ft away on our starboard side and started off-loading the troops. Despite having the collective lever fully down (no power applied), I found that we were being moved sideways and backwards by the wind. Sat on the surface we still had 60 knots of airspeed on the clock and I ended up having to fly the aircraft to try and keep it in position while Tug off-loaded as quickly as possible before we slid into the neighbouring crevasse. As soon as the off-load was complete we bounded into the air and scuttled off down the glacier and back into Antarctic Bay to wait for the others, before breathing a sigh of relief and returning to the ships. Back on board *Tidespring*, Pullthrough and I debriefed, agreed that we had never flown in conditions like these before, and said: 'Thank Christ we'll never have to do that again!' How wrong can you be!

The night aboard *Tidespring* was horrendous, with eighty-knot winds causing serious concerns about damage to the aircraft. On the glacier, things were even worse and, early in the morning the decision was made to airlift the men back to the ships. Mike Tidd was part of that team:

> We launched between snowstorms at about 1030 and headed off into shore but weather conditions forced us to return to the ships to refuel and wait.
>
> An hour or so later we tried again and this time we arrived at the foot of the glacier to find a break in the cloud. As we set off up the glacier we were acutely aware that we were going to be very short of escape options up there.
>
> However, Ian Stanley led us up through the clear patch and, as we approached the top of the glacier, we spotted the smoke grenades that the SAS team had fired to mark their position. They had only moved a few hundred yards from where we had dropped them and were now huddled in the lee of some rocks in an area that was relatively free of crevasses. Their smoke grenades had stained the snow around them making the approach and landing relatively straightforward this time. We landed facing our escape route down the glacier, which at this point was a fairly shallow ice slope leading down about a mile to a ridge, on the other side of which the ice dropped away much more steeply. Tug, my aircrewman, got weaving down the back and soon had our stick of tired, half-frozen troops loaded. As soon as they were all onboard he shut the door, and broke out some hot soup that he had brought along to get some warmth back into the 'grunts'. Meanwhile, I had radioed Ian Stanley and asked permission to depart as I could see a fresh belt of cloud and snow brewing up near our escape route.
>
> As soon as I got the OK, I lifted and headed off down the valley at about 60 knots and 100ft, which should have given me the option of landing on again if the weather got too bad. As it was, the speed with which South Georgia weather changes proved too quick for me. About half a mile along the valley the wind suddenly shifted and without warning I was in complete whiteout in thick driving snow. The only option available was to try and get the aircraft back down on to the ground if I could just find a reference to land by.
>
> I had passed a small clump of rocks a few seconds earlier so I called down to Tug to let him know that we had a problem and banked to the left – a 50/50 decision that probably inadvertently saved both of our lives. Tug threw open the cabin door and leaned out to look for the surface as I tried to turn and regain a landing reference. Unfortunately, what neither of us could see was that we were in a dip in the ice and, as I glanced in at the instruments halfway round the turn, I saw the radalt (radar altimeter) winding down at an alarming rate. I had no idea where the ground had suddenly come from but realising that a collision was inevitable I pulled in power and flared the nose up to cushion the impact. The aircraft hit the ground, left wing low and tail first, doing about 30 knots, sheering the port undercarriage leg off and crashing down and grinding along on its left side. I remember lying in my straps, with a feeling of intense frustration, watching the left-hand side of the cockpit filling up with debris and snow and thinking 'Mrs Tidd isn't going to like being a widow!'
>
> Eventually the aircraft ground to a halt. The inertia switches in the nose had crash-stopped the engines and apart from the wind and my windscreen wiper, which was still squeaking away, it was relatively quiet. I reached down beside me to turn off the

fuel cocks and electrics only to find that the whole lot was buried under snow and broken glass. Tug called through from the cabin that everyone seemed to be in one piece, so I hauled open the starboard cockpit door, climbed up onto the side of the fuselage, and helped Tug get the cabin door fully open.

By this time the other two aircraft had arrived and were able to use the wreckage of mine as visual references to land by and once all survivors had been loaded, the two aircraft waited for a break in the weather and then lifted off in formation and headed off down the glacier. By this time the press of bodies in the back of the Wessex 3 had forced me to unplug from the intercom to make room, and I was probably lost in my own thoughts, as I don't remember much about the flight back to the ships, until we landed on *Antrim*.

Once onboard I climbed out of the aircraft, only to find that *Tidespring*'s second Wessex had also crashed and there was a long and anxious wait before we heard that all aboard were safe and on their way back aboard Humphrey, *Antrim*'s Wessex 3.

Ian Stanley had managed to find a hole in the weather to get in and pick up Ian Georgesson and his team, and the story of that remarkable piece of flying is best left to Ian Stanley himself to describe. Suffice to say that he and his crew managed to pack sixteen armed men into an aircraft cabin that normally feels cramped with four people in it, fly back and land on a heaving deck at well above his normal Maximum All Up Weight [author's note: over 1,000kg above spec.]. Ian was later awarded the DSO and in my opinion it was richly deserved (even if he was a Pinger!)

The loss of 2/3rds of the Task Group's troop-carrying helicopter assets was a major blow to the operational plan but, as it turned out, not a fatal one. HMS *Brilliant*, a Type 22 frigate with two Lynx helicopters embarked, was diverted from the main Falklands Task Force to reinforce the South Georgia Task Group.

Ian Stanley's skill and the unbreakable Wessex 3 airframe had saved the operation, but next day, 23 April, *Tidespring* faced her severest challenge yet, a replenishment operation with the newly arrived *Brambleleaf*.

The two ships moved one hundred miles away from the coast and began the pumpover, having taken HMS *Plymouth* with them, the warship having only about twelve hours fuel remaining.

Unfortunately, the ships ran into a Force 10 gale although that was not their only problem, as Captain Shane Redmond OBE RFA (Rtd) explains:

> During the South Georgia phase it became clear the part weather would play in the re-supply of all units and that some rethinking of how RFAs operate would be essential. The pumpover on 22nd/23rd April emphasised the point that long duration replenishments under the prevailing weather condition had to be avoided wherever possible. Not withstanding this, it was also realised that given the ability to select the replenishment course and speed, RAS between two large and cumbersome ships could be achieved in very much worse conditions than would previously have been thought possible. A further consideration on that day (and throughout the campaign) was the risk of attack when two mission essential units were in such close proximity. (Subsequent discussion with Lt Cdr Horatio Bicain AN, Commanding Officer of the Argentine submarine *Santa Fe*, indicated that such concerns were not without foundation, in fact, he was able to state *Tidespring*'s course and speed during the pumpover with a surprisingly high degree of accuracy). One may well wonder what the effect of a successful attack might have been on the forthcoming deployment

from the UK, particularly in the political sense. On 22nd/23rd April 1982 given the critical fuel state within the group and the absence of any other source of supply, there was simply no option but to press on and get the job done.

The operation had barely begun, however, before both *Endurance* and *Antrim* signalled the presence of a hostile aircraft and Captain Young, commanding HMS *Antrim* and the Task Group, ordered an emergency breakaway. By the next day (24th), however, the ships had proceeded further north and completed their pumpover.

Meanwhile, with HMS *Brilliant* having joined the Task Group on the 24th, the next day brought a much needed change in the Royal Navy's luck, with the near destruction of the Argentine submarine *Santa Fe* by the Task Group helicopters.

The submarine limped into the BAS jetty at Grytviken, after being attacked by the Task Group's Wessex and Lynx helicopters. Quickly realising the demoralising effect this attack must have had upon the garrison, Captain Young and his military staff ordered an immediate attack on the base itself, which was entirely successful. The Argentine troops surrendered, almost without firing a shot.

That was more or less the end of the operation. The Royal Marines took down the blue and white of Argentina and hoisted the Union flag in its place, capturing the tiny Leith garrison and its commander, the infamous Alfredo Astiz, later that day.

This is what the books call the 'Battle for South Georgia' but in reality, it was not won by the soldiers when they occupied Grytviken.

Its outcome was decided two days before, 200 miles away during the *Tidespring/ Brambleleaf* pump over, when Lt Cdr Bicain (commander submarine *Santa Fe*) thought that HMS *Plymouth* was making a depth charge run in his direction when, in fact, she was joining *Tidespring* for an essential fuel replenishment, *Plymouth*, at the time, having very little fuel left.

Bicain broke off his attack, abandoning his self-confessed plan to put four torpedoes into *Tidespring*. The two RFA ships later completed their pumpover, *Tidespring* having replenished *Plymouth* simultaneously.

Had Bicain succeeded in torpedoing Redmond's ship, she would, as her master succinctly puts it, 'have disappeared in a blue flash', having, among other highly inflammable supplies, a swimming pool full of A12 missiles.

The 'blue flash' would certainly have destroyed *Brambleleaf* along with *Tidespring* and left the *Antrim* Group stranded, without fuel and about 1000 miles from the nearest chance of getting any.

Needless to say, the operation to regain South Georgia would have had to start again from scratch.

And South Georgia could not have been left because although it looked like a sideshow from the point of view of certain elements in the UK armed forces, from a logistics point of view, it was essential for a number of very good reasons.

First, because the STUFT needed a reasonably sheltered anchorage to transfer dry goods, mainly food and ammunition, to the store ships, such as *Fort Austin*. Troopships, particularly *Queen Elizabeth II*, also required a safe haven out of flying range of the Argentine mainland to rest their passengers and transfer troops to the smaller vessels making the run into San Carlos water. South Georgia was also ideally placed to act as the anchorage for a 'station' tanker, a role *Blue Rover*, among others, filled for a time.

Food, men and fuel. The three essential ingredients for invasion. And without a safe anchorage such as South Georgia, where else were they to come from?

That evening (17:30 GMT, 25 April), Brian Young sent the following signal, nicely summing up a difficult operation: 'Be pleased to inform Her Majesty that the White Ensign flies alongside the Union Flag at Grytviken.'

The Royal Navy had won but that was not the end of the job for *Tidespring*.

Capturing South Georgia, although it took Whitehall pressure from Young's already overburdened shoulders, added crushingly to the logistics nightmare he faced.

Scrap workers, the crew of Bicain's *Santa Fe*, the commando garrison of Grytviken and Alfred Astiz's special forces unit from Leith all had to be processed, which included trying to identify them, and then incarcerated somewhere they could do no harm before being returned to Ascension for repatriation to Argentina.

Fortunately, he had a possible option on hand – Her Majesty's Royal Fleet Auxiliary *Tidespring*.

Tidespring's role as a prison ship began with a signal from Captain Young, to Shane Redmond, Master of *Tidespring*, asking if he could accommodate some POWs.

Captain Redmond, in proper RFA style, responded with the single word 'Delighted'.

He claims it is the shortest signal he ever wrote, but he might be excused for also claiming it to be the one that got him into the most trouble.

Barely two days after the Argentine surrender, the 27th, saw *Tidespring* back in the bay ready to take on her first load of POWs, the crew of the *Santa Fe*, despondent after the unfortunate death of one of their colleagues, which had occurred while moving the submarine to a safer location.

Shane Redmond and his men, ably assisted by Lt Mike Tidd and his weapons trained flight crew, packed 185 Argentine POWs into the rapidly converted holds and magazines of the old tanker and after a harassing twelve days delivered them to Ascension, safe, well and in better condition than they had been in when they boarded the ship. Having disembarked the POWs, *Tidespring* took delivery of two new Wessex 5s, refilled her fuel tanks and headed south to rejoin the main Task Group, which had been having problems of its own.

(For the full story, see Geoff Puddefoot, *No Sea Too Rough: The story of the Royal Fleet Auxiliary in the Falklands*.)

Operation 'Sutton'

Admiral Woodward's Carrier Battle Group, together with the *Brilliant* Group arrived off the Falklands on the 25th, to be joined on the 29th by HMS *Plymouth* and HMS *Brilliant*, who returned the special forces units, Sqdn D SAS and No 2 SBS to the carriers.

With the arrival of these last two warships, the Carrier Task Group, once again in company with *Olmeda* and *Resource*, began a massive replenishment operation for fuel, ammunition, and stores so that each ship would have reasonably high reserves before entering the soon to be implemented Total Exclusion Zone (TEZ), the Group now being only 500 nautical miles from Port Stanley.

This giant RAS finished the next morning (30th), along with the diplomatic efforts, Alexander Haig, the US negotiator, having blamed Galtieri's junta for the breakdown.

With replenishment complete, Woodward headed his ships for the TEZ.

His task now was threefold. He needed to reduce the effective units in both the Argentine navy and air force to ineffectual levels and then, to blockade the military population of the Falklands, reducing their ability to fight to such a level that the invasion could be conducted with a minimum of both military and civilian casualties.

Between 1 May and 16 May, when the main body of the British amphibious group arrived, Argentina lost its biggest cruiser, *General Belgrano* and British pressure forced the rest of the Argentine navy to withdraw, so that it never again became a major factor in the war.

Unfortunately, Argentina's Air Force (AAF) proved more resilient and managed to cause extensive damage to the Task Force, sinking HMS *Sheffield* and incapacitating several other British warships. Argentine transport runs into the island were also well organised, with C-130 Hercules landing at Port Stanley most nights. Despite the attentions of the AAF, however, the ships and aircraft of the Royal Navy carried out almost daily raids on the island, harassing the youthful Argentine conscripts that made up the majority of the garrison, in an attempt to reduce their morale, while the RFAs continued their round of refuelling and replenishment support to the warships.

Although his men had only managed to partially contain the AAF, with the arrival of the amphibious group, Woodward was committed and on the night of 20 May, Operation 'Sutton', the invasion of the Falkland Islands, got under way.

The assault on the Falklands was to begin with a seaborne landing, destined for San Carlos Water, a sea loch opening off the east side of Falkland Sound, and the landing force itself consisted of:

- *Fort Austin*, tasked to act as antisubmarine and helicopter support ship, acting also as the helicopter refuelling facility.
- *Stromness*, still in her role as troop carrier.
- The LSLs *Sir Lancelot*, *Sir Geraint*, *Sir Percivale*, *Sir Tristram* and *Sir Galahad*, carrying troops but also to be used for the assault.
- The STUFTS *Canberra*, *Norland* and *Europic Ferry*, also carrying troops, would be part of the first wave, while *Elk* was needed to land her cargo of ammunition.
- HMS *Intrepid* and *Fearless* were to provide the landing craft, both LCUs and the bigger LCVPs and HMS *Antrim*, *Broadsword*, *Brilliant*, *Plymouth*, *Yarmouth*, *Argonaut* and *Ardent* were assigned as escorts.

The landing group and escorts detached from the Carrier Battle Group on 20 May, at 14:15 GMT, to begin their westward run, sailing to the north of the Falklands and arriving outside Falkland Sound after dark, bad weather having covered their approach.

HMS *Ardent* and *Antrim* had detached earlier and reached their ordered positions, where the latter would land an SBS strike force and *Ardent* would cover an SAS diversionary attack on Darwin.

By 10:15 Z, *Antrim* and *Yarmouth* had established a patrol line between West and East Falkland and confirmed the absence of enemy submarines. *Antrim* now closed Cat Island, covering the assault ships of the first group, as they made their run.

HMS *Fearless* led *Intrepid* into the Sound at 10:45pm (local time).

Turning towards the shore of East Falkland, they anchored at about 11:20 and began to 'dock down' ready to disembark their LCUs. Meanwhile, the troopships *Canberra*,

Norland and *Stromness*, with *Fort Austin* last and escorted by HMS *Plymouth* and *Brilliant*, arrived and anchored in the Sound soon after the LPDs at about 12:10, almost immediately disembarking the troops to the landing craft.

Gunfire from HMS Antrim and a ruthless assault by the SBS, took care of the observation post on Fanning Head, which was safely in the hands of the Royal Marines by 1:30, ensuring that the ships of the amphibious group were safe from the 106mm recoilless cannon and mortars with which the post was supplied.

Having collected their troops and led by Major Ewen Southby-Tailyour RM, the landing craft made the difficult eight-mile trip down San Carlos Water, with the guns of the Blues and Royals' light tanks jutting over the bows of the LCUs.

Both Marines and Paras landed almost without a shot being fired and occupied their assigned positions in San Carlos Bay, while diversionary attacks being made at Goose Green and HE and star shells off Stanley confirmed the Argentines in their supposition that British were going in US Marine Corps style, that is, by attacking at the point of greatest troop concentrations.

With Port San Carlos and San Carlos Settlement occupied and the beachhead established, the LSLs, led by *Sir Percivale*, moved directly into San Carlos Water, the other ships raising their anchors and following soon after, at about 6:30 Z.

Having arrived safely at their assigned positions, the LSLs anchored and prepared to spend the day unloading. *Sir Percivale*, having anchored off Ajax Bay, kept her single 40mm Bofors gun pointing shoreward, ready to support 45 Commando, then landing, slightly later than planned, from the LCUs.

San Carlos was now designated the Amphibious Operations Area (AOA), Commodore M Clapp RN, being responsible for operations there.

Captain Tony Pitt, Master of *Sir Percivale* remembers the trip well:

At first light, all ships of the Assault Force formed up into a tight box formation with both ships and columns half a mile apart and headed west for the Falkland Islands. The sky was overcast with moderate visibility and ideal for the task. This formation was maintained until 2100 when the various groups broke away to carry out the tasks allocated in the operational orders. *Sir Percival* remained with the other LSLs and *Europic Ferry* and cleared to the northwest of Falkland Islands to await the planned entry into Falkland Sound of this group at approx 1000. *Broadsword* was OTC although she was not programmed to enter the Sound.

It was *Sir Percivale*'s lot to anchor furthest south in San Carlos Water so we had to lead in all the other ships of our group. No specific route had been given to enter Falkland Sound and it was up to the respective Captains to decide the safest. We took a route to the west of Sunk Rock, which was unmarked in order to put maximum distance between Fanning Head and ourselves. Point X was reached on time at 0845 and we assumed Action and Shelter Stations. At this time tracer was sighted in the vicinity of Fanning Head so the passage was approached with some trepidation. On approaching the entrance to San Carlos Water two ships at the north end were identified as *Norland* and an LPD but other ships that should have been in the same area were still anchored in Falkland Sound. It became obvious the operation had been somewhat delayed but to what extent we did not know. We checked with *Fearless* and were told to proceed to our designated anchorage, No 14, off Ajax Bay (Red Beach).

It soon became apparent that Red Beach had not yet been assaulted as a Landing

Craft (Utility) (LCU) full of troops came alongside and proceeded with us to the anchorage. The assault had been planned for 0945 and it was now approaching 1100. On arrival at the anchorage the LCU carried on and we were in a position to watch the assault take place whilst attempting to cover it with our own weapons. Fortunately there was no opposition and we heaved big sighs of relief and congratulated ourselves on having overcome the first hurdle.

The MexeFlote was discharged to the water, assembled and prepared for forthcoming operations. The first Air Raid Warning occurred at 1240 and throughout the rest of the day, for varying periods we were at Action Stations. The last 'all clear' was at 2014. It was soon discovered that the operation that had started so easily was not going to continue that way. The first air attacks were to the north of the inlet where *Norland* and *Canberra* were anchored, but later they concentrated on the ships in Falkland Sound that were less protected by the terrain. Many RN ships were hit during the day but nothing came near the south of San Carlos Water and *Sir Percivale* did not fire a shot in anger.

During the day it was decided that *Sir Percivale* would be off loaded first due to the cargo being more accessible. It was also realised that the off load would have to continue despite the air raids, only stopping when the aircraft were in the vicinity.

Days of air raids followed, with casualties being taken on both sides, including *Sir Galahad* and the oldest of the LSLs, *Sir Lancelot*, the latter hit by three bombs while anchored in San Carlos Sound, all of which fortunately failed to explode.

Perhaps the most serious and significant episode of the war occurred on the 24th, when the AAF surprised the RFA's three big stores ships, *Fort Austin*, *Resource* and *Stromness* at anchor, a bare 400 yards apart, at dawn in San Carlos Sound. A member of *Fort Austin*'s embarked RNSTS complement recalled the episode:

> Dawn on the morning of Monday 24th May, saw the largest gathering of RFAs since the Fleet review. Lined up across San Carlos Water were *Fort Austin*, *Resource* and *Stromness* (all carrying large ammunition loads).
>
> A little astern was *Tidepool* and the five LSLs were anchored at the head of the water.
>
> The three solid support ships were lying abreast of each other at two cables distance (approx 400 ft) and could not spread themselves out because the burning hulk of HMS *Antelope* was ahead with its forward magazine intact.
>
> At 11:30, there was a surprise attack, which placed bombs between the three solid support ships ... the nearest to *Fort Austin* landed fifty feet away but failed to explode.

This attack could quite easily have finished the war in the Argentines' favour.

The British were fairly well supplied with tankers, in a pinch, being able to make use of BP's modified British Rivers class as well as the RFA ships. Of the specialised Ammunition, Food and Equipment Store (AFES) ships, however, they had only four – *Fort Grange*, *Fort Austin*, *Resource* and *Regent* – with *Stromness* designed specifically to resupply only food but also able to RAS munitions if required.

Fort Grange was still a week away, while *Regent* was with the carrier group but with special weapons embarked, whose presence meant she could come no nearer San Carlos than the edge of the TEZ.

A strike that day on any of those three store ships anchored abeam in San Carlos would have probably caused a chain reaction, resulting in an explosion, which to quote one informed RFA source: 'Would have had the destructive force of a small atom bomb.'

It would also have resulted in the destruction of all three RFA ships, leaving the Royal Navy perilously short of ammunition at a time when they needed every missile and shell to fend off the still-dangerous AAF. And that would probably have spelt the end of the war for the Royal Navy.

It was that simple.

Despite this near miss, the invading forces quickly began to make headway, although the loss of *Atlantic Conveyor*, with its load of Chinook helicopters, which also resulted in the deaths of three RFA crew members, did cause serious supply problems.

Goose Green and Darwin were captured by the 2nd Battalion of the Parachute Regiment together with elements of 3 Commando, on 29 May although, unfortunately, the Regiment's commanding officer, Colonel 'H' Jones, was among those killed. On the other side of the island, by the 30th, 45 Commando had secured Douglas Settlement, while 3 Para were firmly ensconced at Teal Inlet and Kilo company, 42 Commando had relieved the SAS on Mount Kent, after the special service men had secured that strong point in a characteristic lightning dash.

Despite sustaining some damage, the LSLs were now operating a shuttle service between Teal Inlet and San Carlos, although operations in the now well established South Georgia anchorage were impeded by the severe weather.

Sir Galahad, which had sustained some bomb damage, was fully operational again. Her Master, Captain Phil Roberts DSO, remembered a mild celebration:

> By 30 May we were ready to sail from San Carlos to proceed to the carrier group to get back our Chinese who by now were embarked in *Sir Tristram*. We had only discharged approximately one hundred tons of ammunition in this time, plus all the vehicles stowed on the upper deck. The ship by this time was like the proverbial tip. We felt rather relieved to sail out of San Carlos that evening and hopefully to restore order if not some decent food, and above all to get out of the firing line for a day or two.
>
> On 31 May, our Chinese crew were returned by helicopter in atrocious weather conditions. They, surprisingly, were all very pleased to be back and straight away set-to to clean up the ship and within an hour had provided us all with a hot meal.
>
> On 1 June we RASed fuel with RFA *Olna*, and restored sanity to the Chief Engineer Officer by getting a fresh supply of cigars. I have never seen someone enjoy a smoke so much before. I decided that it was time I restored my own sanity and sent for my steward. He provided us both with a beautiful gin and tonic with ice and lemon served on a silver tray complete with a bowl of peanuts. Much to the amusement of all on the bridge, we both enjoyed those drinks. They were a happy relief after so much tension.

Operationally, things were going well and the LSLs and a number of other RFAs began to participate in the immense build-up of stores and men that would be necessary for the final push on Port Stanley.

Canberra arrived in the San Carlos anchorage on 2 June, discharged her troops, consisting of the Scots Guards and Welsh Guards, before leaving on the night of the 3rd, while, on the 5th, HMS *Sheathbill*, the Harrier landing pad at San Carlos, became operational.

Despite problems with Brigade organisation, missing equipment and some confusion over transport, by 6 June the Scots Guards had reached Bluff Cove, in support of 2 Para, whose lightning helicopter dash had put them there on the 2nd. Unfortunately, only half the Welsh Guards had reached Bluff Cove and concerns about the safety of the big LPDs forced Commodore Clapp to deploy two of the remaining LSLs to move the rest of the battalion forward.

Consequently, an overloaded *Sir Tristram*, complete with Mexeflote, sailed round on the night of 6 June, and was still in Fitzroy's Port Pleasant anchorage next morning, discharging ammunition for 5 Brigade, her off-load difficulties compounded by a lack of LCUs or similar ship-to-shore transport.

Sir Galahad was in San Carlos, loading vehicles and men of the 16th Field Ambulance, 5 Brigade's medical unit, thirty G Company SAS men and four Rapier missile launchers, the latter intended to supply air cover for the Fitzroy anchorage. She also had a Sea King helicopter embarked.

Captain Phil Roberts, master of *Sir Galahad*, was verbally instructed to embark the remaining 352 Welsh Guards and, sailing at dusk, disembark those troops at Bluff Cove in the early hours of the morning, under cover of darkness, then get back to Fitzroy to offload the Field Ambulance and the Rapiers before dawn, so both operations would be carried out safely under the cover of darkness.

Captain Roberts explains some of the accommodation problems this entailed:

> *Sir Galahad* sailed from San Carlos with over 500 passengers and crew embarked, over 150 in excess of her passenger certificate. COMAW gave signalled approval for the exemption.
>
> The Welsh Guards had to be billeted in the tank deck as the port side troop accommodation had been wrecked by the unexploded bomb on the 24th May. As well as accommodation problems, these extra put a great strain on the catering staff and other ship-board resources.

Both the Rapiers and Guards units were loaded quickly but lack of transport and communications difficulties meant that the Field Ambulance and its vehicles were not aboard until five hours after dusk.

Captain Roberts, knowing that he could not make Bluff Cove, discharge the Welsh Guards and get back to Fitzroy in darkness, signalled Clapp's staff that he intended to stay in San Carlos and sail at dusk the next day.

Soon after, however, he received a signal ordering him to sail but only as far as Fitzroy, where he was to disembark both the Rapiers and the Field Ambulance.

Captain Roberts describes the situation in which he found himself:

> The signal I received from Clapp's staff was not copied to 5 Brigade head quarters, although the Executive officer did inform the O/C troops of the change of destination.
>
> Having already turned in, there was nothing to be gained from calling the Welsh Guards at the time of sailing from San Carlos and this new information would be passed to them in the morning when they were called.
>
> The passage to Fitzroy was conducted in total radar and radio silence so as not to alert the Argentinians of our presence, which meant that the Welsh Guards could not have sent a signal to the rest of their Battalion, anyway.

Captain Roberts is also quite clear about Commodore Clapp's involvement in this incident, as he explains here:

> It should be made clear that Commodore Clapp never intended *Sir Galahad* to go to Bluff Cove. As far as he was concerned, and as he in fact signalled in his initial orders on 6th June, *Sir Galahad* was required to go to Fitzroy (Port Pleasant) on completion of the off-load at Teal Inlet.
>
> It was a misunderstanding by one of his staff that led to a verbal briefing to Capt Roberts, in San Carlos on 7th June, to the effect that *Sir Galahad* was to proceed to Bluff Cove, discharge the Welsh Guards and then proceed to Fitzroy's Port Pleasant, anchoring before daylight in order to off-load the Field Ambulance, SAS and Rapier batteries.
>
> Commodore Clapp was never advised that the low cloud and bad weather that had been affecting Stanley and the east coast of East Falklands, had, in fact, improved considerably, resulting in excellent visibility.
>
> Had he known this, he would never have allowed *Sir Galahad* to sail from San Carlos, as he has made clear elsewhere.

Sir Galahad weighed anchor at 0200 Zulu on the 8th, anchoring in Port Pleasant sometime after first light, 8am local time (approx 1200 Z), about three cables (600 metres) east of *Sir Tristram* and a mile from Fitzroy, the 150-mile trip having proved uneventful.

Weather was bright and sunny with the hills around Port Stanley clearly visible and the single remaining LCU and *Sir Tristram*'s Mexeflote were both loaded with ammunition and waiting for the tide to turn. There had been six LCUs working in the anchorage the previous day but four had returned to *Intrepid* and the other one was making a run to Goose Green to collect 5 Brigade's signal vehicles.

Those responsible for the offload, Majors Todd (RCT) and Southby-Tailyour (RM), immediately boarded *Sir Galahad* in order to get the Guardsmen ashore as soon as possible.

Discussion became heated as a number of alternatives were considered but finally it was decided that the LCU would unload its ammunition and move as many Guards as possible round to Bluff Cove, along with their heavy equipment which they were understandably reluctant to be separated from, although Major Southby-Tailyour has made it clear elsewhere that he would never have allowed such a move in daylight.

Along with the LSLs, they could also use local tractors and trailers, as well as the twenty-foot cutter that the engineers had requisitioned. Meanwhile the single Sea King then available was unloading the Rapier units, but this was slow work, requiring eighteen helicopter lifts to get all four units ashore.

At noon the LCU was alongside *Sir Galahad* but Lt Colonel Roberts, commanding 16 Field Ambulance and senior ranking officer, insisted that his unit should go first. An hour later, the last of the medical team was ashore but now another snag appeared. The LCU ramp had been damaged on the last trip and could not be lowered to allow the heavy equipment to be loaded by way of *Sir Galahad*'s stern doors. Tragically, it was decided to leave the troops aboard while their heavy equipment was offloaded by crane.

Five hours had elapsed since *Sir Galahad* dropped anchor and in that time the Argentinian troops on Mount Harriet, ten miles away had signalled the mainland with the result that the AAF was on its way.

One group bombed HMS *Plymouth* in Falkland Sound, but the jets were too low, none of the bombs exploded and *Plymouth* escaped with superficial damage.

The five Skyhawks of the remaining group had been given the location of the LSLs as Port Fitzroy, which is an inlet to the north of the settlement, while the two vessels were actually in Port Pleasant, to the south.

Finding Port Fitzroy empty and being low on fuel, the jets swept out south over the sea to return home and while making a rising turn, the leader's wingman caught a glimpse of the LSLs.

Simply tightening their turn brought them in line with the ships and the Skyhawks swept in to the attack, three attacking *Sir Galahad*, while the two remaining went for *Sir Tristram*. With his weapon disabled by a broken tracker optic, the sergeant commanding the Rapier troop covering Fitzroy's eastern approach could only watch the ensuing carnage helplessly.

Aboard the LSLs, the aircraft were sighted and heard at about 1715 Z. 'Action stations' was immediately piped but barely seconds later, the aircraft struck.

Sir Tristram was hit by two bombs, both on the starboard side towards the stern. One went straight through the ship without exploding while the other burst inside a compartment, killing the Bosun, Yu Sik Chee and a crewman Yeung Shui Kam and buckling the steel wall of the tank deck. There were soon fires in the steering flat, above which were several pallets of ammunition, and forward, close to a quantity of ammunition and explosives, which still remained aboard.

The three AAF Skyhawks attacking *Sir Galahad* were slightly higher and consequently their bombs developed a more vertical trajectory. One, by sheer bad luck, went through an upper deck hatch and de-flagrated, causing a massive fireball which swept through the tank deck, where most of the Welsh Guards were waiting to disembark. The second exploded in the galley area, killing the butcher, Sung Yuk Fai, instantly and wounding several other crew members, while the third burst in the engine room, killing Third Engineer Officer A J Morris. This last explosion produced clouds of thick, extremely irritant smoke, trapping Second Engineer Officer P A Henry, Third Engineer Officer C F Hailwood and Junior Engineering Officer N Bagnall in the machinery control room. Junior Engineer Officer Bagnall was driven back by the smoke while attempting to escape but was given the only set of breathing apparatus by Second Engineer Officer Henry and ordered to try again. Bagnall eventually succeeded in getting out but Second Engineer Officer Henry, Third Engineer Officer Hailwood and a crew member who was also present, Electrical Fitter Leung Chau, were not seen again.

Meanwhile, on deck, Firesuitman Chiu Yiu Nam, realising that men were still trapped below, pulled on his asbestos suit and went into the flaming tank deck. He managed to lead to safety ten of the Guardsmen who would undoubtedly have died but for his efforts. Third Officer Andy Gudgeon also entered the smoke-filled accommodation, wearing breathing apparatus, although his attempts to save one man, trapped by falling debris, were unsuccessful. Both Paul Henry and Chiu Yiu Nam received the George Medal for their actions while Third Officer Gudgeon received the Queen's Gallantry medal.

Captain Roberts quickly realised that there was no possibility of saving *Sir Galahad* and given the vast quantities of ordnance aboard, his only course was to abandon ship. He managed to give the order over the ship's broadcast system microphone and, having done this, he set about organising the launching of life rafts and lifeboats. He described events thus:

At first light we negotiated the narrow entrance to Port Pleasant and anchored off Fitzroy Settlement about 3 cables to the east of RFA *Sir Tristram*, who was still unloading ammo and stores. The weather was bright and sunny with good visibility – the hills and landmarks around Port Stanley looked very close. *Sir Tristram* had filled both the Mexoflote and one LCU to capacity with ammunition. So the Guards had to wait on board until assets had proceeded to shore, discharged and returned to the ship. The Welsh Guards were anxious to be landed at Bluff Cove where they had originally been ordered to, not Fitzroy. They had been told that the bridge at Fitzroy over to Bluff Cove had been blown and was not yet repaired. So it was that only a handful of RAMC managed to get ashore, and none of the Welsh Guards, by 17:15 when the Officer of the Watch observed two very low flying aircraft approaching the ship fast on the starboard beam. He immediately piped 'Action Stations' and at the same time I entered the wheelhouse. We both hit the deck behind tile chart table.

The ship shuddered with the explosions.

Seconds later, two more aircraft flew low over the ship and again we felt explosions. All ventilation was crash-stopped; fire alarm bells were ringing furiously on the bridge panel. Smoke immediately started to appear through the chartroom door, which had been blown open by the force of the explosions. My immediate reaction was to rush out to the bridge wings to assess the damage.

On the starboard side there were flames and an enormous amount of black smoke coming out of the accommodation and engine room vent fans, and it was much the same on the port side. On looking forward, flames and smoke were shooting out of the after hatch. I tried phoning the engine room by sound powered telephone but there was no reply. It became immediately apparent to me that fires were burning out of control in many places and that the ship could not be saved.

Instinctively, I grabbed the ship's broadcast system microphone, not knowing if it was working, and made the pipe 'Abandon Ship, Abandon Ship'. I learnt later that this pipe had been heard in most parts of the ship. I felt it very important that the after accommodation be evacuated as quickly as possible.

No 4 lifeboat was swung out over the side and had to be lowered shortly afterwards because it was being enveloped in smoke. I proceeded forward to supervise the launching of life rafts. By this time, helicopters were already arriving to take off the wounded, the Mexoflote and LCU were also quickly on the scene as were two lifeboats from *Sir Tristram*.

By 17:50, all the non-seriously injured personnel and crew had been evacuated from the ship. By this time, the whole of the bridge front was burning furiously, with smoke billowing high into the sky. Loud explosions, flames and shrapnel were erupting from the after hatch.

All the remaining injured had been evacuated to the forecastle and were being cared for by 16 Field Ambulance medics, before being winched into a Sea King. The evacuation of the badly wounded was a slow and painful operation. The pilots of the helicopters showed great courage and determination, hovering close to the deck, despite the loud explosions and debris, which was being blown into the air. It was very fortuitous that our foremast had been lowered in order to increase our arc of fire. This enabled the helos to hover four or five feet above the deck, so speeding up the evacuation of the very badly burned Welsh Guards.

At 18:15, the last of the wounded had been lifted off. I bundled my Chief Engineer Officer who had also been wounded up into the helo and then hooked myself on – I was the last to leave my ship. It was a desperately sad moment for me. A well ordered, happy and disciplined ship one moment and a burning inferno the next, and obviously at that time I did not know which or how many of my officers or crew had been killed or injured.

The full story was, of course, well recorded by the BBC camera team and reported on by Brian Hanrahan. For me, and probably my officers, crew and all those troops that we were carrying at the time, and the relatives of those who were killed, it was one of those sad moments of timing because the media used those pictures as their theme for the whole of the Falklands War, showing them time and time again. It certainly is disturbing for me to see them, as it must be for others who were there.

By now, Captain Green, Master of *Sir Tristram*, had also ordered his men to abandon ship, the fires around the remaining ammunition having proved impossible to control. He had clear memories of the attack:

We discharged all that day [7th] and *Sir Galahad* arrived next morning 8th May. Both ships were bombed about 14:00 local time. *Sir Galahad* was very badly hit and so I sent my lifeboats across to assist her.

We apparently had an UXB in the steering flat which was on fire with the entrance blocked off by debris, and the stern trunking above, getting very warm, full of ammunition and cased diesel. I subsequently decided to abandon ship and leave it to the Bomb Disposal people to come and sort out the bomb.

We were evacuated from Fitzroy to *Fearless* and *Intrepid* in San Carlos by helo through the mountains in pitch dark and then a few days later, to British Trent via Atlantic Causeway by helo for the passage to Ascension. Then RAF to Brize Norton where there was a welcoming committee and our families to meet us.

Some of *Sir Galahad*'s crew had been forced to jump from the poop deck, after being cut off by the flames, and liferafts had to floated to these men while the uninjured troops were being evacuated from the tank deck by LCU, lifeboat, liferaft and helicopter, *Sir Tristram* having also sent her boats to help.

The helicopter pilots particularly took incredible risks, bringing their aircraft to within feet of the burning deck and exploding ammunition. At one point, seeing the life rafts being sucked back towards the fiercely burning ship, some of the pilots positioned their machines to produce a back draught, drawing the life rafts away from the hull, despite the explosions and the pall of black smoke surrounding their machines and reducing visibility to zero.

By 17:50 Zulu, all non-injured personnel and most of the ship's crew were off *Sir Galahad* and the wounded had all been moved to the forecastle, the extreme front of the ship. From the bridge front aft, the ship was an entire mass of flames and smoke, with exploding ammunition and flames still erupting from the after hatch.

Of necessity, helicopter evacuation of the wounded was a slow and painful process, made extremely dangerous for both aircraft and crews by the debris and explosions, which periodically ripped the sky apart. Twenty-five minutes later, at 18:15 Zulu, the last of the injured had been removed and, after bundling his badly wounded Chief Engineer into a helicopter, Roberts hooked himself onto the winch cable and was hoisted away from the deck, last man to leave his stricken ship.

In all, forty-three soldiers and seven RFA men were killed at Fitzroy. Wounded from both ships were eventually transferred to the hospital ship *Uganda* for treatment, while the remainder of both crews went first to *Atlantic Causeway*.

Two days later, *Sir Galahad*'s crew were transferred to the tanker *British Test* while *Sir Tristram*'s crew moved to the tanker *British Trent*, both vessels then proceeding to Ascension Island, from where the crews went home by air.

Sir Tristram remained in the Falklands as an accommodation ship until 16 May 1983, when she was transported back to the River Tyne on the Danish heavy lift ship *Dan Lifter* for rebuilding.

Sir Galahad, after a commemorative service on board, was sunk on 25 July, in position 52 16.5S 56 45.35W, where she remains as a designated war grave.

By 14 June, Port Stanley had been recaptured and it was all over. At 8:00pm local (midnight GMT) on 14 June 1982, Menendez and Major General Moore signed the formal Instrument of Surrender.

In Port Stanley, the clearing up had to begin. *Sir Percivale* had the honour of being the first ship into Port Stanley after the ceasefire, on the 17th, as her master well remembers:

> *Sir Percivale* received final instructions to proceed to Port Stanley to arrive at the narrows at 1230 in company with *Sir Bedivere*. We assumed we would meet them somewhere off Port William. Cleared Port Salvador narrows at 0640 and proceeded to Stanley. We kept our fingers crossed that the stated minefield areas were correct and nothing had been laid in Port William. There was no sign of *Sir Bedivere* in the area and at first light we turned into Port William on the final leg. The only vessel in sight was the Argentinian Hospital Ship *Admiral Iridzar* which was at anchor to the west of Port William. We thought that *Sir Bedivere* might already be lying alongside in Port Stanley but no, as we passed through the narrows at 1230 precisely, preceded by a V formation of helicopters, we realised we were the first to arrive and were very honoured to be doing so. We anchored off the Public Jetty and had our several blasts on the ships whistle answered by the cathedral bells. This was a better day for the RFAs and the LSLs in particular.
>
> Launched the Mexeflote and awaited instructions. We resumed our service as a refuelling deck once the helos realised we were around and, appropriately, we achieved landing 1000 during Operation Corporate. A Sea King c/s VS took the final reward.
>
> Later in the day X, Y and Z Companies of 45 Cdo were embarked for Rest and Recreation, all very dirty and tired. Relaxed water rationing for the first time since leaving UK and resolved to make them as comfortable as possible. We sailed Port Stanley at 1930 bound for San Carlos Water and an important meeting with RFA *Fort Grange* for re-supply of provisions, both solid and liquid.

Although Captain Pitt does not mention it, he made sure the RFA had the last word. Safely at anchor in Port Stanley, he sent a signal to the effect that: 'The Blue Ensign now flies over Port Stanley Harbour,' which must have gone down well with the Navy!

South Thule (Operation 'Keyhole') was recaptured on 19 April, leaving the whole island group once again in the hands of the British.

The Falklands campaign was won after one hundred hard-fought days and at the cost of 257 British servicemen, including eleven members of the RFA, and approximately 700 Argentinians, mostly young conscripts. It was in many ways a

Pyrrhic victory since Britain's financial commitment to its Falklands base is estimated at approximately £4 million yearly (MoD sources, despite a number of requests, still refuse to reveal the real figures), which serves to keep a steadily decreasing number of islanders and several thousand sheep on a wind-swept South Atlantic island which many in Whitehall and elsewhere feel should have gone back to the Argentinians years ago.

Although, whatever one's view about the rights (or wrongs) of the South Atlantic war, one significant effect it did have was to herald a complete rethink among the senior HQ staff then responsible for the RFA's operation at Fulham Road's 'madhouse'.

RFA personnel killed in the Falklands War

On board *Sir Galahad*
Third Engineer Officer Christopher Francis Hailwood
Second Engineer Officer Paul Anderson Henry (GM Posthumous)
Third Engineer Officer Andrew John Morris
Electrical Fitter Leung Chau
Butcher Sung Yuk Fai
Seaman N G Por

On board *Sir Tristram*
Seaman Yeung Shui Kam
Bosun Yu Sik Chee

On board *Atlantic Conveyor*
First Radio Officer R Hoole
Laundryman Chan Si Shing
Laundryman Ng Po

Chapter 9

Force Multipliers, Modern Sea War and the New RFA: 1982–99

Despite having only just begun to experience the crippling cuts imposed upon it by the government's 1981 Defence Review, many of the operations conducted by the RFA during the Falklands War still revealed significant deficiencies in the training and equipment needed to undertake the major logistics deployment required of them, operating away from the Royal Navy's much-practised NATO exercise scenario.

With the two exceptions of the new Fort class, the fleet was old and most of the vessels were certainly beginning to show their age. Refits had, in many cases, been poorly completed, with little or no attention paid to the important details that make an RFA ship fit for war duty, such as the integrity of gastight citadels and the adequate operation of torpedo and mine countermeasures systems. Financial constraints also resulted in the radar and sonar equipment aboard the older RFAs being either extremely antiquated or not working at all. Such equipment was sufficient for commercial needs, when it worked, but wholly inadequate, for example, when operating in a theatre such as the South Atlantic against a relatively well trained and equipped enemy. Added to this, a large percentage of RFA ratings were drawn from the Merchant Navy Pool, and they often had little or no specialist RFA training, leaving the captain and his department heads with a very serious shortfall of trained, experienced personnel in vital areas. Internal ship organisation had also proved wholly inadequate for a South Atlantic war, with no provision, at least to begin with, for manning, control or maintenance of weapons, allocation of defence watches (which involved the ship being operational twenty-four hours a day) as well as several other key areas, although most ships quickly instituted systems, largely based on common sense, which seemed to work well.

Almost wholly without any means of self defence, the RFA ships often found themselves exposed to enemy attack, because the Royal Navy, with few enough ships for the job in hand, had no means of fully protecting its civilian support vessels. Nor, of course, were there enough of the specialist RFA ships to operate the supply chain required without help from the totally defenceless STUFT, which only added to the Navy's burden. The loss of *Atlantic Conveyor* and near disaster of 24 May 1982, in San Carlos water, just served to emphasise the thinness of the ice on which the whole logistics effort had been skating.

Loss of several, vitally important RFA ships did not help the supply problem, either. These were vessels designated for immediate sale under the Review, including *Tidepool*, which, embarrassingly for the government, had to be borrowed back from her new Chilean owners in something of a rush, to say the least. Along with the ships, over 1,000 RFA personnel should also have been made redundant just before Operation 'Corporate' began.

Peter Nelson, *Tidepool*'s Chief Officer at the time, takes up the story of her return as she transited the Panama Canal for the *first* time:

> Next stop was the Panama Canal and a break at Rodman US Naval Base where I conformed with Mr Ron Robins (the RFA's Material Manager) instructions to 'tart it up'. Whilst there we handed over the final stores, all but one folio of charts, radios 'except a crystal set' to one of the LSLs on her way home to the UK from Canada. It was then downhill to Chile and we anchored in a small town in the north called Arica. By this time hostilities had broken out in the Falklands and the Task Force was being assembled. I think we must have been the nearest Brit ship to the Falklands at that time.
>
> Anyway, both the Chilean Army and Navy came out to inspect their new ship. Meanwhile, Mrs Thatcher had phoned General Pinochet, asking for her ship back. The Chileans were eager to come with us, even suggesting they mount and man the guns. Unfortunately, they had to be left behind and within 24 hours we were on our way north, arriving off Balboa after dark. We entered the Canal about midnight and really rushed through, sailing into the Atlantic about 6:30 the next morning. The idea was that we weren't seen transiting in daylight. The British Consul provided us with a couple of charts and we set off for Curaçao again.
>
> Captain Rex Cooper met us in Curaçao with a mountain of stores and a crew to bring us up to full strength. The aviation fuel was changed for AVCAT (helicopter fuel), all the stores loaded including a 'few' cans of beer and we set off for Ascension. More gear was loaded there, hoses, connections, wires and all the paraphernalia for RAS and rig building began in earnest. Full marks to the Bosun and crew, who threw everything into it and within a couple of days we were ready for the job.

Even without the clear lessons of the Falklands War, it had long been obvious to many RFA and Royal Navy personnel, including Commodore Dunlop, that major changes, in both equipment and organisation, were long overdue.

The Commodore had even been quoted as being in favour of the RFA not only being operated by the Royal Navy, but managed by it, too, although he later made it quite clear that this was not the case. His plan, in actual fact, was that;

> ... all RFA officers in a responsible position should hold permanent Commissions in the RNR and that conditions of service for all ratings should make it quite clear that, should it be deemed necessary, in the interests of national security, they would be required to sign a similar agreement to the T124X articles of World War II. Should the necessity arise, it would then simply be a question of hauling down the Blue ensign and hoisting the White Ensign with no change of personnel; that is what I meant by the RFA being under the White Ensign.
>
> At no time have I ever subscribed to the view that the RN take over and man the RFA.
>
> What I do feel, without any doubt whatsoever, is that the Service must be administered to undertake the role it is required to fulfil in peace and war, rather than vice versa.

Perhaps characteristically, he could not resist a final broadside:

> In conclusion may I say that I have never failed to be impressed by the cheerfulness, loyalty and dedication shown by the majority of RFA personnel when called upon to partake in operations completely extraneous to the role of the Merchant Navy. It is

my personal opinion that the valuable contribution of the RFA Service to the
Falklands Campaign was in spite of, not because of, the policies created and
administered by RFA management.

The above is quoted from Commodore Dunlop's private papers (courtesy of his
family).

Severely criticised for his views at the time, he retired on 27 November 1982, having
reached statutory retirement age. This, of course, directly contradicts some of the
stories current at the time that he was forced out of the service.

One very senior ex-RFA official, who has asked not to be named, for obvious
reasons, corroborated his views:

Sam's comments were not an isolated opinion. Most thinking COs and a number of
officers held private views regarding the neglect of war preparedness within the
Service during the late 70s and early 80s. Indeed, it could be said that as far as
peacetime requirements were concerned, we were only just fit for purpose.

The problem had nothing to do with the number of ships or manpower for we
had sufficient of both to meet the assessed threat at that time. The real problem was
one of maintenance of the front line fleet and the proper training of our people to
enable us to operate in a hostile, not just a benign, peacetime environment. The
generally truncated and often poor quality refits paid little attention to the upkeep of
ship defence capabilities with one exception, aviation and, even then, non-operational
facilities were often ignored.

As always, there was another side to the problems of ship defence and maintenance,
as Gordon Wilson, the RFA Fleet Manager for Personnel and Operations during the
Falklands War, explains:

In defence of the management team, it would only be fair to point out that formal
Naval plans assumed that RFAs would always be escorted by a warship to provide
defence, and thus would not require extensive self defence equipment. As the Naval
fleet contracted steadily over the years this assumption of warship escorts became
more and more unrealistic, as the Falklands demonstrated. In addition, tighter and
tighter annual budgets meant that RFA refits had to concentrate largely on defects and
improvements essential for safety and seamanship, to the detriment of more
operational needs.

Although much was made in the media at the time about the phenomenal success
of the logistics effort, the supply system and its underlying organisation had been
severely stressed and it was certainly starting to unravel by the early weeks of June
1982. Several of the warships, for example, were down to a single day's ammunition
on the day of the surrender and *Sir Percivale*, by 10 June, had food, at full rations, for
barely two days. What would have happened if the war had dragged on into July is
anyone's guess.

Some idea of the RFA's difficulties can be obtained from examination of the ship's
diaries. Late in the war, *Resource*, the big Fleet Replenishment ship, had been tasked to
re-store from one of the STUFT, *Saxonia*, then anchored in Gold Bay, South Georgia.
Resource's diary recorded at one point:

At first light a RAS was attempted with MV *Saxonia* but excessive rolling caused the RAS to be abandoned because the suspended loads swung dangerously to and fro in *Saxonia*'s hold with a pendulum motion.

Stromness, similarly tasked to restore, finished her RAS with the motor vessel *Lycaon* on the same day, her diary recording:

1512 FAOP [Full Away on Passage]. On sailing South Georgia, embarked 415 troops & 108 Rapier missiles, assorted 200 tons ammo. [Holds filled and remainder of ammo double banked on either side of clearway for almost entire length.]

Good job 'Health & Safety' did not drop by! Joking aside, these two extracts clearly show the incredible lengths the ships and crews were forced to go to in meeting the Royal Navy's supply requirements.

In the end, it was their sheer professionalism along with the point blank, bloody minded refusal of the RFA crews to allow any job to beat them, which, despite horrendous shortfalls in basic equipment and training, allowed the Task Force's supply requirements to be just about met in full. Thankfully, this remarkable feat was also achieved with the loss of only two of the twenty two RFAs deployed, although there was no shortage of critics to insist that this was far more a matter of luck than judgement.

Captain Gordon Butterworth, at the time RFA Chief Marine Superintendent, neatly summed up the attitude of many in the service, when he said:

If there is a job to be done you just got on with it. When all is said and done, if a ship needs fuel, it can't wait and you have to do the job, gale force winds and thirty foot seas notwithstanding.

The end of the war saw the formation of several committees to enquire into its conduct, most notably Lord Frank's, which scrutinised the government's role, along with much of the pre-1982 diplomacy. Perhaps of more interest to the RFA, events at Fitzroy were also the subject of a Naval Board of Enquiry, their report finally entering the public domain in 2007, twenty-five years after the events that it purported to investigate and in a much censored form.

Meanwhile, a post-mortem of a very different type was conducted at Empress State Building, Headquarters of the RFA.

It was perfectly clear to the senior RFA staff there, many of whom had been in the South Atlantic, that the skill, commitment and adaptability of the RFA crews had been the most important factors in the success of the logistics effort, helped out by a very large slice of luck. Equipment and, most especially, training were clearly in need of improvement and so a series of discussions were held about the service's future. As a result, fundamental decisions were made during this period which set the RFA firmly on the road to the highly trained, professional service which was to emerge into the twenty-first century.

First, and arguably the most important decision which arose from these discussions concerned deregistration, that is, the removal of RFA ships from the British Register of Merchant Ships and the effective loss of their merchant ship status. A number of advantages went with deregistration, such as being allowed to defer a routine survey or to fit fire fighting systems more suited to the ship's operational role, although, if deregistered, RFA ships would now no longer be able to enter or leave foreign ports without the diplomatic requirements warships were forced to observe. This was less serious than it sounded because many governments had required formal clearance for RFA visits for a considerable period before this so the eventual clarification of their status as 'Government vessels on non-commercial service' was probably long overdue. Of course, the major advantage which deregistration brought was that now RFA ships could be armed, operating a properly designed armament fit, rather than being covertly equipped with a badly thought out mishmash of weapons as in the past. Deregistration would also acknowledge that the larger ships packed a big military punch by carrying, and operating, up to five armed Sea King helicopters.

Arming RFA ships has always been an issue fraught with problems, some dating back as far as the First World War.

In wartime, an auxiliary which is capable of defending itself and therefore does not require the services of a naval escort has obvious advantages, but set against that is the difficult question of at what point does an armed RFA cease to be an auxiliary and become legally a warship, with all its attached administrative problems. A registered RFA, of course, can theoretically sail where she will, collect cargo, be it fuel oil or dry stores and then leave to replenish a warship or group of warships without any legal complications and it was, of course, this major advantage that weighed against including weapons in an RFA ship's standard fit.

During the Second World War, however, warships were scarce and merchantmen needed to be able to protect themselves. Over 9,500 Allied merchant ships, including RFAs, had some sort of armament and they used those weapons very effectively, destroying scores of U-boats and dozens of enemy aircraft.

The RFA kept its weapons when peace was declared but 1950 saw a change of policy with a general order that all guns and mountings were to be landed at the ship's home port. Deck stiffening and other structural features were to be retained, presumably so the weapons could be repositioned in case of need. Many vessels, however, including some of the early Fort class and the LSLs, were still carrying weapons, boxed up in their holds, long after 1950.

By April 1982, however, no RFA ship had any offensive weapons fitted, in line with the comments made in 1955 by the then Director of Gunnery Division, Naval Staff:

> Guns mounted in afloat support ships have been more for morale purposes than with a view to contributing to any effective anti-aircraft defence.

This, of course, despite the three hundred aircraft shot down by merchant vessels during the Second World War!

In the initial phases of Operation 'Corporate', the RFA ships went south in a rush but upon arrival at Ascension Island, all the LSLs at least, were fitted with 40mm Bofors, mounted in the original positions on the fore deck, except *Sir Percivale* and *Sir Galahad*, which had only a single weapon fitted. Officially, no other RFA received defensive armament and, as previously explained, when the captain of *Tidespring* asked for weapons, just before the *Antrim* group left for South Georgia, he was told by a very senior Royal Navy figure in the Task Force command structure that: 'Giving the RFAs weapons would probably make them more of a danger to themselves than to the enemy.'

Despite Naval misgivings, most of the RFA ships managed to procure some sort of defensive armament, albeit from a variety of sources.

On *Tidespring*, the only ship for which there is any record of crew training, gun crews were trained by the embarked Royal Marines, a marine serving initially as No 1 on the weapon and the RFA crew man serving as No 2, that is, loader. The GMPGs that were the ship's sole armaments, incidentally, had been 'borrowed' from their embarked Wessex helicopter.

Once the RFA man had gained sufficient experience, he took over as No 1, initially under the guidance of a marine, and a second crewmen was appointed as No 2, so that by the time the Royal Marines disembarked, the ship had fully trained gun crews at their weapons.

She also had her own 'home-made' missile launcher, as Lt Mike Tidd describes:

> PO John Humphries, my Scottish armourer, was to display great initiative when, with the help of the ship's engineers, he set about making suitable mountings so that our GPMGs (General Purpose Machine Gun) could provide anti-aircraft fire from the ship's upper deck.
>
> He also created a steerable trolley with two 2in RP half rocket pods strapped to it, which was intended to take on any aircraft attacking us from astern. Whilst the mechanics of this looked feasible, in theory, I think everybody, except PO Humphries, was very glad that we were never called upon to use it in anger!

Interestingly, *Tidespring*'s training regime mirrored in some ways the WWII situation where courses such as 'Merchant Seaman Gunner' and 'Mercantile Machine Gunner' were offered to RFA ratings. Such courses carried the incentive of an allowance of 6d (old pence) and 3d being added to the seaman's pay once he had passed the course, although it is fairly certain that *Tidespring*'s gunners were not so lucky !

As far as their effectiveness went, *Fort Austin*, with her miscellaneous collection of rifles and machine guns, claimed at least one Argentine Dagger shot down, which must have done the crew's morale no end of good.

With deregistration and the increasing certainty that RFAs would now be tasked to serve with the Navy in a force multiplier role, clearly the question of arming RFAs needed to be dealt with once and for all. After much consultation, therefore, it was decided that the new RFAs ships, like the AORs, would be designed to carry a substantial number of weapons, including missiles, 20mm and 30mm BMARC Oerlikons, CHAFF rockets and GPMGs. In addition, a Lieutenant Commander RN was appointed to the RFA for two years, in 1984, to serve as RFA Defensive Weapons Officer.

The process of deregistration itself began in 1985, with the government announcing that future legislation would remove RFA vessels from the Merchant Shipping register. Their intention was that the merchant shipping legislation would cease to have legal effect, although conditions of service would remain the same.

Needless to say, this created a certain amount of concern among the crews, who viewed procedures such as regular ship surveys by Lloyd's Register, for example, as their overall assurance on ship safety. With these concerns in mind and in order to implement the change in status with as little friction as possible, a process of consultation with trade unions and other interested bodies was begun. At the same time, an in-house deregistration team was formed, and with the job of explaining the changes to the whole workforce.

The RFAs had been registered with the Department of Transport or its predecessors since 1911, when they probably fitted the merchant shipping definition, that is, plying for profit or reward, quite well.

War service changed all this, especially the embarkation and arming of ASW helicopters, which had begun well prior to the Falklands, as well as the impromptu fitting of weapons which was such a prominent feature of that war. *Fort Victoria* and *Fort George*, the new AORs, of course, could not be classed as merchant ships by any stretch of the imagination and with their introduction, the RFA would be forced to rethink its merchant navy pretensions.

Deregistration, it was felt, would solve all the problems.

From the crew perspective, a deal was eventually worked out with the unions which included a number of conditions:

- Professional certification by the Department of Transport (DoT) would continue.
- Sea time in RFAs still qualified as merchant service.
- RFAs would only employ registered seafarers.
- National Maritime Board membership would be maintained as would the use of the NMB Code of Conduct.
- RFAs would continue to use DoT Articles of Agreement.
- Final decisions on certificates of competency would remain with the DoT.
- The MoD would act as 'regulator', and thus responsible for maintaining safety standards.
- Accomodation would be at or above DoT standards.
- The DoT and Lloyd's Register would still be responsible for inspections.

The whole issue, however, proved too complex for a simple solution and after a certain amount of compromise, instead of deregistration, in 1989, an Order in Council (The Merchant Shipping (MOD) OiC 1989 No 1991) was issued which allowed RFAs to undergo a 'change of status'.

This meant they remained British registered merchant ships, with a 'letter of understanding', in fact, being passed between MoD (Navy) and the DoT, to the effect that they would conform to the requirements of most of the merchant shipping legislation, but as 'government ships on non-commercial service'. This allowed RFAs to operate unrestricted by the legal constraints of the Merchant Shipping Act, while still implementing a set of working conditions that satisfied the crews and without many of the restrictions imposed upon warships.

Which, one cannot help feeling, may have been a more satisfactory solution to some of those concerned, in the long run, anyway. Although, of course, whether the situation was deliberately engineered to that end must remain a matter only for conjecture.

The ships which would be subject to this 'change of status' were also being improved to cope with it and the new work load this would involve.

Sir Tristram was returned from the Falklands and rebuilt, becoming some twenty-nine feet longer and having several additional features added, the most significant being the replacement of aluminium by steel in her superstructure, much of the loss of life at Fitzroy being attributed to the poor structural stability of aluminium at high temperatures.

A new *Sir Galahad* was commissioned and a number of the older LSLs were entered into the Ship Life Extension Programme (SLEP). *Diligence*, formerly the offshore support ship *Stena Inspector*, was acquired as a heavy repair ship, while *Argus* joined the fleet as a helicopter training ship, replacing the elderly *Engadine*. *Sir Caradoc*, formerly *Grey Master*, and *Sir Lamorak*, formerly *Lakespan Ontario*, were taken over by the Admiralty and introduced into the fleet in 1983, temporarily replacing the two LSLs put out of service by the Argentine air force. Several new Leaf class tankers were also taken up on bareboat charter during this period and a number of existing Ol, Rover and Leaf class ships were tasked for limited solid stores support. These vessels carried small amounts of solid stores in prepared packs, while several were also provided with basic mechanical handling equipment.

Perhaps most significant of all, in 1992, the first of a whole new generation of RFAs left the slips of the Harland & Wolff Belfast shipyard, with the launching of the first AOR, *Fort Victoria*.

This, the first wholly new RFA to be launched since the process of deregistration, clearly indicated the progress of 'navalisation' within the service and its move towards the 'Force Multiplier' concept, whereby RFAs would assume some of the duties formerly assigned to warships.

Known technically as an Auxiliary Oiler Replenishment (AOR), she was a 'one-stop ship', designed to deliver both fuel and dry stores, including munitions.

Equipped with four RAS rigs amidships, a Hudson reel for astern refuelling, the latest 996 surveillance radar (eventually), an operations room, twelve-bed hospital and hangar and maintenance facilities for up to five of the new Merlin helicopters, *Fort Victoria* could cope with the most exacting demands encountered in the logistics role she would be required to play. Most significantly, she was eventually well armed, being permanently equipped with 30mm cannon, two Phalanx close in weapons systems (CIWS), as well as two separate decoy systems, Sea Gnat and the Type 182, although the Vertical Sea Wolf system which had been discussed for her was fitted but never put into a state where it could be used.

Her adoption into the RFA fleet was not without significant problems, however. *Fort Victoria*'s first Commanding Officer, Captain Shane Redmond OBE RFA (rtd), describes some of the difficulties he and his crew encountered:

> The birth of *Fort Victoria* was not an easy one. Indeed, it could even be said there were serious complications. The lead ship in a new and forward looking generation of AORs (Auxiliary Oiler Replenishment), the project had been under discussion for nearly ten years when the contract was finally placed with the Belfast shipbuilders Harland & Wolff, in the late summer of 1988.
>
> (I have always felt at odds with the official designation AOR as I thought it tended to belittle a ship conceived at the edge of then current technology, fast, well armed and with an outstanding aviation capability and of course, providing a one stop replenishment facility. Quite clearly a force multiplier in her own right and deserving of a more glamorous NATO designation.)
>
> Despite the problems in Northern Ireland at that time and the numerous corrections to the build plan normal in any lead project, the initial construction phase went as well as could reasonably be expected. Builder's sea trials followed in June of 1992.
>
> Prior to trials, Harlands, with MoD agreement, decided that the final fitting out and the rectification of any emergent work, post trials, should be subcontracted to

Cammell Lairds of Birkenhead. The wisdom of this decision would have been difficult to question at the time.

Unfortunately, at a meeting with the Yard's Managing Director in late March 1993, I was advised that Cammell Laird (Birkenhead) were ceasing operations and that the caisson accessing the basin the ship was in, would be sealed during the second week of April. In a somewhat hurried ceremony I was instructed to accept the ship 'as is' from Harland & Wolff. We subsequently sailed for Portsmouth on the 5th April 1993 with a considerable amount of work still outstanding – I believe, something in the region of 15,000–20,000 items by the time we arrived!

Portsmouth ... and yet another workforce which would have to get to grips with not only the geography of *Fort Victoria* but also a considerable number of quite serious emergent or inherent defects, not least of which were those relating to safety and habitability. Add to this the mounting pressure to complete the build and get on with sea trials and it is easy to see why tensions developed at senior level between ships staff and the project leaders, Director General (Ships) at Bath.

The ship had become a problem, well behind schedule, substantially over budget and with a worrying number of outstanding items relating to both the build project and a seemingly endless stream of emergent work. Tension between my staff and the Project leaders, while a fact, was also unfortunate, due almost entirely to the tabling and discussion surrounding this emergent work – defects raised by the ship as we became increasingly familiar with the ship and her systems. The general feeling amongst my Heads of Department was that Bath seemed somewhat embarrassed by the situation they found themselves in. No doubt the Project Team would have been rather glad to see the back of *Fort Victoria*.

Unfortunately the Naval Base were caught in the middle and despite their difficult position did all that could be done to work their way through a substantial list of work in a thoroughly professional manner.

By the end of July and despite outstanding work, the ship was declared ready to commence her Part Four trials based on Portland. I was therefore invited to sail from Portsmouth on the afternoon of 5th August 1993.

Unfortunately, but not surprisingly, before we could get used to having the ship to ourselves, systems started to fail and we were reluctantly forced to anchor in Weymouth Bay to carry out temporary repairs. The inevitable result of this was to leave us with no alternative but an embarrassing return to Portsmouth. If my recollections are correct, there we remained for approximately six more months, finally resuming our long over due sea trials early in the New Year.

So ended a difficult and trying period for myself, Mike Mission my Chief Engineer Officer and to a lesser extent, the ship's Heads of Department. The pressure to accept a ship in a less than satisfactory state was enormous and indeed often included veiled threats to have personnel transferred who were considered to be 'obstructive' simply because they insisted on correct procedures being followed, particularly where safety was concerned.

To in some way illustrate the difficulties encountered during that period perhaps the best example is that of the sewage treatment plant.

Mike and his engineers were of the opinion that the after plant located adjacent to and accessed via the ratings accommodation may have been releasing methane, a potentially life threatening gas, into the habited area.

Though noted, little notice was taken of ship's staff concerns until the Health &

Safety Executive at Basingstoke were contacted. The result of test confirmed Mike's suspicions and the ship's company were evacuated to shore accommodation. Subsequent recommendations included modification to all units' gas tight access doors and the fitting of alarmed detectors in compartments housing the treatment plants. On the morning of our departure for trials Mike (CEO) was asked to accept that remedial work had been completed. However the detectors were not in place and he declined to accept responsibility for the plant. Just before 12 noon I had a visit from a Commander RN insisting that I sort out my 'Chief' and sail at 1330 as scheduled. Failing this he would get my 'chief' relieved by a more accommodating individual. At this point I went through the roof and said in terms not open to interpretation that if my CEO is removed I go, if I go the ship's company go and if that happens, the ship goes nowhere. The simple answer is fit the ****** detectors, the cost is minimal. The work was completed in double quick time and we sailed on the same tide that day. This was but one of a number of stupid, not to say down right dangerous, pressures we were subjected to at this stage.

Perhaps it is also worth mentioning one more incident, both ludicrous and annoying when viewed in the overall concept of safe ship operations.

Radar (and the legislation governing its capability and use) is without doubt the single most important development in safe navigation since the introduction of the chronometer. The ARPA navigational and anti-collision radar fitted in *Fort Victoria* was basically out dated having its origins in the late 70s/early 80s.

In my opinion and that of my Navigator, the set simply did not conform to the 'new build' requirements at that time. It had failed repeatedly on test and also on a number of occasions at sea during earlier trials. However, the ship builders insisted it was compliant and fit for purpose as a consequence of which MoD (N) was not prepared to meet the relatively insignificant cost of updating to a current model, regardless of poor performance or indeed, my views as Commanding Officer.

Stationary in the English Channel surrounded by an impenetrable morning fog and without functioning navigational radar, the RFA's newest and most expensive vessel sat for half a day while the manufacturer's technician struggled to get the equipment up and running. Eventually the technician had to admit that set was inoperative and that in his opinion nothing more could be done. I discontinued the trials and after the fog thinned, returned to Portsmouth where a new, modern radar unit was awaiting our arrival.

These are, of course, my recollections and may well differ from those of others also associated with the build and introduction into service of a fine ship.

But then, there are always two sides to any story!

A final addition to the fleet was made in 1996, with the chartering of the motor vessel *Celestine*. Designed as a roll-on/roll-off ferry, she was renamed *Sea Crusader* and along with a second vessel of similar type, *Stena Ausonia*, subsequently renamed *Sea Centurion*, was expected to give the Royal Navy a much needed increase in heavy lift capacity, replacing, in part, the now ageing LSLs.

The acquisition of a simple, cheap unarmed roll-on/roll-off (ro-ro) ferry, capable of catering to the army's transport needs, without incurring the maintenance costs of the LSLs, had been considered briefly after the now infamous 1981 Defence Review, although the Falklands war had brought further discussion on the matter to an end. Many in the RFA saw these ro-ros as less useful than a purpose-built RFA, however, and they were soon returned to their owners, *Sea Centurion* in 2002 and *Sea Crusader* in 2003. These were replaced by the Point class, which, although owned by MoD, are under commercial management and not crewed by RFA personnel.

Helicopters and their deployment are a major part of the RFA's modern force multiplier role. With the importance of this role increasing in the immediate period post-Falklands, especially because many of the Royal Navy's smaller warships could not operate Sea King helicopters, negotiations began in 1983 for the acquisition of the US Navy Arapaho system.

RFA fleet list 1990

Fast fleet replenishment tankers
Tidespring
Olmeda, Olna, Olwen
Black Rover, Blue Rover, Gold Rover, Green Rover, Grey Rover
Bayleaf, Brambleleaf, Oakleaf, Orangeleaf
Store ships
Regent, Resource
Fort Grange, Fort Rosalie (ex *Fort Austin*)
Landing ships
Sir Bedivere, Sir Galahad, Sir Geraint, Sir Percivale, Sir Tristram
Specialist ships
Diligence, Argus

Total: 24 vessels with a workforce of about 2500

Basically, the Arapaho concept was designed around a number of standard ISO marine containers equipped with stores, workshops and accommodation for air and ground crews.

To begin, the system looked good, comprising hangars for four Sea Kings, spare deck space and two operating spots as well as flight command, a briefing room, workshops, power generation, fuel supply, fire fighting equipment, ordnance crew quarters and a galley. It looked even better with the manufacturer's claim that it could all be fitted and operational in twelve hours! It turned out to have only one drawback. It was completely unsatisfactory for handling aircraft!

Reliant (originally the Harrison Line containership *Astronomer*) was equipped with this system and subsequently sent to support the army in Beirut, being responsible for their final evacuation in February 1984. Upon returning to the UK, she proceeded to the Falklands on what was expected to be a major deployment but the Arapaho system proved to be so bad that she was recalled. Stripped of her purpose-built containers, she was sold back into conventional merchant service in 1986 and the Arapaho concept was abandoned, but not before it had cost the Royal Navy £30 million.

In a more successful change to helicopter operations as well as a further move towards RFA autonomy, an RFA Aviation Support Unit was established at RNAS Culdrose, in 1990, to administer the RN personnel embarked on RFAs, who were responsible for helicopter operations and the vessel's defensive weapons, among other things. It was, incidentally, freely admitted at the time that this new facility was driven by the needs of the new AOR class and *Argus*, with their greatly increased helicopter complements.

So, in line with the Service's increasingly military orientation, RFA personnel were offered training in aviation to complement this increased use of helicopters. In particular, the rating Helicopter Controller was introduced, now allowing increased use of ratings in the vital business of helicopter deployment.

This provided clear evidence that now the crew of an RFA was beginning to really be seen as an integrated whole, at least in terms of responsibilities and training, without perhaps, quite the rigid demarcation between officers and seamen as had previously existed. Further emphasising this 'whole ship' concept, in vessels with RN Supply & Transport staff (known as the 'STONNERY') embarked, those staff played an equal part in activities such as firefighting parties and guns crews.

Ships, however well designed and free from legal restraint they may be, are only as good as the men who man them.

This is reflected, at least initially, in training and personnel development and, in one of the more significant events of this post-Falklands period, Warsash College, now Warsash Maritime Academy, part of Southampton Solent University, was commissioned, in 1985, to conduct what became known as the 'Warsash' study.

Warsash was basically a thorough review of manpower utilisation. A special project team was appointed, termed the Manpower Management Programme, tasked to examine and offer recommendations about systems, appointing, appraisal, career development, promotion, training and education.

Incidentally, part of the Warsash team's study involved psychometric evaluation of the individual and as a direct result of this type of advanced study, many of the techniques used to train RFA personnel were re-evaluated.

In 1991, Warsash conducted a second study, 'the Way Ahead', also tasked to offer recommendations on some fundamental changes to the way the RFA was organised and operated.

In line with the introduction of its new ships and militarisation of the Service, as well as some of Warsash's recommendations, RFA training courses rapidly began to improve, both in variety and content. One of these, the thirteen-week Commanding Officer Designate run by the Royal Navy at HMS *Dryad*, was the first course of its type especially for RFA captains and chief officers, although RFA officers had, in fact, been attending this and other courses of a similar type since 1982, well before Warsash. Also available for the first time was the Royal Navy's Principal Warfare Officer's course, in line with the RFA's new weapon's policy.

This training process clearly needed Service-wide co-ordination so an RFA chief officer was appointed at headquarters, in 1987, as Training Controller. His job included, among other duties, the production of a comprehensive training booklet (the Course Prospectus), which allowed RFA personnel to know what courses were actually on offer. At the same time, the first Record of Courses and Individual Training (ROCIT) books were to be introduced. Issued to all RFA personnel, they were designed to enable individuals to keep a record of their own progress in the service.

As well as the specialist courses run by the Royal Navy training establishments, RFA officers also began regularly attending the Royal Navy Staff Course (RNSC) run by the Royal Naval College at Greenwich from 1996, such courses being specifically tailored to equip them with the skills necessary to operate in a high profile role in any of the UK's military establishments. This was to have fundamental implications when control of the RFA was transferred to the Royal Navy in 1999.

Only a snapshot of the training available for RFA personnel after the revealing experiences of the Falklands is presented here, of course. Nor does it include the new areas of responsibility, in weaponry and other departments, which came into force during this period. In fact, over eighty courses were available to RFA staff by the end of the 1980s.

Incidentally, while on the subject of information dissemination throughout the Service, the RFA began publication of its own newspaper, *Gunline*, in 1985, which eventually replaced the old-style news magazine, *Force Four*.

Although much attenuated, this list of training courses does, however, illustrate the emphasis the RFA management was now placing on courses in tactics, weapons and fire and damage control. Essentially warfare training, this was, once again, clearly in line with the force multiplier role which senior officers expected the Service to be playing with their new generation of ships, led by the two new Fort class.

It certainly compares very favourably with the situation before 1982, here described by a retired senior officer, Captain Shane Redmond:

> Personnel were either selected for specific courses or we asked if we could attend. No published list was available, that I am aware of, so word of mouth also played a part. Attendance was mandatory though by no means all embracing!
>
> *Courses – Officers*
>
> Admiralty Gyro (Sperry type) at Ditton Park, Slough. RN course
> Unit Security Officers (USO) Course at various locations. R class only. RN course*
> Flight Deck Officer (FDO) at Portland N/Base. RN course*
> Helo Controller (HCO) at Portland N/Base. RN course*
> *Note*: * These were mandatory for appointment to all aviation capable RFAs.
>
> Lieutenant's Course at RNC Greenwich. RN course
> Senior Management Course in house. RFA
> RFA PRO Course in house. RFA
> NBCD and Firefighting at PHOENIX, Portsmouth (mandatory for R Class). RN course
>
> Sperry and S G Brown both provided Merchant Navy type Gyros to the RFA and operated their own training courses. Though not statutory, they were essential (also attended by other customers' officers)
>
> *Courses – POs and ratings*
>
> (I cannot recall anything before mid 1960s)
>
> Flight deck training was generally provided 'on the job' during work-up but a number of separate courses were also run at Portland in the 1970s for POs. RN course
>
> Firefighting at PHOENIX, Portsmouth. Mainly POs and usually initiated by the RFA or the ship. RN course
>
> GEC MK II rig course at Chapman's Works, Newcastle. RFA/ship initiated. RFA course

RIB (Rigid Inflatable Boat) at Portland – mainly for ratings. RFA/ship initiated. RN course

I have no details of the number of spaces or the number of those trained though, with the exception of USO, FDO and HCO, pre-joining training did not always occur. In fact, many of the RN courses only offered the RFA one or a fairly small number of places.

Certainly, six months after passing through Portland, crew changes meant that a very high percentage of a ship's company were untrained in the RFA/RN sense and it was often left up to the ship to organise, for example, flight deck training, in order to stay operational. There was also a need to keep certain personnel up to date; for example, HCOs.

Records were kept by the relevant RFA personnel department and the ship. In the case of the HCO and FDO, they were kept by the individual officer.
The only training provided for Pool ratings was either while working up at Portland or that provided by the ship internally.

The first RFA officer to take the PWO course was First Officer P T Hanton, although this first placement on the PWO's course was actually the result of a cancellation! Captain Redmond again:

I sent the first RFA Officer to attend a PWO course, 1st Officer Phil Hanton to *Dryad* in 1984. Phil was my Staff Officer in HQ, when one afternoon the phone rang and we were offered a cancellation on the PWO course for the following week. This was our first break through, following plenty of approaches to DNOT, and was too good an opportunity to miss. I lost an outstanding Staff Officer and the RFA got its first PWO. This was followed by our first Navigator to attend the FNO (Frigate Navigator's) course. Up to the time I left, in 1996, we were taking up spare capacity without formal allocation.

Principal warfare officers (PWO) are command advisers on warfare procedures and tactics. As gunnery specialists, they also conduct all aspects of above water warfare practices as well as running the operations room, providing command with a clear tactical picture. Both the AORs and *Argus* had a PWO on the complement.
First Officer Hanton seemed to fit in easily with the RN officers on the course, while dealing with its unfamiliar complexities. Although the RFA does and probably always will operate as a unit in its own right within the UK's naval organisation, in terms of training, knowledge and often experience, there was certainly starting to be fewer differences between the officers of both services. Navalisation, although in a much modified form, appeared to be proceeding painlessly by the back door.
'Black Sam' Dunlop would surely have approved.
Coinciding with the improved training, employment practices were also rationalised. In 1986, the Directorate of Naval Manpower Audit instigated a thorough review of RFA manning procedures, including the role of RN parties and RNSTS embarked civilians.
Prior to this, however, terms of employment had been re-negotiated, with the result that ratings were moved to a consolidated salary scheme, in line with conditions which had been in place for petty officers for several years.

Gordon Wilson, who was Fleet Manager for Personnel and Operations during the Falklands War, was later extensively involved with these changes to working conditions and has kindly commented upon them:

> Contract POs had been on all-hours worked salary prior to 1982. I negotiated the ratings' 'no-strike' deal with the National Union of Seamen (NUS) as a direct result of our Falklands experience, and the need to reassure the RN that the RFA would always be there (I was bidding then, successfully as it turned out, for the *Argus* to be an RFA, not an RN vessel). I also negotiated the ratings' salary with the NUS (who were very much in favour of it) and the Treasury.
>
> It was the next natural step after the PO's deal, and would have happened earlier had the Falklands not intervened. It had been publicly stated before the Falklands that ratings salary would follow once the CPOs/POs salaries had bedded down.

There was some difficulty about the acceptance of this 'consolidated salary' scheme in its early stages, its introduction initially being rejected by the workforce on the first ballot. Some minor changes were soon made and the new scheme came into force from 1 April 1988, guaranteeing all RFA personnel, contracted or not, a fixed income, and paying salaries, monthly, directly into a bank account. Pay scales were adjusted to allow 'all hours working', thus doing away with the need for overtime payments, which had been a source of difficulty for many years. This package of improvements also included a 'no-strike' deal and improved pension provision.

Complementing these changes, recruitment was reorganised and improved, with the introduction, in 1989, of a 'dedicated' Recruitment Cell, headed by a chief officer. Alongside this Cell and operated by it, was the Ratings Adult Entry Scheme and, at the same time, the Junior Ratings Training unit was also introduced, using the experience gained from the operation of the very successful Cadet Training Units for Deck, Supply and Engineering officers. Of perhaps even more fundamental significance to the general well being of the service was an earlier introduction, the Rating to Officer scheme, which saw young ratings being trained for their Class 4 (fourth officer) certificate at Glasgow College.

One vitally important result of these improvements was that by the end of 1990, a fully contracted work force was well within sight. This was crucial to the progress of the new style Service since it would ensure that, in future, the RFA would no longer have to depend upon untrained personnel or inexperienced officers from the Merchant Navy Pool to man its ships.

Change was not confined to crews and ships, either. Initial reorganisation of the RFA senior management had also begun.

In June1986, the posts of Commodore RFA and the senior shore-based Chief Marine Superintendent were merged under the title Commodore RFA. At the same time, a similar merging of the posts of Commodore Chief Engineer and the shore post of Chief Technical Superintendent also took place. Their assistants still retained the title 'Superintendent', however.

A much revised, more navalised, rank structure was also introduced at the same time. Changes included the introduction of the post of Senior Captain and Senior Marine Engineering Officer. Under the new scheme, radio officers became communications officers, while pursers were now designated supply officers. Overall control of the fleet still rested with the civil servants of the Royal Navy Supply and

Transport Service, however, which some RFA officers still saw as less than desirable.

Another radical improvement came in 1991, with the rewriting of BR875, the *RFA Handbook*. Known to one and all as 'The Bible', it was substantially updated and rewritten in four volumes, entitled *Administration, Operating Standards, Warfare*, and *Ship Maintenance and Repairs*.

This new *Handbook* proved to be just a forerunner, however. With the new role the RFA was being asked to undertake and the experience of high level management and administration many of its officers now had, in 1993, further, absolutely fundamental, changes were made to the Service's most senior staff.

Most importantly, in the view of some RFA personnel, control of the RFA was finally transferred from the Director General Supplies & Transport (Naval) to the Commodore RFA (COMRFA), making him 'type' commander of the RFA Flotilla and placing him in full command of the Service, under the Commander in Chief Fleet (CINCFLEET).

This time, the title superintendent disappeared, leaving the COMRFA to be assisted by chief staff officers instead. These CSOs now became the three specialist heads of department responsible for Operations and Warfare (X), Engineering and Systems (E) and Policy and Finance (S), all with the rank of captain.

At the same time, the Commodore (E), formerly Commodore Chief Engineer, was transferred to the organisation of the Director General Fleet Support (Ships) at Bath. This department was responsible at the time for managing the engineering support for the Royal Navy, RFA and all other MoD-owned ships.

The growing number of RFA officers appointed from 1983 onwards to the staff of a number of defence and Royal Navy establishments also reflected this new level of integration between the Services.

The RFA headquarters remained at the 'Madhouse', in London's Earls Court, until later relocated to Whale Island, Portsmouth Naval Base.

Neatly capping all these other, more radical, changes was the introduction of a new uniform, incorporating new rank badges. Approved in 1987, it had then been postponed on grounds of design and supply difficulties, only to finally arrive in 1993, coinciding neatly with the advent of COMRFA.

Implementation of these changes, in some cases, took place over a considerable period of time, but by 1992–3, the Service was beginning to take on much of its future shape. One consequence of this was that many long established RFA personnel found the new organisation not to their liking and so resigned. Foreign nationals were also largely replaced by British personnel, thus avoiding the contractual and communication problems that their employment had led to in the past. And for the first time, women began to make a significant contribution, the first female officer cadets being admitted to Warsash in 1993, before moving later to the Cadet Training Unit in *Fort Austin*.

Commodore Richard Thorn, who was COMRFA from April 1989 to 1994, gives an account of his experiences during those years and the sometimes rocky road the RFA was following:

In May of 1989, I relieved Commodore Barry Rutterford as Commodore RFA and AD 76 with executive authority within my branch of DST (Ships and Fuel). Barry Rutterford was responsible for combining the posts of Commodore and Chief Marine

Superintendent into the new shore based position with executive responsibility. The previous Commodore – Commodore Sam Dunlop CBE DSO – had served with great distinction in RFA *Fort Austin* during the Falklands conflict. He had also been quoted in the *Daily Telegraph* as being in favour of the RFA being not only operated by the Royal Navy, but managed by it too. He was severely, and in my opinion, unfairly criticised for stating this view.

Quietly, and happily, the Chief Marine Superintendent, Captain Gordon Butterworth CBE, managed to have the RFA formally recognised as a Service with its own heraldic device. Barry Rutterford also incurred the displeasure of very senior Civil Servants for being outspoken about what he believed.

All this seems to me important background to the events leading up to a great and important change in the life of the RFA Service. My own experiences – first RFA officer to attend the Lieutenant's course at Greenwich Naval College, various other Royal Naval courses, command of eleven RFAs, and periods ashore as a Marine Superintendent without executive authority – had led me to believe that the quality of the serving officers, petty officers and ratings within the RFA were such that they were both ready and able to take a more positive role in their own management and future – in which they all had a vested interest. I had private conversations with both civil servants and naval officers to see if my views were shared. The Chief of Fleet Support, Admiral Sir Jock Slater, asked the question: 'What management arrangements for the RFA would best serve the interests of the Royal Navy?' (That is my recollection of the gist of the question).

I was specifically directed to give an answer as I was the most senior RFA officer within the Royal Naval Supply and Transport Service. I gave my answer and detailed reasons for it. I passionately believed the time had arrived for the Officers, Petty Officers and men of the RFA to show their abilities to manage their own affairs to the satisfaction of the Royal Navy and the nation.

As a body of professionally qualified seamen, engineers, communicators, supply officers and other disciplines brought up under modern educational facilities, I believed that we could stand level in ability with both Naval Officers and Civil servants.

On one hand, I was accused of being a 'closet' naval officer and invited to 'Reconsider my position' and on the other – I was asked if I thought it appropriate for me to become a rear-admiral – (I responded absolutely not, as there was and is no culture of such a title in the Merchant Navy or the RFA – in fact it was my opinion at that time, Commodore as a rank, was probably more appropriate for some RN Officers of the senior Flag rank!) I was also told privately by a very Senior Naval officer that he appreciated my stance, but was unable to give any assistance and that I should 'Nail my colours to the mast'.

From this, it may be deduced that life was not easy, but I was determined that in a period of great change and reorganisation within both the Military and the Ministry of Defence – that the RFA, unlike the WRNS and other unfortunate sections of the whole – should survive as a viable professional civilian manned specialist service within the RN structure. The analogy was the Royal Marines who had also moved under the overall management of the Commander-in-Chief Fleet.

Part of this important period in the history of the RFA was 'The Way Ahead Study' the findings of which brought about a Ministerial announcement in the form of a Parliamentary Written Answer in February of 1992, following a Navy Board agreed set of proposals for the way ahead on the management of the RFA Service. The outcome of all this was that COMRFA – as a Type Commander for the RFA Service sitting on the board of the Commander in Chief Fleet alongside his Royal Naval and Royal Marine counterparts – became a reality.

I would like to make two important points – plus a third, and a general observation. This great change and achievement in the life of the RFA Service is the culmination of the work of a great many people, some of whom – key players – I have mentioned. The RFA Service remains alive and well as a result.

I am sure that purist historians will be fascinated to delve into relevant Ministry papers on the subject, upon their release into the public domain 30 years after the events. I have kept names out of my description of events where possible – I am sure that they know who they are!

If I have achieved anything, I am proud to be associated with the establishment of the sensible precedent that the Commodore of the RFA is chosen from the RFA Service and that he should be the best man for the job – regardless of age or discipline. That the post should be held for a minimum of three years and a maximum of five years – I believe that that is a good senior management term of office.

Nearly 14 years on from my own retirement from this great service – envied, and to a degree copied by the United States Military Sealift command – my successors, Commodores Squire, Lannin, and Thornton have done a great job. The last two having served with me as Executive Officer and Navigator in RFA *Fort Austin* – Sam Dunlop, I hope, would be proud of us!

Viewpoints, of course, differ and several senior RFA officers felt that management by the RNSTS still had a number of significant advantages and that complete 'navalisation' of the RFA might be less than desirable.

Reflecting these differences within the Service, another perspective on this transitional period is given here by Gordon Wilson, who, as an RN Supply & Transport Officer, was Fleet Manager for Personnel & Operations during the Falklands campaign. He was a member of the RFA Management Board from then until late 1986, and had served aboard RFAs:

The Falklands Conflict, perhaps inevitably, marked a true watershed for the RFA. During the 1970s, Sea King helicopters had become a very important part of the fighting fleet. However, they were too big to be carried on any warship other than an aircraft carrier. Most RFAs already had flight decks fitted, and the larger RFAs also had hangars and full support facilities. This capability to transport and operate helicopters became invaluable to the Royal Navy, leading to RFAs being integrated more and more into naval operations as well as carrying out their traditional role of logistic support. In turn, this meant that RFAs were employed in or near the front line much of the time, sometimes operating independently, a role which had not been envisaged in the strategic planning assumptions for the RFA Service.

In the aftermath of the Falklands Conflict it became very clear that big changes were going to have to be made. First among these was whether the RFA fleet should be defensively armed. The lack of any inherent capability to defend itself, coupled with the impracticality of the much reduced RN fleet providing constant protection, had been a major difficulty in the Falklands, frequently placing RFAs at risk. Since it was highly likely that the Royal Navy would continue to shrink in size, driving more tasks towards the RFA and also reducing the likelihood of providing close escorts during operations, the conclusion was reached at HQ – after much debate about alternatives and consequences – that RFAs should in future be armed. It was recognised during consideration of this large topic that the decision would lead to a major change in direction for the development of the RFA Service, which indeed it did. The consequences could be described in short as militarisation, and would question the civilian nature of the Service and its management.

One incident of particular relevance to this issue sticks in my mind. RFA *Fort Austin* was kept down in the Falklands long after most ships had returned home, to provide helicopter air cover. The official line on her 4 fully armed Sea Kings (each packing a punch greater than a WW II frigate!) was that they operated off the deck of the RFA, but were tasked and controlled from the carrier. They weren't really, and this was very evident when the two carriers came home, leaving *Fort Austin* on her own. Then she ran out of her cargo of food, meaning she was to all intents now a naval warship (and a powerful one at that). That's when my Director, Tony Kemp, said to me, '... and this is a *merchant* ship???'

Clearly, we had to get back to the 'old' RFA, or take the fleet to a whole new level.

We chose the latter. There was an immediate expansion of training within naval establishments, including weapons, electronics and communications, while the number of RFA personnel seconded permanently to a variety of naval establishments increased substantially. Guns and other defensive weaponry were fitted to the ships and extra ships were acquired to fill new roles (*eg*, the helicopter training ship RFA *Argus* and the forward heavy engineering repair ship RFA *Diligence* – both converted merchant ships). Warfare, safety and operational training were all introduced or expanded. Salaries (to cover all hours worked) were extended to cover all ratings, which encouraged a more stable, better trained workforce, and a distinctive uniform for ratings was introduced. 'No strike' agreements were reached with the maritime trade unions, and the carriage of wives at sea was phased out. RFA officers were given wider training, and included in general naval or defence training courses (*eg*, the National Defence College, the Joint Services Staff College and the Royal Naval Staff College). In the light of these and other fundamental changes it was recognised that retaining the ships on the merchant register was no longer appropriate, and work began to deregister the fleet – work which culminated in the RFA's change of status in 1989.

It was abundantly clear from the outset that arming the ships would trigger a sea change in the direction of the future development of the RFA, and also that the change would not be to everyone's taste. It would affect all levels of the Service, including the overall management structure. Many of the RFA's personnel joined for a life following the RN around the world, but not for full blooded operations in the front line. Consequently a significant number of people chose to resign, or took opportunities to leave as the RFA moved ever closer to the Royal Navy.

The emphasis at HQ was also predictably undergoing change. RFA officers were receiving much wider training and experience, developing skills in personnel management, industrial relations, and inter-departmental liaison hitherto provided by civilian staff of the Royal Naval Supply & Transport Service. The extra RFA staff embedded within the Navy's training establishments had now begun to provide much closer liaison with the many naval authorities involved in RFA operations, and management of ship maintenance was also transferred from London to the MoD in Bath. The time was therefore ripe, as had been foreseen when the RFA's change of direction was agreed, for management of the RFA fleet to transfer from civilian hands to the RFA's own personnel, and for that management to be placed under the direct control of Commander-in-Chief, Fleet, at Northwood.

Given the views of these two very senior members of HQ staff during the RFA's transitional period, it is clear that RNSTS personnel were generally supportive of the partial militarisation of the Service and actively encouraged its development in this direction. It was, perhaps, inevitable that such an organisation as the RFA should eventually be managed, at all levels, by its own officers and RNSTS staff, in the main, showed a positive attitude to this change and an unqualified acceptance of it.

Clearly, however views may have differed, it was the good of the Service that was at the forefront of everyone's mind.

Stores personnel, or the 'STONNERY', of course, are still very much a part of RFA crews, being civil servants now drawn from the Naval Bases and Supply Agency, which replaced the Royal Naval Supply and Transport Service. They sign articles and are allocated to defence watches just like any other member of the ship's company.

Chapter 10

Saddam Hussein, Bosnia and Humanitarian Aid

Despite its immense shake-up in organisation, the RFA still had to carry on its normal work and, during this period, it was involved in supplying places as far apart as the South Atlantic, Iraq, the Gulf and Bosnia.

With the repossession of the Falkland Islands and the need for logistics support to the recently established garrison, the RFA was tasked to a new and stimulating environment. This intriguing new deployment is described here by one of the Service's senior officers:

> Ever since the 1982 Campaign to successfully recover the Falklands the RFA has provided a continual presence in the region. Initially, up until late 1986, the presence was significant in the form of OL and/or Tide, Fort, Rover and Sir Class ships as a standard package to support an equally significant RN force of ships.
>
> The establishment, however, of the Mount Pleasant Airport Complex with its runways and hangar provided an opportunity to reduce the level of ships due to the newly acquired ability to rapidly reinforce and defend the Falkland Islands by air. The standard RFA presence was rapidly reduced to a single Rover Class which has seen all 5 of the original class serving in the area although the task has in the main been conducted by *Gold Rover* and, the now sadly decommissioned, *Grey Rover*.
>
> The main role of the Rover Class is to support the efforts of Commander British Forces South Atlantic Islands (CBFSAI) in defending the Islands from potential Argentine aggression. This is primarily achieved by providing Afloat Combat Support to the resident Castle Class Offshore Patrol Vessels (OPV) and their accompanying destroyers and frigates, as well as a plethora of other tasks including Defence Diplomacy visits to outlying settlements, South America, South Africa, West Africa and British Dependencies e.g. South Georgia and Tristan da Cunha. As can be seen the ship has a large parish effectively covering the South Atlantic from the Canaries south. Hence the title: Atlantic Patrol Task (South).
>
> Since 1982, when no facilities were available to RFAs, the amount of shore support and amenities available to ships and their ships' companies have developed beyond comprehension. A fully equipped port was opened on East Falkland at East Cove Military Port in 1986, which has road links to the international airport at Mount Pleasant as well as into the capital Port Stanley. The facilities on offer include swimming pools, sports fields, internet cafes, cinemas, bars, hire Land Rovers and a twice weekly connection to the UK; it is now probably easier to join a ship in the Falklands than some well known Scottish ports! Logistic support is comprehensive and cargo can be loaded at a Single Point Mooring in a matter of hours.
>
> The Falklands terrain and coast line is certainly amongst the most striking and beautiful in the world and when coupled with the opportunity to visit such places as South Georgia, Montevideo, Rio and Cape Town to name but a few places, it makes

this one of the most popular and operationally enjoyable drafts available to RFA personnel.

Each Rover Class vessel spends in the region of 30 months on station with the Officers and Ratings changing on a regular basis at roughly 4 to 6 month intervals. The South Atlantic winter provides challenging weather conditions but the respite of calm conditions are only ever 48 hours steaming to the North. A patrol cycle with the destroyers and frigates to and from the West African area has been established which means that it is rare to spend longer than 8 weeks continuously off the Falklands. Regular maintenance visits to South American ports are extremely popular.

In summary, Atlantic Patrol Task (South) provides the RFA with a highly popular, rewarding and ongoing duty. It also reinforces the ability of the RFA to provide supremely effective Military Effect to a theatre of operations that has been in a State of Military Vigilance continuously for 25 years. Long may this Flexible Global Reach continue.

Mr D Soden was part of the RNSTS complement aboard *Fort Austin* and RFA *Reliant*, just after the war:

RFA *Fort Austin* deployed to the Falklands Islands in February 1983, replacing *Fort Grange* which was return to the UK for a refit. Deployment to the Falkland Islands was to last until July when the ship was to be replaced by either *Reliant* or *Fort Grange*.

After handover *Fort Austin* settled into the routine of issuing supplies to the HM Ships/STUFT ships in the area. Transfer was normally achieved either by passing the stores to a tug for onward delivery, the ship's workboat or by alongside transfer. The RAS option was hardly ever undertaken. For the majority of the deployment, the ship remained at anchor in San Carlos Water with the exception of a monthly two day visit to Port Stanley and a once only RNR visit to South Georgia. Shore leave was a rarity. In San Carlos Water all you had for company was the *Scottish Eagle* (STUFT tanker), the Rapier batteries located on the hills and the resident albatross.

Within a few months of the ship's arrival, the Islands were placed on a high state of alert. This was due to it being the first anniversary of the Falklands war ensuring that the Argentine Military undertook regular incursions into the no go zone.

Besides receiving regular mail from the UK, life on the ship was fairly mundane and often crew members thought of home. For immediate contact with home your only option was to visit the Radio Room and use the very expensive Marisat Satellite telephone system. After entering the Radio Room the duty Radio Officer would ensure that you understood that to use the telephone system it would cost £6 a minute and during the phone call the Radio Officer would time the call by the use of a stop watch. The Radio Room staff had on occasions had to ensure that you were in the right condition to be able to make the call. To that end I have known people to be asked to walk a straight line that had been placed on the deck and another method was to ask them to say tongue twisting words like 'chrysanthemum' – it really did work and thanks to the Radio Room some people did save a lot of money.

During one of the ship's stand off days, she anchored near to Speedwell Island (the island is located in the Falkland Sound). From the ship you could identify a number of red roofed buildings on the Island but were unsure to the number of inhabitants, so the workboat was launched and a party sent ashore with some provisions as a gift for the inhabitants. About six of us ventured ashore and were met by the local farmer, his wife and two daughters (one being 18 years old) who happened to be the only inhabitants on the island. We were invited into their home and we talked to them about what life is like living on such a remote island. The wife mentioned that she obtained essential supplies by contacting the Falkland Islands Company who would deliver her requirements to the island by boat every two weeks. If clothing was required it would be obtained by looking at a catalogue and placing an order and delivery could take up to 6 months.

The remoteness of the island brought into question what the family did to entertain themselves. They mentioned that they played board games, completed crosswords and read books but also found great joy in listening to the plays broadcast on the Falkland Islands Radio.

The farmer's wife then produced a photograph showing a picture of a Sea King helicopter (probably from RFA *Fort Grange*) which had landed on the Island over the previous Christmas. The picture showed someone dressed as Father Christmas coming out of the helicopter and she remarked it was the greatest day of her life. After saying our good byes we returned to the ship.

The farmer agreed that other crew members could visit the island. That afternoon some 60 people landed on the island (probably with the idea of sighting the 18 year old girl) and the word came back that the farmer and his family were nowhere to be seen with the likely reason that they had hid away because they could not handle seeing so many people all at once.

That night your thoughts went to the family ashore especially as you lay in your comfortable en suite cabin.

During the ship's deployment news arrived to say *Reliant* would not be replacing *Fort Austin* as it was stuck in the Birkenhead shipyard because of industrial action and we would now have to wait for *Fort Grange* to undertake a refit, store up and, after completing FOST, head for the Falkland Islands. *Fort Austin* was eventually relieved and left for the UK in early December.

It must be said that the majority of the crew of *Fort Austin* remained with the ship for the full deployment.

STO(N) staff were first appointed to the RFA *Reliant* (formerly MV *Astronomer*) in 1984 when the ship was deployed to Lebanon in support of the British Army in Beirut. The STO(N) department's main role on the ship was the management of spares required to keep the embarked squadron of 5 Sea King helicopters airborne. Other tasks included the control of the ships frozen provisions, general naval stores and NAAFI items.

I joined the ship in 1985 before it left for a deployment to the Falkland Islands

The STO(N) department consisted of 4 officers and 3 PO/ratings, who were all accommodated in a structure that was built at the stern of the ship and was known as the 'Hilton'.

What I can remember about my cabin is that the porthole was square and big enough for a person's body to get through. Underneath the bunk was a rather lengthy knotted rope which was to be used as a means of escape if the exit of the Hilton was on fire.

Meal time in the officer's mess was quite an unusual set up as the dining room was not large enough to accommodate all the officers at one sitting – so that meant two sittings had to be employed. When the meal time approached officers gathered near the dining room doors and then it was the survival of the fittest as to who got a seat. If you were unlucky you had to wait for the next sitting.

We worked in a series of containers located in the ship's hold forward of the bridge structure. Access to the containers was either by a lift operating from the main deck (out of bounds during bad weather/flying operations) or by descending three vertical ladders whose entrance was down a side passage on the starboard side of the ship. Once down in the containers the staff would normally remain there until break times. The days would normally start with a deluge of requests for spares from the embarked flight and, on average, over 40 signal store related demands would be raised each day requesting spares from the UK. Signal traffic was horrendous. Adding to our problems, the accounting system was manually operated and one member of the STO(N) team was responsible for keeping the ledgers up to date.

During 'Action Stations' the STO(N) department's role was to be in charge of the 3in rocket team (which was located on the Monkey Island). In proceeding to action stations, you would first have to come up three vertical ladders, proceed back to the 'Hilton' complex to collect your equipment and then climb up to the Monkey Island. By the time you arrived at the 3in rocket system, total exhaustion had set in!

During the ship's deployment to the Falklands, it made a visit to South Georgia.

Late one Sunday afternoon while we were there, the tannoy system requested that the STO(N) duty officer attend the flight deck with mechanical handling equipment. Unaware of what was happening, the duty officer soon realised that one of the embarked helicopters was heading for the ship with an underslung load. It was not until the load had landed on the flight deck did they realise that the load was a headless reindeer, a gift from the local military detachment. I can still see that reindeer now being moved off the flight with its legs up in the air. The reindeer did not last long on the ship and was eventually disposed of at sea.

Operation 'Offcut' also got under way in 1983, with *Reliant* tasked to support the Royal Navy in Lebanon.

Problems in Lebanon began in June 1982, when the Israelis breached the ceasefire after the attempted assassination of their ambassador in London and a suspected build-up of Palestinian armaments in South Lebanon.

Violence escalated and in February 1983, a small Royal Navy contingent, including HMS *Fearless*, joined the predominantly American Multi National Force (MNF). Royal Navy involvement consisted mainly of assisting the Army by the deployment of Sea King HC.4 helicopters in transport, supply and medical evacuation roles.

When HMS *Fearless* was relieved, *Reliant* was tasked to take over the helicopter deployment role and, in 1984, was involved in the evacuation of 5000 UK nationals.

The region itself still remains volatile, fuelled by the complications of Middle Eastern politics and its inherent religious overtones although, fortunately, British Service personnel no longer have a major land role in Lebanon.

Royal Navy involvement in the Middle East continued with the evacuation of UK nationals from Aden in 1986. The Royal Yacht *Britannia* and *Brambleleaf* were both involved and according to the account by two members of the crew, writing in *Gunline*, there were some unpleasant moments.

Brambleleaf had left Mombasa on the morning of 11 January 1986, due to rendezvous with *Britannia*, after which the RFA would accompany *Britannia* to Sri Lanka.

News of the attempted coup, which started the trouble, reached *Brambleleaf* on the 13th and, having arrived in the vicinity of their rendezvous with *Britannia* two days later, on the 15th, she received a report that *Britannia* was now standing by off Aden. The morning of the 17th saw *Brambleleaf* patrolling an area twenty-five miles south of Aden, while *Britannia* made arrangements for the evacuation of the UK nationals in the country.

Finally cleared for evacuation, *Britannia* collected over 400 evacuees and, on the afternoon of the 18th, sailed for Djibouti, leaving *Brambleleaf* and HMS *Newcastle* to finish the job.

HMS *Newcastle* sent an evacuation team across to *Brambleleaf* and the Leaf began her approach to the evacuation beach on the evening of the 18th.

Four miles off, *Brambleleaf* launched a Pacific 22 rigid inflatable boat (RIB), complete with the Royal Navy evacuation team and an RFA crew. The RIB had just reported that there was heavy fighting but no sign of any more refugees when it broke down!

Another sea boat was immediately launched and with both boats now in the water, all hell suddenly broke loose.

Both ship and sea boats came under fire from anti-tank rockets and shells so *Brambleleaf* withdrew, darkening ship in record time as she went, while the sea boats zigzagged their way back towards her and safety.

That was more or less the end of *Brambleleaf*'s wild adventures. They spent the rest of the time replenishing *Britannia* and HMS *Newcastle* before anchoring in Aden Harbour on the 21st, to collect any remaining evacuees. None materialised and *Brambleleaf* eventually continued an uneventful deployment, accompanying *Britannia* on her Sri Lanka trip.

It was the Middle East again in 1987, when the RFA supported Royal Navy ships during their mine clearance operations in the Gulf of Oman, between Iran and Iraq, in a deployment designated Operation 'Cimnel'. *Diligence* and *Regent* were deployed during the whole of this period as engineering and logistics support for the ships of the Royal Navy, underlining, once again, the indispensable role the specialist RFA ships now play in many Royal Navy operations.

Operation 'Cimnel', of course, was really only the beginning of Britain's involvement in the Gulf during this period.

Instability and conflict had been a characteristic of this region even before 1969 when the former Shah of Iran sent ships displaying the Iranian national flag up the Shatt-al-Arab waterway. This waterway had been entirely allocated to Iraq under the terms of a 1937 treaty, defining the borders between the two countries.

Diplomatic relations were severed in 1970, then restored in 1975, after a new border had been negotiated but it was after the fall of the Shah in 1979 that the real trouble began.

Government in Iran now rested in the hands of a priestly (Shi'ite Muslim) administration. Iraq's leadership and most of its rich middle class were Sunni, headed, from 1979, by Saddam Hussein and it seemed to them that the Iranian clerics were coming to have altogether too great a hold on Iraq's much poorer Shi'ite majority.

Events escalated and on 22 September, Iraq invaded Iran. At this point, Saddam Hussein had help from the United States, Russia, Europe and several Arab states as well as financial backing from the Arab states of the Persian Gulf, all of which saw Saddam Hussein as 'an agent of the civilised world' against a revolutionary Iran. For the time being, they ignored Saddam's use of chemical weapons against the Kurds and Iranians and Iraq's desperate efforts to develop nuclear weapons.

By 1988, the war had reached a bloody stalemate, with estimates running as high as one million Iranians and Iraqi killed. Iraq was also left with a war debt of $75 billion.

So Saddam needed money, not least because much of his debt was to the United States and this dependence on a country that many saw as a traditional enemy, conflicted with his much publicised stance on Arab nationalism.

Besides, Saddam saw the war as having spared Kuwait, at least, from the imminent threat of Iranian domination, which he maintained meant that Kuwait's share of the Iraqi war debt, some $30 billion, should be 'forgiven'. Moreover, not only did Kuwait, with a population of two million compared to Iraq's twenty-five million, hold similar size oil reserves, but historically, many in Iraq had long felt that Kuwait had only come into existence by an imperialistic trick of the British in 1922. To many in Iraq, including Saddam Hussein, Kuwait was part of their country.

Iraq finally invaded Kuwait on 2 August 1990, their president having convinced himself that his value to the Americans outweighed any concerns the United States might have had about Kuwait's oil, which then totalled about 10 per cent of the world's total reserves. He was wrong, although it took the Americans some time to decide that.

After a period of negotiation and threats following the invasion as well as a UN Security Council deadline for withdrawal, which Saddam blithely ignored, on 16 January 1991, a US-led coalition launched a blistering attack on Iraq, codenamed 'Desert Storm', beginning with round-the-clock ground and aerial missile strikes. Days later, a fast moving ground force, consisting mostly of British and US armoured and infantry units, swept into Kuwait.

By February, the over manned and under equipped Iraqi Army had been summarily ejected from Kuwait and coalition forces were occupying the southern portion of Iraq as far as the Euphrates river.

The Royal Navy had considerable involvement in the Gulf War, codenamed Operation 'Granby', being much the most experienced of the coalition forces, because of a ten-year involvement in the Armilla Patrol. Their force was designated Task Group 321.1, and consisted of a number of warships and RFAs.

This Armilla Patrol experience was to prove particularly valuable because one of the Security Council's first moves was to establish a trade embargo on Iraq. Nothing was allowed in or out in the hope that, with the drying up of his money supply, Saddam would be forced to surrender.

Royal Navy vessels stopped over 2500 ships and boarded about 600, while coalition ships challenged over 12,000 merchant vessels, boarded 1100 of these and diverted sixty, these last vessels containing over one million tons of cargo destined for Saddam's war effort.

The Royal Navy were also an essential part of the later maritime campaign. This was divided into three phases, involving firstly, constant air activity by both land based Tomahawk land attack Cruise missiles and carrier based air strikes.

Phase two, under the umbrella of the aerial assault, consisted of the destruction of the Iraqi anti-maritime forces and their surface navy with a final phase planned to take both the US and British navies close inshore where they could launch an amphibious force and/or a naval bombardment as required. Despite the large number of countries contributing to the coalition forces, only Royal Navy and US Navy ships had any part in the actual fighting.

During Phase Two, Royal Navy Lynx helicopters, with their Sea Skua missile system, destroyed over a quarter of the Iraqi surface forces with no loss to themselves, paving the way for the coalition surface fleet to safely approach the Kuwaiti coastline, its way cleared through the dense minefields by British Hunt class mine hunters. By 16 February, the combined naval force was approaching the coast, prior to bombardment by the 16in guns of the American battleships. Just before the Iraqi surrender, on 25 February, HMS *Gloucester* detected and 'splashed' the only Silkworm missile attack the Iraqis managed to launch, just short of USS *Missouri*, one of these major USN battleships.

Along with these key units, the RFA, as usual, was in the thick of it, operating within fifty miles of the Royal Navy's forward position.

Diligence's divers were assisting in the repair of USS *Tripoli*, previously hit by mines while *Argus*'s surgical teams were attending to casualties from USS *Princeton*, which had also been mined. *Olna* was operating a non-stop delivery service to British and American units in their frontline stations screening the capital ships while *Fort Grange*, like *Olna*, another Falklands veteran, carried on a continuous Sea King shuttle, moving food and stores into all the escorts over frighteningly short transit distances. The LSLs were also kept hard at work moving stores from the Task Group's base ports, initially from the United Arab Emirates and then from Bahrain.

By 28 February, President Bush had announced the end of the war. Then the cleanup had to begin, dousing the oilfield fires the Iraqis had started once they saw no chance of winning and repairing the damage caused by missiles and shells from both sides.

Resource also took part in Operation 'Haven', supporting British forces supplying aid to Kurdish refugees on the Turkey–Iraq border. She arrived in the eastern Mediterranean port of Iskendrun, on 15 May 1991, with enough equipment to build and equip a tent city and feed 8000 people for a month, which was soon offloaded and taken up into the mountains for the use of British forces. After a period spent in the region, *Resource* left for the UK on 22 July, where she de-stored for a much needed refit.

Later, during the trouble over UN inspections of the Iraqi weapons establishments between 1997 and 1999, the Navy was once again involved. Diligence, the new one-stop ships *Fort George* and *Fort Victoria*, *Fort Austin* and *Brambleleaf* all deployed in support of the Royal Navy and coalition forces at various times during that period.

RFAs deployed to the Gulf (1990–2)

Argus, Bayleaf, Diligence, Fort Grange, Olna, Orangeleaf, Resource, Sir Bedivere, Sir Galahad, Sir Percivale, Sir Tristram

---

Almost before the Gulf war had properly ended, the RFA found themselves in the thick of it again, this time in the land-locked waters of the Adriatic.

The Balkans has always been an area characterised by complex political shifts and Britain, particularly, has had her fair share of problems in that region, dating back as far as the end of the nineteenth century and also involving the origins of the First World War.

With the destabilisation of the Soviet Union and demise of the Warsaw Pact, however, independence was declared by Croatia and Slovenia in 1991 and Bosnia and Herzegovina in 1992. These regions split from the former Yugoslavia, later to become Serbia and Montenegro, leading, in 1992, to what came to be known as the Bosnian war, which went on until the Dayton Accord of 1995.

The reasons behind the war are complex, but by 1992 Serbs and Croats were involved in fighting all over Bosnia and Herzegovina, with support from both Croatia, Serbia and Montenegro.

Successive involvement by both the European Community and UN both failed to produce a peaceful solution and eventually NATO intervened. Their intervention and aggressive use of artillery by the Allied Rapid Reaction Force brought about the Dayton Accord of November 1995.

NATO had responsibility for enforcing the peace after the Accord and there is still a NATO presence in the region.

The RFAs were involved during the whole of the period 1992–5, as part of Operation 'Grapple', later Operation 'Hamden'. Operating both in the Adriatic port of Split in Croatia and at sea, they supported both the Royal Navy and the British land-based forces.

Split was certainly not a safe berth, as these short extracts from *Resource*'s daily orders make clear:

Extract from assessment by RMT representative:

In response to recent enquiries of the situation in Split, Croatia by the MoD, the crew of RFA 'Resource' have decided to voice their own opinions of the matter.

The recent weeks have seen an increase in gunfire in close proximity to the vessels in Split.
a) 11 May – A bullet thudded in to the shot mat at Resource's gangway.
b) 15 May – A burst of automatic fire was heard by OOD (the duty officer) aboard 'Sir Percivale' which came close enough to make him take cover.
c) 16 May – 1900, two of our people walking ashore just outside the dock gate heard two shots followed by a burst of 5 or 6 rounds. They heard the bullets pass them and hit the trees and bushes close to them. On turning round they saw a man with a rifle watching them.

Personnel ashore have been warned by locals of an increase in animosity towards the British in general. They have been told: 'There are many strangers coming into Split'.

Due to the recent fighting, the increase in more militant refugees has become apparent. They have been told that the Croatian attitude is becoming belligerent due to the British not helping the Croats to fight the Serbs, thus making the British pro-Serb.

Daily Orders

Security in Split:
It's coming up to the week end again and one or two crime preventive points have emerged. Stay with the crowds and avoid getting cornered in lonely streets. It's not a good idea to wear your jewellery in a visible manner and only take a minimum of money ashore with you. Having a 'mugger purse' might help to avoid a free kicking, it's considered tactically not a good idea to take on the local heavies.

The worst of the local thugs are the HOS, who are on leave in town and have attempted to intimidate our people. Reputed to be Croatians dressed in black uniforms but not always so as they have foreign nationals amongst their forces and may also be dressed in civvies. They are certainly all pugnacious and generally spoiling for a fight.

RFA vessels deployed to Bosnia (1992–5)

Argus, Bayleaf, Fort Austin, Fort Grange, Olna, Olwen, Orangeleaf, Resource, Sea Centurion, Sea Crusader, Sir Bedivere, Sir Percivale

---

David Soden was then part of the 'Stonnery' detachment aboard *Resource*, which took part in the Bosnia operation. He remembers the port of Split, where the RFAs usually unloaded, very well:

> During my time onboard RFA *Resource* in Split I witnessed the period when Croatia was at war and staff onboard had to be very careful when entering the centre of Split at night because of possible conflict with the Croatian army who used Split as an R and R location.
>
> The ship was tied up alongside in the port, which was in a very unhealthy location, on one side was an asbestos factory and on the other a sulphur pit which would ignite in the summer because of the heat, while ship's stern was next to one of the town's main sewage outlets.
>
> On a few occasions, maybe due to a wedding or other events, the local Croats would spray gun fire into the air. On a few occasions, whilst crossing the main deck, I saw clearly that the gun fire was aimed over the top of the ship. In the possible event that somebody might be wounded by a stray bullet, it was decided that QM hut (located at the top of the gangway) should be surrounded by sand bags. Luckily nobody was hit.
>
> Whilst in Split, the ship's role was to supply both food and ammunition to the Army in Bosnia. The ammunition was stored in the holds and was always well shored in as the ship was always on short notice to sail. This shoring process was not made easy by the Army, who after losing a quantity of ammunition in Bosnia, insisted that each Friday the ammunition held on the ship should be unshored to enable the stock held to be checked. The shoring/unshoring saga continued until the ship was replaced by RFA *Fort Grange*.

Making the best of things has always been something the RFA is particularly good at and the mooring at Split provided a well marked example of this talent. David Soden again:

> When RFA *Resource* was tied up alongside in Split, the daily movement of cargo meant that the ship would have to be trimmed at the end of each working day. Besides trimming the ship for normal ship's stability, of much greater importance was the need to ensure that the Sky TV picture was maintained. To this end, a quantity of pig iron ballast was retained on the main deck and a combination of the Supply & Transport department moving the ballast and the duty officer ensuring that the ship was kept upright meant that morale and the Sky TV picture was maintained.

During the succeeding years of the decade, the RFA saw further involvement in the Armilla Patrol (Operation 'Bolton') as well as the handover of Hong Kong to China in 1997. *Sir Percivale* was the last RFA to leave Hong Kong harbour prior to the handover.

Argus, Bayleaf and *Fort Austin* returned to the Adriatic in 1999, during Operation 'Magellan', when the British Army, as part of the NATO force, was involved in peacekeeping duties in Kosovo.

The Falklands campaign has been described as the RFA's finest hour, but it also marked the beginning of a period of immense change, highlighting major challenges in areas such as training, organisation and equipment, which needed urgent attention if the RFA was to continue providing afloat support to a rapidly modernising Royal Navy.

As one might expect, the whole Service rose to these challenges and by the turn of the century, most of the necessary skills and organisation were in place, along with the modern vessels needed to carry out the replenishment and operational duties the RFA was finding demanded of it.

Chapter 11

The Twenty-first Century: 2000–?

A new era opened for the RFA with the launch of the Fort class AORs. One-stop replenishment was now a reality but the Navy still had a requirement for an 'auxiliary oiler' to replace the ageing Ol class, which had been in service since 1965. In order to meet this requirement, a new class of tanker was ordered in 1997 and designated the Wave class, a name which will certainly have a familiar ring to old-time RFA men.

Wave Knight, the first of this new Wave class of large fast fleet tankers was launched in 2000, with her sister ship, *Wave Ruler* coming off the slips a year later.

Similar in size and capacity to the old Ol class vessels which they were replacing, they have a top speed of eighteen knots and a cargo capacity of 16,000 cubic metres, which includes aviation fuel, water and dry stores. In addition, they are equipped with 30mm cannon and fittings for Phalanx close in weapons system (CIWS), along with hangar and maintenance facilities for the big Merlin helicopter.

Tenders were invited for the construction of these two new vessels in 1996 and on 12 March the following year, a contract worth £200 million was placed with VSEL (Vickers Shipbuilding & Engineering Ltd), which managed to fight off strong competition from BAE Sea Systems (BAESEMA), Govan. There appears to have been some political disagreement over the order with Michael Forsyth, the Scottish Secretary, believing the contract should have been awarded to the Govan dockyard. Forsyth no doubt feared for his tiny majority in the Stirling constituency because upon losing the order, the Clyde shipyard was likely to shed at least 300 jobs, a circumstance unlikely to improve the government's popularity in an area already under the SNP umbrella.

Wave Knight was laid down on 22 May 1998 at the Vickers yard in Barrow-in-Furness, Cumbria. She was constructed in units, which were transported to Devonshire Dock Hall at Barrow and combined into twelve blocks. These were largely outfitted before being taken to the superberth where these were assembled. Despite subsequent delays in construction due to the innovative nature of this method of construction, *Wave Knight* was eventually launched in autumn 2000, although she was not actually out of the builder's hands and ready to begin trials until 2002.

This first of the new Wave class left the Clyde on 16 October 2002, with a full RFA crew aboard, arriving at Plymouth for the first time on 4 November. She quickly embarked on a programme of mooring trials, harbour checks and safety training, with some inevitable defect rectification thrown in.

Rigs were stretched with RFA *Black Rover* on the 30th as well as streaming of her Hudson reel equipment and a receiving rigs exercise, with *Brambleleaf* tasked as receiving ship. The honour of her first full RAS went to HMS *Sutherland* and after further RAS trials, safety exercises with the Navy's recently adopted Merlin helicopter and rectification of minor defects, she was accepted into service on 8 April 2003.

Wave Ruler, although she had to be transferred to Govan for completion, launched on schedule in February 2001 and following a similar period of work up, she was also accepted into service later the following year.

Comparisons between the crew complements of two tankers (*Wave Knight*: 78; *Olna*: 62) show that, despite the immense improvements in training and technology, crew numbers have changed very little in the years between the commissioning of these vessels. Incidentally, a similar sized merchant ship will carry a much smaller crew than an RFA, usually only twenty to twenty-five officers and ratings. This is because most of a commercial merchant ship's work is done in port, while RFAs do theirs at sea.

There are one or two obvious differences between *Olna* and *Wave Knight*, perhaps the most important being that the Wave class now have a whole new systems engineering department, replacing electrical as well as part of communications, and very necessary because so much technology aboard the Wave class is computer controlled. Medical requirements are taken care of by sick berth attendants aboard the Waves instead of the solitary surgeon aboard the Ol class and the new class have a RFA Helicopter Controller and some twenty RN maintenance staff instead of *Olna*'s thirty-two-strong Royal Navy aviation party. The old style purser, of course, is now a logistics supply officer and his orders are controlled via a computer rather than contained in the accumulated mountains of paperwork which once bedevilled this department.

Comparisons between the Rover class reveal a similar pattern. Crew numbers in 2008 are slightly higher, there is a systems engineering department, and a helicopter controller is also embarked in this class, rated at leading hand. Otherwise, little seems to have changed. New vessels are still being planned for the RFA fleet, of course, although the latest class, first launched in 2005, was something of a departure, even for the RFA.

Belonging to the Bay class, these vessels are designated Landing Ship Dock (Auxiliary) – LSD(A) – and are intended as a replacement for the ageing LSLs, although their logistic capability far exceeds the old 'Knights of the Round Table' class, being more akin to the Royal Navy's LPDs, HMS *Fearless* and *Intrepid*.

	Bay Class	SLEPed Sir Class (eg, Sir Bedivere)
Length/beam	176m/26.5m	139m/19.6m
Displacement (full load)	16,220 tonnes	8585 tonnes
Complement	71 (20 Officers, 51 OR)	59 (20 Officers, 39 OR)
Troops	350 (700+ in war state)	340
Access	Stern dock and side ramps	Bow ramp only
Vehicles	24 Challenger tanks 150 trucks	18 Challenger tanks 20 trucks
Helicopters	2 spot flight deck for Merlin Chinook and US V22 Osprey	1 Chinook or Merlin
Landing craft	1 LCU MK 10 operated from floodable dock, two LCVP Mk 5 and Mexeflote carried on deck and offloaded by crane.	2 Mexeflotes
Armament (when fitted)	4 × 30 mm BMARC cannon Phalanx CIWS	2 × 30mm Bofors

Capable of operating LCVPs and a single ninety-six-feet-long LCU from their stern dock, these ships can also deploy Mexeflotes as well as twenty-four battle tanks that enter or leave the ship by way of either stern or side ramps. There is a Chinook capable flight deck and although no hangar or maintenance support is included in the original build, hangar facilities can be carried in collapsible form. Steering is by way of a single joystick on the bridge and this class is also equipped with a computer controlled satellite positioning system linked to the newly developed azimuth thruster propulsion units, making these vessels capable of holding position very precisely. Self defence is well catered for with the inclusion of four 30mm cannon and fittings for Phalanx CIWS along with a Royal Navy party to operate them.

A vast improvement on the Round Table class, they are thirty-seven metres longer, nearly seven metres wider, can operate more helicopters, carry twice as many vehicles and deploy those vehicles safely from over the horizon in a landing craft they carry rather than having to beach. And to do all this, they only need twenty more crew.

All in all, the perfect expression of the 'Force Multiplier' concept and very well capable of taking up either a supply, humanitarian or combatant role, whichever is needed. Incidentally, it is expected that these ships will normally operate as part of the Royal Navy Amphibious Task Group (ATG).

Beautiful, immensely useful, well-equipped ships, modern and up to date as tomorrow. Although, surprisingly enough, for a while no one was quite sure when, or even if, they might enter service.

Construction of the first of the Bay class began as far back as 1998, when the UK Ministry of Defence Procurement Executive (now the Defence Equipment & Support Agency) issued a solicitation for a vessel, then designated Alternative Landing Ship Logistic.

This ship was to replace the LSLs, required to have a minimum payload of 350 troops, 500 lane metres of vehicles and seventy tonnes of war maintenance reserves (WMR) (stores, fuel, ammunition, etc.). Facilities were to be provided to embark and operate both helicopters and Mexeflotes, with provision for vehicles to offload into landing craft in conditions up to sea state 3.

Defence projections suggested that all amphibious requirements could be met with four new ships of this type, along with a retained, recently SLEPed *Sir Bedivere*. This was felt to be particularly advantageous as each new ship was expected to cost only as much as a reconstruction of one of the thirty year old LSLs.

Informal proposals together with rough costings based on these specifications were eventually received from ten UK and foreign shipyards.

Invitations to tender for two ALSLs, with options for three more vessels in the same class, were issued to five UK shipbuilders in April 2000, with the specs now changed to increase the WMR to 106 tonnes. An original budget of £87 million had also increased to £138 million for the two ships. Finally, just three firm tenders were received, from Appledore Shipbuilders Ltd (North Devon), BAE Systems Marine (Govan, Scotland) and Swan Hunter (Tyneside) on 13 June 2000.

After a period of consideration, a contract for four ALSLs was awarded to Swan Hunter. However, in order to get the new ships introduced more quickly, the MoD decided that BAE Systems Marine should construct two of these at their Govan shipyard, to the same Swan Hunter design and for a similar price.

In order to save money at the design and development stage, Swan Hunter had not designed their vessel from scratch but had chosen to base it on a similar ship, the Royal Netherlands Navys LPD, HRMS *Rotterdam*, originally built by Royal Schelde as a variant of their Enforcer family.

Swan Hunter and BAE were contracted to do the building while the Dutch company, Royal Schelde, would supply design and naval architectural services. The final contract for two ships each was worth some £210 million to Swan Hunter, with £120 million going to BAE. This was expected to create 1000 new jobs at Swan and some 600 at Govan, BAE's Clyde yard. At this stage, all four ships were expected to enter service somewhere between the end of 2004 and autumn 2005.

Problems, however, bedevilled the project from the start and by December 2003, due to technical and design difficulties at both Schelde and Swan Hunter, *Largs Bay* and *Lyme Bay*, the two Tyneside ships were a year behind schedule, although the first Govan ship, *Mounts Bay* originally scheduled for launch in October 2003, did leave the slips in April 2004. The bad news was that her sistership, *Cardigan Bay*, would not be delivered until sometime in 2006. Compensation payments, then estimated by BAE at £20 million, and an increase in costs also meant that, according to the National Audit office (NOA), the unit cost of each ship had now risen to £91.5 million, some £366 million for all four, £36 million up on the 2000 estimate.

On 24 February, 2005, the Minister for Armed Forces, Adam Ingram issued a statement, in an attempt to clarify the situation. In part it said:

> The original contract price for the … costs of the two Swan Hunter Landing Ship Dock (Auxiliary) ships, *Largs Bay* and *Lyme Bay* was £148 million [author's note: this was in 2000] and the anticipated cost is now £235 million. The MoD has made a provision of £40 million for delay and dislocation costs in respect of the two LSD(A)s that BAE Systems are building and has already made an initial payment of £16 million.

Later in the statement, he added:

> However, in September 2003, when the company announced that it could not absorb the risk and complete the contract at the agreed price and timescale, both financial and timescale risks were, in effect, transferred to the MoD.

So the MoD had admitted that it had taken over all financial and timescale risks from Swan as far back as September 2003. Furthermore, in March 2005, Newcastle's *Evening Chronicle* revealed that Swan Hunter had accepted an £84 million pound 'lifeline'. This was on condition that it implemented a management restructuring and accepted technical management from BaE because, as the owner of the yard, Jaap Kroese, bluntly put it: 'We will work together with BaE because we simply do not have the design capability to do it ourselves.'

Swan's troubles were not over, however. Engineering tests conducted during April 2005 showed major problems with the two Swan Hunter ships which would take another £20 million to put right. Swan wanted more money, although MoD sources emphasised that both *Lyme Bay* and *Largs Bay* were virtually complete. Swan Hunter would be retained as the lead yard, because the MoD claimed this represented the best value for money for the taxpayer, although BAE's *Mounts Bay* would now be lead ship, for functions such as speed trials.

Mounts Bay began sea trials in September 2005, having first moved under power in

April. The RFA took delivery on 10 December 2005, and after training and first of class trials was expected to enter service in spring 2006, although she did not actually begin her operational life until August.

Meanwhile, in spring 2005, Swan Hunter tried to interest the MoD in converting *Lyme Bay* into a joint casualty treatment ship, a plan, incidentally, which MoD had already shelved. Perhaps inevitably, Swan's offer was rejected and *Lyme Bay*, the first of the Swan ships was floated out on 3 September 2005, after the planned operation on 26 August (a bank holiday weekend!) was aborted due to, of all things, there being insufficient water in the dry dock!

Swan Hunter was optimistically hoping the ship would begin sea trials around November 2005, be delivered in December and enter service in summer 2006. This time it was gremlins in the electrical system which prevented her completion and by February 2006, the MoD were seeking bids for a 'get well programme' for both Swan Hunter ships, with BAE Naval ships looking as if it would take the contract.

Costs for the Swan vessels had now increased, according to Adam Ingram, Minister of State for the Armed Forces, to £236 million, which included £62 million for the provision of lead yard equipment in support of the two BAE ships and £11 million-worth of spares for all four vessels. The BAE total build cost for two vessels was £176 million. Both yards thought they would need more money before the ships were completed.

Total cost so far (3 November 2005): £412 million
Original estimated cost (2000): £268 million
Difference: £144 million

Largs Bay began trials on 2 March 2006 and was accepted by the RFA 'in good condition' about seven weeks later, on 25 April, although it was not clear whether her defect list had been fully attended to. *Cardigan Bay* was delivered to her owners in August 2006, while the last of the four, *Lyme Bay*, was finally completed by BAE Systems and handed over to the RFA on 2 August 2007.

The MoD actually terminated its contract with Swan Hunter early in 2007 and *Lyme Bay* was towed to BAE's Govan yard where she was successfully completed.

Final settlement figures:

Swan Hunter (*Largs Bay* and *Lyme Bay*, two years late): £ 309 million
(£99 million over budget)

BAE Systems (*Mounts Bay* (on time) and *Cardigan Bay* (one year late)): £187 million
(£65 million over budget)

In fairness, it needs to be pointed out that most of BAE's over-budget costs and late delivery were caused by problems with Swan Hunter.

Fleet maintenance has always been a major part of the RFA's yearly budget, amounting to around £100 million and, until recently, this money has been allocated, as and when required, to suppliers and contractors by competitive tender, in line with Public Sector Procurement rules.

In 2004, however, a Category Management team, designated Commercial Ship Maintenance (CMT), was set up with the task of improving this procedure and, it was hoped, thereby saving some £30 million from the RFA's annual ship repair bill. After due deliberation, they came up with a number of strikingly innovative recommendations.

To begin with, the team recommended that ships should be grouped in clusters for maintenance with contracts based on a 'Through Life Support' (TLS) scheme, replacing the 100s of uneconomic, individual contracts which were currently in place. Each cluster would be the responsibility of one contractor, thereby improving efficiency and ensuring operational requirements could be more smoothly met. Alongside this, internal and external changes in RFA organisation should be introduced so as to support these TLS strategies.

Both traditional suppliers, MoD, Treasury and C-in-C Fleet needed to be convinced but, by December 2005, the first TLS contract was let, for *Argus*. This contract was between the RFA and both A & P Falmouth Ltd (ship repairers) and Rolls Royce (power generation), covering the support requirements for *Argus* for five years. It has proved remarkably successful, producing savings of more than £4.5 million, which constitutes a 20 per cent reduction in maintenance costs. Together with these financial benefits, the ship is now routinely maintained in her best condition ever, with her availability now beyond the RFA team's stated operational readiness requirements.

With the RFA now being called on to operate on a world wide scale, maintenance can often be carried out more economically away from the UK.

With this in mind and in line with the RFA 'Global Reach' initiative, a second pilot scheme was launched in March 2006, for *Brambleleaf*. Worth £6 million, the twelve-month contract included operational support in Dubai as well as a refit in Singapore and eventually delivered savings of £400,000, without interfering with the ship's operational commitments. A similar UK-based package for *Fort George* delivered savings of £2.3 million (15 per cent). Incidentally, this may stir some memories for older RFA men, because Hong Kong and Singapore were often used for RFA refits during the 1960s and the 1970s.

Having worked out the TLS Statement of Technical Requirements (SoTR) and developed a 'Should Cost of Ownership by Year' model for each vessel, the TLS invitation to tender for the six ship clusters was issued in August 2007, with contracts awarded for the work to a number of suppliers, both ship repairers and specialist manufacturers, in June 2008.

With its long-term future in mind, RFA resources have relocated to suppliers' sites near the new TLS contractors so as to ensure that the TLS is embedded and sustained throughout the supplier community. These changes also complement a wider MoD reorganisation to incorporate 'new build' procurement with the exisiting TLS scheme, bringing both ship building and maintenance under the umbrella of an Afloat Support Directorate of the Defence Equipment and Support Organisation. This will presumably ensure that new ship design incorporates low cost maintenance features as standard at the design stage, thus ensuring maximum operational efficiency and minimum cost, whatever new additions the future holds for the RFA fleet.

As of April 2008, the fleet consisted of sixteen vessels, in a number of classes, each with widely varying and specialised characteristics, crewed by 2520 men and women, of whom around 25 per cent are officers.

Composition of Ship Clusters and Contractors (June 2008)

Cluster1
Argus
Contractor: A & P Falmouth (this contract was placed in December 2005 as a pilot
for the TLS strategy)
Cluster 2
Cardigan Bay, Largs Bay, Lyme Bay, Mounts Bay
Contractor: A & P Falmouth
Cluster 3
Bayleaf, Orangeleaf, Black Rover, Gold Rover
Contractor: Northwestern Ship Repair & Shipbuilders Ltd
Cluster 4
Diligence, Wave Knight, Wave Ruler
Contractor: Northwestern Ship Repair & Shipbuilders Ltd
Cluster 5
Fort Austin, Fort Rosalie
Contractor: Northwestern Ship Repair & Shipbuilders Ltd
Cluster 6
Fort George, Fort Victoria
Contractor: Northwestern Ship Repair & Shipbuilders Ltd

Contracts to provide specialist equipment for the upkeep work of the RFAs have
also been awarded to Lloyd's Register, Bristol, for classification services to ensure
each ship meets maintenance standards, Hempel Ltd, Cwmbran, for the supply of
paint, and Trimline Ltd, Southampton to provide furnishings. Another contract,
for provision of specialist engineering services, is expected to be let later in 2008.

A final change to headquarters organisation took place during 2001–2 with the
introduction of the RFA Bureau and a change of status for the Commodore. COMRFA
is now designated as a one-star level Assistant Chief of Staff (Sustainability),
responsible to the Chief of Staff (Support). He, in turn, reports to a three star level
Deputy Commander in Chief.

As head of the RFA, the Commodore has responsibility for planning, exercise and
management of all matters relating to logistics and sustainability of all British
maritime forces as well as having a place on the board of the C-in-C Fleet. He is also
the biggest employer of registered seamen in the UK.

In line with this change in command structure and the RFA's integration into the
organisation of both the Royal Navy and MoD, RFA officers now serve in many of the
specialised departments attached to both and their numbers have increased
tremendously in the years between the post Falkland period of reorganisation and the
present.

As well as being part of the MoD and Royal Navy logistic organisation, many of
these officers, petty officers and ratings are also permanently attached to the staff of
several of the Royal Navy training centres, including the Britannia Royal Naval College,
Dartmouth.

Of course, this smooth integration with both MoD and the Royal Navy is only possible because of the high levels of training the officers seconded to these establishments receive during their careers. And that all starts for many of them with an RFA cadetship. Beginning a career in the RFA as an officer cadet in 2008 is a highly selective procedure, necessarily, of course, because the job is very demanding right from the outset, and requires high quality personnel for its efficient delivery.

Initially, a candidate must be over sixteen years of age, British and have good passes (B) in mathematics, English language and science plus C passes in at least two more subjects. This allows entry to the three year Higher National Diploma (HND) course in Nautical Science for Deck Cadets or Marine Engineering for Engineering Cadets. Both courses entail spending half of this training period in college and the other half at sea. Having passed the final course exam, the cadet then sits an oral exam for the award of the MCA certificate of competency, which signals the end of the cadetship and his transfer to an RFA as Third officer, able to stand a watch on the bridge or in the engine room. Both HND courses can be 'topped up' up to allow the award of either BSc in Marine Operations Management for deck officers or BSc in Marine Engineering and Management for the engineering branch. Older candidates with higher initial entry qualifications can go straight on to the relevant BSc course.

Before getting on this course, however, every candidate first undergoes a psychometric test at their local Army Careers Information Office, before then attending an RFA Interview Board (RFAIB).

This board, which takes place at HMS *Sultan*, is very intensive, consisting of two and a half days of aptitude, fitness and leadership tests, together with planning exercises and culminating in an interview on the final day. Candidates who pass their board are short listed for a career in the RFA. Prior to starting the HND/BSc at a naval college, every officer trainee attends the seven-week induction course at Britannia Royal Naval College, Dartmouth.

Older, pre-qualified candidates are also employed. Deck officers need an Officer in Charge of Navigational Watch Certificate of Competency (STCW 95), engineers need an Officer in Charge of Engineering Watch Certificate of Competency (STCW 95), LSOs can enter with a variety of relevant HNDs while systems engineering officers are usually qualified either to HND or graduate level in electronics or electrical engineering or have extensive, relevant experience.

Officer candidates have to pass the Admiralty interview board, similar to the cadet's RFAIB, in that it is also two days of tests, before proceeding to Britannia Royal Naval College for the six week induction course and then to their first sea going appointment with the RFA.

Once qualified, a third officer studies for a mate's certificate before undertaking his master's 'ticket', required for command of any merchant vessel, which, of course, includes all RFAs. Many RFA second officers hold a master's certificate, while it is mandatory for promotion to first and chief officer.

Training for ratings follows an essentially similar pattern. No formal qualifications are required but there is a written test, followed by an interview. Successful candidates then proceed to a Royal Navy establishment for training in their specialisation.

Seamen initially go to HMS *Phoenix* for STCW95 Basic Safety training before undergoing the RFA Seaman Grade 2 (SG2) course at HMS *Raleigh*. Communications (Communication Rating at HMS *Collingwood*), Catering (Catering Asst [Cook/Stwd] at HMS *Raleigh*) and Engineering ratings (Motor Man 2 at HMS *Sultan*) all complete training courses for their own particular specialisation before attending the Phoenix safety course. First sea appointments usually follow, although several of the training courses also include some sea time. Every new rating completes one or more task books while at sea, which upon completion, lead them to a nationally recognised qualification, at NVQ2 level.

Once their initial qualification period is over, there is an extensive collection of specialised training courses for both officers and ratings, many of which are run by the Royal Navy.

Britannia College's RFA officer induction course, introduced in 2002, seems to be popular with all candidates, whatever their age and specialisation.

The course is of six weeks duration and consists of RFA induction, naval general training, seamanship, basic leadership development, through life skills, essential staff skills and warfare. Candidates also visit several RFAs during the course to gain first-hand experience of life aboard.

There is a mix of physical training and classroom theory with essays and assessed presentations adding to the work load. Of the twenty candidates on the very first RFA course, several were women.

This is now by no means unusual. Women first began to be recruited to the RFA in 1993, when the first officer cadets were admitted to Warsash, the RFA officer's training college. Since then, they have entered the service in ever increasing numbers, in almost all departments, both as officers and ratings, and have proved themselves every bit as capable and adaptable as their male colleagues.

It was all a bit different back in the early 1950s, when this senior RFA officer, now retired, joined the Service:

> Over the years I have been asked by family and friends why 'I chose to go to sea'. The truth is I have no honest answer to the question except perhaps to say that from an early age I had always felt that this was what I wanted to do.
>
> In the early 1950s, careers advice had not as yet become a part of school life. There was therefore little constructive careers or job information available to students. I certainly had no idea of what was involved, the advantages, disadvantages and the many other questions that any teenager would expect to ask and have answered by careers advisors today. In any event opportunities were limited in what was still post war Britain, except of course within the framework of the Armed Services and – the Merchant Navy.
>
> Against this background of limited knowledge, I blindly took the first steps towards a life at sea. With a reasonable educational background there were two avenues open to me both of which would eventually lead to Officer Status. The main stream was via one of the pre-sea but fee paying training establishments for example, HMS *Conway*, HMS *Worcester* or Pangbourne Nautical College and completing their two year course or alternatively, by applying to a particular shipping company for direct entry as a Cadet or Apprentice. In all but a few cases this was a no cost option for parents.
>
> Apart from the academic and practical advantage to be gained from the college course, you were certainly not a novice in nautical terms the day you joined your first ship. In addition, the time spent in pre-sea training had the effect of reducing a Cadet's indentured period from four to three years sea service in the qualifying time required to sit the first of three professional examinations. As far as I was concerned,

this meant that I was a Certificated Officer at the minimum age of twenty, six months to a year ahead of those joining via the direct entry system.

And so it was that at the age of 14 years and nine months I started my pre-sea training which was to last two years. A harsh regime of rigid discipline by today's standards and one where even the smallest offence would result in painful punishment on the receiving end of a 'teaser', a 3-foot length of rope back spliced and whipped at one end. Swung from shoulder height it definitely put the school cane in the shade where pain was concerned. Notwithstanding this, the academic side of life was straight forward, GCEs and nautical subjects at least to Certificate of Competency level. Practical seamanship was part of the daily routine and there was little you did not know about basic skills by the time you left.

Another question I am often asked is why did I join the RFA. Well, my pre-sea training establishment provided a booklet outlining the various types of Merchant Navy shipping companies accepting Cadets with pre-sea training. This was the only careers advice I can remember but the booklet did give considerable information on their trading areas, types of ships and salaries and thus became the major factor in where you ended up. The Captain Superintendent became the final arbiter as to whether a particular application went forward or not based on what the companies were looking for and the individual cadet's profile. For example, P&O got the good kids, the not so clever went to the tanker companies or something like that.

Where was the RFA at that time? – off the scale or, at best, close to the bottom of the heap! Of course personal preference did play a part, at least that's my excuse! Having had an application accepted the next step in the RFA process (and probably the same for other Companies) was a brief interview at Old Admiralty Building, followed by a 'we will let you know'. However, on the way out the lady who seemed to run the RFA's Cadets handed me a clothing list and said I was in!

So my sea time began. I joined my first RFA on a dark and damp November's evening at Chatham. RFA *Fort Dunvegan*, a WWII Canadian built store carrier running between Chatham, Gibraltar and Malta which was due to sail the following day. Thereafter. two further RFA's as a Cadet, *Wave Prince*, an uneventful time and finally *Tidereach* where I had the somewhat embarrassing experience of joining not via the gangway, but in a cargo net as the ship slipped from the jetty at Hebburn-on-Tyne. This was certainly an eventful period, with my first experience of working with the Fleet and of course, the Suez operation in the closing months of 1956.

In addition to the routine of life at sea we were also provided with a detailed correspondence course intended to cover the academic or written side of the Second Mates (FG) certificate examination. Most if not all of the subject matter had already been covered during my two years pre-sea period and as a consequence served as little more than a refresher course. Papers were sent off monthly, corrected and returned via the Captain (who in most cases took an interest in the results). Failure to complete the task papers within the time frame was not a popular option with the 'Company' and invariably resulted in a letter, again via the Captain, reminding you that your qualifying 'sea time' was at stake. Even so, I have yet to meet an ex Cadet who completed the whole course.

On leave the following summer, the career break came in the form of a telegram instructing me to join RFA *Somersby* at Wallsend on the Tyne as Temporary Acting Third Officer. And so to all intents and purposes my Cadetship ended and I found myself on the bridge as a watch keeping officer at the tender age of eighteen and a half. The so called hands-on experience was invaluable and made all the difference when

I came to stand in front of a Board of Trade examiner some eighteen months later.

The early promotion of Cadets to that of Watch-keeping Officers was of necessity quite common place and a direct result of a severe shortage of qualified Officers during the late 1950s. In any event the advantages of this promotion were numerous, not least of which was an increase in leave and salary. Overnight, my leave rate went from one month a year to three and salary from ten pounds a month to over 40. This was in addition to the statutory three months study leaves (plus one month extra for a re-take), the net result of which was that money and time while studying was not a problem.

A new century with new ships had arrived, but for the RFA, the same old problems reappeared, beginning in Africa, during 2000.

Sierra Leone is a former British colony that was granted independence in 1961. Civil war has raged there between the established government of President A T Kabbah and the rebel Revolutionary United Front (RUF) since early 1999.

The RFA involvement began in 2000, when British Army, Royal Navy and RAF units were deployed to reinforce the UN peacekeeping forces already present, after the breakdown of the Lome Peace Agreement.

Following this breakdown, the RUF took some 500 UN peacekeepers prisoners and killed a number of others. In response to the perceived danger to UK nationals, the 1st Battalion, the Parachute Regiment, was flown into Senegal, from where they quickly moved to seize Sierra Leone airport, which was then used to evacuate noncombatants. The Paras continued to hold the airport and patrol Freetown, allowing UN supplies to be flown in safely. Operations ended on 15 June 2000, after government troops captured the RUF leader.

During much of this period, *Sir Percivale* was based in Freetown, where she was pivotal in the overall organisation of British efforts to support the Sierra Leone government. Among her many jobs was supporting a mobile hospital erected on the jetty next to her berth in order to provide medical facilities for nearly one thousand British troops involved in this operation. The hospital had both a fully equipped operating theatre and intensive care unit, with a thirty strong staff to run. *Sir Percivale*'s crew also carried out some building and maintenance work at the local Cape Community School before the end of their deployment.

RFAs deployed to Sierra Leone

Argus (deployed in place of HMS *Fearless* after latter suffered engine-room fire), *Fort Grange, Sir Bedivere, Sir Percivale, Sir Tristram*

The Service also found itself in action in Afghanistan from October 2001 to the end of 2002, supporting units of the Royal Navy, during the course of the US Army's Operation 'Enduring Freedom'. Although major British deployment ended in 2002, British forces remain on peacekeeping duties and tragically a number have been killed, including Sarah Bryant, a corporal in the Intelligence Corps, the first female member of the British armed forces to be killed there.

RFAs deployed for Afghanistan

Bayleaf, Brambleleaf, Diligence, Fort Rosalie, Fort Victoria, Sir Percivale, Sir Tristram

---

Gulf involvement began again in 2003, when, after a period of frustrating negotiation over Iraq's development of weapons of mass destruction, Coalition forces finally invaded Iraq from bases in Kuwait and other friendly Middle East countries on 23 March 2003.

Beginning once again with a massive aerial strike from ships in the Gulf, Royal Marines and US Marines stormed ashore, quickly spearheading a lightning strike towards Baghdad. British Challenger tanks destroyed fourteen Iraqi tanks near Basra four days later and by 9 April, US tanks were in the centre of Baghdad, with the Iraqi regime nowhere in sight. The MoD announced the start of British troop rotation on 29 April 2003. British forces are still in theatre, attempting to restore control to the elected Iraqi authorities.

The RFAs were involved in all aspects of these operations, from supporting the mine sweepers clearing a way into Um Qasr to supplying the needs of HMS *Ark Royal*. *Sir Galahad* was the first vessel into Um Qasr after the channel had been swept and her cargo included food, bottled water, medical aid and equipment for building shelters to house the beleaguered civilian population.

As well as conducting in their more usual supply operations, *Fort Austin*, *Fort Rosalie* and the giant AOR, *Fort Victoria* also deployed their Sea King and Merlin helicopters in support of the Royal Marines during the 'Royals' operations on the Al Faw peninsular, emphasising the RFA's now well-established 'force multiplier' role.

Argus, a primary casualty reception facility of one hundred beds was available and it was here that British, US and Iraq casualties received initial treatment. Incidentally, one US Marine who participated in training aboard *Argus* was so impressed that he told all his colleagues to get a tattoo reading 'If injured, take to Argus'!

Writing in *Gunline*, Commodore Jamie Miller, COMATG neatly summed up the RFA's contribution: '... what my Amphibious Task Group has achieved over the past two years of operations and exercises could not have been done without the resolute and unfailing support of the RFA community'.

The RFAs are still permanently deployed with the Royal Navy's Armilla patrol in the Persian Gulf.

RFAs deployed to Gulf in 2003

Argus, Bayleaf, Brambleleaf, Diligence, Fort Austin, Fort Rosalie, Fort Victoria, Orangeleaf, Sea Crusader, Sir Galahad, Sir Percivale, Sir Tristram

---

The RFA's traditional humanitarian role has not been neglected with its increasingly military commitments, either. Wherever disaster threatens happens around the globe, the RFA is often there, to such an extent that several ships in the Service have received a humanitarian award in the form of the Wilkinson Sword of Peace, one of the latest being *Sir Galahad*, after she took much-needed supplies into Um Qasr at the end of the 2003 Iraq war.

Fort George was also involved in relief work, during the Mozambique floods in 2000. In what must have been two very hectic weeks, the AOR used her embarked Sea King helicopters from 820 Naval Air Squadron to deliver over 500 tons of essential supplies to villages cut off by the floods. For this action and their later work in Sierra Leone, the whole ship received a Commendation from C-in-C Fleet. Her Master, Captain L Coupland, was later also awarded a Queen's Commendation for Valuable Service.

Diligence was similarly tasked to participate in the cleanup operations after the Asian Tsunami in 2004, a disaster which left over 300,000 people dead. Members of her crew were extensively involved in helping to rebuild the badly damaged infrastructure of the areas which were in the path of the tidal wave. Among other tasks, they repaired electrical generators and desalination plants on the Maldives as well as clearing a local church of rubble. Most the congregation had died in the church when the tsunami struck and, after the site had been cleared, *Diligence*'s Chaplain, Fr Charles Howard, rededicated the building.

There is apparently no limit to the versatility of RFA crews and their ships. In yet another change to their traditional role, RFAs are extensively involved in policing, and often preventing, the drug trafficking carried out by fast boats off the coasts of Central America and the Caribbean.

These drug runners use fast, seventy-knot, power boats, which operate at night to avoid the US Coast Guard patrols. To combat this, RFAs such as *Wave Knight* and *Wave Ruler* deploy their Lynx Mk 3 helicopters. Aboard the aircraft are specially trained Royal Marines snipers who use AW50 sniper rifles, loaded with armour-piercing rounds, to disable the power boat's outboard motors, should the smugglers fail to respond to a warning burst from the Lynx's 0.50 calibre machine gun. The RFAs are very effective.

During 2006–7, *Wave Ruler* captured eleven tons of cocaine, worth a staggering £420 million if it had reached the streets of the United States, while *Lyme Bay*, on her first deployment after commissioning in January 2008, caught a Venezuelan fishing boat, *Astromelia*, carrying bales of cocaine. The crew managed to dump their illegal cargo over the side from where the Bay class's sea boat promptly recovered it, before overtaking the fishing boat and putting a US Coast Guard law enforcement detachment aboard her. The bales later proved to hold cocaine worth £20 million.

The RFA deployments still have their lighter side, however. *Wave Knight*'s crew had a taste of this when they found themselves at the sharp end of a particularly arduous deployment in 2005.

Upon their ship's arrival in Cartagena, the ship's company was asked to host a 'Miss Colombia' night! Needless to say, the crew (at least the male part) responded in true RFA fashion, even escorting the girls down the red carpet upon their arrival. As the one of the crew was heard to remark: 'It's a tough job ... but somebody's got to do it.'

The Future?

Unquestionably, the most important government initiative to affect the RFA for many years is the MARS project.

The Military Afloat Reach and Sustainability (MARS) project first saw the light of day in July 2002, when an Integrated Project Team (IPT) was established at the Defence Procurement Agency, in Abbey Wood, near Bristol.

The team was asked to examine a number of aspects of the RFA's operations at sea with a view to making financial savings. Even privatisation was not ruled out and, in fact, this had already been introduced with the Point class. These were commercially managed and crewed ro-ro ferries, which had been responsible for much of the Army's heavy lift capacity since 2002. Owned by the MoD, they are chartered out to commercial firms, exactly like ordinary merchant ships, when the Army is not using them. Most importantly, these ro-ros were only used for major deployments and exercises, situations where the MoD expected, or rather, perhaps hoped to have plenty of notice.

At the risk of being accused of labouring the point, what was going to happen if the RFA disappeared and all the Army and Royal Navy's logistics fleet were owned on this basis, given that wars often happen at extremely short notice?

Remember Saddam Hussein's invasion of Kuwait, which sparked the 1992 Gulf War and, before that, more especially, the Falklands War? How long would it have taken the Royal Navy to go south with the sort of logistics support the RFA deployed in days, if all of its afloat support had to be returned from charter, recrewed and retrained?

And just to emphasise the way ministerial thought was turning, during the earlier House of Commons debate on defence procurement, Armed Forces Minister Adam Ingram had said in a statement, announcing the establishment of the MARS Project: 'We will welcome innovative proposals, which might include public-private partnership arrangements. I hope for an imaginative and enthusiastic response from British industry.'

Without going into too many details, by 2004, the MoD had decided that eleven new ships were to be built and operated by the RFA, at a projected cost of £2.5 billion.

Information and assessment from several other well informed quarters, however, suggested that, in fact, efficient delivery of an amphibious force with carrier and warship cover would require something like twenty ships, although some of the freighting requirement could be met by chartered STUFT.

Of course, it is hardly surprising to find that, almost immediately, pressure began to be applied to the Royal Navy to accept cheaper, commercially owned ships, brought in under charter to MoD, as an alternative to MARS. Sufficient new hulls were not available, however, and it was decided to extend the service of the existing RFAs, while the MoD looked around for what they called 'lead contractor (integrator)'.

Although no such contractor had yet come forward, by 2006, the MoD had a list of the ships which they would require under MARS as follows:

- Five fleet tankers (ready 2011–15)
- Three logistics vessels, with sea-basing facilities (ready 2016–20)
- One fleet tanker, specifically equipped for the new carrier class (ready 2021)
- Two solid support vessels

Unfortunately, with a lead contractor still not forthcoming, by August 2007, the MoD had down-sized the original plan and divided it into several smaller projects, which they hoped would be faster moving. The first of these, designated 'military

Concept of Operations for MARS Ships

The MARS Project is charged with acquiring the next generation of RFA ships. As can be interpreted from the role of the Royal Fleet Auxiliary and the nature of RAS operations, the collective roles of the MARS ships include, but are not limited to:

(a) Replenishment of Naval ships operating in task groups or as single units while underway or at anchor, utilising various RAS techniques including VERTREP (VERTical REPlenishment by helicopter), surface transfer and rafted-up transfer utilising ships' cranes. Replenishment operations may be conducted by day or night, and some may be conducted simultaneously.

(b) Support to amphibious operations in a potentially hostile environment (extreme environmental conditions and/or under threat of hostile action). Operations may be conducted by day or night utilising a range of boats and craft in up to mid Sea State 4, or by helicopter lift, in addition to those methods outlined above.

(c) Aviation facilities capable of providing helicopter operations in support of Naval combatant ships or in support of an amphibious task group and landing force, by day and night. Facilities are to include maintenance of helicopters for a fully capable aviation arrangement on a fleet tanker.

(d) Base for armed forces operations, including an HQ element, and the ability to operate specialist boats.

Fleet Tanker Outline Requirements

Based on an expansion of the concept of operations of the MARS ships outlined above, the MARS Project have undertaken concept design studies to ascertain the principal ship characteristics for the Fleet Tankers. These are outlined in the following paragraphs.

Within the RFA flotilla, the MARS Fleet Tankers will:

(a) Provide replenishment of logistics to Naval task groups and Naval combatant and auxiliary ships providing:
    i.   F76 Marine Gas Oil (a Petroleum Class III clean product);
    ii.   F44 Aviation Kerosene (a Petroleum Class III clean product);
    iii. F34 Aviation Kerosene (a Petroleum Class II clean product); and
    iv. potable water.

(b) Be capable of conducting replenishment operations in daylight hours or at night, underway or at anchor, utilising various techniques including connected abeam replenishment.

(c) Provide aviation facilities to enable helicopter operations, refuelling and maintenance.

In addition to the above, the MARS Fleet Tankers must be:

(a) Constructed with quality equipment and material of proven reliability;

(b) Interoperable to NATO standards and with NATO assets;

(c) Designed to increase reliability, facilitate ease of maintenance, repair or replacement and minimise through life costs;

(d) Designed with open architectures that facilitate support and readily enable

future capability upgrades and incorporation of emerging technologies; and
(e) Capable of operations worldwide, seasonally unrestricted: from Tropical to Arctic:
   i.   Hot: Seawater temperature up to +32degC (gradual degradation of performance to +38degC); and
   ii. Cold: Air temperature down to –35degC (Grade D steel or tougher required) and 1st Year Ice capable.

INDICATIVE (to be confirmed) characteristics of the MARS Fleet Tankers are:
(a) Petroleum Class II and III compliant and reconfigurable and fully pumpable cargo capacity of 18000cz;
(b) Potable water cargo capacity of 1300m³;
(c) Carriage of 8 fully laden 20ft ISO containers;
(d) Sustained speed (in deep condition, Sea State 5, six months out of dock and at end of life) of 15 knots (estimated contract speed in calm seas and deep water, clean hull and deep condition of 17–18 knots);
(e) Range of 7000nm at 15knots;
(f) RAS rigs to include three abeam tensioned jackstay rigs, one astern fuelling reel, one over the bow reception point;
(g) Helicopter deck and facilities for maintenance and refuelling;
(h) Accommodation for up to 90 persons of mixed gender to UK Flag merchant standards;
(i) Ship life of 25 years;
(j) Fully OCIMF compliant;
(k) Classification to LR Naval Ship Rules with Naval Ship Auxiliary notation (noting structure will be to the new Common Structural Rules with some enhancements); and
(l) Medium speed diesel propulsion operating on MGO fuel.

Note: Based on specifications issued as part of DE&S MARS IPT (August 2007) and published at <navy-matters.beedall.com>

tanker' was made the subject of an 'Invitation to Participate in Dialogue', based on a number of requirements listed in 'Concept of Operation of MARS Ships'.

The MoD issued its 'Invitation to Participate in Dialogue' to industry for up to six fleet tankers at an expected cost of £800 million in December 2007 and on 21 May 2008, they announced that four companies have been short listed – Fincantieri (Italy), Hyundai (Republic of Korea), Navantia (Spain) and BAE Systems with BMT DSL and DSME (Republic of Korea). Their proposals were to be tested for value for money and the MoD expected to select one of the companies to design and build the new ships in early 2009. None of the bidders intend to build the fleet tankers in the UK.

Unfortunately, all this is now so much waste paper, because, on 11 December, 2008, the Defence Secretary, John Hutton announced that: 'there was scope for alternative approaches … which is likely to result in the deferral of the fleet tanker element of the project'. Just what those 'alternative approaches' will be is, as yet, unclear.

Several other projects have been discussed alongside MARS, although, to date, none have passed the drawing board or committee stage. These include:

A joint casualty treatment ship (JCTS)

Originally designed as a better replacement for hospital ships, a JCTS was intended not to be subject to Red Cross provision and would thus have been able to operate forward in a combat area and recycle wounded personnel. These new ships were intended to be very well equipped, their specification including 150 beds, four operating theatres, a laboratory and X-ray, CT scan, ultrasound and intensive care facilities.

Unfortunately, the project was cancelled in 2005, the ship's intended role being partially taken over by *Argus*. *Argus* was refitted in 2001 to improve her permanent medical facilitates and allow her to be quickly tasked as a one-hundred-bed primary casualty receiving ship (PCRS)/emergency hospital with out further dockyard work.

Further modifications to her medical facilities were begun in January 2009 as part of a £23 million refit. The work is to be carried out by A & P Group's Falmouth facility under the RFA support contract awarded to this company in 2008.

Aviation support ship (ASS)

Proposed after the salutary experiences with helicopter forward support, or rather lack of it, during Operation 'Iraq Freedom'. Funding was unavailable and this role will be filled by an updated *Argus* until 2020, when the forward aviation role will be taken over by units of the planned MARS project, which will have extensive aviation facilities. However, what these will consist of exactly has not been made clear yet.

Operational maintenance and repair ship (OMAR)

Due 2014 to replace *Diligence*. No tender has been approved as yet.

Begun as a miscellaneous collection of partly converted freighting tankers and cargo tramps, the transition to a high tech, immensely versatile RFA fleet fit for the challenges of the twenty-first century was clearly marked by the introduction of the early Tide class, which ushered in the new era of purpose-built RAS capable ships. Development of the Service in terms of its personnel, however, is nowhere near as clear cut.

Even as late as the eve of the Falklands War, in April 1982, personnel contracts were neither mandatory nor universal and most of the crews were still signed on from the Merchant Navy pool, often for a single voyage. As a consequence of this, training was a hit and miss affair largely conducted on a piecemeal basis by the relevant ship with an occasional place allocated for RFA personnel at one of the naval training schools. Seen as an integrated, operational Service, the RFA still lacked continuity and a well organised personnel and training structure, although it still did its job very well.

With the Argentine surrender in Port Stanley, however, an immense period of reorganisation and change began. This resulted in the emergence of an RFA finally commanded and run throughout entirely by RFA personnel, with fully contracted crews aboard the ships specifically trained for the job they had to do.

With its internal reorganisation completed, the RFA is now a Service in its own right. Most of its Merchant Navy ties are cut and it is led by seamen who know their job from bridge to RAS deck.

Commodore R C Thornton, the retiring COMRFA, has offered his own personal overview of the RFA, as he approached the end of his own term as Commodore in September 2008:

If you ask the Head of Service to write an article describing the state of the RFA as it is today, you ought not to be surprised if that view is subjective and biased towards an upbeat evaluation. After all, as I approach the end of my term and move into retirement, adverse comment might reflect on my ability and performance and who in their right mind would admit to being less than perfect? So I will do my best to offer an objective and balanced view of the RFA of today, both the good and the bad, because in my opinion, this will be of greater value to the informed reader.

As I write, we have just passed our 103rd birthday and been honoured to receive our own Queen's Colour, presented on behalf of Her Majesty the Queen, by our Commodore-in-Chief, His Royal Highness the Earl of Wessex at a ceremony on board *Largs Bay* in Portsmouth. It was a great day and confirmed the position of the RFA as part of the wider Naval Service, yet most certainly reinforced our very special identity. The RFA Association was present to witness, support and participate in the event and demonstrated their relationship to the RFA Service. The Association is growing steadily and also enjoys Royal patronage.

Also present on that day were representatives of the Carmen, the Fuellers and the Master Mariners, the three City of London Livery Companies who have one or more ships affiliated to them. We hosted the Mayors of Cities and Boroughs who also share special links with our ships and of course several Lady Sponsors. I point this out because I see this as a significant rise in our profile and representative of a wider engagement with many influential people. Our principal contractors were also present, demonstrating a longer-term stable relationship with them for our ship repair and support services. It would be remiss of me not to point out the recent amalgamation of the RFA support team and the procurement team under the leadership of Commodore(E), this is a very significant step forward for us as a Service and puts us in the van of change in that area. All were present or represented.

Of course, the area closest to my heart is that of the people of the RFA. The Commander-in-Chief commented very favourably on the spirit of the people and noted a real 'spring in their step and a smile on their faces'. This was immensely pleasing for me as the performance and potential of the people of the RFA is not wanting. We have taken significant steps forward with initial and career training as we rise to the challenges of higher tempo and greater military expectation. Recruiting is now managed under Captain Naval Recruiting and gives us access to a much bigger pool of people. All officers (direct entry, cadet or rating to officer) must now pass the Admiralty Interview Board before attendance at a bespoke course at BRNC Dartmouth. Ratings have bespoke and fully accredited initial training courses at *Raleigh* (for Seamen, Chefs, Stewards and Stores Accountants) at *Collingwood* for our Communicators and most recently, *Sultan* for Engineers including the rating apprentice scheme. The standards are rising and will ensure that we are well fitted for the job we have to do.

I have reservations about some of what I describe as baggage in our terms and conditions, born of history. Some of this baggage is good and some is not and we must address the bad and get rid of it if we are to remain agile and therefore versatile. Strategic development work is currently being conducted within Project Darwin where the RFA Continuous Improvement Team seeks to address such issues.

The short-term pressures of successive planning rounds I feel are corrosive and tend to hinder the efficient development of the whole. That said, with only 16 ships and 2300 people, we punch well above our weight and are currently deployed in the Caribbean, the South Atlantic, Indian Ocean, Arabian Gulf, Mediterranean, Black Sea and, of course, European waters closer to home. We have an enviable record of availability and delivery and rise to most of the challenges that any Navy faces in the post cold-war era. Asymmetric threats are what we wrestle with in the choke points of the world and this means we must manage a whole new range of weapons and tactics to counter them. The demands upon our people are unrelenting and it is such pressures that have required me to pursue Sponsored Reserve Status for the personnel of the RFA. There are still doubters out there, but all new entrants are required to volunteer and we are now over the 55% mark.

Our new capabilities, including people, were all on display as we received the Queen's Colour that is now displayed alongside that of the Royal Navy and the Royal Naval Reserve here in Navy HQ on Whale Island.

In summary, the RFA of today is in good shape despite a challenging operational and resource climate. Future potential is excellent but as always we must rise to the challenges and hang on tight to our particular identity as we line up the processes of the RN and the RFA. If we do this, I can safely say that we are and will remain, a 'World Leader in Versatile, Valued and Integrated Afloat Support'.

It is this that has been recognised with the presentation of our very first Queen's Colour.

RFA fleet list April 2009

Helicopter training and casualty receiving ship
Argus
Forward repair and heavy lift ship
Diligence
Bay class
Cardigan Bay, Largs Bay, Lyme Bay, Mounts Bay
Old Fort class
Fort Austin, Fort Rosalie (ex *Fort Grange*)
New Fort class
Fort George, Fort Victoria
Wave Class
Wave Knight, Wave Ruler
Rover Class
Black Rover, Gold Rover
Leaf Class
Bayleaf, Orangeleaf

Total: 16 vessels crewed by 2520 personnel.

Epilogue

In this and the preceding chapters, discussion has centred on the evolution and development of the RFA in the years since 1950, in terms of both ships and personnel. There have been many changes, some good and a few perhaps not so good but, since the Second World War, it is very clear that the RFA has been forced to take a new direction, away from its Merchant Navy origins and leading towards what many have crudely termed the 'navalisation' of the Service. This last is not a process I'd care to try and quantify and even now I'm not quite sure that 'navalisation' is actually what's happened.

This was finally and unequivocally brought home to me quite soon after the publication of *No Sea Too Rough*, my book about the RFA in the Falklands, when I was offered the chance to visit one of the Service's newest ships, *Largs Bay*.

Now, I have no experience of Service life at all, but beginning with that first entry into the ward room, there was an air about that ship of brisk, self reliant efficiency. Do not get me wrong, there was no barking of orders or clicking of heels, in fact, I do not think I heard a raised voice or even an order issued in my whole time aboard, although it became abundantly clear during the subsequent tour of the big LSD(A) that the whole crew were very proud of her.

It was something quite intangible, a clear understanding between all the members of the crew, from the captain down, that everyone knew their job and could be quite safely left to get on with it, without interference or unnecessary supervision. This crew knew they could handle anything that was thrown at them because their skill and trust in each other, and in their ship, would see them through.

Looking back, it is plain that, whatever has changed about the Service, and we all must accept that much has, 'navalisation' is too simplistic a concept to apply to it.

Yes, certainly, there is more discipline, ships are more complex, standards of recruits and training has improved out of all recognition, contracts are universal. But, even with all that, the men and women of the RFA still stand apart, the demands of their job emphasising a need for self discipline and self reliance, quite different from the other services' more regimented approach.

They are not and never will be simply naval officers and ratings in a different uniform, however close co-operation between the services may be. The job they do makes them different and most seem to take a fierce and considerable pride in that difference.

They are the 'Grey Funnel Line'.
The Royal Navy's totally reliable, one-stop, supermarket, still:
Ready For Anything.

Ship Data Tables

Wave Class (1)

Tonnage: 8141–8199 gross, 4545–4664 net, 11,600–11,955 deadweight, 16,650 full load displacement as designed
Length: 492ft 8in
Beam: 64ft 4in
Draught: 28ft 6in
Depth: 35ft 6in
Machinery: 2 × geared steam turbines, 6800shp, water tube boilers, single shaft
Speed: 14.5–15 knots
Complement: 60 RFA

These were standard Ministry of War Transport 12,000 ton tankers, many originally given 'Empire' name prefixes by the original owners, Ministry of War Transport, although these were eventually taken over as Wave class ships and out of a class of twenty-one, the Admiralty took all but one. *Wave King*, *Wave Emperor*, *Wave Governor* and *Wave Monarch* were ready in time to serve with the British Pacific Fleet, and the rest were managed commercially until they were accepted into the RFA.

Eight of the class were modified as fast fleet tankers, with the rest being used as freighting tankers with some replenishment capability. The ships in this class differed from one another in some respects – Wave Baron, *Wave Chief*, *Wave Commander*, *Wave Conqueror*, *Wave Duke* and *Wave Laird* all had Metrovick geared turbines; the rest had Parsons geared turbines. *Wave Liberator* had a slightly different bridge to the other ships in the class. These were not really satisfactory ships and the various lessons learned were taken into consideration in the early Tide class. The cargo capacity was approximately 8,000 tons of FFO, 750 tons of diesel and 950 tons of aviation fuel, although the Waves could also carry fresh water and had a limited stores capability.

Name	Builder	Laid down	Launched	Completed
Wave Victor (A220)	Furness	16.11.42	30.9.43	2.44
Wave Master (A193)	Laing	1943	25.5.44	12.44
Wave Knight (A249)	Laing	–	22.10.45	5.46
Wave Prince (A207)	Laing	1945	27.7.45	3.46
Wave Sovereign (A211)	Furness	10.5.44	20.11.45	2.46
Wave Baron (A242)	Furness	1.9.44	19.2.46	6.46
Wave Chief (A265)	Harland & Wolff	–	4.4.46	27.8.46
Wave Ruler (A212)	Furness	27.10.44	17.1.46	4.46
Wave Commander (A244)	Furness	1.4.43	21.4.44	8.44
Wave Conqueror (A245)	Furness	16.12.42	27.11.43	3.44
Wave Duke (A246)	Laing	–	16.11.44	4.45
Wave Emperor (A100)	Furness	15.9.43	16.10.44	20.12.44
Wave King (A182)	Harland & Wolff	23.3.43	6.4.44	21.7.44
Wave Liberator (A248)	Furness	1.3.43	9.2.44	6.44
Wave Monarch (A108)	Harland & Wolff	17.6.43	6.7.44	3.11.44
Wave Protector (A215)	Furness	15.6.43	20.7.44	10.44
Wave Governor (A247)	Furness	30.11.43	30.11.44	8.3.45
Wave Regent (A210)	Furness	28.4.44	29.3.45	31.5.45
Wave Laird (A119)	Laing	1945	3.4.46	9.46
Wave Premier (A129)	Furness	6.7.45	27.6.46	12.46

The following ships were modified to perform Fast Fleet Replenishment duties:

Wave Baron was managed by Gow, Harrison and Co Ltd, Glasgow, on behalf of the Ministry of War Transport, while building as *Empire Flodden*, under which name she was launched. She was modernised in refit during 1961–2, and had a further refit, at Swansea, in 1966. *Wave Baron* was laid up at Devonport in December 1969 and was for sale at Plymouth in February 1972. She was sold to a Dutch trading house with the intention of scrapping and resold to Spanish breakers. She arrived at Bilbao on 23 April 1972 for breaking up.

Wave Chief was launched as *Empire Edgehill*. She was completed for the RFA and commissioned on 30 August 1946. She had a varied career. She ran aground in the Johore Strait and suffered bottom damage, and served in the Korean War, for which she won a Battle Honour. She served in the first Cod War with Iceland during 1958–61. This was the only vessel of the class with a complete foremast and topmast. *Wave Chief* was extensively modernised in the early 1960s and escorted Sir Alec Rose around Cape Horn in his yacht in April 1968. Taken out of service in August 1974 and laid up at Rosyth, *Wave Chief* arrived at Inverkeithing on 13 November 1974 to be broken up.

Wave Knight was managed in the early part of her career by Tankers Ltd, an associate company of Athel Line Ltd, and entered RFA service in May 1946. She served in the Korean War and in the first Cod War. Laid up at Plymouth, she was sold to Belgian breakers and arrived at Willebroek in tow on 19 October 1964 to be broken up.

Wave Master was managed by Eagle Oil & Shipping Co Ltd as *Empire Salisbury* until she was accepted into the RFA in 1946. She was commissioned in December 1946. Taken out of service on 23 September 1962 and laid up at Singapore, she was sold in April 1963 to be broken up at Jurong, where she arrived in tow the following month.

Wave Prince was managed by Athel Line Ltd as *Empire Herald* until she was accepted into the RFA Fleet. She was commissioned on 12 February 1947. This ship refitted and modernised in 1961–2 and was part of the fleet that visited Stockholm for the British Trade Fair that year. She acted as escort oiler for the Royal Yacht during the Queen's visit to Australia. *Wave Prince* arrived at Plymouth in April 1966 and was laid up; she was for sale in May 1971. She left Plymouth in tow on 5 December 1971 and arrived at Burriana on 16 December for scrapping.

Wave Ruler was managed by Eagle Oil & Shipping Co Ltd upon completion as *Empire Evesham*. She was present at the Christmas Island nuclear tests, having left Rosyth on 22 December 1956 and arriving at Christmas Island on 1 February 1957. During that voyage she had boiler trouble. She was also in active service during the first Cod War. The ship relieved *Wave Victor* as Air Ministry fuel hulk at Gan Island in October 1970. *Wave Ruler* was sold in January 1976 'as lies' for scrapping and towed to Singapore. However, at the end of December 1976 she was lying off Johore, Malaysia, and in the following year was towed to Taiwan for breaking up.

Wave Sovereign, which was ordered on 29 May 1943, was commissioned with the RFA on 28 February 1946. She was present at the Christmas Island nuclear tests and supported Royal Navy ships during the first Cod War. She was taken out of service in 1966 at Singapore and sold in June 1967 for breaking up locally.

Wave Victor was under management of Anglo-Saxon Petroleum Co Ltd as *Empire Bounty* upon completion, and was taken into RFA service in 1946. On 17 January 1954, bound Swansea, *Wave Victor* had a fire in the engine room and drifted out of control. Several tugs and lifeboats and the corvette HMS *Carisbrooke Castle* went to her aid, but by the time these vessels arrived the fire was well alight and out of control. The crew abandoned ship because of risk of explosion in the bunkers and the vessel continued drifting. Later several crew members and a fire-fighting team reboarded her and brought the fire under control. She was towed back to Swansea, and then to Wallsend for repairs. She provided support during the first Cod War and was Air Ministry fuel hulk at Gan from 1960 (left Falmouth 2 March, arrived Gan 30 March) to 1971, when she was replaced by *Wave Ruler*. She was towed to Singapore for scrapping, but in March 1975 was reported as a hulk at Manila Bay in March 1975. She was scrapped in 1981.

The following ships of the class were used mainly as freighting tankers, although these did have some RAS capability:

Wave Commander was managed by the Athel Line Ltd, London, upon completion as *Empire Paladin*, and in 1946 was taken into RFA service as *Wave Commander*. Apart from a collision in the Strait of Gibraltar in 1954, *Wave Commander* had a relatively uneventful career, and was for sale at Devonport, where she had arrived on 22 October 1958. She arrived at Inverkeithing in tow on 9 May 1959 for breaking up by Thomas W Ward Ltd.

Wave Conqueror, completed as *Empire Law*, was placed under the management of Anglo-Saxon Petroleum Co Ltd, London, and entered RFA service in 1946 as *Wave Conqueror*. She arrived at Sheerness on 31 December 1957 and was laid up and was sold to H G Pounds, Portsmouth in 1958. *Wave Conqueror* became a fuel hulk at Le Havre in 1959 and was broken up at La Spezia, where she arrived in tow on 23 April 1960.

Wave Duke was under the management of British Tanker Co Ltd upon completion as *Empire Mars*. On 10 January 1946 she was sold to the Admiralty and from that date until 27 January 1948 the manager was Hadley Shipping Co Ltd under her new name *Wave Duke*. She was taken into service into RFA service on 16 November 1946. On 25 March 1957, Wave Duke left Houston for the UK with a full cargo of oil and struck a submerged wreck in the Houston Channel and sustained damage. She was still in the Channel two weeks later and had transshipped cargo to the tanker Derwentdale. On 30 April 1960 she was taken out of service and laid up at Devonport. *Wave Duke* was for sale at Plymouth in October 1969. She left Plymouth in tow and arrived at Bilbao on 25 December 1969 for scrapping and work began the following month.

Wave Emperor, which was ordered on 3 February 1943, served with the British Pacific Fleet Train during the Second World War, and for which she had the pendant number B523. In 1959, she was for sale 'as lies' at Portland. *Wave Emperor* was sold to BISCO and arrived at Barrow-in-Furness on 19 June 1960 for breaking up by Thomas W Ward Ltd.

Wave Governor served with the British Pacific Fleet Train during the Second World War, under the pendant number B524. On 30 April 1959 she arrived at Rosyth, was taken out of service and laid up. On 9 August 1960, she was moved to the local scrapyard of Shipbreaking Industries Ltd.

Wave King was the first of the class acquired by the Admiralty, having been under construction as *Empire Sheba*. She was taken into service the day following completion. *Wave King* served with the British Pacific Fleet Train under the pendant number B525, and on 9 August 1956 she sustained serious damage when she struck a rock when on voyage from Rio de Janeiro to Belem. She returned to the UK and was docked at South Shields. *Wave King* was taken out of service in 1956 and laid up at Portsmouth, and was sold in March 1960 to H G Pounds, Portsmouth, and was resold to BISCO for breaking up by Thomas W Ward Ltd, Barrow-in-Furness, where she arrived in tow on 16 April 1960.

Wave Laird was launched as *Empire Dunbar* and was completed in September 1946 for RFA service. She was supply ship to HMS *Protector* in the Antarctic and the Falkland Islands, and was a support ship in the first Cod War. *Wave Laird* arrived at Plymouth on 19 October 1960, was taken out of service 1961, and after a long lay-up at Plymouth, where she was for sale in October 1969, she was sold to Spanish breakers and arrived at Gandia in February 1970.

Wave Liberator was managed by British Tanker Co Ltd, London, on completion as *Empire Milner*. On 10 January 1946 she was sold to the Admiralty and from that date until 10 January 1948 the manager was Hadley Shipping Co Ltd under her new name *Wave Liberator*. She entered RFA service later in 1946. *Wave Liberator* was at Bombay at the end of 1958 for sale 'as lies' with unrepaired collision damage. She was sold to Hong Kong Towing and Salvage Co, and left Bombay in tow on 5 April 1959 and arrived at Hong Kong on 4 May for scrapping.

Wave Monarch was laid down as *Empire Venus*, but completed for the RFA. She served with the British Pacific Fleet Train during the latter part of the Second World War, under the pennant number B526. She was sold in March 1960 to H G Pounds, Portsmouth, and became a oil hulk at Le Havre, replacing *Wave Conqueror*. She changed hands again in 1960 and passed to Société Mirolene, was renamed *Noema*, and continued as a storage hulk. She arrived at Bilbao on 8 April 1964 for breaking up.

Wave Premier, which was laid down as *Empire Marston*, but not launched as such, had a typical career with the RFA. On 9 June 1959 she arrived at Rosyth, was taken out of service, and laid up. She was sold less than one year later to British Iron & Steel Corp (BISCO), and on 11 June moved to the Shipbreaking Industries Ltd scrapyard at Rosyth.

Wave Protector was managed by Anglo-Saxon Petroleum Co Ltd upon completion as *Empire Protector*, entering RFA service in 1946. She replaced *War Hindoo* as oiling store hulk at Grand Harbour, Malta, in March 1958. *Wave Protector* was for sale at Malta 'as lies' and was sold for scrap to Italian interests. She arrived at Le Grazie in August 1963.

Wave Regent had a normal and uneventful RFA career. She arrived at Devonport on 3 May 1959 to be laid up, and arrived at Faslane on 29 June 1960 for breaking up.

Fort Class (1)

Tonnage: 7201–7332 gross, 3771–4184 net; *Fort Rosalie, Fort Sandusky* 6391 deadweight, rest 7720–9520 deadweight, 9790 displacement
Length overall: *Fort Beauharnois, Fort Duquesne* 439ft 2in; others 441ft 6in
Beam: 57ft 2in
Draught: 26ft 11in–27ft
Machinery: Triple expansion engine, 2500ihp, single shaft
Speed: 10–11 knots
Range: 11,000nm / 10 knots
Complement: 115

This class of ship was built in Canada as part of the Emergency War Tonnage programme; they differed from the US Liberty ships in that they were of a riveted construction, whereas the Liberty ships were all welded.

The ships in this class were all managed by commercial interests on behalf of the Ministry of War Transport during the Second World War and for a time afterwards until they were transferred to the RFA. There were three types of these ships – the North Sands type conformed to the original design supplied to Canada by J L Thompson & Sons, Sunderland. Designed as coal burners, they had three Scotch boilers and were shelter-deck type ships. The Victory type was also of shelter deck design, although these had two water tube boilers and burned oil, thereby reducing costs and crew. The Canadian type was designed to burn either coal or oil, and had Scotch boilers fitted. Of these designs *Fort Duquesne, Fort Langley, Fort Beauharnois, Fort Charlotte, Fort Constantine* and *Fort Dunvegan* were Victory types, and *Fort Rosalie* and *Fort Sandusky* were Canadian type. Named after Canadian forts, the style of naming has been carried on with more recent RFA vessels.

Name	Builder	Laid down	Launched	Completed
Fort Beauharnois (A285)	West Coast	–	29.10.44	10.44
Fort Charlotte (A236)	West Coast	–	5.4.44	4.44
Fort Constantine (A237)	Burrard	–	11.3.44	25.4.44
Fort Dunvegan (A160)	Burrard	–	28.2.44	14.4.44
Fort Duquesne (A229)	West Coast	–	28.9.44	25.11.44
Fort Langley (A230)	Victoria	–	31.10.44	18.5.45
Fort Rosalie (A186)	United	29.8.44	18.11.44	7.7.45
Fort Sandusky (A316)	United	11.9.44	25.11.44	1.8.45

Fort Beauharnois was launched as *Fort Grand Rapids*, completed as *Cornish Park*, and was renamed *Fort Beauharnois* in May 1945. Upon completion she was managed by Alfred Holt & Co, Liverpool, for Ministry of War Transport. She joined the RFA fleet in 1950. She was a stores issuing ship employed on the Chatham–Gibraltar–Malta run. She was present at the Christmas Island nuclear tests in 1957 and was employed freighting between the UK and the Far East during 1960–2. In 1959, she arrived at Leith on 22 January for refit, and while at the shipyard there was a fire on board. In 1962 she was offered for sale 'as lies' Malta, and on 8 November 1962 arrived at Spezia for breaking up.

Fort Charlotte was launched as *Buffalo Park*, and was renamed in 1945. She was managed by Eastern & Australian Steam Ship Co Ltd, London, for the Ministry of War Transport. She was a stores issuing ship that joined the RFA fleet on 11 June 1948, was involved in the Korean War and was also present at the Christmas Island nuclear tests in 1957. Employed on the UK–Malta run from 1960, she was then transferred to Hong Kong, where she was taken out of service in 1967 at Singapore. She was sold to local breakers in January 1968.

Fort Constantine was completed as a stores issuing ship, air, and intended to operate with aircraft carriers and forward air bases in the Pacific. In addition to her merchant navy crew, she carried a unit from the Admiralty Victualling Division. She was managed by Ellerman & Bucknall Steamship Co, London, for Ministry of War Transport upon delivery. By 1948 management was in the hands of W H Seager & Co, Cardiff. Acquired by the Admiralty in 1948, *Fort Constantine* started her RFA career on the Mediterranean–Far East freighting run. She was present at the Christmas Island nuclear tests. She was then employed between Chatham, Gibraltar and Malta. She was laid up at Plymouth in 1965. The ship was sold to German interests in September 1969 and broken up at Hamburg, where she arrived on 24 October.

Fort Dunvegan was originally managed by Ellerman & Bucknall Steamship Co Ltd on behalf of Ministry of War Transport. She was a latecomer to the RFA fleet, which she joined on 19 March 1951. She was another stores issuing ship and was first employed on freighting runs from the UK to Malta. She was the first RFA ship to fly a commodore's burgee and was transferred to the Far East in 1960, remaining there until 1968, when she was taken out of service. *Fort Dunvegan* was broken up at Kaohsiung later that year.

Fort Duquesne was launched as *Queensborough Park* and completed as *Fort Duquesne* under the management of Alfred Holt & Co, Liverpool, on behalf of Ministry of War Transport. She was the final member of the stores issuing fleet. She joined the RFA on 16 September 1947 and was attached to the Mediterranean fleet. She had a special flight deck fitted in 1951 and was used for VERTREP trials with Royal Navy Dragonfly helicopters. The ship took part in the Suez Operations in 1956. *Fort Duquesne* was taken out of service in April 1967 at Chatham, and sold for breaking up at Tamise, Belgium, where she arrived on 29 June.

Fort Langley was launched as *Montebello Park* and completed as *Fort Langley* under the management of Alfred Holt & Co, Liverpool, on behalf of Ministry of War Transport. Management was transferred to G Nisbet & Co, Glasgow, in 1948, and this arrangement continued for a few years. She entered service with the RFA as an armament stores ship in May 1954, and later was fitted with a small helicopter landing platform aft. *Fort Langley* was taken out of service in February 1970 at Plymouth and officially returned to the Canadian government. She was then sold to Marine Salvage Co Ltd, of Port Colbourne, Ontario, and resold for breaking up at Bilbao, where she arrived on 21 July.

Fort Rosalie was the first of the class allocated to the Admiralty and completed to their requirements; she was one of the ships in the Pacific Fleet Train, operated under the management of Ellerman Lines as an MFA. The ship was acquired by the RFA on 20 November 1947 and was converted to an armaments store ship at Portsmouth in 1958. She served on the Far East Station during 1949–51, and made several voyages to Australia and South Africa, where she loaded ammunition stored in both countries during the war. The ship was present at the Christmas Island nuclear tests in 1957, having arrived at Christmas Island on 10 April from Portsmouth. She was fitted with cargo lifts during 1959–60. Taken out of service on 1 May 1972, and laid up at Rosyth, *Fort Rosalie* was, together with *Fort Sandusky*, returned officially to the Canadian government. Both were sold to Spanish breakers and left Rosyth in tow on 24 January 1973 to and arrived at Castellon on 10 February to be broken up.

Fort Sandusky was managed by Ellerman Lines, London, for the Ministry of War Transport following delivery in August 1945, and management was transferred to W H Seager & Co, Cardiff in 1948. The ship was acquired by the RFA on 13 January 1949, converted to an armament store ship and assigned to the Far East Station, from where she made voyages to Australia and South Africa with her sister *Fort Rosalie* to return ammunition stored in these countries from the war. The ship took part in operations during the Suez crisis of 1956 and was finally laid up at Rosyth following decommissioning on 13 February 1972. Together with *Fort Rosalie*, *Fort Sandusky* was returned to the Canadian government. Both were sold to Spanish breakers and left Rosyth in tow on 24 January 1973 and arrived at Castellon on 10 February to be broken up.

Fleet Oiler *Olna*

Tonnages: 12,660 gross, 7412 net, 17,500 deadweight, 17,000 displacement
Length overall: 583ft 5in
Beam: 70ft 2in
Draught: 31ft 8in
Depth: 40ft 6in

Machinery: 2 × BTH steam turbines, 11,000shp, driving two generators 4200kW/3000V ac, connected to electric motor, single shaft
Speed: 16.5 knots
Complement: 77 RFA, 183 RN

This tanker was under construction, together with a sistership, for Anglo-Saxon Petroleum Co Ltd, London. Both were acquired by the Admiralty for RFA operation, but the later vessel was returned to her original owner. *Olna* was originally commissioned as HMS *Olna*, with a Devonport crew and a Lieutenant Commander RNR in command.

Name	Builder	Laid down	Launched	Completed
Olna (A216)	Swan Hunter	–	28.12.44	8.5.45

Olna was originally built as *Hyalina* for Anglo-Saxon Petroleum Co Ltd, London (Shell), and was the first of two sisterships that were of turbo-electric drive. She was commissioned into the RFA as *Olna* on 20 March. 1946 was not a good year for *Olna* – on 13 May, she caused damage to the Commission Quay, North Shields, while berthing, and on 29 August she ran aground in the river at Abadan. She was refloated four days later. She took part in the Coronation fleet review on 15 June 1953, she was involved in Operation 'Musketeer', the Suez crisis campaign, in 1956, and in 1957 was in Operation 'Grapple', the nuclear bomb tests. *Olna* was sold in December 1966 for breaking up, left Plymouth in tow on 6 January 1967 and arrived at Castellon, Spain, on 19 January for scrapping.

Her sistership, intended name *Oleander*, planned as Anglo-Saxon's *Helicina* was taken over by the Admiralty while under construction, but after hostilities ceased, she was returned to Anglo-Saxon and assumed her original name.

Eddy Class

Tonnages: 2156–2224 gross; 841–901 net; 2193–2286 deadweight; 4165 tons full load displacement
Length overall: 286ft 5in–287ft 8in
Beam: 44ft 1in–46ft 4in
Draught: 17ft 3in
Machinery: 3-cylinder triple-expansion engine (Lobnitz made the engines for all of this class), 1750ihp; two scotch boilers, single shaft
Speed: 12 knots
Complement: 38

Designed as coastal and harbour tankers, even as they were building, their function as station oilers was rapidly becoming obsolete with the advances made in replenishment at sea. They were a piece of misplanning. There were eight ships in the class, although another two were cancelled in 1953. Those that did enter service, with one exception, had relatively short careers for RFA vessels.

Name	Builder	Launched	In service
Eddybay (A107)	Caledon	29.11.51	29.11.52
Eddybeach (A132)	Caledon	24.4.51	8.12.51
Eddycliff (A190)	Blythswood	25.8.52	10.2.53
Eddycreek (A258)	Lobnitz	19.1.53	11.9.53
Eddyfirth (A261)	Lobnitz	10.9.53	25.4.54
Eddyness (A295)	Blyth	22.10.53	11.10.54
Eddyreef (A202)	Caledon	28.5.53	23.10.53
Eddyrock (A198)	Blyth	16.12.52	7.6.53
Eddycove (A205)	Ordered 1951, cancelled 1953		
Eddymull (A287)	Ordered 1951, cancelled 1953		

Eddybay was laid down on 23 March 1951. She was based in the Mediterranean, mainly on Gibraltar where she was employed as a white oils carrier. In the last years of her life, she was loaned to the RAF as a petrol carrier and as a semi-hulk at Gibraltar. She left Gibraltar on 26 August 1963 in tow for Portsmouth, where she arrived on 10 September. She taken out of service on 9 November 1962. *Eddybay* was sold at first to Pounds Shipowners & Shipbreakers Ltd, Portsmouth, and resold to Belgian breakers. On 29 August 1964, she arrived at Antwerp en route for Willebroek for scrapping.

Eddybeach was laid down on 20 March 1950. She was based in the Mediterranean, mainly at Gibraltar for much of her career, and acted as a water carrier during times of severe shortage there. She was taken out of service on 27 May 1962 at Devonport, and sold to Greek interests in 1963. The ship was converted to a fish factory vessel and renamed *Mykinai*, at first under Greek flag and later Argentinian. On 7 October 1974, the vessel sank alongside a quay after a bomb exploded in her engine room. She was raised in November, laid up unrepaired, and sank again, at moorings, on 2 September 1979.

Eddycliff spent the majority of her career at Malta as the station tanker. Taken out of service in August 1963 at Devonport, she was sold in 1966 at Malta to Greek interests, converted to a fish factory vessel, and renamed *Knossos*. She was sold to Argentinian interests in 1986. Since then she seems to have slipped off the radar.

Eddycreek was based for most of her career at Hong Kong supporting the Far East Fleet. Taken out of service on 25 July 1960 at Devonport, she was sold in November 1963 to Paul R Abela, of Surrey, and while still under British flag but with Italian crew, ran aground off Capraia Island during a gale on Christmas Day 1963 when on voyage from Naples to Genoa. She was refloated in damaged condition and sold to breakers at Leghorn in February 1964.

Eddyfirth, laid down on 28 April 1952 and delivered on 10 February 1954, was, in the later part of her career, a popular sight at most of the UK naval bases. Before this, however, she spent much time in the Mediterranean based on Malta, where she supported the minesweeping flotillas. It would appear that she survived the axe because she was utilised to perform a role removed from her original station oiler role, which was latterly as a white oil carrier, collecting naval aviation turbine fuel (Avcat) from refineries and distributing it around the UK and Mediterranean as required. *Eddyfirth* was taken out of service in April 1961 and sold to Spanish breakers in January 1982. She was broken up at Seville, where work commenced on 28 March 1983.

Eddyness was based mainly in the UK on harbour and coastal freighting duties; she was laid up between from about 1961 and taken out of service on 29 January 1963. *Eddyness* was for sale at Plymouth in November 1969. She was broken up at Valencia, where she arrived on 24 February 1970.

Eddyreef does not seem to have had a remarkable career and was taken out of service in 1958 and was laid up at Devonport. She arrived in tow at Willebroek in April 1964 for breaking up.

Eddyrock was based on Singapore and supported ships of the Royal Navy there during the Indonesian crisis, especially the Inshore Squadron. Taken out of service in March 1967, she was sold on 27 June 1967 to commercial interests in Singapore and renamed *Aletta* in 1968. On 16 December 1976, she arrived at Jurong for breaking up, and work commenced on 31 March 1977.

The two other vessels in this class – *Eddycove* and *Eddymull* – were ordered in 1951 but subsequently cancelled.

Early Tide Class

Tonnages (as built): *Tide Austral* 13,165 gross; others 13,146 gross; *Tide Austral* 7171 net; others 7119 net; *Tide Austral, Tidereach*, 18,292 deadweight; others 16,913 deadweight
Displacement tons: 9040 light; 25,940 full load
Length: *Tide Austral, Tidereach* 583ft 2in; others 583ft 4in
Beam: 71ft 4in
Draught: 32ft 1in
Depth: 40ft 6in
Machinery: 2 × Pametrada steam turbines with double reduction gearing, 16,000shp, 3 × Babcock & Wilcox watertube boilers, single shaft
Speed: 17–18 knots
Armament: *Tidereach* fitted for light AA, but not fitted; *Tide Austral* fitted with 8 × 40mm AA after transfer to RAN
Complement: 90

These were Admiralty-designed fleet tankers, using lessons learned from the Wave class and other ships used in the Second World War. These ships had ice-strengthened hulls and were intended for front line support duties; they were fitted, with abeam refuelling rigs, auto-tensioning jackstay winches as well as astern refuelling capabilities.

Name	Builder	Laid down	Launched	Completed
Tide Austral (A95)	Harland & Wolff	5.8.52	1.9.54	28.5.55
Tiderace (A97)	Thompson	30.8.53	30.8.54	24.1.56
Tiderange (A98)	Laing	1.7.53	1.7.54	26.3.56
Tidereach (A96)	Swan Hunter	2.6.53	2.6.54	30.8.55

Tide Austral was built for the Royal Australian Navy but because of financial problems and manpower shortage, she was loaned to the Royal Navy upon completion. The ship was taken over by Australia on 15 August 1962 and was commissioned as HMAS *Supply* on 7 September 1962. She served with the RAN at Mururoa Atoll, Vietnam and around the Pacific area. She was rebuilt in 1974 with a number of improvements to the ship. She was finally decommissioned on 16 December 1985. In February 1987, she arrived at Kaohsiung, Taiwan, to be broken up.

Tiderace was commissioned into the RFA on 25 January 1956 and served with the fleet in a number of areas. She was renamed *Tideflow* on 28 June 1958, after confusion during the Suez crisis, when the wrong ship was ordered to return to Malta. She underwent a major refit at Smith's Dock, North Shields, where she arrived on 1 May 1963. *Tideflow* was decommissioned in November 1975 at Devonport. She left Plymouth in tow on 4 May 1976 and arrived at Bilbao, Spain, on 10 May, to be broken up.

Tiderange undertook builder's trials on 26 March 1956, and was commissioned into the RFA on 30 August. Like her two sisters, she saw service with the fleet on a variety of stations. She was renamed *Tidesurge* on 28 June 1958. Following a major refit at Swan Hunter & Wigham Richardson, she left the River Tyne for trials on 3 March 1963. The ship was decommissioned in May 1976 at Portsmouth, and was entered on the sales list at Portsmouth on 10 February 1977. She was sold quite promptly and left Portsmouth in tow on 19 April for Valencia to be broken up.

Tidereach was commissioned on 30 August 1955. She had a major refit at the Cammell Laird shipyard in Birkenhead in 1966. *Tidereach* completed her last operational RAS in March 1978 and was soon after decommissioned, destored, and laid up at Portsmouth. On 22 February 1979, she was sold to Dutch interests and resold to breakers at Bilbao. She left Portsmouth in tow on 16 March and arrived at Bilbao four days later. Breaking up commenced in August 1981.

Armament Store Issuing Ships

Tonnages (as first taken into service): *Resurgent* 9301 gross, 3781 net; *Retainer* 9511 gross, 3902 net; 8669 deadweight, 14,400 full load displacement
Length overall: 477ft 2in
Beam: 62ft 2in
Draught: 25ft 1in
Depth: 35ft
Machinery: 1 × 6-cylinder Scotts'/Doxford diesel engine, 6500bhp, single shaft
Speed: 15 knots
Aircraft: Small landing platform aft
Complement: 132 RFA, 34 naval stores staff

Ordered for the Hong Kong–Indonesia passenger and cargo service of China Navigation Co Ltd, London, these ships, formerly named *Changchow* and *Chungking*, never entered that service due to the internal warfare against the Dutch authorities in Indonesia. The ships, which originally had accommodation for forty-eight first class passengers and 576 steerage and deck passengers, were surplus to requirements before completed. Both were chartered to the French company Messageries Maritimes to run on its Marseilles–Panama–South Pacific service. Both were purchased by the Admiralty on 29 February 1952 and the charters continued under other management. In their RFA role, which lasted well over two decades, the vessels were in service mainly east of Suez.

Name	Builder	Laid down	Launched	Completed
Resurgent (A280)	Scotts'	7.6.49	31.7.50	15.2.51
Retainer (A329)	Scotts'	11.10.48	19.1.50	11.50

Resurgent (ex *Changchow*) was purchased by the Admiralty on 29 February 1952 and was managed by British India Steam Navigation Co Ltd, London, from 19 December 1952 to 1957, when she was converted for her RFA role. She entered service in July 1957 and was taken out of service on 18 August 1979. She was laid up at Rosyth. On March 18 1981, *Resurgent* was sold to Panamanian interests for resale for scrap. She left Rosyth in tow on 5 May 1981 Spain, and arrived at Aviles on 13 May, where some superstructure was remove to lighten the ship. She was then moved to Gijon, where she arrived on 15 May for scrapping.

Retainer (ex *Chungking*), was acquired by the Admiralty in 1952, and was managed by Buries Markes Ltd, London, from 25 April 1953. She was taken over for conversion for her RFA role in July 1954 and this was completed in April 1955 at the Palmers' Hebburn shipyard. Following two years of service, in September 1956 *Retainer* arrived again at the Palmers' Hebburn yard to undergo extensive overhaul, which was completed in August 1957, and which resulted in considerable increase in stores-carrying capacity. A further refit took place in 1962 at Hebburn, where she arrived on 18 May from Milford Haven. At Singapore in November 1964, she was fitted with gun platforms abreast the lift in No 1 hold. While being refitted on the Clyde, on 1 March 1971, *Retainer* was holed by the ore carrier *St Margarets*, which was being towed up river. She left Portsmouth for Rosyth in April 1978, was taken out of service, destored and laid up. In the following year, she was sold to Dutch interests and resold to Spanish breakers. *Retainer* left Rosyth in tow on 29 October 1979 and arrived at Barcelona on 19 November for scrapping.

Surf Class Tankers

Tonnages: 7742 gross, 4361 net (*Surf Patrol*), 4274 net (*Surf Pioneer*), 11,500 deadweight, 15,800 full load displacement
Length overall: 469ft 6in
Beam: 60ft 6in
Draught: 27ft 8in
Depth: 34ft 1in
Machinery: 4-cylinder Richardsons Westgarth diesel, 4400bhp (*Surf Patrol*), 4-cylinder NEME diesel, 4250bhp (*Surf Pioneer*), single shaft
Speed: 12.5 knots, 13.75 knots maximum
Complement: –

These two freighting tankers were ordered by Polish owners but were acquired on 14 July 1951 by The Admiralty while building and were intended for RFA service connected with the Korean War.

Name	Builder	Launched	In service
Surf Patrol (A357)	Bartram	7.2.51	17.7.51
Surf Pioneer (A365)	Bartram	23.4.51	28.11.51

Surf Patrol was launched at the Sunderland shipyard of Bartram & Sons Ltd as *Tatry*, and was the first to enter service in the RFA – on 7 July 1951. She was taken out of service on 11 May 1961 and spent several years in lay-up at Plymouth/Devonport before sale to commercial interests in December 1969. She went to a member company of the Chandris group and was renamed *Marisurf*. She arrived at Split on 21 July 1980 to be broken up.

Surf Pioneer, building as *Beskidy*, entered service on 28 November 1951. She was taken out of service on 13 August 1960 and laid up at Devonport. She was sold ten years later to Spanish breakers and arrived at Burriana on 28 February 1970 for scrapping.

A third tanker, which was loosely described as Surf class, was the former Korean-flagged *Yung Hao*, built at the Harima shipyard at Aioi, Japan, and completed in February 1939 for Japanese owners. She was of 10,519 tons gross, fitted with steam turbines, and originally capable of nineteen knots in service. She was seized during the Korean War, in April 1951, renamed *Surf Pilot*, taken to Singapore and laid up. She did not enter active service with the RFA but was included in the listings until March 1960, when she was broken up at Singapore.

Second Leaf Class Tankers

Tonnages:	Gross	Net	Deadweight (full load)	Displacement
Appleleaf	11,588	6559	16,900	22,980
Bayleaf	12,123	6940	17,930	–
Brambleleaf	12,123	7042	17,960	–
Cherryleaf (1953)	12,402	7338	18,560	–
Cherryleaf (1963)	14,027	7764	19,770	18,560
Orangeleaf	12,481	6949	17,475	–
Pearleaf	12,353	7051	18,045	23,900
Plumleaf	12,692	7306	18,562	24,940

Dimensions	Length oa	Beam	Draught	Depth
Appleleaf	557ft 7in	68ft	29ft 10in	38ft
Bayleaf	556ft 6in	71ft 5in	30ft 6in	39ft 3in
Brambleleaf	556ft 8in	71ft 4in	30ft 6in	39ft 3in
Cherryleaf (1953)	554ft	72ft 9in	30ft 8in	41ft 2in
Cherryleaf (1963)	556ft 5in	72ft	29ft 6in	39ft 4in
Orangeleaf	559ft 4in	72ft	30ft 6in	39ft 3in
Pearleaf	568ft	72ft	30ft	39ft
Plumleaf	562ft	72ft 1in	31ft	39ft 1in

Machinery:
Appleleaf, Bayleaf, Brambleleaf, Orangeleaf 1 × NEME/Doxford 6-cylinder diesel, 6800bhp, single shaft
Cherryleaf (1953) 1 × NEME/Doxford 6-cylinder diesel, 6600bhp, single shaft
Cherryleaf (1963) 1 × MAN 7-cylinder diesel, 8400bhp, single shaft
Pearleaf 1 × Rowan/Doxford 6-cylinder diesel, 8000bhp, single shaft
Plumleaf 1 × NEME/Doxford 6-cylinder diesel, 9500bhp, single shaft

Speeds: *Cherryleaf* (1953) 13.5 knots; *Bayleaf, Brambleleaf, Plumleaf* 14 knots; *Cherryleaf* (1963) 14.5 knots; *Orangeleaf, Pearleaf* 15 knots

In 1959–60, seven tankers were taken over on bareboat charter from commercial owners, and six were employed as freighting tankers and the exception, *Orangeleaf*, served as a replenishment tanker. An eighth tanker of this period, the later *Cherryleaf*, was added in 1973, when she also took on the same pendant number, A82, which had been allocated to her predecessor.

Name	Builder	Laid down	Launched	Completed
Appleleaf (A83)	Bartram	–	22.4.55	9.55
Bayleaf (A79)	Furness	28.9.53	28.10.54	30.3.55
Brambleleaf (A81)	Furness	26.5.52	16.4.53	8.1.54
Cherryleaf (A82)	Laing	–	28.5.53	12.53
Cherryleaf (A82)	Rheinstahl	–	16.10.62	21.2.63
Orangeleaf (A80)	Furness	27.11.53	8.2.55	6.55
Pearleaf (A77)	Blythswood	–	15.10.59	31.1.60
Plumleaf (A78)	Blyth	-	29.3.60	8.60

Appleleaf was completed as *George Lyras* by Sunderland builders Bartram & Son in September 1955 for Marine Enterprises Ltd, which was beneficially owned by London Greek company Lyras Brothers Ltd. Lyras was doubtless pleased with the opportunity to put the vessel back into service, for she had been laid up at Kiel from 10 November 1958, and operation by the RFA started on 17 April 1959. On 26 April 1963, *Appleleaf* left Old Kilpatrick for Aden, but on voyage she had engine trouble and put into Gibraltar on 3 May. In October 1967, *Appleleaf* was part of the Aden taskforce. The RFA charter ceased at the end of 1969 prior to sale of the tanker in January 1970. Under her new name, *Damon*, the vessel was in service until 1 March 1979, when she caught fire while repairing at San Pedro, Argentina. She was sold to local breakers and arrived at the scrapyard on 6 June 1980.

Bayleaf was built for London & Overseas Freighters Ltd, London, as *London Integrity*, and was taken on charter on 16 June 1959 for operation by the RFA. On 8 October 1972, while berthing in Grand Harbour, Malta, *Bayleaf* was blown close to rocks inside the breakwater when strong north-easterly winds struck. She later berthed at Palatorial Wharf and discharged her cargo. In March 1973, she reverted to her owners and her original name. She was sold 7 January 1977 for breaking up and arrived at Burriana on 25 January 1977 for scrapping.

Brambleleaf was another of the commercially owned tankers taken on bareboat charter on 22 May 1959, and left Falmouth on 28 May for Trinidad on her first RFA voyage. She was completed in 1954 as *London Loyalty* for London & Overseas Freighters Ltd. On 6 April 1963, *Brambleleaf* left Ras Tanura for Gibraltar (for orders), and soon after had engine trouble. She left Bahrain one month later to recommence her voyage to Gibraltar. She had an extensive refit at the Swan Hunter shipyards on the River Tyne in 1966. When the charter ended, in April 1972, the vessel went immediately to associates of London & Overseas and was renamed *Mayfair Loyalty* under Liberian flag. She spent the last couple of years of her life at the Italian port of Spezia. First laid up on 9 September 1974, she was sold to local breakers on 27 February 1976. Scrapping began in July 1976.

Cherryleaf was completed in 1953 as *Laurelwood* for Molasses & General Transport Co Ltd, which was managed by J I Jacobs & Co Ltd, London. Her charter commenced in 1959 and she left Cardiff on 16 May for Trinidad on her first RFA voyage as *Cherryleaf*. She served as *Cherryleaf* until she arrived at Devonport on 25 August 1965 and was laid up; she was then returned to her owners. Her further sale was swift, and without reversion to the name *Laurelwood*, the tanker was sold to Greek interests and renamed *Agios Constantinos*. She had two further changes of name – to *Aeas* in 1967 and to *Irenes Fortune* in 1972 – and was delivered to shipbreakers at Laurium, Greece, in January 1976.

Cherryleaf was completed by Rheinstahl Nordseewerke, Emden, in 1963 as *Overseas Adventurer* for London & Overseas Bulk Carriers Ltd. She was taken up on charter for operation by the RFA on 5 March 1973 and renamed. The charter ended in 1980, when the tanker reverted to her original name, for just one year, and she was sold to Saudi Arabian interests in 1981 and renamed *Petrostar XVI*. During the Iran–Iraq hostilities, she was attacked by Iranian helicopter gunships and struck by rockets about 5nm NE of Halul Island on 5 April 1986, when on voyage from Bahrain to Sharjah with 17,000 tons of fuel oil. She was on fire in the engine room and accommodation; the fire was extinguished later that day, and the tanker was towed into Sharjah on 9 April. The tanker was declared a constructive total loss and she was sold to Taiwan breakers, arriving at Kaohsiung on 24 January 1987.

Orangeleaf was built for The South Georgia Co Ltd, a subsidiary of Chr Salvesen & Co, Leith, and was completed in June 1955 as *Southern Satellite*. Her charter for operation by the RFA started on 22 May 1959, and continued until 1978, during which time she had a refit at Swansea in 1966. Of the seven Leaf class tankers taken on charter in 1959–60, this was the only one used as a replenishment tanker – the others were freighting. In July 1978, *Orangeleaf* arrived at Singapore for handing back to her owners and the tanker was sold soon after to Korean breakers at Seoul, where she arrived on 14 September.

Pearleaf was ordered by London Greek shipping firm A G Pappadakis and before launching was purchased for £1.28 million by Jacobs & Partners Ltd, London, an associate of John I Jacobs & Co Ltd. The purchase was made solely with the RFA charter in mind. She left the River Clyde on 31 January 1960 on completion of trials, during which she achieved 15.75 knots fully laden. She was at the Jubilee Review at Spithead on 28 June 1977. She served in the Falklands campaign. Her charter continued for well over two decades and ended on 9 May 1986. She was sold to Saudi Arabian interests to become the static tanker *Nejmat El Petrol XIX* and was broken up at Gadani Beach, Pakistan, in 1993.

Plumleaf was under construction for Wm Cory & Son Ltd, London, and was launched as *Corheath*. However, she did not enter service under that name because her charter was agreed before completion and she ran trials as *Plumleaf*. She served in the Falklands campaign. When the charter of *Plumleaf* ended in 1986, due to corporate changes that had taken place in the many intervening years since she started RFA service, she was now owned by Blue Funnel Bulkships Ltd, a part of the Ocean Group of Liverpool. *Plumleaf* did not revert to her original name and was sold to breakers at Kaohsiung, where she arrived on 17 December 1986.

Air Stores Support Ship *Reliant*

Tonnages: 8438 gross, 3630 net, 9290 deadweight, 13,737 full load displacement
Length overall: 468ft 10in
Beam: 61ft 6in
Draught: 26ft 3in
Depth: 39ft 9in
Machinery: 6-cylinder Hawthorn Leslie/Doxford diesel engine, 7500bhp, single shaft
Speed: 16 knots
Complement: 102–110 RFA and stores personnel

Name	Builder	Launched	Completed
Reliant (A132)	Laing	9.9.53	3.54

The stores support ship *Reliant* was built by Sir James Laing & Sons Ltd, Sunderland, as the commercially owned freighter *Somersby*, owned by Ropner Shipping Co Ltd, West Hartlepool. *Somersby* entered service as a cargo liner, mainly on Gulf of Mexico to UK service, and it had accommodation for twelve passengers. However, due to poor results, she went on to tramping from May 1956. The vessel was purchased by the Admiralty in early 1957 and arrived at Smith's Dock, North Shields, on 1 August for inspection prior to handing over. On 11 August, she became RFA *Somersby* and soon began service on freighting, and was used in connection with the destoring of Trincomalee, after the closure of that base. In February 1958, *Somersby* arrived again at Smith's Dock and underwent an extensive seven-month conversion into a stores issuing ship. *Somersby* left the Tyne on 8 September and arrived at Rosyth the following day. She was renamed *Reliant* at Rosyth on 23 September 1958. On 4 November 1958, she left Chatham for the Far East Station as the first air stores issuing ship. She could now replenish aircraft and commando carriers at sea.

Reliant returned to the UK in autumn 1960 for further conversion, and upon completion of this, she was again deployed to the Far East Station. She now had a large helicopter cargo platform built over the poop deckhouse – but had no hangar facilities – and her new refrigeration unit had a capacity of 30,300 cubic feet. *Reliant* had a further refit, at Hong Kong, in 1962. *Reliant* was destored and laid up at Rosyth in April 1973, only to be reactivated in May 1974. She was taken out of service on 7 May 1976 at Rosyth, was destored, and placed on the sales list on 28 August. She left Rosyth in tow arrived at Inverkeithing on 23 August 1977 for breaking up by Thomas W Ward Ltd.

Stores Ships *Hebe* and *Bacchus*

Tonnages: 4823 gross, 2441 net, 5425 deadweight (*Bacchus*), 5218 deadweight (*Hebe*), 8173 displacement
Length overall: 379ft 3in
Beam: 55ft 2in
Draught: 22ft
Depth: 31ft
Machinery: 5-cylinder Swan Hunter/Sulzer SRD68 diesel engine, 5500bhp, single shaft
Speed: 14–15 knots
Range: Bunkers 630 tons fuel oil, 18 tons/day maximum
Complement: 36 (accommodation for 54)

These two store ships, built by Henry Robb Ltd, Leith, were owned by British India Steam Navigation Co Ltd, London (a member of the P&O group), and were on charter for nineteen years for operation by the RFA. Due to internal changes in the P&O group, registered ownership of the vessels was changed to Peninsular & Oriental Steam Navigation Co in April 1973.

Name	Builder	Laid down	Launched	In service
Bacchus (A404)	Henry Robb	18.4.61	4.6.62	8.11.62
Hebe (A406)	Henry Robb	18.4.61	7.3.62	4.6.62

Bacchus was the third RFA ship to bear this name. She was designed to carry naval stores from the UK to overseas naval bases, and she pioneered containerisation with 'CHACONS', which were small wooden containers that were developed at Chatham Dockyard. Much of her sea time was spent on the overseas freighting run between Ceylon, Singapore and Hong Kong. Upon leaving Limassol on 29 November 1977,

Bacchus made contact with the motor vessel *Frontier* and both vessels sustained damage. *Bacchus* came off charter on 8 September 1981 and left Chatham on 1 October upon return to her owners. She was promptly sold and was renamed *Cherry Lanka* on 6 November. She was in service for another four years and arrived at Gadani Beach, Pakistan, in December 1985 for scrapping.

Hebe arrived at Malta on 9 July 1962 on completion of her first voyage from the UK. She was severely damaged by a fire, in Gibraltar on 30 November 1978. Most of the bridge and accommodation was destroyed, with one rating killed. Subsequent investigation showed the cause of the fire to be arson and a crew member was charged with arson and convicted. The RFA charter was cancelled in December and the ship was returned to her owners. *Hebe* was sold on 8 June 1979, renamed *Good Guardian*, and left Gibraltar in tow on 13 June for repairs in Greece. She arrived at Piræus on 20 June. She was renamed *Guardian* in 1981 and *Wafa* in 1987. The ship arrived at Famagusta for scrapping on 16 September 1987. The loss to the RFA of the services of *Hebe* was estimated at £1 million.

Later Tide Class

Tonnages: 14,130 gross, 7411 net, 17,400 deadweight, 27,400 displacement
Length overall: 583ft 8in
Beam: 71ft 3in
Draught: 32ft 1in
Depth: 40ft 6in
Aircraft: 3 × Westland Wessex helicopters
Machinery: 2 × Hawthorn Leslie/Pametrada geared turbines, 15,000shp, 2 × Foster Wheeler superheat boilers, single shaft
Speed: 17 knots
Complement: 110 plus embarked RN flight party

These two ships were slightly larger than the previous ships of the early Tide class, and incorporated several improvements. *Tidepool* and *Tidespring* were the first tankers constructed with a flight deck, a hangar and workshop facilities to enable them to maintain an embarked flight. There was even a swimming pool, albeit small, in front of the hangars.

Name	Builder	Ordered	Laid down	Launched	In service
Tidespring (A75)	Hawthorn Leslie	28.2.61	24.7.61	3.5.62	18.1.63
Tidepool (A76)	Hawthorn Leslie	28.2.61	4.12.61	11.12.62	28.6.63

Tidespring took part in the second and third Cod Wars and was present at the Queen's Silver Jubilee Review at Spithead on 28 June 1977. This ship held the record for the longest duration on patrol during the Beira Patrol. In 1982, the ship was one of the first in theatre during the Falklands campaign, where she assisted in the recapture of South Georgia. The ship repatriated 198 POWs to Ascension Island, before sailing south again to join the rest of the fleet. The Falklands campaign extended the life of this ship, which was due to have been scrapped under the 1981 Defence Review. *Tidespring* went on to serve a further nine years and was taken out of service on 13 December 1991. She left Portsmouth on 20 March 1992 in tow and arrived at Alang, India, on 2 July 1992 for breaking up.

Tidepool started final trials on 28 June 1963 prior to delivery. She supported ships on the Beira Patrol in the mid-1960s, and arrived at the Hebburn yard of Vickers on 9 December 1966 for refit. She supported RN ships during the 1976 Cod War and was sold to Chile in 1982, just as the Falklands War broke out. Britain asked for her return from the Chilean navy, although the ship was actually in a port in northern Chile when this request was made. Her RFA crew immediately sailed her back through the Panama Canal. She was taken out of service on 13 August 1982 and returned to Chile. She was renamed *Almirante Jorge Montt*. She was decommissioned from the Chilean navy on 15 December 1997.

Round Table Class Landing Ship Logistic (LSL)

Tonnages: *Sir Lancelot*: 6390 gross, 3315 net, 2180 deadweight; *Sir Bedivere*: 6474 gross, 3489 net, 2404 deadweight; others: 4473 gross, 2179 net, 2404 deadweight
Displacement: 6,407 tons full load
Length overall: *Sir Lancelot*: 415ft; *Sir Galahad*, *Sir Geraint*: 412ft; others: 413ft 5in

Beam: *Sir Lancelot:* 59ft 9in; *Sir Galahad, Sir Geraint:* 58ft 9in; others: 58ft 10in
Draught: *Sir Lancelot:* 12ft 10in; others: 13ft 1in
Machinery: 2 × diesel engines (*Sir Lancelot:* 12-cylinder Denny/Sulzer, 9520bhp; *Sir Bedivere:* 10-cylinder Mirrlees-Blackstone, 9400bhp; others 10-cylinder Mirrlees National, 9400bhp; two shafts, bow thruster)
Speed: 17 knots
Range: 9200nm / 15 knots
Complement: 68 RFA crew, with provision for up to 350 troops

Constructed to replace the LSTs of Second World War vintage, these ships were designed for amphibious operations in support of larger amphibious ships. This class of ship had both a bow and stern door leading directly onto the main vehicle deck, as well as having internal ramps connecting the upper and lower decks.

With shallow draft and bow thrusters, these ships were designed to be beached to facilitate disembarkation of troops and vehicles through the bow or stern door. They all had landing spots on their main vehicle deck, as well as a dedicated flight deck at the rear of the main superstructure, although there were no hangar or maintenance facilities.

Originally owned by the Ministry of Transport and at the end of the 1960s by Board of Trade Sea Transport Branch, the vessels were managed by British India Steam Navigation Co Ltd. The colour scheme was white hull with a thin blue band near the waterline, buff funnel, masts and cranes. They were taken over fully by the RFA in 1970, when they were allocated pendant numbers.

Name	Builder	Ordered	Laid down	Launched	Completed
Sir Lancelot (L3029)	Fairfield	1961	29.6.62	25.6.63	16.1.64
Sir Galahad (L3005)	Stephen	1964	22.2.65	19.4.66	17.12.66
Sir Bedivere (L3004)	Hawthorn Leslie	1964	28.10.65	20.7.66	18.5.67
Sir Tristram (L3505)	Hawthorn Leslie	1965	14.3.66	12.12.66	14.9.67
Sir Geraint (L3027)	Stephen	1964	21.2.65	26.1.67	12.7.67
Sir Percivale (L3036)	Hawthorn Leslie	1965	27.7.66	4.10.67	23.3.68

Sir Lancelot was the first ship of this type and when ordered in 1961 it was announced that her cost of construction would be £1.75 million. After a few uneventful years, *Sir Lancelot* was in collision with the Algerian motor vessel *Djurdjura* on 19 February 1977 off Calshot Pillar Buoy; extensive damage above the waterline forced her to return to Marchwood. She took part in the Falklands campaign, being hit three times by bombs while in the San Carlos anchorage, although fortunately, none of the bombs exploded. She was sold in 1989 to UK shipowners Lowline and renamed *Lowline Lancer*, and later became a floating casino based in Cape Town. In 1994, she was commissioned into the Singapore Navy as *Perseverance*. She was sold to the private naval support company Glenn Defense Marine Asia in 2003 and renamed *Glenn Braveheart*, and in 2008 was renamed briefly as *Ark*, and arrived at Chittagong on 12 March to be broken up.

Sir Galahad also took part in the Falklands campaign, and on 8 June 1982 she was bombed and badly damaged with great loss of life. She was sunk as a war grave on 25 June 1982 by HMS *Onyx*. A new ship bearing this name was launched on 25 November 1987.

Sir Bedivere was the first ship into the Stanley anchorage after the Argentine surrender. This ship undertook the Service Life Extension Programme (SLEP), in which she was extensively modified and upgraded because it was planned that she would stay in service until 2011. However, the ship was taken out of service on 18 February 2008 and in 2009 was sold to Brazil. She was refitted at Falmouth and became the Brazilian navy's *Almirante Saboia*, commissioned as such on 21 May 2009.

Sir Tristram served in the Falklands campaign, in which she was badly damaged on 8 June 1982. After the war, the ship was brought back to the UK on the heavy lift ship *Dan Lifter*. She left Port Stanley on 16 May 1983 and arrived in the River Tyne on 13 June; she was put into the water the following day. *Sir Tristram* entered dry dock at Wallsend on 10 August 1984 and was extensively rebuilt and lengthened. She was remeasured at 6824 tons gross, 2443 tons deadweight, with overall length of 442ft 8in. She remained in service until 17 December 2005. At present there are plans to use her in a training role.

Sir Geraint had an uneventful early career. She was at the Jubilee Review at Spithead on 28 June 1977, and two years later, on 21 June 1979, she was in collision with the German motor tanker *Tarpenbek* off the Isle of Wight, and *Tarpenbek* sank. There were no injuries, but *Sir Geraint*'s bow door was buckled and starboard door holed. She also took part in the Falklands campaign, although did not benefit from SLEP due to cost.

A further mishap occurred in 1988, when, in September, she ran aground during exercises off Norway. She refloated and proceeded to Aalesund for inspection. She was taken out of service on 1 May 2003, and on 19 July 2004 was towed from Portsmouth to Southampton. In July 2005, she was sold to breakers in Pakistan, briefly bearing the name *Sir G*, and arrived at Gadani Beach on 22 October 2005 to be broken up.

Sir Percivale had a quiet first twelve years of service, with some time spent in the Pacific. She took part in the Falklands campaign, during which she was involved in the supply runs to Teal Inlet, and she was the first British ship to re-enter Stanley harbour. The ship also served in the Gulf War in 1991 and twice deployed to support British operations in the Balkans. In 1996, *Sir Percivale* took part in combined exercises with Jordan, followed by Green Wader 96, the first exercise of the then newly formed Amphibious Squadron of the Joint Rapid Deployment Force. In 1997, the ship took part in the large Ocean Wave 97 deployment to the Far East and was present for the handover of Hong Kong to China. Following this, *Sir Percivale* escorted the ships of the former Hong Kong Squadron (3 Peacock class patrol vessels) to their new owners in the Philippines. During other parts of Ocean Wave, the ship took Royal Marines to Brunei, Singapore and Thailand for exercises. In 1998, *Sir Percivale* took part in practice amphibious assaults in Norway, France and Spain. In 2000, the ship was deployed to Sierra Leone to support British forces training the army of that country. Since then the ship has been involved in operations connected with Afghanistan and Iraq. The ship was to have a SLEP refit, but the refit of *Sir Bedivere* proved so costly that this plan was abandoned and new ships were procured instead. *Sir Percivale* was taken out of service on 17 August 2004 and was laid up at Marchwood.

Helicopter Support and Training Ship

Tonnages: 6384 gross, 2848 net, 4520 deadweight, 8950 full load displacement
Length overall: 424ft 1in
Beam: 58ft 5in
Draught: 22ft 1in
Depth: 35ft 4in
Machinery: 5-cylinder Wallsend/Sulzer RD68 diesel engine, 5500bhp, single shaft
Speed: 16 knots
Aircraft: Support capability for 4 × Westland Wessex, or 2 × Westland Sea King, or 2 × Westland Wasp
Complement: 63 RFA, 32 RN + 131 training

Name	Builder	Ordered	Laid down	Launched	In service
Engadine (K08)	Henry Robb	18.8.64	9.8.65	16.9.66	15.12.67

The need for *Engadine* was seen in the earlier 1960s when more and more helicopters were deployed from Royal Navy aircraft carriers and other surface warships. The ship was ordered in August 1964, from Henry Robb Ltd of Leith and was taken into service in December 1967. Her scheduled launch had been delayed by one day due to high winds. She replaced HMS *Lofoten*.

Home port for *Engadine* was Portland for the whole of its career. During the Lebanon crisis of 1976, she was deployed as part of contingency plans to evacuate British citizens. She attended the Silver Jubilee fleet review on 28 June 1977, and took part in the Falklands campaign, during which she operated as a helicopter support and refuelling base in San Carlos Water. By the mid-1980s, *Engadine* was coming to the end of her useful life, and as a replacement the containership *Contender Bezant* was purchased for conversion and became *Argus*. *Engadine* was taken out of service in March 1989 and laid up at Devonport. She was sold to owners in Greece and arrived at Piræus on 18 February 1990, where it was intended for a new service that failed to materialise and the ship was laid up. She was eventually sold to Indian shipbreakers and arrived at Alang on 7 May 1996 for scrapping.

Regent Class AEFS

Tonnages: 18,029 gross, 8040 net, 19,000 deadweight, 22,890 full load displacement
Length overall: 640ft 1in
Beam: 77ft 1in
Draught: 26ft 3in
Depth: 49ft 6in
Machinery: 2 × AEI double reduction geared turbines, 20,000shp, single shaft

Speed: 21 knots
Aircraft: 1 × Wessex HU5 helicopter
Complement: 125 RFA, plus 44 STON and embarked RN air crew

These two ships were specifically designed as Ammunition, Explosives, Food and Stores (AEFS) to operate with aircraft carriers and commando carriers and other large fleet units, to keep them supplied with missiles, bombs and other ammunition and stores. They were the only two ships in the fleet that had a permanent Royal Navy flight allocated at the time of their launch.

Name	Builder	Ordered	Laid down	Launched	Delivered
Resource (A480)	Scotts'	24.1.63	19.6.64	11.2.66	16.5.67
Regent (A486)	Harland & Wolff	24.1.63	4.9.64	9.3.66	6.6.67

Resource was part of several deployments throughout her career, serving throughout the world. She attended the Jubilee Review at Spithead on 28 June 1977. In 1982, she sailed south with the Falklands task force and was one of the first vessels to pick up survivors from HMS *Sheffield*. The ship was placed in reserve at Rosyth in 1991 and lay there until she was required to support UN and IFOR forces in the former Yugoslavia. In 1994, she returned to the UK for refit, on completion of which she returned to Split, where she remained alongside until 1997, and she was taken out of service on 1 May 1997. *Resource* was sold to Electra Marine for breaking up, and left Devonport on 24 June 1997 under the name *Resourceful* for the voyage to India, and arrived at Alang on 20 August 1997.

Regent was one of the ships that evacuated British nationals from Cyprus during the Turkish invasion period. In 1982, she was also one of the ships that took part in the Falklands War, along with her sister. She also took part in the first Gulf war, when she was attached to the *Ark Royal* group in the Mediterranean. *Regent*, together with *Resource*, and RMAS *Kinterbury* were reported at the beginning of September 1992 to have been involved in dumping suprplus munitions about 400 miles from Land's End. *Regent* was taken out of service in October 1992 and laid up at Devonport, from where she sailed on 21 January 1993 under the new name *Shahzadelal* for Alang in India, where she arrived on 19 February 1993 to be broken up.

Dale Class Tankers

(*Derwentdale, Dewdale* and *Ennerdale*)

Particulars are for *Derwentdale, Dewdale, Ennerdale*, respectively.

Tonnages:

Gross:	42,343	35,642	29,189
Net:	28,288	24,504	18,066
Deadweight:	73,375	63,588	49,209
Displacement:	88,555	67,000	62,000
Length overall:	798ft 11in	774ft 6in	710ft
Beam:	117ft 10in	107ft 10in	98ft 7in
Draught:	42ft 6in	41ft 5in	37ft 6in
Depth	55ft 4in	55ft	51ft 10in

Machinery:
Derwentdale 9-cylinder Hitachi/B&W diesel, 20,700bhp, single shaft
Dewdale 9-cylinder H&W/B&W diesel, 17,000bhp, single shaft
Ennerdale 8-cylinder Krupp/B&W diesel, 16,800bhp, single shaft

Speed:	15.5 knots	15 knots	15.5 knots
Complement:	56	51	51

These three tankers, built to varying designs, were at the time the largest vessels in the RFA fleet and were on long-term charter from 1967 to support Royal Navy and Allied fleet operations east of Suez. They were not fitted with equipment to allow them to replenish ships at sea, and were classified instead as 'mobile reserve tankers'.

Name	Builder	Launched	Completed
Derwentdale (A221)	Hitachi Zosen, Innoshima	18.1.64	4.64
Dewdale (A129)	Harland & Wolff, Belfast	5.3.65	2.7.65
Ennerdale (A213)	Kieler Howaldtswerke, Kiel	31.8.63	1963

Derwentdale was completed as *Halcyon Breeze* for Caribbean Tankers Ltd and managed by Court Line (Ship Management) Ltd, London. She commenced charter on 17 June 1967 and arrived in the River Tyne three days later for conversion by Swan Hunter (Dry Docks) Ltd to bring her up to RFA standards. The charter ended in 1975, when the vessel was sold by her owners and renamed *Alnadji*. She was in service under this name for a few years and arrived at Kaohsiung, Taiwan, on 9 May 1982 for scrapping.

Dewdale was built as *Edenfield* for Hunting (Eden) Tankers Ltd and managed by Hunting & Son Ltd, Newcastle. She arrived at Birkenhead on 14 August 1967 for conversion by Harland & Wolff to bring her up to RFA standards and was renamed *Dewdale*. She saw service with the Aden task force during the British withdrawal, and was also active on the Beira patrols. The charter lasted until September 1977, when the vessel was returned to her owners. She then resumed the name *Edenfield*. Sold fairly soon after she became *World Field*, and arrived at Kaohsiung on 6 August 1982 to be broken up.

Ennerdale was taken on charter in 1967 from Anglo-Norness Shipping Co Ltd, which was managed by Naess, Denholm & Co Ltd, London. The tanker was completed by Kieler Howaldtswerke, Kiel, in 1963 as *Naess Scotsman*. The tanker arrived at Vickers Ltd Shipbuilding Group shipyard at Hebburn in October 1967 for refit to bring her up to RFA standards and was renamed *Ennerdale*. On 1 June 1970, loaded with 41,500 tons of refined furnace oil and gasoil, some of which was destined for the frigate HMS *Andromeda*, she sank on a sandbank after striking uncharted submerged stone pinnacles and badly holing her starboard side, seven miles off Port Victoria, Mahe, Seychelles, in 04 29 36N 55 31 22E. Her eighteen British officers and forty-two seamen from the Seychelles all safely abandoned the tanker, from which there was a heavy leakage of oil. The wreck was subsequently destroyed with explosives fired from Wessex helicopters to prevent further spillage threatening the Seychelles.

Olynthus Class Fast Fleet Replenishment Tankers

Tonnages (as built): *Olwen*: 18,604 gross, 9392 net, 22,350 deadweight; *Olna*: 18,582 gross, 9367 net, 22,350 deadweight; *Olmeda*: 18,586 gross, 9380 net, 22,270 deadweight
Displacement (full load): *Olwen*: 33,773; *Olna*: 36,605; *Olmeda*: 33,240
Length overall: 648ft
Beam: 84ft 2in
Draught: 34ft
Depth: 44ft
Machinery: *Olwen*, *Olna* 2 × Hawthorn Leslie/Pametrada double reduction geared turbines; *Olmeda* 2 × Wallsend/Pametrada double reduction geared turbines 26,500shp, 2 × Babcock and Wilcox superheat boilers, single shaft, bow thruster
Speed: 21 knots
Range: 10,000nm / 16 knots
Armament: 2 × 20mm; 2 chaff launchers
Aircraft: 3 × Westland Wessex or Westland Sea King
Complement: 88 RFA, 40 RN

When launched, these ships were considered a very advanced, sophisticated design and an improvement on the slower, smaller Tide class. It was originally planned that there would be be six vessels in this class, but only three were built.

Name	Builder	Order	Laid down	Launched	In service
Olwen (A122)	Hawthorn Leslie	4.2.63	11.7.63	10.7.64	21.6.65
Olna (A123)	Hawthorn Leslie	–	2.7.64	28.7.65	1.4.66
Olmeda (A124)	Swan Hunter	4.2.63	27.8.63	19.11.64	18.10.65

Olwen was launched as *Olynthus* and she underwent builder's trials on 8 June 1965, sea trials on 15–17 June, and was delivered on 21 June. She was renamed in October 1967 to avoid confusion with the submarine HMS *Olympus*. The ship provided support for RN ships during the final Cod War. She was in attendance at the Jubilee Review at Spithead on 28 June 1977. In 1978, she ran aground on the Shambles. In refit during the Falklands campaign, she only managed to arrive after the Argentinian surrender. *Olwen* served in the 1991 Gulf conflict, and was deployed to the Adriatic in support of NATO forces in the mid 1990s. *Olwen* was taken out of service in 1999 and laid up at Portsmouth. She was sold to Eckhardt & Co, Germany, in December 2000 and resold to Turkish breakers; she left Portsmouth in tow on 2 February 2001. The voyage was not without problems – on 19 February she broke adrift in a storm off Gibraltar when her tug lost all power. A Spanish tug from Algeciras came to her aid. However, in circumstances similar to those that affected the sale of *Olna*, she was reactivated in Greece, and renamed *Kea* for the voyage to India. She arrived at Alang on 21 July 2001.

Olna spent her early life in support of various deployments, although in 1966, she did go to the aid of a ship that had sunk in the Arabian Sea. During the Falklands campaign she sailed as part of the second wave of ships and was part of the *Bristol* group. In March 1985, *Olna* was involved with HMS *Endurance* in the rescue of personnel of the services expedition to Brabant Island, off the Antarctic peninsula, and took those involved back to Port Stanley. In 1990–1, she was part of the British task force deployment to the Gulf. The ship was placed in mothballs at Gibraltar during 1999–2000, although she was reactivated in 2000 for intended operations off Sierra Leone. However, she did not go to Sierra Leone, but instead relieved other RFA ships in an exercise off Scotland. She then returned to reserve and was taken out of service on 24 September 2000 and laid up at Portsmouth. She was originally sold to Eckhardt & Co of Germany in December 2000, resold to Turkish shipbreakers in 2001, and left in tow from Portsmouth on 9 March. However, due to the large amount of asbestos found to be on board, this sale to Turkey fell through, and she proceeded to Greece, having been sold on to Indian breakers. In Greece, she was reactivated for the voyage through the Suez Canal, having been renamed *Kos* in May. She arrived at the breaker's yard at Alang on 20 June.

Olmeda was the second of the class to be launched, as *Oleander*. She ran acceptance trials on 18 October 1965 and left the River Tyne on 23 October for Portsmouth. She was renamed on 4 December 1967 to avoid confusion with the *Leander* class frigate HMS *Leander*. The ship saw extensive service during the Falklands War, taking part in Operation 'Keyhole', the recapture of the island of Thule, after the main hostilities had ended. *Olmeda* did not serve in Persian Gulf during the Gulf War; however, she supported HMS *Ark Royal* in the Mediterranean, where she acted as station tanker. *Olmeda*'s career came to an end much earlier than her sisterships, when she was taken out of service in January 1994 and laid up at Portsmouth. She was sold to Indian shipbreakers, and renamed *Niaxco* for the voyage to Alang, where she arrived on 17 August 1994.

Ness Class Fleet Stores Ships

Tonnages (as built): *Lyness* 12,372 gross, 4717 net, 7832 deadweight; *Stromness, Tarbatness* 12,359 gross, 4744 net, 7782 deadweight; 16,792 full load displacement
Length: 523ft 4in
Beam: 72ft 3in
Draught: 25ft 6in
Depth: 44ft 6in
Machinery: 8-cylinder Wallsend/Sulzer RD76 supercharged diesel engine, 12,800bhp, single shaft
Speed: 17–18 knots
Aviation: Fitted with flight deck for helicopter but no hangar facilities
Complement: 110 RFA, 50 STON

This class replaced the wartime Forts and was seen as a vast improvement. Carrying around 40,000 items of palletised naval, victualling and air stores, this meant VERTREP loads could be quickly moved around the four holds by fork lift trucks along the centre clearway to one or more of the four RAS points. The ships were fitted with a flight deck, served by a dedicated stores lift, although they had no hangar facility.

All of these ships were purchased by the US Navy and saw further service with the Military Sealift Command (MSC), after upgrading, which included a hangar for embarked helicopter, as front line combat stores ships.

Name	Builder	Ordered	Laid down	Launched	Completed
Lyness (A339)	Swan Hunter	7.12.64	7.7.65	7.4.66	22.12.66
Stromness (A344)	Swan Hunter	7.12.64	5.10.65	16.9.66	30.3.67
Tarbatness (A345)	Swan Hunter	7.12.64	15.4.66	23.2.67	10.8.67

Lyness was designed as a naval stores and victualling ship, although she also carried a limited amount of air stores. After running preliminary trials on 13 December 1966, she was accepted into service on 22 December. She was later converted to an aviation stores ship. *Lyness* attended the Silver Jubilee Fleet Review on 28 June 1977. In 1979, it was announced that *Lyness*, having spent her career as an air stores support ship, would, with the withdrawal of the aircraft carrier HMS *Ark Royal*, be destored and restored as a general stores support ship. She was sold to the US Navy in 1980 and left Plymouth on 1 December for Norfolk VA. She transferred to the MSC on 18 January 1981 and became USNS *Sirius* (T-AFS 8). *Sirius* was decommissioned on 1 July 2005, and transferred to the Texas Maritime Academy as the training ship *Texas Clipper III*.

Stromness was an air, naval and victualling ship, known throughout the fleet as the 'Super Sampan', largely because she had Hong Kong Chinese crew. Like her sister *Lyness*, she attended the Silver Jubilee Fleet Review and was to be disposed of under the terms of the 1981 Defence Review. However, she was reactivated to serve in the Falklands campaign, and her crew restored her in record time. *Stromness* sailed south with a full complement of stores, as well as 350 men of 40 Commando, Royal Marines for the landing beach in San Carlos Water. Stromness left Devonport on 2 December 1982 for refit in Gibraltar, and in April 1983 to the US Navy and renamed USNS *Saturn* (T-AFS 10). The ship was finally decommissioned on 1 July 2005.

Tarbatness was similar to the other ships in the class, except she carried more air stores, so that she could support carrier operations. *Tarbatness* had Maltese crew for much of her service life. On 26 January 1977, together with *Tidepool* and *Green Rover*, *Tarbatness* left Portsmouth to spend four months on Atlantic Group deployment, supporting the helicopter carrier HMS *Tiger*, nuclear submarine HMS *Churchill* and six units of the 7th Frigate Squadron. She was laid up in Gibraltar in 1980. She left the River Tyne on 23 September 1981 with an RFA crew and on 5 November 1982 she was transferred to the US Navy and renamed USNS *Spica* (T-AFS 9). The ship was finally decommissioned on 26 January 2008.

Rover Class Small Fleet Tankers

Tonnages:	Gross	Net	Deadweight	Displacement (full load)
Green Rover	7503	3186	6822	11,520
Grey Rover	7509	3185	6822	11,520
Blue Rover	7511	3186	7060	11,520
Gold Rover	7574	3256	6799	11,520
Black Rover	7574	3256	6799	11,522

Length overall: 461ft 4in
Beam: 63ft 2in
Draught: 24ft
Depth: 33ft 6in
Machinery: 2 × 16-cylinder Ruston & Hornsby diesels, 16,000bhp, on first three vessels, later replaced by 2 × 16-cylinder Crossley-Pielstick PA4 diesels, 15,382bhp; *Gold Rover*, *Black Rover* were fitted with 2 × 16-cylinder Crossley-Pielstick PA4 diesels, 15,360bhp; single shaft, bow thruster
Speed: 18 knots
Range: 15,000 miles / 15 knots
Armament: 2 × 20mm Oerlikon, 2 × 7.62mm MG
Aircraft: Helicopter deck, no hangar
Complement: 54

These are small fleet tankers designed to operate with frigates or small fleet units. The class was launched in two batches; the first group were *Green Rover*, *Grey Rover* and *Blue Rover* (ordered January 1968), followed four years later by *Gold Rover* and *Black Rover* (ordered November 1971), which differed very slightly from the earlier three.

The main engines fitted to the first three vessels of this class were two 16-cylinder Ruston & Hornsby diesels of 16,000bhp that were found to be unreliable; they were changed for two 16-cylinder Crossley-Pielstick units of 15,360bhp, and fitting of these was completed in March 1973 (*Blue Rover*), June 1974 (*Green Rover*), and September 1975 (*Grey Rover*). These ships carry diesel, aviation spirit, lubricating oil and fresh water along with a limited amount of dry and refrigerated stores. They all had a flight deck to facilitate VERTREP operations, though no hangar.

Name	Builder	Laid down	Launched	In service
Green Rover (A268)	Swan Hunter	28.2.68	19.12.68	15.8.69
Grey Rover (A269)	Swan Hunter	28.2.68	17.4.69	10.4.70
Blue Rover (A270)	Swan Hunter	30.12.68	11.11.69	15.7.70
Gold Rover (A271)	Swan Hunter	–	7.3.73	22.3.74
Black Rover (A273)	Swan Hunter	–	30.8.73	22.8.74

Green Rover conducted successful trials of Harrier jet landings on her flight deck, while moored in the River Thames. On 26 January 1977, together with *Tidepool* and *Tarbatness*, *Green Rover* left Portsmouth to spend four months on Atlantic Group deployment, supporting the helicopter carrier HMS *Tiger*, nuclear submarine HMS *Churchill* and six units of the 7th Frigate Squadron. Taken out of service in 1992, she was sold to the Indonesian Navy and renamed KRI *Arun* (903). She is still in service as a tanker and flagship of the Indonesian Navy Training Command.

Grey Rover early in 1970 replaced Black Ranger on training duties at Portland. She stood by to evacuate British nationals from Lebanon, and was at Malta in 1977, when the naval base there was being run down. In December 1978, *Grey Rover* was ordered to stand by off Iran after civilian unrest and the possibility of the evacuation of British nationals. In November 1983, *Grey Rover* was back off Lebanon during Operation 'Offcut', the naval support for British troops in the multinational force in Lebanon. After her final South Atlantic tour, she sailed for the Caribbean where she took part in the biggest drugs bust in recent times, with a haul of approximately £350 million of cocaine. *Grey Rover* finally sailed into Portsmouth on 15 March 2006, and was taken out of service.

Blue Rover was the support tanker for the Royal Yacht's tour of the Pacific during 1971–2, and had to be towed to Singapore by *Britannia*, after losing her rudder. The ship took part in the Falklands campaign in 1982, being based at South Georgia as station oiler for a time. She was taken out of service in February 1993. *Blue Rover* was sold to the Portuguese Navy in March 1993 and renamed *Berrio*.

Gold Rover was the first RFA ship to fly the flag of an RN flag officer, when she flew the flag of FO 2nd flotilla during a deployment to the Pacific in 1975. *Gold Rover* attended the Jubilee Review in the Solent on 28 June 1977. She was also one of the ships sent to help with flood relief operations off Jamaica in 1986. In January 2000, she had to be towed in to Devonport after breaking down off the Lizard. During 2006 she was very busy. She was in Nigeria for the 50th anniversary of the Nigerian Navy and as part of Operation Vela, off Sierra Leone. On 6 October she, along with Royal Navy frigate HMS *Argyll* and Royal Marines from 40 Commando, seized more than two tonnes of cocaine during a major drugs haul off West Africa. The illegal drugs, which were found in an unregistered vessel, had a UK street value of some £60 million. In 2006, *Gold Rover* was part of a Royal Navy amphibious task group, the 'Vela' deployment, on route to Sierra Leone, where she and other ships were taking part in a major amphibious exercise. While on the way to West Africa, *Gold Rover* was contributing to the global fight against terrorism and the Royal Navy's maritime security operations activity. She was due to decommission in 2009.

Black Rover was present in Malta for the independence ceremonies, and assisted with evacuation operations when Turkey invaded Cyprus in 1974. In 1977, she accompanied HMS *Kent* on a deployment through the Bosporus into the Black sea. *Black Rover* has been APT (S), support tanker with a number of deployments and task groups, and in 2008 she was tasked as FOST tanker. In 2000, *Black Rover* took part in Exercise 'Unified Spirit' and the Joint Task Force Exercise (JTFEX) 01-1. The combined exercise, which took place off the US east coast and in the Caribbean, began on 9 October and included the USS *Harry S Truman* Battle Group, USS *Nassau* Amphibious Ready Group, and fourteen NATO ships from Canada, France, Germany and the UK. By February 2001, *Black Rover* had set sail from Devonport at the start of an eleven-month deployment as Atlantic Patrol Tanker (South). Along with HMS *Glasgow*, she went to support British forces in and around Sierra Leone. Later in 2001, *Black Rover* went to the Falklands and returned home in December. She was deployed in June 2005 and its tasking included assisting with post-Tsunami reconstruction and participation in multinational exercises in the Far East as the UK's component of the Five Power Defence Arrangement. She now has the role of Flag Officer Sea Training (FOST) Tanker, and in September 2006 she hosted the RFA recruitment video film crew. *Black Rover*'s role as FOST tanker allowed the film-makers to capture many of the RFA's abilities. Due to the busy nature of the FOST schedule, the film crew experienced a wide variety of exercises and evolutions during their time on board. *Black Rover* is expected to decommission in 2010.

Fort Class Fleet Replenishment Ships

Tonnages: *Fort Rosalie*: 16,049 gross, 6778 net, 8300 deadweight; *Fort Austin*: 16,054 gross, 6728 net, 8165 deadweight; 23,482 full load displacement
Length overall: 603ft 9in
Beam: 78ft 10in
Draught: 29ft 6in
Depth: 48ft 10in
Machinery: 1 × 8-cylinder Scotts'/Sulzer 8RND90 diesel engine, 22,300bhp, single shaft, bow thruster
Speed: 21 knots
Armament: 2 × 20mm GAM-BO1, 4 × 7.62mm GPMGs
Aircraft: 4 × Sea Kings (2 flight decks)
Complement: 140 (114) RFA, 44 (36) STON, 20 (45) embarked RN naval air unit; doctor and 5-bed hospital

These ships were purpose designed to replenish warships with ammunition, stores and fresh water while underway. They can support up to four Sea King or Merlin helicopters, either on the main flight deck, or from the 'emergency' pad on top of the hangar roof, the aircraft being used mainly for re-supply role, although they have been used in the anti-submarine role, thereby making these ships potent force multipliers.

Name	Builder	Ordered	Laid down	Launched	Completed
Fort Rosalie (A385)	Scott Lithgow	28.4.72	9.11.73	9.12.76	6.4.78
Fort Austin (A386)	Scott Lithgow	28.4.72	9.12.75	9.3.78	11.5.79

Fort Rosalie was launched *Fort Grange* and arrived at her home port, Plymouth, on 15 April 1978. She entered service shortly afterwards. Under this name, she sailed for the Falklands with 824 Naval Air Squadron C flight embarked, and provided much needed support for the task force. In February 1986, while stationed in the Falklands Protection Zone, the ship was visited by Prime Minister Thatcher. *Fort Grange* also saw service in the Gulf conflict in the early 1990s with 846 Naval Air Squadron.

From April 1997 to January 2000, *Fort Grange* was stationed, with her sister, at Split in the former Yugoslavia during the troubles there. During a refit on the Tyne, the ship was renamed *Fort Rosalie* on 1 June 2000 after confusion arose with the new ship *Fort George* – mail intended for the latter ended up on *Fort Grange*; she left the Tyne on 14 June under her new name. By the end of June, *Fort Rosalie* was at Gibraltar, where she oversaw repairs to the damaged HMS *Tireless*, and also gave support and hotel services to the crew of *Tireless*. In January 2003, *Fort Rosalie* along with other RFAs sailed for the Gulf for Operation 'Telic'. In August 2006, the ship attended the Devonport Navy Days, representing the RFA. *Fort Rosalie* was at Birkenhead for a £28 million refit by Northwestern Ship Repair & Shipbuilders from May 2008 until 2009.

Fort Austin entered RFA service in June 1979, having been accepted from the builders on 22 June. Like her sister, she took part in the Falklands campaign. With Commodore Sam Dunlop as her master, she took part in the landings at San Carlos, taking much needed ammunition to the troops. In May 2000, the ship was part of the fleet deployed to Sierra Leone. Together with HMS *Argyll*, *Fort Austin* took part in the fourth major drugs bust in two months, in an operation in the Atlantic that ended on 5 November 2006. In 2007, *Fort Austin* commenced a major refit and modernisation at the A & P Tyne shipyard at Hebburn, on the River Tyne. She left the Tyne on 23 November and successfully completed sea trials. The refit included the updating of several systems, including bridge and command, and helicopter landing aids.

Aviation Training Ship

Argus

Tonnages: 26,421 gross, 7926 net, 12,221 deadweight, 28,081 tonnes full load displacement
Length overall: 175.12m
Beam: 30.64m
Draught: 8.197m
Depth: 17.0m
Machinery: 2 × Lindholmen/Pielstick 18PC2.5V 18-cylinder diesels, 23,400bhp, two shafts, bow thruster

Speed: 18 knots
Armament: 2 × 20mm Oerlikon GAM-BO1, 4 × 7.62mm GPMGs, Seagnat chaff launchers
Aircraft: Five pads for Westland Sea Kings, CH-47 Chinooks, Westland Merlins, or Westland Lynx; can transport Sea Harrier FA2s
Complement: 80 RFA, 35 RN, 137 RN air squadron

Name	Builder	Launched	Completed
Argus (A135)	Breda	28.11.80	7.81

The aviation training ship *Argus*, which doubles as a primary casualty receiving ship, was built by Cantieri Navale Breda SpA, Venice, and completed as the containership *Contender Bezant*. The ship was requisitioned in 1982 for service in the Falklands campaign. In an unusual course of events, *Container Bezant* arrived at Belfast on 29 March 1984, and she was actually purchased by Harland & Wolff Ltd, with the intention of sale to the MoD during or upon completion of the four-year conversion at its shipyard. The ship entered RFA service in 1988, replacing *Engadine* in the aviation training role. She was formally renamed *Argus* at Belfast on 23 March 1987.

Argus has proven to be a versatile vessel, serving in many campaigns and operations. *Argus* was fitted with a fully functional hospital for the 1991 Gulf crisis, and this has since been added to, providing one hundred beds. In recent conflicts, the ship's role as a primary casualty receiving ship (referred to as such rather than a hospital ship because the vessel is armed) has been more prominent than its aviation training duties. The last time the hospital was fully utilised was off Freetown in 2000–1.

The ship deployed to the Arabian Gulf in 1991 for service in the Gulf conflict, and also saw service in the Adriatic in 1993 and 1999 supporting British operations in Bosnia and in connection with Kosovo respectively. During this period, *Argus* operated in part as an LPH, but her unsuitability for this role was a major factor in the commissioning of HMS *Ocean*. In 2003, *Argus* was deployed again to the Gulf as part of a thirty-three-ship fleet to support a British amphibious assault of the Al-Faw peninsula. *Argus* operated in its PCRS role. In 2007, the ship was refitted with upgraded hospital facilities, generators and aviation systems to give an operational life until 2020. In 2008, she deployed to the Middle East to act as a platform for Sea King ASaCs7 helicopters.

Being a former container ship, *Argus* does not have a traditional aircraft carrier layout – the superstructure is located forward, with a long flight deck aft. The ship has a small secondary superstructure approximately two thirds down the flight deck, containing the ship's exhaust funnel. This small deck is used by small helicopters to simulate landing on the flight deck of a destroyer or frigate.

Third Leaf Class Tankers

Tonnages:	Gross	Net	Deadweight	Displacement (full load)
Appleleaf	20,440	10,680	33,750	40,870
Bayleaf	20,086	11,522	29,999	37,390
Brambleleaf	20,440	10,680	33,257	40,870
Oakleaf	24,608	14,934	34,800	49,377(39310)
Orangeleaf	19,976	13,642	33,751	40,870

Dimensions (metres)	Length oa	Beam	Draught	Depth
Appleleaf	170.69	25.96	11.864	15.68
Bayleaf	170.69	25.94	11.045	15.68
Brambleleaf	170.69	25.9	11.864	15.65
Oakleaf	173.69	32.26	10.221	14.91
Orangeleaf	170.69	25.91	11.864	15.65

Machinery: *Appleleaf, Bayleaf, Brambleleaf, Orangeleaf* 2 × 14-cylinder Crossley Premier-Pielstick PC2 V14 (14PC 2V) diesels, 14,000bhp, single shaft; *Oakleaf* 1 × 4-cylinder Uddevalla/B&W diesel, 12,250bhp, single shaft, bow thruster

Speeds: *Appleleaf, Bayleaf, Brambleleaf, Orangeleaf* 15 knots (16.5 knots maximum); *Oakleaf* 14.5 knots (15.5 knots maximum)
Complement: *Appleleaf, Bayleaf, Brambleleaf, Orangeleaf* 56 RFA; *Oakleaf* 36 RFA
Armament: *Oakleaf* 2 × 7.62mm GPMGs; *Bayleaf, Orangeleaf* 2 × 20mm GAM-BO1, 4 × 7.62mm GPMGs

Four of the five tankers in this class were under construction at the former Cammell Laird Shipbuilders Ltd yard at Birkenhead and were originally ordered by John Hudson Fuel & Shipping Ltd, London, which was unable to accept delivery. The changes of name and registered ownership that followed were complex and are not fully covered in the brief histories set out below.

Name	Builder	Laid down	Launched	Completed
Appleleaf (A79)	Cammell Laird	–	24.7.75	9.79
Bayleaf (A109)	Cammell Laird	1.2.75	27.10.81	4.82
Brambleleaf (A81)	Cammell Laird	23.7.74	22.1.76	2.80
Oakleaf (A111)	Uddevallavarvet	–	2.7.81	1981
Orangeleaf (A110)	Cammell Laird	–	12.2.75	7.79

Appleleaf was launched as *Hudson Cavalier* and then spent a long period in the Mersey in lay up prior to completion. She arrived in the River Tyne on 10 December 1978 for conversion for RFA duties and she commenced service in February 1979. She had been purchased by Matheson & Co Ltd, London (manager Jardine, Matheson & Co Ltd) and renamed *Appleleaf* for RFA charter. *Appleleaf* was sold in 1989 and renamed *Westralia*, and upon further sale in 2007 was renamed *Shiraz*.

Bayleaf, laid down as *Hudson Sound*, was registered in the name of owner Lombard Leasing Services Ltd and was completed as *Bayleaf*. She was commissioned into RFA service on (26 March 1982), having effectively been purchased by the MoD, but the leasing arrangement continued. She returned to Devonport on 31 August 1982 after her maiden voyage to the Falklands. On 16 September 2002, when supporting Royal Navy and Allied warships in the Arabian Gulf, *Bayleaf* rescued six sailors from the Guinea-registered cargo ship *Falcon*. From October 2008 to June 2009, she was at Birkenhead for an extensive refit. She is expected to decommission in 2010.

Brambleleaf, launched as *Hudson Deep*, was registered in the name of Finance for Shipping Ltd, with managers as Jardine Matheson & Co Ltd. She was contracted for charter in February 1979 and was refitted on the Mersey for her RFA role (commissioned on 20 February 1980). She entered service on 26 March 1982. In the mid-1980s she was purchased outright by the MoD and the leasing arrangement continued. She taken out of service in 2007, two years earlier than expected. During August 2009, it was reported that she had been sold to breakers at Ghent, Belgium.

Oakleaf was built at Uddevalla, Sweden, and completed for Swedish owners as *Oktania*. In 1985 she was sold to James Fisher & Sons plc, Barrow, for charter for operation by the RFA. She was converted for RFA purposes at a cost of £5 million by Falmouth Shiprepair Ltd. This conversion was completed on 12 August 1986, and she was commissioned and renamed *Oakleaf* two days later. She was taken out of service in 2007, three years earlier than expected.

Orangeleaf was launched as *Hudson Progress* and was for a while laid up. She was sold to become *Balder London*, registered in the name of Lloyds Industrial Leasing Ltd, under the British flag, and beneficially owned for a while by Parley Augustsson & Co, of Norway. Before joining the RFA, *Balder London* carried aviation fuel from Ascension Island to the Falklands in 1982, and at the end of the conflict was at San Carlos Water. She entered service with the RFA in 1984, having arrived at Falmouth on 9 March for refit and commissioned there on 2 May. She received battle honours for taking part in the Kuwait campaign in 1991. In mid-August 1992, *Orangeleaf* and HMS *Cardiff* supported local authorities in relief work in the Bahamas, following hurricane Andrew. During early to mid-1994, *Orangeleaf* took part in deployment with a French carrier battle group centred on *Charles de Gaulle* in the Indian Ocean. She also took part on Operation 'Telic' (the second Gulf War). In July 2005, she was at the International Fleet Review in the Solent. She is due to decommission in 2009.

Sir Caradoc and Sir Lamorak

Tonnages: *Sir Caradoc* 2049 gross, 920 net, 3302 deadweight; *Sir Lamorak* 1585 gross, 549 net, 2677 deadweight
Length overall: *Sir Caradoc* 124.01m; *Sir Lamorak* 109.51m
Beam: *Sir Caradoc* 15.03m; *Sir Lamorak* 20.43m
Draught: *Sir Caradoc* 4.979m; *Sir Lamorak* 4.934m
Depth: *Sir Caradoc* 11.61m; *Sir Lamorak* 12.5m
Machinery: *Sir Caradoc* 4 × 9-cylinder Normo diesels, 5040bhp, two shafts, two bow thrusters; *Sir Lamorak* 2 × 8-cylinder Pielstick diesels, 8000bhp, two shafts, bow thruster
Speed: *Sir Caradoc* 16 knots; *Sir Lamorak* 17 knots
Complement: 24
Armament: None
Aircraft: None

These vessels were chartered to fill the gap caused by the loss of or damage to vessels of the Round Table class LSLs during the Falklands campaign. Both were taken into RFA service in March 1983.

Name	Builder	Laid down	Launched	Completed
Sir Caradoc (L3522)	Trosvik	13.12.71	11.8.72	12.72
Sir Lamorak (L3532)	Ankerlokken	–	9.72	12.72

Sir Caradoc was launched as *Grey Master* at the Trosvik shipyard, Brevik, Norway. She entered RFA service on 17 March 1983, and taken out of service in June 1988. In July 1988, her Norwegian owners sold her and she became *Stamveien*, and later changes of owner saw her with the new names *Hua Lu* (1994), *Morning Star II* (2002) and *Royal Nusantara* (2006).

Sir Lamorak was completed in December 1972 at the Ankerlokken shipyard, in Floro, Norway, as *Anu*. She had several former names due to changes of owner or charter, and these were *Anu* (1974), *Norcliff* (1974–80), *Lune Bridge* (1980), *Lady Catherine* (1980–1), *Lakespan Ontario* (1981–3). She entered the RFA fleet on 11 March 1983 as *Sir Lamorak*, and was taken out of service on 20 January 1986 and returned to her owners. After this, her 'tradition' of changes continued, and she was renamed *Merchant Trader* (1986), *Mols Trader* (1987), *Mads Mols* (1987), *Pride of Portsmouth* (1989), *Norman Commodore* (1991), and *Fjardvagen* (1995).

Helicopter Base Ship *Reliant*

Tonnages: 28,156 gross, 16,916 net, 23,120 deadweight
Length overall: 204.22m
Beam: 30.99m
Draught: 10.021m
Depth: 15.6m
Machinery: 2 × 10-cylinder Cegielski/Sulzer diesel engines, 29,000bhp, single shaft, bow thruster
Speed: 21 knots
Complement: –

Name	Builder	Launched	Completed
Reliant (A131)	Stocznia Gdanska, Gdansk	6.7.76	20.1.77

Reliant was built in Poland as the type B463 cellular containership *Astronomer* and was delivered to Charente Steamship Co Ltd, Liverpool, managed by T & J Harrison Ltd. In May 1982, she became the largest of four vessels chartered by the Ministry of Defence for conversion into aircraft ferries for service in the Falklands campaign. She completed conversion in one week and left Devonport in June with thirteen helicopters. *Astronomer* was taken up on further charter and on 25 April 1983 arrived at Birkenhead for conversion into a helicopter base ship and emerged from the conversion as *Reliant*. The charter was purchased by the Ministry of Defence, which effectively became owner of the vessel, and the cost of the whole exercise was quoted as £25 million. *Reliant* was formally acquired on 16 November 1983 and re-entered service on 3 December. She had been fitted with the Arapaho containerised aircraft handling system, hangar and flight deck.

In January 1984, *Reliant* relieved HMS *Fearless* as support ship to the British UN forces in Lebanon, and in the following month evacuated the British troops and 500 civilians from Lebanon to Cyprus. After this, *Reliant* returned to the UK, and then proceeded to the Falklands for what was expected to be an extended deployment. However, the Arapaho system proved to be unsatisfactory for handling aircraft and the deployment was curtailed. The charter had been due to end in January 1987. The ship was taken out of service on 25 July 1986 and the fittings were removed by Seaforth Welding Co Ltd.

On 27 October 1986, *Reliant* was sold to Hong Kong owners, reconverted for commercial service, and renamed *Admiralty Island*. She was sold on to become *Wealthy River* in April 1989 and on 9 July 1998 arrived at Alang to be broken up.

Strategic Lift Ships

Sea Centurion and *Sea Crusader*

Tonnages: *Sea Centurion* 21,104 gross, 6331 net, 12,350 deadweight, 22,000 full load displacement; *Sea Crusader* 23,986 gross, 7195 net, 9677 deadweight, 18,031 full load displacement
Length overall: *Sea Centurion* (182.6m); *Sea Crusader* 162.49m
Beam: *Sea Centurion* 25.8m; *Sea Crusader* 25.64m
Draught: *Sea Centurion* 7.4m; *Sea Crusader* 6.521m
Depth: *Sea Centurion* 8.3m; *Sea Crusader* 15.45m
Machinery: *Sea Centurion* 4 × 8-cylinder NSDF/Sulzer 8ZA40S diesels, 31,323bhp, two shafts, two bow thrusters; *Sea Crusader* 2 × 7-cylinder Kawasaki/MAN-B&W 7L40/54 diesels, 13,383bhp, 2 shafts
Speed: *Sea Centurion* 22 knots; *Sea Crusader* 17.5 knots
Complement: 17
Armament: None
Aircraft: None

Name	Builder	Laid down	Launched	Completed
Sea Centurion (A98)	Esercizio	15.6.96	7.97	7.98
Sea Crusader (A96)	Kawasaki	18.3.96	7.6.96	1996

Sea Centurion was built by Societa Esercizio Cantieri, Viareggio, Italy, and launched as *Stena Ausonia* for Stena Ausonia Ltd. She was later named *Und Ege*. As a conventional roll-on/roll-off vessel, she has 2700-metre lane capacity. She was taken up on RFA charter and taken into service on 18 October 1998 as *Sea Centurion*. She was taken out of service on 25 July 2002 and returned to her owners. Her subsequent names have been *Mont Ventoux* (2003), *Stena Forwarder* (2005) and *Ark Forwarder* (2007).

Sea Crusader was built by Kawasaki Heavy Industries, Sakaide, Japan, and launched as *Celestine*. She entered service in the RFA as *Sea Crusader* on 10 October 1996, and her intended charter was in 1998 extended until a replacement could be brought into service. She was returned to her owners following decommissioning on 7 August 2003 and reverted to her original name of *Celestine*.

Fort Class Auxiliary Oiler Replenishment

Tonnage: 28,821 gross, 8646 net, 16,061 deadweight (*Fort George*), 16,967 deadweight (*Fort Victoria*); 31,565 full load displacement
Length overall: 669ft 1in
Beam: 99ft 8in
Draught: 31ft 10in
Depth: 56ft 1in
Machinery: 2 × 16-cylinder Allen/Crossley-Pielstick diesel engines, 25,083bhp, two shafts
Speed: 20 knots
Armament: 2 × Phalanx CIWS point defence guns (fitted 1998); 2 × GAM-BO1 20mm
Aircraft: 3 × Merlin Mk 1 helicopters
Complement: 95 RFA, 24 STON, 15 RN

These ships combine the roles of a fleet support tanker and stores ship, a concept that is known in naval circles as the 'one stop ship'. These ships, originally planned as a class of six, have four dual-purpose rigs amidships, which allow replenishment of two ships simultaneously, with both fuel and stores from the same RAS point. The ships are also fitted with a Hudson Reel, which allows them to conduct replenishment over the stern, a two-spot flight deck, and hangar facilities that enable them to carry up to five Sea Kings, or Merlin helicopters for VERTREP operations or other tasks. Both are expected to decommission in 2019.

Name	Builder	Ordered	Laid down	Launched	In service
Fort George (A388)	Swan Hunter	18.12.87	9.3.89	1.3.91	16.7.93
Fort Victoria (A387)	Harland & Wolff	23.4.86	–	4.5.90	24.6.94

Fort George was launched in 1991, by Lady Slater, wife of the then Commander-in-Chief Fleet. During a refit on the Tyne in 1999, she was fitted with a Vulcan Phalanx close in weapons system (CIWS), for anti aircraft protection and in March 2000 she embarked a flight of five Sea King helicopters before deployment to the Mozambique Channel to assist with relief operations following flooding in that country. In May 2000, she was one of the ships tasked to support British operations off Sierra Leone. On 26 September 2000, during Mediterranean deployment, she rescued passengers and crew from the Greek ferry Express Saminia, which had run aground and sank during a storm. She arrived at Birkenhead at the end of 2007 for refit.

Fort Victoria became the centre of attention, shortly after launch, because she was the target for two IRA bombs. The first exploded in the engine room causing damage and flooding that was quickly dealt with by emergency crews, while the other bomb was successfully located and defused. The knock-on effect of this was late delivery of the vessel. In early 2003, Fort Victoria was deployed on Operation 'Telic'. In 2007, the ship was placed in 'extended readiness' at Portsmouth, but on 2 November arrived in tow in the River Mersey to await refit at Birkenhead. Fort George had already arrived at Birkenhead at the end of 2007 for refit.

Repair Ship Diligence

Tonnages: 8048 gross, 2424 net, 4941 deadweight, 10,765 tonnes full load displacement
Length overall: 111.49m
Beam: 20.99m
Draught: 7.0m
Depth: 8.31m
Machinery: diesel-electric drive; five Nohab-Polar 16-cylinder diesels, total 18,000bhp, driving 5 generators each 2520kW/6000V ac, connected to 4 electric motors each of m1495shp and SR geared to screw shaft, one shaft, two 360 degrees azimuth thrusters, two bow thrusters
Speed: 10.5–12 knots
Armament: 4 × 20mm Oerlikon, 4 × 7.62mm GPMG
Aircraft: Deck landing spot for Westland Sea King, or Westland Lynx, or CH-47 Chinook helicopter
Complement: 38 RFA, 147 RN

Name	Builder	Laid down	Launched	Completed
Diligence (A132)	Öresundsvarvet	28.1.80	3.4.80	12.1.81

The fleet repair ship Diligence was built by Öresundsvarvet AB, Landskrona, Sweden, and completed in 1981 as an oil rig support ship. The vessel first served the RFA during the Falklands campaign as a commercially owned ship taken up from the trade (STUFT). As Stena Inspector, the ship repaired many British vessels. Stena Inspector was purchased by the government in October 1983 for £25 million from Stena (UK) Line and renamed Diligence. She went to the Clyde Dock Engineering Ltd facility, where she was converted and military features added, including a large workshop for hull and machinery repairs, supply facilities, accommodation, armament and communications centres.

Entering RFA service at Portland on 12 March 1984, she is designed to provide forward repair and maintenance facilities to ships and submarines operating away from home ports and in addition to workshops she also provides overside facilities. For Royal Navy vessels, Diligence provides a large workshop facility that is equipped with specialist machinery and spares. Diligence is the Royal Navy's primary battle damage repair unit, and at short notice can react to situations worldwide. A key feature is her dynamic-positioning system, which can keep the vessel static in poor conditions, using thrusters and the variable-pitch propeller. She has a helicopter deck on the roof of her bridge. Another great advantage is that her hull is built to the highest ice class specification.

At the end of the Iran–Iraq war, the Strait of Hormuz was mined and *Diligence* supported the multinational minesweeping operation to clear that vital seaway. *Diligence* also helped repair HMS *Southampton*, which was damaged following collision. The ship returned to the Gulf in 1990 to support operations during the Gulf War and repaired, among many others, US ships damaged by mines. During Operation Ocean Wave 97, *Diligence* deployed to the Far East as a submarine support ship. The following year, the ship supported the 3rd Mine Countermeasures Squadron in the Persian Gulf. Following just two weeks back in the UK, *Diligence* departed for the south Atlantic, and returned to Faslane in December 1998. In early 1999, the ship again deployed to the Falklands region.

In 2001, there was a large exercise in Oman, and *Diligence* supported four mine countermeasures vessels involved. Its next wartime assignment came with the large task force deployed against Iraq in 2003, which *Diligence* supported the largest British fleet deployed since the Falklands. More recently she was off Sierra Leone with the Vela task force. When the ship returned to UK in November 2006, she had the longest deployment of an RFA in recent times. From her departure from Portsmouth, it was five and a half years before *Diligence* returned home. In that time she has visited twenty-five countries, voyaged 150,000 miles through the Mediterranean to the Persian Gulf, across the Indian Ocean to India, Sri Lanka and Singapore, the South China Sea to the Philippines and from South Africa across the Atlantic to the Falklands and South America. Many countries were visited more than once.

The twenty-five-year-old ship was given a £16 million overhaul during 2007 at Northwestern Shiprepairers & Shipbuilders, Birkenhead. During the refit, which was completed in December 2007, most of the interior was upgraded with the intention of extending the ship's service life until 2014.

Sir Galahad

Tonnages: 8861 gross, 2658 net, 3077 deadweight, 8751 full load displacement
Length overall: 140.47m
Beam: 20.02m
Draught: 4.574m
Depth: 8.56m
Machinery: 2 × 9-cylinder Mirrlees-Blackstone KMR9Mk3 diesels, total 13,310bhp, two shafts, bow thruster
Speed: 14 knots cruising, 17 knots maximum
Complement: 49 RFA, 400 troops
Aircraft: 4 × Westland Wessex, or 2 × Westland Sea King, or 2 × Westland Wasp (one pad aft for Sea King or smaller, one pad amidships for Chinook or smaller)
Armament: 2 × 20mm Oerlikon, 2 × 7.62 MG

Name	Builder	Ordered	Laid down	Launched	Delivered
Sir Galahad (L3005)	Swan Hunter	6.9.84	12.5.85	13.12.86	25.11.87

Sir Galahad, which entered service in 1988, was a landing ship logistical (LSL) and is now in service with the Brazilian navy as *Garcia D'Avila*. This new *Sir Galahad* was given the identical pendant number to her namesake that was sunk in the Falklands campaign. She was a combined landing craft and ferry with two flight decks for helicopters and bow and stern doors. There was capacity for around 400 troops and 3440 tonnes of supplies.

The ship has seen service in two wars since she was built, both against Iraq. She was deployed in 1991 for Operation 'Granby' and in 2003 for Operation 'Telic'. Her role in both conflicts was transport of supplies. In the second Gulf War, *Sir Galahad* transported humanitarian aid, docking in Umm Qasr on 28 March 2003. On 26 April 2007, it was announced that she was to be sold and she made her last 'voyage' with the RFA on 20 July, sailing from Marchwood to Portsmouth, to be taken out of service. She was formally handed over to her new owners, the Brazilian navy, on 13 November 2007, and was commissioned into the Brazilian navy as *Garcia D'Avila* on 4 December.

Wave Class Fast Fleet Tankers

Displacement: 31,500 tons full load
Length overall: 196.5m
Beam: 28.25m
Draught: 9.97m
Machinery: diesel-electric – 4 × 12-cylinder Wärtsilä Vasa V32 diesels, 2 × GEC Alstom motors, total 27,200bhp, single shaft, bow thruster, stern thruster
Speed: 18 knots
Range: 10,000nm / 15 knots, 8000nm / 18 knots
Armament: 2 × 30mm cannon; 4 × 7.62mm GPMG; fitted for but not with two Vulcan Phalanx
Aircraft: 1 × Merlin helicopter
Complement: 72 RFA, 26 RN for helicopter operations and weapons

These ships were designed and built to replace the Olynthus class (*Olwen*, *Olna* and *Olmeda*); they can operate in support of most of the Royal Navy's task groups, or independently as a force multiplier. The ships can carry 3000 cu m of fuel, 500 cu m of dry cargo and up to 380 cu m of fresh water. They are capable of operating Merlin helicopters, and have a large hangar with maintenance facilities. Both are expected to leave service in 2028.

Name	Builder	Ordered	Laid down	Launched	In service
Wave Knight (A389)	BAE, Barrow	12.3.97	22.5.98	29.9.00	8.4.03
Wave Ruler (A390)	BAE, Govan	12.3.97	–	10.2.01	27.4.03

Wave Knight is the second ship to bear the name; the first was a Wave class oiler completed in 1945. She has operated in a number of roles, most notably as APT (N) when she successfully seized a large quantity of illegal drugs. On 18 April 2009, Royal Navy personnel operating from *Wave Knight* in the Gulf of Aden, intercepted and fended off two pirate attacks with its armament. The pirates were attacking two merchant ships.

Wave Ruler is also the second ship to bear the name, the first being a Wave class oiler completed in 1946. As APT (N) she has, like her sister ship, been instrumental in the seizure of large quantities of illegal drugs. In August 2008, she was in the Caribbean following Hurricane Gustav and assisted in the relief efforts, and in November 2008 provided humanitarian relief to the Cayman Islands following Hurricane Paloma. On 3 October 2008, *Wave Ruler* docked in Havana, Cuba. This was only the second time since the country's revolution fifty years before that a Royal Navy ship had visited the country. The five-day stay was part of an ongoing anti-drugs operation in the Caribbean.

Bay Class LSD (A)

Displacement: 16,160 tons full load
Length overall: 579 feet 5 inches
Beam: 86 feet 7 inches
Draught: 16 feet 9 inches
Machinery: Two Wärtsilä 8L26 engines, two Wärtsilä 12V26 engines, azimuth thrusters.
Speed: 18 knots
Range: 8000nm / 15 knots
Armament: 2 × 7.62 Mk 44 Miniguns, 6 × 7.62mm L7 GPMGs
Aircraft: Twin spot flight deck with limited facilities to transport and operate Merlin or Chinook helicopters, and V-22 Osprey tiltrotor aircraft
Complement: 59

The design of this class of ships is based on the Dutch *Enforcer* class. They are intended to take over from the ageing Round Table class of LSLs and will provide a much larger capacity, with capacity for 356 troops, thirty-two Challenger tanks, or 150 light trucks, a large number of containers as well as two LCVP or one LCU, which are floated out from the flooded stern dock. They can also carry two Mexeflotes attached to the ship's side.

Name	Builder	Ordered	Laid down	Launched	In service
Largs Bay (L3006)	Swan Hunter	19.12.00	1.10.01	18.7.03	2.1.07
Mounts Bay (L3008)	BAE Systems	19.11.01	14.1.02	19.4.04	15.9.06
Lyme Bay (L3007)	Swan Hunter/BAE	19.12.00	1.10.01	26.8.05	8.8.07
Cardigan Bay (L3009)	BAE Systems	19.11.01	–	9.4.05	6.3.07

Largs Bay was the second of the class to be launched, or rather floated out of the dock in which she was constructed. She was dedicated on 17 December 2006, took part in 'Southwest Scimitar', a training exercise with HMS Ark Royal and HMS Albion. In a mishap on 3 March 2007, when bound for Plymouth, *Largs Bay* reported that she had lost engine power and steering and was drifting five miles west of Eddystone light as a result of an engine room fire. On 6 March she arrived at Plymouth Sound with tugs assisting it to Delta Buoy. In November 2007, she was the first of the Bay class deployed to the Caribbean area, and the latest deployment (2009) is to the Falklands. *Largs Bay* was fitted to receive Phalanx CIWS 30mm DS30B cannon in 2008–09.

Mounts Bay was the first of the class to be launched. In autumn 2006, she was fitted with the Bowman communications system, when she was part of the deployment of naval ships off Sierra Leone. On return from this deployment, she immediately began loading trucks and equipment for Exercise 'Clockwork' in Norway, operating north of the Arctic Circle. On return to the UK she continued to be busy with a variety of taskings.

Lyme Bay was also built initially by Swan Hunter, where the two ships were known affectionately as 'Larger and Lime', however, because of delays and cost over-runs the incomplete ship was transferred to BAE Systems at Govan for completion. Lyme Bay was built in a dock and was floated out starting on 26 August 2005, but this was not completed until 3 September. She left the Tyne on 17 July 2006 and arrived on the River Clyde on 22 July. She was accepted into service on 2 August 2007.

Cardigan Bay was launched one day late owing to adverse weather conditions. She entered service on 6 March 2007 in Portland.

Appendix 1

Chronology of World Events and RFA Involvement 1950–2008

1950
Building begun – Eddybeach, Surf Patrol (as Tatry), Surf Pioneer (as Beskidy)
Launched – Retainer (as Chungking), Resurgent (as Chungchow)
Completed – Retainer (as Chungking)
Transferred or taken over by Admiralty – RRS Discovery II (manned and managed by Director of Stores)
Laid up or sold – Fortol

Guns and mountings removed from RFAs and landed at home port
Spabeck converted to high test peroxide (HTP) fuel carrier
Fort Duquesne fitted with small helicopter platform by Malta dockyard prior to trials
Sea Salvor involved in salvage of cargo ships *Etivebank* and *Benledi*
Introduction of funnel bands to indicate ship's function

Further modifications to pension provision
Albert Medal awarded to AB M R Ellis (killed on 6 July 1950 – medal awarded 23 January 1951)
Donkeyman Harold Prior awarded Kings Commendation for Brave Conduct from same incident

Korean War begins (25 June 1950–27 July 1953)
(British Army, Royal Navy and United Nations involved. War ends 1953)

1951
Building begun – Eddybay
Launched – Eddybay, Eddybeach, Surf Patrol, Surf Pioneer
Completed – Resurgent (as Chungchow), Surf Patrol, Surf Pioneer, Eddybeach
Transferred or taken over by Admiralty – Fort Amherst, Fort Dunvegan, Rippledyke (as Empire Tesbury), Surf Patrol, Surf Pioneer
Laid up or sold – War Afridi

Eddycove/Eddymull: ordered but subsequently cancelled
Fort Duquesne: First helicopter trials on an RFA (Westland Dragonflies used)
Fort Duquesne also trialled Clark-Chapman one-ton automatic tensioning winch
NAV *Bedenham* severely damaged by depth charges exploding at Gibraltar. Ship then sank
Maine: lost propeller on westward passage through Shimonoseki Strait and was towed in by USS *Relaier* (AARS 42) with USS *Yuma* (ATF94)

Captain S G Kent and Chief Engineer H Ringshaw both from Maine subject of a letter of appreciation from Headquarters 8th US Army, Korea
Captain S G Kent appointed first Commodore RFA

1952
Building begun – *Tide Austral* (Tide class: first purpose-built fast fleet tankers), *Eddyfirth*
New hospital ship laid down at Barclay Curle 20 February – order cancelled 11 July
Launched – *Eddycliff*, *Eddyrock*
Completed – *Eddybay*
Transferred or taken over by Admiralty – *Retainer* (as *Chungking* managed by British India Steam
Navigation Co.), *Resurgent* (as *Chungchow*), *Seafox* (small aircraft transport), *Amherst* (as *Fort Amherst*)
Laid up or sold – *Olcades* (fire damage), *Prestol*

Operation 'Hurricane'
First atom tests, off Monte Bello Islands
Cyprus emergency
British troops and Royal Navy involved; ends with independence under President Makarios (1959)
Kenyan insurgency, Mau Mau revolt
British Army involved. Ends with independence under President Kenneth Kaunda

1953
Building begun – *Tiderace*, *Tidereach*, *Tiderange*
Launched – *Eddycreek*, *Eddyreef*, *Eddyness*, *Eddyfirth*, *Brambleleaf* (as *London Loyalty*), *Cherryleaf* (as *Laurelwood*), *Reliant* (as *Somersby*)
Completed – *Cherryleaf* (as *Laurelwood*), *Eddycliff*, *Eddyreef*, *Eddyrock*
Transferred or taken over by Admiralty – *Resurgent* (as *Chungchow*, managed by Buries Markes)
Laid up or sold – *Boxol*, *Limol*
Seafox reclassified as stores victualling ship

Maine received Presidential Unit Citation of the Republic of Korea
Wave Ruler ran aground on sandbank outside Swansea docks on 28 September, after being disabled on the 19th. She was refloated after her cargo was pumped to her sister ship *Wave Monarch*
St Edward's Crowns adopted for badges and buttons
Black Ranger: crew of ss *Mountcharles* rescued from disabled ship off Padstow

Korean War
War ends, with partition of country into communist North and democratic South
Disaster relief
Flooding in UK and the Netherlands; deployed along with naval helicopters
Coronation Fleet Review

1954
Launched – *Tiderange*, *Tidereach*, *Tiderace*, *Tide Austral*, *Bayleaf* (as *London Integrity*)
Completed – *Brambleleaf* (as *London Loyalty*), *Reliant* (as *Somersby*), *Eddyfirth*, *Eddyness*
Transferred or taken over by Admiralty – *Fort Langley*
Laid up or sold – *Maine*

Wave Victor suffered engine room fire off Ilfracombe. Crew abandoned ship. Vessel salvaged and towed to Swansea Sheilds for repair
Wave Commander in collision with BP tanker off Gibraltar
King Salvor converted to submarine rescue bell ship, operating the US-designed rescue bell
Renamed HMS *Kingfisher*, she was to act as tender to the Clyde-based Third Submarine Squadron
Olna plays role of German oiler in film *Battle of the River Plate*

Engineer cadetship scheme introduced
Captain W Brunswick Brown appointed Commodore RFA
Captain L J Mack, Master of *Rowanol*, made honorary citizen of Greek town Karlovasi after rescuing three of its citizens

1955
Launched – *Orangeleaf* (as *Southern Satellite*), *Appleleaf* (as *George Lyras*)
Completed – *Bayleaf* (as *London Integrity*), *Tide Austral, Tidereach, Orangeleaf* (as *Southern Satellite*),
Appleleaf (as *George Lyras*)
Laid up or sold – *Denbydale*, HMS *Bulawayo*

Spabeck used to transport high test peroxide (HTP) for submarine experiments
Fort Rosalie dumps 1500 tons of atomic waste off Land's End

Captain T H Card appointed Commodore RFA

1956
Completed – *Tiderace, Tiderange*
Transferred or taken over by Admiralty – *Reliant* (RFA's first air stores issuing ship) (as *Somersby*,
chartered by Admiralty, initially for three months)

Blue Ranger collides with destroyer HMS *Chieftain* in Mediterranean
Echodale: First night flight by RN helicopter to an RFA
Wave King struck a rock off Brazil and badly damaged

Replenishment at sea and station allowances introduced

Suez (Operation 'Musketeer')
British army and Royal Navy involved, ends same year (1956) with arrival of UN peacekeeping forces
and reopening of Suez Canal, although canal is now nationalised
Task grp 324 (Red Sea group – Operation 'Toreador') – *Wave Sovereign*
Task grp 325.8 (Logistics group – supporting carriers) – *Olna, Retainer, Tiderace* and *Tiderange*
RFAs also involved in Suez Canal clearance

Operation 'Mosaic' (atom test)
Eddyrock deployed

Disaster relief
Greek earthquake: RFAs deployed with Royal Navy vessels sent to assist
Cyprus: RFAs deployed with Royal Navy vessels sent to assist

1957
Transferred or taken over by Admiralty – *Reliant* (as *Somersby*: freighting), *Resurgent* (for conversion
to armaments issuing ship)
Laid up or sold – *Spabeck* (temporary)

Nuclear powered tanker Discussion of construction of nuclear powered tanker for RFA (single
screw, 65,000 tons deadweight)

Captain T Elder appointed Commodore RFA

Operation 'Grapple' (atom test on Christmas Island)

Disaster relief
Turkish earthquake: RFAs deployed to assist Royal Navy
Ceylon floods: RFAs deployed to assist Royal Navy

Accident at sea:
Wave Master assists search for German sailing vessel *Pamir*

Mutiny
Wave Govenor's Lascar crew refused to man the ship and were discharged ashore in Trinidad. Forty new West Indian seamen signed on as crew

1958
Building begun – *Plumleaf* (as *Corheath*)
Completed – *Resurgent, Reliant*
Transferred or taken over by Admiralty – *Reliant* (first air stores supply ship in service)
Laid up or sold – *Ennerdale, War Afridi, War Hindoo, Wave Conqueror* (defective engines), *Belgol, Celerol, Fortol, Larchol, Prestol, Serbol, Wave Commander, Wave Conqueror*

Leaf class First bareboat charter by Admiralty, vessels operating as RFAs, predominantly this class (Leafs)

Tide class *Tiderace* renamed *Tideflow*, *Tiderange* renamed *Tidesurge*

Technical Advisers retitled Marine Superintendents and Deputy Marine Superintendents
Technical Assistants retitled Marine Engineering Superintendents and Deputy Engineering Superintendents

Salvage
Wave Knight in company with RN ships: after collision between MT *Melika* and MV *Fernand Gilbert Cedardale* took 23,000 tons of crude aboard from *Melika*. *Sea Salvor* also deployed

1959
Launched – *Pearleaf*
Transferred or taken over by Admiralty – *Appleleaf* (as *George Lyras*), *Cherryleaf* (as *Laurelwood*), *Brambleleaf* (as *London Loyalty*), *Bayleaf* (as *London Integrity*), and *Orangeleaf* (as *Southern Satellite*)
Laid up or sold – *Abbeydale, Arndale, Bishopdale, Boxol, Cedardale, Derwentdale, Dewdale, Dingledale, Eaglesdale, Elderol, Easdale, Echodale, Ennerdale, Limol, Petrobus, Wave Commander, Wave Governor, Wave Liberator, Wave Emperor, Wave Regent, Wave Premier*

Review of manning levels. Distinction made between RAS-capable ships and other RFAs
Ranks of Senior Master and Senior Chief Engineering officer introduced into RFA

Cyprus emergency
Blue Ranger and *Brown Ranger* deployed to island

First Cod War (31 August 1959–20 July 1961)
RFAs deployed: *Wave Baron, Wave Chief, Wave Ruler* (badly damaged), *Wave Victor, Wave Sovereign, Wave Laird, Wave Master, Wave Prince, Black Ranger, Olna, Tideflow* and *Tidesurge*

Salvage
Fort Beauharnois deployed to recover British cargo vessel *Beaverbank*

1960
Launched – *Plumleaf* (as *Corheath*)
Completed – *Pearleaf, Plumleaf*
Transferred or taken over by Admiralty – *Pearleaf, Plumleaf*
Laid up or sold – *Broomdale, Eddycreek, War Brahmin, Wave Monarch, Wave Duke, Wave King, Surf Pioneer, Rippledyke*

War Sepoy removed from entrance to Dover. Sunk there as Second World War block ship
Cederdale and *Sea Salvor* receive salvage award
Reliant returns to UK for second stage of conversion
Fort Charlotte record RAS(s) 51.55 tons/hour

Way Ahead sub working party considered naval manning of RFAs
Introduction of RAS Proficiency Bonus for deck and engine-room ratings
First Commodore Chief Engineer appointed RFA

Malayan emergency (ended 31 July)

Black Ranger in collision with submarine HMS *Thule*
Allegedly signal sent: 'Only Thules rush in where Rangers fear to tread'

Eddycreek and *Wave Victor* in use as Gan station tankers, refuelling RAF, reflecting the way air transport is fast superseding troopships

1961
Building begun – *Bacchus, Hebe, Tidepool, Tidespring*
Laid up or sold – *Echodale, Surf Patrol*

Sir Lancelot design agreed
Reliant conversion completed

Tideflow and RN frigate HMS *Falmouth* in collision off Lyme Bay during anti-submarine exercise. *Falmouth* holed, but able to make Portland under own power
Fort Dunvegan: Opium found aboard
Wave Victor fuelling hulk for RAF at Gan

Company Service Contracts for UK POs and ratings in foreign-going RFAs, tankers and stores issuing ships introduced
RFA second officer attended lieutenant's course at RN Staff College, Greenwich

Kuwait crisis
Fort Dunvegan (as air stores/victualling ship), *Fort Sandusky, Fort Charlotte, Wave Master, Wave Ruler, Gold Ranger, Olna, Resurgent, Retainer, Reliant, Tidereach, Orangeleaf* and *Pearleaf* deployed to support operation

1962
Building begun – *Sir Lancelot*
Launched – *Hebe, Bacchus, Tidespring, Tidepool,* RRS *Discovery* (manning/management by DoS), *Cherryleaf* (as *Overseas Adventurer*)
Completed – *Hebe, Bacchus*
Transferred or taken over by Admiralty – *Bacchus, Hebe*
Laid up or sold – *Bacchus, Fort Beauharnois, Fort Constantine, Wave Master, Eddybay*
Lost – *Green Ranger*

Reliant: Opium found aboard

First use of term Front Line support ships in Statement on Defence Estimates
Tide Austral handed over to the Royal Australian Navy and commissioned as HMAS *Tide Austral* on 15 August at Southampton and as HMAS *Supply* at Portsmouth on 7 September 1962
Pennant numbers painted on RFAs

Captain A E Curtain OBE RD appointed Commodore RFA
New HQ – Empress State Building – the Mad House

Indonesian confrontation (1962–August 1966)
RFAs deployed included: *Gold Ranger, Eddyrock, Fort Charlotte, Wave Sovereign, Tidereach*
Brunei
Gold Ranger deployed

1963
Ordered – *Regent, Resource, Olynthus, Olna* and *Oleander* (R class ships are first RFAs with purpose-built helicopter pads)
Launched – *Sir Lancelot, Ennerdale* (as *Naess Scotsman*)
Completed – *Tidespring, Tidepool, Cherryleaf, Ennerdale*
Laid up or sold – *Airsprite, Eddybay, Eddybeach, Eddycliff, Eddycreek, Eddyness, Eddyreef, Amherst, Nasprite, Wave Protector, Philol*

First training course for RFA petty officers

Zanzibar
Hebe deployed to evacuate UK nationals

1964
Ordered – *Sir Galahad, Sir Geraint, Sir Bedivere, Engadine* (helicopter training ship), *Lyness, Stromness, Tarbatness*
Building begun – *Regent, Resource, Olna*
Launched – *Derwentdale* (as *Halcyon Breeze*), *Regent, Oleander, Olynthus*
Completed – *Sir Lancelot, Derwentdale*
Laid up or sold – *Wave Knight*

Captain E Paine CBE appointed Commodore RFA
Admiralty integrated into Ministry of Defence as Navy Department
Board of Admiralty becomes Admiralty Board
NAS 767 at Culdrose training Wessex for service on RFAs
RFA radio officers begin attending long course at HMS *Collingwood*

Persian Gulf
RFA support to Royal Navy ships involved in anti-smuggling, piracy and security operations

Tanganyika
Army mutiny: RN aircraft carrier deployed with *Tideflow* in support

1965
Ordered – *Sir Tristram, Sir Percivale,*
Building begun – *Sir Galahad, Sir Geraint, Lyness, Engadine, Stromness, Sir Bedivere, Dewdale* (as *Edenfield*)
Completed – *Olynthus, Oleander, Dewdale*
Laid up or sold – *Oakol, Airsprite*

RNSTS
Formation on 1 January by merger of four departments

Secretary of State for Defence becomes registered owner of RFAs
RFA ratings allowed use of NAAFI facilities
Cadet replaces apprentice for RFA officers under training

Aden emergency ends in 1967 with independence

Indonesian confrontation
Royal Navy patrols with RFA support

1966
Building begun – *Sir Percivale, Sir Tristam, Tarbatness*
Launched – *Regent, Resource, Olna, Lyness, Sir Galahad, Sir Bedivere, Sir Tristram, Engadine, Stromness*

Completed – *Sir Galahad, Lyness, Olna*
Laid up or sold – *Spabeck, Cherryleaf, Olna*

Regent/Resource: Permanent helicopter flights assigned
Freighting tankers rerated as support oilers
Captain G O Evans CBE, DSO appointed Commodore RFA
Fleet Manager RFA, attached to HQ staff of DFMT(N) and ranked as Assistant Director, introduced
to manage fleet. Post later split into Fleet Manager (Tankers) and Fleet Manager (Dry Cargo and
LSLs)
Electronics Superintendent appointed for first time

Beira Patrol (1 March 1966–13 June 1975)
Blockade of Mozambique port of Beira to prevent oil imports
Endurance record of 90 days continually at sea set by *Tidespring* during this operation

Rescue
Olna deployed in rescue operation involving *World Liberty* (Liberia)
Olna deployed in rescue of crew of *Zaneta* (Liberia)
Pearleaf deployed in rescue of crew of tanker *Mare Nostrum* (Italy)

1967
Launched – *Sir Percivale, Sir Geraint, Tarbatness*
Completed – *Stromness, Regent, Resource, Sir Bedivere, Sir Geraint, Sir Tristram, Engadine, Tarbatness*
Laid up or sold – *Eddyrock, Wave Sovereign, Fort Duquesne, Fort Charlotte*

Olynthus renamed *Olwen*
Oleander renamed *Olmeda*

Short Miscellaneous Air Courses become available for officers and ratings
Centralised pay scheme for officers. Officer's pay now settled monthly
Post of C-in-C Mediterranean Fleet abolished. RFAs now responsibility of C-in-C Home Fleet,
redesignated C-in-C Western Fleet

Aden crisis
Aden becomes independent – involved in troop evacuation
RFAs deployed: *Dewdale, Appleleaf, Olna, Retainer, Reliant, Resurgent, Stromness, Fort Sandusky,*
Tidespring and *Tideflow*

NATO's Standing Naval Force Atlantic (STANAVFORLANT) formed
RFA contributes occasional tanker

Arab–Israel Six Day War (23 May–10 June)
RFA support of HMS *Hermes* Group after Egyptian threat to blockade Strait of Tiran

1968
Building begun – *Blue Rover, Green Rover* and *Grey Rover*
Launched – *Green Rover*
Completed – *Sir Percivale*

RN lose aircraft carriers and Middle East and Far East stations run down

Captain J Dines CBE RD appointed Commodore RFA

Guinea Gulf patrol
Carried on until Suez Canal reopened, this was a RAS refuelling patrol off St Helena by Wave and
Rover class ships using Freetown to load and Simonstown to load and for repairs

Aden
RFA ships support RN ships on standby during peace talks
Disaster relief
Sea Salvor and four minesweepers deployed after earthquake in NW Sicily

1969
Launched – *Blue Rover, Grey Rover*
Completed – *Green Rover*
Laid up or sold – *Birchol, Oakol, Teakol, Fort Constantine, Wave Baron, Wave Duke, Wave Laird, Surf Patrol, Surf Pioneer, Fort Langley, Eddyness*

Engadine: first deck landing by Westland Sea King
Ennerdale: first awarded Wilkinson Sword of Peace

New victualling system tried – so successful it is extended to whole fleet
RFA ensign introduced fleetwide. Gold anchor now vertical on ensign, ensign with horizontal gold anchor retained by newly formed RMAS

1970
Completed – *Grey Rover, Blue Rover*
Laid up or sold – *Appleleaf, Bishopdale, Black Ranger, Spa, Rowanol*

Ennerdale lost (no casualties)

LSLs transferred to management and Marchwood Military Port is designated their base port

Apollo XIII
Ennerdale, Tarbatness and *Tideflow* in place for Apollo XIII splashdown incident

Disaster relief
Operation 'Burlap' (East Pakistan cyclone relief). RFAs deployed: *Sir Galahad, Resource, Olwen, Stromness*

1971
Ordered – *Black Rover, Gold Rover*
Building begun – *Sir Caradoc* (as *Grey Master*)
Laid up or sold – *Blue Ranger, Robert Dundas, Wave Victor, Wave Prince*

Green Rover: Harrier VSTOL landing in Thames

Captain H O L'Estrange DSC RD appointed Commodore RFA
Commander Far East Fleet abolished and so Western and Eastern Fleets became the Fleet under C-in-C Fleet. Fleet RFAs programmed by RFA officer appointed as Operations Room Logistics officer (later Fleet Logistics Officer)
RFA superintendents are retitled
Catering and accounts duties integrated under title Purser (1 January)

Operation 'Bracken' (Gulf 1–31 December)
Royal Navy ships and RFA s deployed to ensure safe withdrawal from British bases
Operation 'Lymelight' (Live BBC TV broadcast from English Channel)
Olmeda and *Regent* deployed

1972
Ordered – *Fort Austin, Fort Grange*
Launched – *Sir Caradoc* (as *Grey Master*), *Sir Lamorak* (as *Anu*)
Completed – *Sir Lamorak* (as *Anu*)

Laid up or sold – *Wave Baron, Fort Sandusky, Fort Rosalie, Brambleleaf, Gold Ranger*

Resource: Improved GEC RAS gear trialled

Captain G A Robson appointed Commodore RFA

Honduras: (26 January–7 February)
HMS *Ark Royal* Task Group, with one RFA and amphibious force including *Sir Bedivere, Sir Geraint* and *Sir Tristram* deployed to prevent invasion of British Honduras

Malta
Evacuation of Malta: *Bayleaf, Sir Geraint, Lyness* deployed
Operation 'Motorman'
Internal security duties in Northern Ireland, involving movement of troops using LSLs
Iceland (7 September–31 December)
RFAs support RN ships on patrol
Operation 'Zealous'
Tidepool, Tidesurge and *Tidereach* standing by for Uganda evacuation
Disaster relief
Tidespring, Stromness deployed in wake of Rodriguez Island (Indian Ocean) cyclone

1973
Building begun – *Appleleaf, Fort Grange*
Launched – *Gold Rover, Black Rover*
Completed – *Sir Caradoc* (as *Grey Master*)
Transferred or taken over by MoD – *Cherryleaf* (as *Overseas Adventurer*)
Laid up or sold – *Bayleaf, Black Ranger, Reliant*

Engadine: Helicopter trials support unit formed at RNAS Culdrose

Iceland (Second Cod War: 1 January–14 May)
Wave Chief and *Blue Rover* deployed with Royal Navy on patrol duties
Rescue
Olwen rescued twenty people during fire on Norwegian tanker *Fernwave*
Resource attended fire on Liberian tanker *Naess Spirit*
Sir Tristram rescue of deep submergence sub *Pisces III*
Salvage
Resurgent: Cypriot MV *Nejma* towed to Majorca

1974
Building begun – *Brambleleaf* (as *Hudson Deep*)
Completed – *Gold Rover, Black Rover*
Laid up or sold – *Derwentdale, Wave Chief, Brown Ranger*

Grey Rover/Blue Rover re-engined
Reliant returned to service after refit

RFAs have ship's safety officer appointed under Health and Safety Act (1974)

Cyprus
Regent, Olwen, Olna, Gold Rover standing by with RN ships after Turkish invasion
Suez Canal
Bacchus: Clearance of war debris from Canal

1975
Building begun – *Fort Austin, Bayleaf* (as *Hudson Sound*)
Launched – *Orangeleaf* (as *Hudson Progress*), *Appleleaf* (as *Hudson Cavalier*)
Laid up or sold – Robert Middleton, Tideflow

Engadine: VSTOL trials
Plumleaf: First vessel through newly opened Suez Canal
General Council of British Shipping takes over as central organisation representing UK shipowners:
RFA represented as MoD shipowner

Cyprus
Olmeda standing by with RN ships east of Malta
Iceland (Third Cod War: 24 November 1975–1 June 1976)
Green Rover, Blue Rover, Olwen, Tidepool, Tidereach deployed with RN vessels
Beira Patrol
Tidesurge last vessel deployed. Terminated this year
Evacuation
Cambodia/Vietnam
Operation 'Faldage': *Olna* and RN vessels stand by off Kom Pong Som to evacuate British nationals
Operation 'Stella': *Green Rover* and RN vessels evacuate refugees
Angola
Orangeleaf and RN vessel deployed for possible evacuation of British nationals

1976
Launched – *Reliant* (as *Astronomer*), *Fort Grange, Brambleleaf* (as *Hudson Deep*)
Laid up or sold – *Wave Ruler, Tideflow, Reliant*

Lyness deployed with HMS *Ark Royal* for BBC TV documentary *Sailor*, detailing involvement
Blue Rover/Grey Rover: Refuelling trials with commercial tankers

Cod Wars: Iceland
Olwen in support of patrolling RN vessels
Falklands
Shackleton's Falklands survey. *Tidesurge* and HMS *Eskimo* deployed to Falklands to prevent invasion
Shackleton later recommends islanders receive £13 million for improvements, inflaming situation
further
Evacuation
Grey Rover and *Stromness* off Lebanon for Britons
Engadine off Gibraltar

1977
Transferred or taken over by Admiralty – *Reliant* (as *Astronomer*)
Laid up or sold – *Spaburn, Spalake, Dewdale, Tidesurge*

Tarbatness: Maltese crew replaced with UK personnel
Gold Rover: Experimental RAS with MT *British Tamar*
Stromness: Landing trials of Harrier GR3

Captain S C ('Black Sam') Dunlop appointed Commodore RFA

Operation 'Journeyman'
Covert naval presence off Falklands during talks with Argentine government, to counter possibility
of invasion
Operation 'Pallium'
Sir Geraint deployed to Pitcairn Island with RE detachment to improve landing facilities; postage
stamp issued

Spithead Review
RFAs deployed: *Engadine, Sir Tristram, Gold Rover, Tidespring, Olwen, Stromness, Sir Geraint, Pearleaf*

1978
Launched – *Fort Austin*
Completed – *Fort Grange*
Laid up or sold – *Tidereach, Retainer, Orangeleaf, Empire Gull, Tarbatness* (sales tour)

Hebe badly damaged by fire, one crew member accused of arson. Later changed to murder

Order-in-Council 121 amended to cover basic sea training

Iran
Grey Rover and RN vessels stand by for evacuation of British nationals

1979
Completed – *Fort Austin, Orangeleaf* (as *Balder London*)
Transferred or taken over by MoD – *Appleleaf* (as *Hudson Cavalier*)
Laid up or sold – *Resurgent, Retainer*

Resource: Trial of shore test point for RAS Mk2 rig at RN Armament depot, Glen Douglas
Olmeda: First fit of SatNav equipment
Olwen: Harrier deck landing
Resource ran trials

RFA discipline now covered by Merchant Navy Code of Conduct
Master, *Sir Geraint*, convicted of misconduct; certificate revoked

Operation 'Culex'
Bacchus, Fort Grange deployed following influx of illegal immigrants into Hong Kong
Malta
Closure of Naval base. *Bacchus, Sir Lancelot, Tarbatness, Olna* deployed with RN vessels
Evacuation
Cherryleaf and RN vessel off Grenada for evacuation of British nationals
Disaster relief
Cherryleaf deployed with RN vessels during Hurricanes David and Frederic

1980
Building begun – *Diligence* (as *Stena Inspector*)
Launched – *Diligence, Argus* (as *Contender Bezant*)
Transferred or taken over by MoD – *Brambleleaf* (as *Hudson Deep*)
Laid up or sold – *Cherryleaf, Tarbatness, Lyness*

Armilla Patrol (October 1980–)
British presence established in the Gulf of Oman/Strait of Hormuz in case of escalation in the Iran–Iraq war. *Stromness* and *Olwen* first RFAs deployed
Iran–Iraq conflict
Fort Austin, Olna, Olmeda deployed

1981
Launched – *Oakleaf* (as *Oktania*), *Bayleaf* (as *Hudson Sound*)
Completed – *Diligence* (as *Stena Inspector*), *Argus* (as *Contender Bezant*)
Laid up or sold – *Lyness, Tarbatness, Eddyfirth, Resurgent, Bacchus*

First tanker safety course for RFA petty officers held at Warsash Nautical College

1982
Completed – *Bayleaf* (as *Hudson Sound*)
Transferred or taken over by MoD – *Reliant* (as *Astronomer*)
Laid up or sold – *Stromness* (returned to service 1 April), *Tidepool* (returned by Chile for duration of Falklands campaign)

Emergency life support apparatus (ELSA) introduced into RFAs

Falklands campaign (2 April–14 June)
Recovery of the Falkland Islands group after illegal Argentine invasion
Operation 'Corporate' Recovery of British territory in South Atlantic
Operation 'Paraquat' Recovery of South Georgia (*Tidespring, Brambleleaf*)
Operation 'Sutton' Recovery of the Falkland Islands

1983
Transferred or taken over by MoD – *Sir Caradoc* (as *Grey Master*), *Sir Lamorak* (as *Lakespan Ontario*), *Brambleleaf, Diligence* (as *Stena Inspector*)
Laid up or sold – *Stromness*

Captain J G M Coull appointed Commodore RFA
First course on dynamic positioning system (*Diligence*) for RFA officers
Arapaho system: Negotiations begin with US for purchase

Falklands support
RFA ships supporting RN ships in Falkland Islands Protective Zone
Operation 'Matchstick'
Destruction of Argentine base on South Thule: *Tidespring* deployed to support HMS *Ariadne*

Operation 'Offcut' (from 18 November)
Blue Rover, Grey Rover, Brambleleaf, Reliant deployed with RN vessels to support British troops included in multi-national force in Lebanon

1984
Ordered – *Sir Galahad*
Transferred or taken over by MoD – *Diligence, Argus* (as *Contender Bezant*), *Orangeleaf* (as *Balder London*)

Reliant in service with Arapaho containerised helicopter system

First Defensive Weapons Officer appointed (RN lieutenant commander)
RFA Aviation Support Unit (ASU) formed at Culdrose
Marchwood memorial unveiled
Death at sea: Two personnel killed, four injured aboard *Olwen*

Lebanon
Reliant deployed to relieve HMS *Fearless* and evacuate British nationals
Falklands
RFA support reduced to as required. *Diligence* permanently assigned (diving facilities)

1985
Building begun – *Sir Galahad*
Completed – *Sir Tristram*

Captain B H Rutterford appointed Commodore RFA
Warsash Study commissioned: Assessment of RFA manning practices

Purser (3/O/(S)) induction training course introduced. Supply Officers Training Unit established to run this course
First issue of *Gunline*
RFA Service crest officially approved by HM the Queen

1986
Ordered – *Fort Victoria*
Launched – *Sir Galahad*
Laid up or sold – *Sir Lamorak* (charter expired), *Pearleaf, Plumleaf, Reliant*

Reliant: Arapaho container equipment removed
Black Rover: Seamen's strike

Commodore RFA now includes duties of shore based Marine Superintendent
New RFA rank structure introduced
Several senior HQ posts established
Consolidated Ratings Salary: Proposal that this be introduced
Directorate of Naval Manpower Audit instigates review of manning RFA procedures and NUS introduce guidelines to reduce risk of strikes on RFAs

Training
RFA officers on first C O Designate course specifically for personnel
First officer undertakes RN Principal Warfare Officer Course
RFA engineering/electrical officers on Bond instrumentation course
RFA weapons maintenance course introduced at HMS Collingwood/Cambridge
Communications Officer's Long Course

Aden
Brambleleaf deployed with Royal Yacht to evacuate British and foreign nationals

1987
Ordered – *Fort George*
Completed – *Sir Galahad*

Diligence: £2 million refit
Oakleaf: computer installed for stores and stock management
ICS25 Integrated Communications system fitted to *Olwen, Olna, Argus, Sir Galahad, Olmeda* and all new constructions and refits
Refits section established under Director General Ship Repairs

RFA Staff Officer post established with MoD Directorate of Naval Ware
Training Controller appointed at Headquarters
RFA rate Petty Officer (Stores) introduced
HQ team set up to study Warsash Study
MNB agree War Zone pay (Gulf *not* included)

Operation 'Cimnel' (later Operation 'Calendar II')
Diligence and *Regent* deployed with RN vessels in mine clearance operation
Operation 'Purple Warrior'
Biggest RN deployment since Falklands

Korean War Memorial opened by HM Queen
Remembrance Sunday: RFA represented at Albert Hall and Cenotaph

1988
Building begun – *Fort Victoria*
Transferred or taken over by MoD – *Argus*
Laid up or sold – *Green Rover*, *Sir Caradoc* (returned to owners)

RFA introduces Cubitts navigational aid
RFA Ratings Consolidated Salary introduced
RFA POs and ratings paid Defensive Weapons Allowance whether ship fitted with weapons or not
RFA Chaplain appointed

Disaster relief
Hurricane Gilbert (Grand Cayman and Jamaica), *Oakleaf* deployed with RN vessels

1989
Building begun – *Fort George*
Laid up or sold – *Sir Lancelot*, *Engadine*, *Appleleaf*

Captain R M Thorn appointed Commodore RFA
New RFA common rank structure introduced
Order in Council 1989 – changes to status of RFA vessels to government vessels on non-commercial charter
Rating helicopter controllers introduced

Disaster relief
Fort Austin deployed in aftermath of Hurricane Dean (Bermuda)
Brambleleaf and RN ships deployed in wake of Hurricane Hugo (Caribbean)

1990
Launched – *Fort Victoria*

Fort Victoria: Terrorist bomb in engine room; no casualties

Operation 'Eldorado'
Tidespring deployed with RN vessels off Liberia for possible evacuation

Operation 'Granby' (the Gulf War 2 August 1990-31 August 1991)
Iraq invades Kuwait. *Fort Grange*, *Olna* and *Diligence* deployed initially. *Sir Bedivere*, *Sir Tristram*, *Sir Galahad* and *Sir Percivale* deployed to freight supplies later. *Argus* deployed later as primary casualty/evacuation ship in Gulf

1991
Launched – *Fort George*
Laid up or sold – *Tidespring*

RFA Handbook (the Bible) rewritten
'Way Ahead' study commissioned

Gulf
Olmeda, *Regent*, *Orangeleaf* deployed
Operation 'Desert Storm': Invasion of Iraq
Operation Haven: Kurdish refugee support on Iraq–Turkey border

Operation 'Manna'
Fort George deployed in wake of Bangladesh cyclone

1992
Laid up or sold – *Regent, Resource*

Warsash Manning Trial introduced
RFA Meritiorious Conduct scheme introduced
RFAs allocated British Forces Post Office (BFPO) numbers

Operation 'Grapple'
Sir Bedivere, Resource and *Argus* deployed to former Yugoslavia (*ie*, Bosnia) to support British element of UN Protection Force

Orient '92
Fort Austin and *Olwen* deployed with RN vessels to Far East

Disaster relief
Orangeleaf deployed with RN ships in wake of Hurricane Andrew (Caribbean)

1993
Completed – *Fort George, Fort Victoria*
Laid up or sold – *Blue Rover*

RFA reorganisation introduced: now headed up by Commodore RFA (Type Commander (Flotilla)), not a civil servant in the person of Director Supply and Transport
New offices at Portsmouth Naval base replace the old 'Mad House'
Marine Superintendent and Technical Superintendent now designated Chief Staff Officers

Operation 'Grapple' (later Operation 'Hamden')
RFAs still deployed to assist British contingent in Bosnia
Operation 'Snowdon'
Oakleaf and RN vessel deployed to Haiti during political unrest

1994
Completed – *Fort Victoria*
Laid up or sold – *Olmeda*

Sir Bedivere arrived Rosyth for SLEP programme
Captain N D Squire appointed Commodore RFA
Operation 'Hamden'
Fort Grange supporting carrier group operating in Adriatic
Operation 'Spartan' (17–30 September)
Oakleaf deployed to Haitito support RN ships
Operation 'Driver' (9 October–15 November)
RFA ships on Armilla Patrol deployed to Northern Gulf

1995
International Standards of Training, Certification and Watchkeeping amended (STCW 95)
FOST Portland closed: transferred to HMS *Drake* Plymouth (FOST Plymouth)
Operation 'Hamden' (January–20 November 1996)
RFAs still deployed
Operation 'Chantress'
Sir Galahad deployed to Angola

Disaster relief
Oakleaf deployed with RN units to Anguilla in wake of Hurricane Luis

1996
***Building begun** – Sea Crusader* (as *Celestine*), *Sea Centurion* (as *Stena Ausonia*)
***Launched** – Sea Crusader* (as *Celestine*)
***Completed** – Sea Crusader* (as *Celestine*)
***Transferred or taken over by fleet** – Sea Crusader* (as *Celestine*)

Joint Rapid Deployment Force (JRDF) formed

RNSTS
Ceases operation. Supply role taken over by MoD Naval Bases and Supplies Agency. This Agency
and Marchwood Defence Sea Mounting Centre absorbed into new Warship Support Agency (*WSA*),
which in turn, is part of MoD Defence Logistics Organisation (*DLO*)
Exercise RUKUS 906
First joint exercises between Royal Navy, USN and Russian navy. *Black Rover* deployed with RN units
Operation 'Hamden' (January–20 November 1996)
RFAs still deployed. *Oakleaf* and *Fort Grange* deployed to support HMS *Invincible* during Harrier
operations

1997
***Ordered** – Wave Knight, Wave Ruler*
***Launched** – Sea Centurion* (as *Stena Ausonia*)
***Laid up or sold** – Resource*

Armilla Patrol/Operation Bolton (Gulf of Oman and Persian Gulf)
RFAs deployed with RN units to maintain UN embargo of Iraq
Yugoslavia
RFAs deployed to support UK forces present as part of Stabilisation Force (SFOR)
Operation 'Caxton'
Black Rover deployed for evacuation after volcanic eruption on Montserrat
Operation 'Tiller'
Argus and *Orangeleaf* deployed Sierra Leone for possible evacuation
Hong Kong (Handover to People's Republic of China)
Sir Percivale last out prior to handover

1998
***Building begun** – Wave Knight, Wave Ruler*
***Completed** – Sea Centurion* (as *Stena Ausonia*)

Armilla Patrol/Operation 'Bolton' (Gulf of Oman and Persian Gulf)
Fort Victoria, Fort George, Bayleaf, Brambleleaf and *Diligence* deployed with RN units to maintain UN
embargo of Iraq
Operation 'Resilient'
Orangeleaf, Oakleaf deployed with RN units for evacuation (Sierra Leone)
Disaster relief
Black Rover supporting RN units following Hurricane George (St Kitts and Montserrat) and
Hurricane Mitch (Honduras)
Sir Tristram (Operation 'Tellar') deployed in wake of Hurricane Mitch

1999
***Transferred or taken over by Fleet** – Sea Centurion* (as *Stena Ausonia*)
***Laid up or sold** – Olwen, Olna*

Black Rover, Sir Tristram share Wilkinson Sword of Peace Award

Captain P J Lannin appointed RFA Commodore and Assistant Chief of Staff (Sustainability)

Sierra Leone
Oakleaf, Gold Rover, Grey Rover deployed to support RN units
Operation 'Bolton' (Iraq deployment)
Brambleleaf, Fort Austin deployed to support RN units
Operation 'Magellan' (Kosovo deployment)
Fort Austin, Argus, Bayleaf deployed in support NATO Balkans force (KFOR)

Twenty-first Century

2000
Ordered – *Largs Bay, Lyme Bay*
Launched – *Wave Knight*

Fort Grange renamed *Fort Rosalie*
Olna returned to service temporarily before being laid up again

Operation 'Palliser'/'Barras' (Sierra Leone)
Sir Geraint, Sir Tristram, Sir Percivale deployed to support UK forces
Amphibious Ready Group (ARG): deployed with this group (Sierra Leone)
Disaster relief
Mozambique: *Fort George* deployed for flood relief (Wilkinson Sword of Peace awarded)
Naval Task Group 2000
Seven British warships and support ships undertaking voyage around world to celebrate new Millennium. *Bayleaf, Diligence* and *Fort George* deployed to accompany group
Greek ferry disaster
Fort George deployed Sea Kings to rescue survivors after Greek registered ferry *Express Saminia* sank off Greek island of Paros

2001
Ordered – *Cardigan Bay, Mounts Bay*
Building begun – *Largs Bay, Lyme Bay*
Launched – *Wave Ruler*

Commemorative postage stamps South Georgia/South Sandwich Islands

Exercise 'Argonaut'
RFAs deployed in support of RN units
Operation 'Silkman' (Sierra Leone)
LSLs deployed to Freetown
Operation 'Enduring Freedom' (Afghanistan)
US led

Rescue at sea
Diligence: twenty sailors rescued from MV *Bella 1* following engine failure
Fort Austin: twenty sailors rescued from sinking inflatable boat

2002
Building begun – *Mounts Bay*
Laid up or sold – *Sea Centurion, Sir Geraint*

Argus: Three crew members injured during deck-handling exercise when a Sea King from 848 NAS crashed soon after take-off

Bureau introduced/COMFRA integrated into C-in-C Fleet organisation and now based at Portsmouth
RFA Association created
STCW in force for every British Merchant Navy officer (including masters)

Operation 'Oracle' (anti-smuggling operations against Iraq)
RFAs deployed to support RN ships
Operation 'Veritas'
UK contribution to Operation Enduring Freedom: LSL deployed in support 45 Commando

2003
Launched – Largs Bay
Completed – Wave Knight, Wave Ruler
Laid up or sold – Sir Geraint, Sea Crusader

Captain R C Thornton appointed Commodore(X) RFA and Assistant Chief of Staff (Sustainability)
Second officer RFA appointed Flag Lieutenant to First Sea Lord
First RFA Officer's training course established at Britannia Naval College
RFA Medical Assistants re-classified as Medical Technicians

Operation 'Telic'
RFAs deployed to Gulf in support of RN vessels
Um Qasr Sir Galahad, Sir Percivale deliver humanitarian aid
Aviation Fort Victoria: first deployment of Merlin MH1 aircraft

2004
Launched – Mounts Bay
Transferred or taken over by Fleet – Oakleaf (purchased at end of bareboat charter)
Laid up or sold – Sir Percivale (decommissioned in preparation for extended readiness)

Wave Ruler First RAS with Mexican navy, after training

New computer system (Magellan Human Resources) introduced
Supply Department renamed Logistics Supply Department. Supply officers and ratings renamed Logistics Supply staff

Wilkinson Sword of Peace award
Award to *Sir Galahad* for work in Iraq
D-Day: 60th anniversary
Wave Knight, Sir Percivale deployed
Exercise Rapid Alliance
RFAs deployed as part of UK contribution Aurora Deployment
Disaster relief
Wave Ruler deployed with RN units in wake of Hurricane Ivan (Cayman Islands)
Operation 'Garron' *Diligence* deployed in wake of Asian tsunami

2005 (Royal Fleet Auxiliary centenary year)
Launched – Cardigan Bay, Lyme Bay
Completed – Mounts Bay

Diligence supported the newly formed Iraqi Navy in the Northern Arabian Gulf

New RFA Cadet insignia introduced

Anti-drug smuggling operations
RFA tanker supporting West Indies Guard Ship and US Coast Guard
Armilla Patrol (Gulf of Oman and Persian Gulf)
RFA tanker deployed with RN units
Disaster relief
Operation 'Garron' *Diligence, Bayleaf* deployed in wake of Asian tsunami
MARSTRIKE 05:
Fort George deployed with RN Strike Force for Middle East exercises

2006
Completed and taken over by Fleet – *Mounts Bay*
Laid up or sold – *Grey Rover, Sir Galahad*

Gold Rover: 50th anniversary of Nigerian Navy; Operation 'Vela': off Sierra Leone
Wave Ruler seized over £1 billion-worth of cocaine drugs during September–November

Operation 'Aquila 06'
Fort Victoria deployed with RN ships for evacuation of UK nationals from Israel and Lebanon

2007
Completed – *Cardigan Bay, Lyme Bay*

Orangeleaf completed SLEP programme extending operational life until 2017
Argus – £12 million upgrade at Falmouth, which then became her base port
Sir Bedivere appointed mother ship and afloat training platform for Iraqi navy and marines
Gold Rover – medical supplies to Tristan da Cunha

HRH the Earl of Wessex visits RFA HQ at Whale Island

Humanitarian aid
Wave Knight deployed to Dominican Republic after Tropical Storm Noel

2008
Laid up or sold – *Sir Bedivere*

Largs Bay: £20 million drugs haul from fishing boat stopped off Barbados
Lyme Bay deployed to Tristan da Cunha to help rebuild harbour; starts Tall Ships Race in Liverpool (23 July)
Wave Ruler: £420 million-worth of drugs captured; relief work during Hurricane Gustav and Hurricane Paloma
Fort Rosalie caught fire in refit at Birkenhead, resulting in slight damage to the ship and, fortunately, no injuries

Queen's Colour
Presentation of the Queen's Colour by His Highness the Earl of Wessex aboard *Largs Bay* on 18 July

Appendix 2

Modern Replenishment at Sea

By 1950, despite the atmosphere of postwar austerity, development of the replenishment process that had begun during the later stages of the Second World War still continued apace.

Liquid replenishment-at-sea had become more or less routine although ships such as the Wave class, which carried out many of the refuelling operations, were not purpose built for the job, having been rapidly converted from their freighting tanker role.

With the introduction of the early Tide class, in 1954, all this was to change. The early Tides were purpose-built fast fleet replenishment tankers. Over 500 feet long and seventy feet wide, they were capable of eighteen knots and with three RAS rigs on each side and astern refuelling arrangements, they could replenish three ships simultaneously, even if one was an aircraft carrier.

Along with their other modifications, an increased derrick length and the introduction of two additional troughs meant that replenishment could now take place with the ships nearly 200 feet apart, greatly increasing the ease with which the process could be carried out in rough weather, because, in addition, the vessels maintained station by use of the engines alone, hawser and breast ropes having been quietly and unofficially dispensed with.

As a further increase in efficiency, the troughs now carried two lengths of five-inch fuel hose and a three-inch fresh water hose, all capable of being used simultaneously. Later experiments, particularly those concerned with replenishment in heavy weather, resulted in development of a new abeam rig, incorporating a jackstay to support the three troughs, while the newly devised Clarke Chapman self-tensioning winch kept the rig taut.

With a few modifications, this self-tensioning abeam rig is that in use today. For the astern method, a new non-stretch bonded fuelling hose was introduced, allowing the hose to be simply trailed astern from the tanker, without any supporting wires, until it is grappled and connected by the receiving ship, at which point the pump over can start.

A number of connecting systems have entered service over the years, with the result that now RFA ships are fitted with both the USN/NATO 'probe and drogue' system as well as the predominantly British Quick Release Mk II (QR Mk II).

In the USN system, connection is made by the probe travelling down the jackstay and entering the drogue with sufficient force to seat itself correctly in the retaining clips. This has resulted in the development of a non-tensioned jackstay and a winch incorporating a slipping clutch, fitted alongside the standard RFA equipment.

The early Tides served as the model for many of the RFA tankers that entered service later, in particular, the new Tides, *Tidespring* and *Tidepool*, introduced in 1963, and which were still in service up to the time of the Falklands War, in 1982. Later vessels have improved facilities for the crew like fully enclosed RAS control (RASCO), first introduced on the R class.

Chief Officer Chris Puxley took part in many replenishment operations aboard the early Tide class *Tideflow*. He had this to say about the RFA's experiences with HMS *Ark Royal*:

Refuelling the 'Ark' was always an impressive event, especially at night.

Both ships were usually darkened, eliminating all unnecessary lighting, so as a result we were all working under gloomy red floodlights. As we closed in to keep station on her starboard side the 'carrier loomed enormously into our field of vision, with the accommodation island towering high above us on the RAS deck. Three luminous nylon gunlines were fired by rifle across to our deck from the separate, red lit RAS pockets of the carrier, two to establish a link for each replenishment rig and one for the distance line and telephone wires to be attached to, up near the bows. Almost as a matter of routine, the two jackstay refuelling rigs and the distance line and phones would then be hauled back across to the 'carrier', with the large loops of fuel hoses spanning the sea and the searching white breakers thrown up between the two ships. Personnel on the decks of both ships could be seen moving about, mainly by the little light carried on their inflatable lifejackets. The distance line up forrard, with its tiny indicator lights apparently dancing on it in the wind, kept the bridge teams informed of our distance apart. Steam winches rattled throughout the RAS as their operators paid out or hauled in the three hose trays riding under each of the two automatically tensioned jackstay wires. They were compensating for the movement of the two ships and kept the tension off the pressurised hoses as the fuel was pumped across. The replenishment operation probably lasted for between one and two hours. On completion of fuelling, the hoses were blown through with air before being disconnected. When the hoses had been hauled back to the tanker, the jackstays were uncoupled and slipped. Still under cover of darkness, the tanker then slowly pulled away from the carrier, whilst the crew began re-stowing and securing the gear, ready for the next customer.

Even loading a freighting tanker, such as *Brambleleaf* had its complications. Chris Puxley again:

When in port and loading or discharging the cargo, the 2nd Officer and myself would keep cargo watches. This meant monitoring the loading or discharging process carefully, transferring the flow of oil from one tank to another as they became full or empty. When loading from a refinery, the cargo came aboard very quickly; making a fearsome crackling noise as it raced through the deck manifold. You needed to keep your wits about you so as to change tanks at the precise moment when the oil in the tank reached the required height, usually just a couple of rungs on the ladder from the top of the tank. Often we loaded two or three different products at the same time, requiring the deftness of a one armed paperhanger! If you were not prepared and the tank overflowed, the consequences would be catastrophic. The ship was getting on in years and some of the valves were quite stiff to turn, and especially difficult to close against a torrent of oil.

Present-day replenishment operations

Prior to the replenishment start time in the case of a fuel RAS, all required products are flushed through the rig to ensure that clean products of the required standard are available. For a solid RAS the loads need to be made up ready for dispatch. Once this has taken place the rig requires laying out; this requires all ropes and ancillary equipment to be connected to the rig. This includes but is not limited to the following equipment:

- Hose line
- Messenger lines
- Distance line
- Telephone line
- Signal bats
- Tool bag
- Gunline and rifle

The rig may also be required to be altered depending on the customer's requirement.

Replenishment can be divided into three main areas, these being abeam, stern, and vertical replenishment by helicopter (VERTREP). These can then subdivided into three delivery methods dependent on the customer's requirements.

Beam replenishment can take the format of RAS (L) (liquid) or RAS (S) (solid), RAS (L) can be delivered by large derrick or jackstay method. There are two jackstay methods; firstly the probe which is usually the preferred method of delivery, and secondly the quick release connection (QRC)/NATO 'B' method. The rig can be adapted to any of these methods, however, it is normal for it to be built and remain in one of the aforementioned states.

Large derrick can also be delivered in two formats; as with the jackstay this can take the format of either QRC/NATO B. The large derrick is a lot simpler to change from one connection to the other and only takes around fifteen minutes to change from one to the other.

The stern RAS (L) can be delivered by two different formats, depending on the ship's fit. The take two formats consist of the conventional stern rig, which is laid on the deck of the tanker on rollers, consisting of thirty-foot hoses joined together or alternatively, the Hudson reel, which consists of a 'lay flat' hose in one continuous length, except for the last fifteen feet, which is the same as the conventional type stern hose. For the receiving vessel it makes little difference which delivery method is used.

Beam replenishment in the RAS (S) format can be divided into two main forms: light jackstay and heavy jackstay. The light jackstay is used for the transfer of personnel or for stores up to the weight of 250kg. The light jackstay is purely manned by personnel with no machinery involved and is therefore manpower intensive, sometimes using all available ship's company.

Heavy jackstay is used for the transfer of heavy loads of stores, including ammunition, up to a maximum weight per load of two tonnes. There are three main methods of delivery and these are dependent on the ship's fit. These can come in the format of fixed high point, and GEC Mk 1A and GEC Mk 2. Within these fits there are various methods of additional equipment that can be used, depending on the receiving vessel's receiving position and equipment. This equipment can be in the form of drop reel traveller, which allows the lowering and recovery of loads from heavy jackstays to the deck on vessels which do not have the availability to lower the receiving end to the deck.

Regardless of the type of abeam rig used, or the stores to be transferred, that is, liquid, solids or personnel, there is little difference in the basic procedures to follow. Procedures for the stern rig are, of course, different. The procedures are adaptable to suit the various rigs and reception units used. However, I will go through the generic procedures for the rigs.

It is normal for the receiving ship to make an approach on the delivering vessel from astern and take up the correct position, which is abeam at a normal working distance of between twenty-four and fifty-five metres and at a speed of between ten and sixteen knots. First contact between the vessels is by line throwing rifle, normally fired by the receiving vessel. The rifle has been adapted to fire a soft nosed projectile to which is connected a light thin nylon line. Once this has been successfully passed, it is in turn connected to progressively thicker ropes to which are attached all ancillary lines including the messenger used for recovering equipment, telephone line used for secure communication between the two vessels and distance lines used to indicate the distance between the two vessels All these lines are removed as they come inboard on the receiving vessel and moved to their respective points, until eventually the main wire span is hauled across. This is attached by the receiving ship by a slip and then the rope used to heave the wire across is removed. The far end of this rope is in turn attached to the hose end, or the hook in the case of the solid replenishment. Once the receiving vessel indicate that the jackstay is connected, the tension is gradually put on the wire using the automatic tension winch (ATW). This enables the wire to be kept at a constant tension and in effect give a ridge wire for the hoses or hook to be pulled across by the receiving vessel. In the case of the probe rig, the probe enters the receiver on the receiving ship, and if enough momentum is available the indicators on the back of the receiver will indicate a correct connection. Should this not happen then the delivering ship will heave the probe out and another try will commence. In the case of a heavy jackstay QRC or NATO 'B' rig the hoses are heaved across the tensioned jackstay and a manual connection is made on the receiving vessel's deck. In the case of a solids RAS, once the jackstay has been tensioned there is a test weight of two tons passed across the rig to prove that all machinery is working properly and capable of supporting the weight. Once this has been done in all cases the rig is now ready for use and pumping or load transfer can commence.

Should an emergency of any description take place during the replenishment, then an emergency breakaway will commence, controlled by the delivering vessel. This will take the role of returning/recovering all equipment in a rapid but safe manner to the delivering ship. Should this not be possible, the ropes will be cut or kept by whichever vessel has them at that particular time. This will then be transferred to the delivery vessel at a safer time after the incident has passed.

Once the replenishment has been completed and all intended stores/fuel have been passed all equipment ropes and wires will be recovered by the delivery ship in a methodical process. This will be recovery of the hoses/hook, followed by all ropes that remain across to the receiving vessel including the telephone line and, lastly, distance line. The vessels can then move apart and continue on their passage.

VERTREP is the transfer of stores in an under-slung net using a helicopter. This is a common evolution for replenishment of stores, lube oil and certain types of ammunition. Replenishment may take place at any time of day or night and in its entirety is a hazardous operation, not least because by the close proximity of the vessels to each other. Should a vital piece of machinery fail on either vessel, i.e. main engine, steering equipment, then a collision could occur very quickly. The weather can play an important part and it is not uncommon for the deck to become awash, and in extreme conditions this could sweep overboard loose equipment and even personnel. All available personal protection equipment, including automatic water-activated lifejackets, are worn by all personnel involved in the evolution, and safety lines are rigged in all areas where safety rails have been removed. However, this does not always prevent the worst predicament of a man overboard, in this case the two ships would initiate an emergency breakaway and launch a rescue boat to recover the unfortunate sailor.

Post-1982, replenishment operations have continued to evolve, and now new and more efficient replenishment rigs and equipment are fitted to newer vessels. These are partially computer controlled, although they still require skilled input from a qualified operator. This does allow the operator to move the loads at higher speeds during a solids RAS, as the computer equates the distance between the two vessels and stops the load on both vessels over the required spot.

Future innovations may include rigs to transfer ever heavier loads of up to five tonnes. This would present considerable engineering challenges but rapid progress is being made in these areas.

Although fraught with technical and navigational difficulties, replenishment operations can have their funny side, as in this one described by Richard Fearnley RFA (Rtd), who was Radio Officer aboard an Ol class ship during the period in question:

Replenishment at sea has always been a major part of the expertise of the Royal Fleet Auxiliary; I have been aboard a supply ship supplying stores to warships on both port and starboard sides of our vessel, with a Vertrep underway at the same time.

This Vertrep operation included a Sea King helicopter with a pallet of supplies slung beneath it taking off from our flight deck, with the port and starboard replenishment rigs all operating at the same time and as if that wasn't enough, our ship was steering a figure of eight at 10 knots.

I have also undertaken RAS under sea conditions that would frighten most seafarers, with Atlantic breakers coming over the bow and the water between the RASing ships literally boiling.

You have to remember that whilst underway the supply and receiving ships come within 30 metres of each other, whereas most ships on sighting one another at sea would normally pass with at least a mile apart, so this RAS operation is a complex piece of navigation for all concerned.

My story starts in the Mediterranean, where it was a perfect day in every sense of the word, with the sun shining, sea state '0' and no swell. We, however, were in the midst of a major NATO exercise, with Greeks, Turks, Americans, Italians and what seemed every nation under the sun all wanting oil from us at the time.

We were one of the biggest Fleet Support Tankers at sea within the NATO fleet at that time, an 'Ol' class

I went onto the bridge, with a sheaf of weather reports and signals plus the usual navigation warnings under my arm as an old ex-American frigate with smoke belching from its flue steamed up beside us, ready for a RAS of FFO (Furnace Fuel Oil). The gunlines went over, and the phone lines connected and the usual pleasantries were exchanged.

We sent over Scotch and cigarettes, whilst the Greek vessel sent over Ouzo and a strikingly disgusting brand of cigarettes nobody had ever heard of! The Captain reminded me of 'Greeks bearing gifts' and smiled and handed the goodies over to me as nobody else wanted them!

Pumping started and our Captain, one of the Scottish no nonsense breed, started to tell this amazing story to while away the time, as the bridge was quite crowded with the Captain, the Officer of the Watch, the Chief Officer, two Quartermasters, and two of my signalmen, and as the RAS would take at least an hour or so his story would be well received and went something like this:

Some time in the early 60s and not long after NATO had been established the Americans decided they needed to bring their fleet into the Mediterranean and work with the British, who incidentally still clung on to their Mediterranean Fleet, being based at Malta and Gibraltar.

An exercise was duly set up and the vessels of most NATO nations joined in, with war simulation and replenishment at sea being one of the major parts of the programme to be undertaken.

The first ship to come alongside the replenishing tanker was an American frigate, and it swept up alongside the RFA, with the 'Stars and Stripes' playing over the tannoy. Gunlines went over, and the US Captain on the bridge wing saluted the rust streaked old RFA alongside his newly painted ship.

Pumping started, and within half an hour the ship had taken on its fuel and had disconnected and the American steamed off into the sunset.

The next ship to come alongside was an old ex-American frigate, who had seen action during the 2nd World War, and liberally smoked her way alongside and wallowed in the wake of the RFA.

The Captain on the bridge wing waved, and our gunlines were fired and the hoses connected. This was also in the days of having no phones, so our signalman waved his flags, but to no avail! No response!

A good hour passed and pumping had ceased and the lines brought in, and our hose rigs winched onboard and our Captain gestured to the Greek ship that the exercise was over and that he could make his way.

Nothing happened.

The Captain then ordered the signalman to send 'Exercise Complete'. The signalman waved his flags several times, but again nothing happened. The Captain then brought out his megaphone and shouted across to the Greek Captain that the exercise was over and he was to proceed!

Still nothing happened.

The Greek Captain just waved back and his ship stayed on station alongside the RFA tanker. The Captain then made a pipe (broadcast over the ship's PA system). 'Do you hear there, do you hear there – any member of the ships company who can speak Greek please come to the bridge. I say again. Any member of the ships company that can speak Greek please come to the bridge.'

Not a soul came up to the bridge, and everyone looked at each other wondering what to do next?

Protocol between NATO countries was quite exacting, and we had certainly followed the rule book thoroughly, as we didn't want to offend the Greeks in any way. Suddenly some fifteen minutes after the pipe, a dirty and greasy stoker appeared from the engine room, as it had taken him all this time to get from the bottom plates to the bridge, and he went up to the Captain and said: 'I speak Greek, Captain, what do you want?'

The Captain looked at the stoker somewhat bemused, and indicated his dilemma and pointed to the Greek frigate still keeping perfect station alongside the ship, and the Captain told the stoker to tell the Greek Captain that the exercise was over and could he proceed!

The stoker nodded his head and went onto the bridge wing, with the megaphone in hand and waved at the Greek Captain to get his attention, and then yelled:

'Hey Greeky! Why don't you **** off – the exercise is over yeh!'

With that the Greek Captain acknowledged the order and his ship steamed off into the sunset, with black smoke belching from its funnel!

We were all laughing on the bridge, as the Greek ship had finished its RAS, and with a wave our two ships parted company, and we were wondering whether the Greek captain was telling the same story, but the other way around!

Appendix 3

Battle Honours

Battle Honours have been awarded to ships of the Royal Navy since the time of the Spanish Armada; these awards are made by the Navy Board on the recommendation of the Battle Honours Committee, and since its inception in 1905, the Royal Fleet Auxiliary has been awarded Battle Honours for various actions.

Listed below are the actions and ships that have been awarded a Battle Honour since 1950.

Korea

Brown Ranger 1950, *Green Ranger* 1951–2, *Maine* 1950, *Wave Baron* 1952, *Wave Chief* 1951–3, *Wave Knight* 1951–3, *Wave Laird* 1950–1, *Wave Premier* 1950–2, *Wave Prince* 1950–3 and *Wave Sovereign* 1952–3.

Falklands 1982

Appleleaf, Bayleaf, Blue Rover, Brambleleaf, Engadine, Fort Austin, Fort Grange, Olmeda, Olna, Pearleaf, Plumleaf, Regent, Resource, Sir Bedivere, Sir Galahad, Sir Geraint, Sir Lancelot, Sir Percivale, Sir Tristram, Stromness, Tidepool and *Tidespring.*

Kuwait 1991

Argus, Bayleaf, Diligence, Fort Grange, Olna, Sir Bedivere, Sir Galahad, Sir Percivale and *Sir Tristram.*

Appendix 4

Marchwood Military Port

By Major (Retd) Robin H G Barton MBE

Background

I was commissioned into the Royal Army Service Corps (RASC) in 1949, and trained as a flotilla officer for the operation of coastal and harbour small craft. I once commanded a platoon of DUKWs and other strange amphibians. In February 1953, I took my platoon to the Netherlands to assist with the consequences of the disastrous seawater flooding. In 1964, prior to the formation of the Royal Corps of Transport (RCT) and the merging of the water transport functions of the Royal Engineers and the RASC, I attended an eighteen-month, RE-managed, Long Transportation Course (qualification symbol TN). This was the first time I had served at Marchwood. The course covered the whole spectrum of military port operating involving the loading and discharge of commercial shipping in ports and across beaches. Marchwood at this time was the training base for all military port operating trades including 'freight handlers.'

Facilities centred on one double-sided jetty with about 5.5 metres of water and a hard which had been developed in the Second World War as a major base for the construction and assembly of the floating roadways for Mulberry Harbour. This jetty was constructed for the import of aggregate and Portland cement for the bulk production of concrete for the 'beetles' and for the assembly in the water of the beetles and 'whales' that comprised Mulberry's ten miles of floating roadway. A major bonus was that Marchwood was rail served. A small commercial freighter alongside was the principal training facility.

My Training

The Long TN course provided a thorough grounding in the best port operating practice. It included lengthy practical attachments to the London docks (Port of London Authority), Liverpool Docks (Mersey Docks & Harbour Board) and a major shipping company, in my case Liverpool's Harrison Line. There were also extensive exercises in the West Country following the concept of the Port Emergency Planning (PEP) scheme in which ocean-going ships, moored in deep water, would be discharged by coastal shipping and lighterage into minor ports or across beaches. Other modules included practical railway training with attachments to railway regions, in my case Eastern Region of British Railways.

We emerged with practical experience of just about everything concerned with getting cargo through a port and into a ship, and then the process in reverse. I had personally been sent to the top of a mast to inspect it and deep into ballast tanks, the latter an act of pure sadism. At Marchwood, there was very little passage of cargo, military or otherwise, through the port; training was pre-eminent. There were rumbles of a miraculous new Landing Ship Logistic to be named *Sir Lancelot*, but none of us had ever seen it. At the conclusion of the course in 1965, and at the time of the formation of the RCT, I was posted on exchange to the US Army Transportation Center at Fort Eustis, Virginia. I was engaged in training US Army stevedore companies and small craft crews, prior to their deployment to Vietnam. I took part in the extensive Logistics Over the Shore (LOTS) operations on Virginia's Atlantic beaches, and these employed some very impressive US Navy auxiliary ships. I was in the United States during the Aden withdrawal operation, in which *Sir Lancelot* was blooded. I returned to UK late in 1968 and was appointed OC 52 Port Squadron RCT at Marchwood.

Marchwood 1968 and the national dock strike

I arrived back in Marchwood just in time for the great national dock strike of 1968. By now, the new LSLs were coming into service. These were operated, as the troopships had been, by the British India Steam Navigation Co Ltd (BI) with British officers and Chinese crews. They were smart and shiny in their traditional 'blue band margarine' livery. Some of the capacity was employed on the regular resupply of the British Army of the Rhine (BAOR) with military cargo from Marchwood to Antwerp. General cargo in containers was largely shipped through commercial ports. The dock strike proved to be a catalyst. Cargo for BAOR that would have been shipped commercially was diverted to Marchwood for shipment by LSL and even the RCT's own LCTs. Container handling was improvised and craneage had to be hired, but it was a start. The LCTs managed to take twenty or more containers in the tank decks. Various unsavoury looking characters in small boats hung around like a ring of wolves, and more collected at the gates, but no interruption was attempted. A breakthrough had been made and a new principle established.

Commercial cargo could be routed through a military port for transportation in service ships.

Marchwood operations

The 17 Port Regiment RCT had two port squadrons – 51 and 52. Typically, one squadron would operate the military port for a period of months while the other would concentrate on training, exercises and standby for deployment overseas. The roles would then be rotated. The 'duty' port squadron would deal with every aspect of assembling and loading export cargo, and the discharge and clearance of incoming cargo. After the dock strike a more formal, dedicated line of communication was established through Antwerp for the re-supply of BAOR, and utilising the LSLs. Most important was the transportation of armour, and ammunition and explosives.

Marchwood, benefiting from its extensive land area requisitioned in wartime, held a valuable explosives licence. Ammunition safety was of paramount importance. We used to joke that if Marchwood had a bad day, Winchester would have a beach! Hyperbole, of course, but anyone with a glazing contract in Southampton would have enjoyed a luxurious retirement. Relations with the LSLs had the highest priority. I personally met every incoming LSL to greet the captain and chief officer, whatever the hour. I think I knew enough about the sea to comprehend their problems and many became personal friends.

The LSLs were tasked by MoD Army Q (Mov) 1. There was constant training going on between ourselves and the LSLs at every level. The LSL detachments from the squadrons were deployed with the LSLs to discharge the ships at a foreign port, as necessary. Much training was done with Mexeflote to improve efficiency and safety. If an LSL deployed side-carrying Mexeflote, the RCT crew would keep continuous watch on it while at sea, and of course operate it when launched. *Sir Lancelot*, the class prototype, always had problems with Mexeflote. She could not side-carry a raft in its standard configuration of three cells three wide. Thus one rake had to be taken apart and carried as individual cells on deck. This caused all sorts of launching problems when joining up the individual cells in the water, which was difficult and highly dangerous. The five 'production' LSLs with a raised foredeck had no such problems and could side-carry complete rafts. The squadrons always took part when the LSLs did their annual beaching trials at Lulworth or Worbarrow Bay.

Libya withdrawal operation

In September 1969, Libya's Revolutionary Command Council under Colonel Gaddafi deposed King Idris and assumed control of the country. In December, Britain announced that it would withdraw its military presence, mainly RAF El Adem and an army training base at Tobruk, by 31 March 1970. At short notice, I was appointed Port Commandant Tobruk. I deployed with about one half of my squadron to Libya and the majority of us arrived at El Adem on 1 January 1970. The balance, with two full sized Mexeflote rafts, our heavy equipment and MHE, arrived on *Sir Geraint* on 16 January. We occupied much of Tobruk harbour's limited facilities, including a hard and one deep-water jetty of inadequate length, accessed by a weak bridge. *Empire Gull*, which was already in theatre as the Mediterranean supply ship, was available for the operation. This was a fascinating, tough old steam ship from another age, with about two thirds of the cargo capacity of the LSL. It had bow ramp loading stressed for tanks and fifteen-ton derricks, but was not drive-through. This caused problems when loading large vehicles, which had to be backed on. Our mission was to bring out everything of value from El Adem, the training base and the military infrastructure. *Empire Gull* was really the star of the show. She made seven sailings to Cyprus and one to Malta. Three LSLs, *Sir Geraint*, *Sir Percivale* and *Sir Tristram*, made a total of nine sailings between them, eight to Marchwood and one to Malta.

The LSLs in the early stages concentrated on the shipment of armour (thirty-three MBTs), other A vehicles, abnormal loads and 945 tons deadweight of bombs, ammunition and explosives, mainly from El Adem. In addition, three commercial ships were chartered to make single voyages to the UK. A total of 772 vehicles were recovered. Overall, cargo shipments totalled 38,902 tons. Tobruk was an area taken by surprise. There was no containerisation or even palletisation. This was thousands of tons of general cargo in its most chaotic and labour-intensive state. The final act of withdrawal was made on 28 March 1970 with the simultaneous sailing, fully laden, of *Sir Geraint* and *Empire Gull*. *Sir Geraint* also carried the senior officers, our Infantry screen and ourselves. It was full to the last bunk, because the airfield had long since been closed. We departed three days early to successfully wrong-foot Gaddafi's rent-a-mob. My last memory of Tobruk is of the harbourmaster's tug planing along behind *Sir Geraint* like a pram dinghy while its crew wrestled to release the tow wire. (Much amusement – it's a hard world!) To my mind it absolutely proved the concept of the new LSLs with Mexeflote lighterage, working with a well-trained port squadron, to handle a complex situation covering the whole spectrum of military equipment at short notice in a basically hostile, foreign location.

Marchwood after Libya

Empire Gull had so proved herself in Libya that it she was retained in service. She came back to Marchwood to form the backbone of the dedicated line of communication to BAOR. In all weathers, she plodded her relentless way back and forth to Antwerp, thus freeing an LSL for wider operations. At about this time, the LSL fleet began to change over from BI operation to join the RFA and MoD Navy. This was a slow process as one by one the Chinese crews withdrew, old friends appeared in slightly different uniforms, the blue bands disappeared and the ships came back from refit in battleship grey, all except *Empire Gull*. The 'Black Pig' remained stubbornly black until the end. There were new faces everywhere and we were off once again on an endless round of Mexeflote training and beaching exercises. Perhaps the most noticeable and immediate change came in radio communications. The Marconi radio officers of BI management lacked the equipment and training to meet current service communications requirements. The RFA soon brought that area bang up to date.

Marchwood in the 1970s

In late 1970, having been to British Transport Staff College, I became Senior Instructor of Port Division of what became the School of Transport. This was co-located at Marchwood. Port Division trained all other ranks in the port trades and all RCT officers at some stage in their careers. Specialist courses were held for all officers joining 17 Port Regiment. Training was still given in the traditional 'sticks and string' disciplines of stevedoring and a retired freighter, *Woodlark*, was retained for that purpose. However, training was evolving more and more to the modern world of containerisation, roll-on/roll-off (ro-ro) shipping and of course the LSLs. Liaison with the LSLs was paramount and every opportunity was taken for trainees at every level to gain practical, hands-on experience aboard these. Some exercises were specifically held for our training purposes. Eventually, an RCT warrant officer (WO2) was added to the complement of each LSL to assist the captain in the management of military matters and training.

The 1970s saw an increasing pattern of major exercises and operations involving the LSLs and the port squadrons, mounted from Marchwood. The winter 'Hardfall' series took the Royal Marines to Norway. A major amphibious exercise in the Netherlands, before the completion of the North Sea Barrier between the islands, involved an LSL, LCTs, a commercial ship and the whole of 17 Port Regiment. All the material successfully landed was maintenance cargo for BAOR diverted through the exercise. Perhaps the biggest of all was Exercise 'Forte 76', a tri-national logistics exercise (Britain/France/Germany) directed by the French. By now I was second-in-command of 17 Port Regiment and in charge of the regiment's contribution. The British commitment included *Sir Lancelot*, *Empire Gull*, RCT LCTs and RCLs and a port squadron.

An amphibious, logistic landing was made at Merville-Franceville-Plage near the mouth of the Caen Canal and close to the D-Day beaches. A whole week's supply of BAOR maintenance cargo was landed across the beach into a transit area that was normally the seafront car park, for clearance via a railhead. This included a decent tonnage of live ammunition and explosives! This would never be authorised today but luckily for me all went well.

At the end, in a moment of relaxation, *Sir Lancelot* provided some exquisite entertainment. She was anchored off with her stern ramp fully extended. Something serious failed at the outboard end and it collapsed into the water seconds after the chief officer had dived off the end for a swim! (I think his name was Bob Day?) There was so much laughter that there was unseemly delay in fishing 'choff' out of the oggin. There then followed the unusual spectacle of *Sir Lancelot* steaming up and down at ever increasing speeds to get this wretched ramp to plane high enough for some brave souls to get wires onto it. It was eventually recovered and secured, never to move again. But there was a problem. With no stern ramp there was no way of getting our heavy plant from the beach into the ship by Mexeflote. The French came up with a brilliant solution. (They wanted to get home too!) *Sir Lancelot* was cleared to enter the port of Caen via the canal. Turning round in the final basin had bits of greenery stuck in the guardrails at both ends of the ship. All our plant and equipment eventually made it the docks to be loaded through the bow or craned on. Then there was a real run ashore. By the time we sailed the next morning the word had got around. Old-and-bold veterans lined the canal and there were euphoric scenes at Pegasus Bridge. There was some real 'entente cordiale' that day.

The Falklands (Operation 'Corporate')

As 1982 approached, I was in an engineering R&D appointment and anticipating retirement. I was recalled to 17 Port Regiment at Marchwood to be second-in-command for the second time.

As the Falklands situation deteriorated, I was called to the MoD to advise on lighterage and improvised means of discharging STUFT shipping. As Operation 'Corporate' was implemented, two LSLs with Mexeflote and port operating equipment sailed immediately from Marchwood for Ascension Island. Some personnel flew. Others who deployed will comment on this. At Marchwood the problem was loading commercial taken-up ships with the inadequate depth of water at our single jetty.

Under emergency exemptions, Marchwood personnel took part in the loading of STUFT ships throughout the port of Southampton. Ammunition in large quantities was lightered by Mexeflote to *Europic Ferry* (she was instantly nicknamed 'erotic fairy'). We worked night and day stowing and shoring. An army mobile crane (with operator) was chained and welded to her upper deck for overside discharge. Marchwood became a vast assembly area for vehicles and cargo to be called forward to Southampton as required. Marchwood teams also assisted in the stowage of many ships elsewhere from Southampton. I remember in particular the ill-fated *Atlantic Conveyor* at Plymouth. Small Marchwood detachments, with plant as necessary, went with the majority of commercial ships. Throughout the operation, what was left of 17 Port Regiment beavered away to provide base support and reinforcements of personnel and material. Later, I was a member of the team that drew up the specification for the replacement *Sir Galahad*. My area was, of course, Mexeflote and cargo handling.

After the operation, over many months Marchwood received back shiploads of recovered vehicles, damaged or otherwise, salvage, and thousands of tons of stores, much of it by LSL. The worst event occurred in late autumn when eighty war dead were repatriated by LSL to Marchwood in a standard twenty-foot container. Families and press were present as the container, shrouded in the biggest union flags we could get, was taken to an improvised mortuary in the main cargo shed for individual processing and placing in coffins prior to release for funerals all over the country. It was all over national television that night. No one who was present will ever forget this chilling and emotional experience. It must have been dictated by transport limitations but it should never have been allowed. The bodies should have been decently coffined elsewhere before being returned to the UK with the level of dignity that obtains today.

Port rebuild

The Falklands campaign was the catalyst that resulted in the eventual rebuild of the Marchwood Military Port. After years of justifications and presentations, the Marchwood rebuild earned its green light.

At one final presentation, aboard an LSL, the QMG said informally, 'When I got this job I was told to get the Army some decent boots and sort out Marchwood.' With the temerity that comes with increasing years I had the cheek to say, 'At Marchwood, General, we are not too fussed about the boot's. To my intense relief the great man laughed, otherwise it would have been the Tower for me. The rebuild was completed for, I believe, about £18 million, almost peanuts today. It provides the magnificent Falklands deep water jetty, which can accept almost any service or commercial logistic ship. It also provides for the separation of the training and administrative functions to the rear of the area, leaving the waterfront clear for port operations and the assembly of cargo. There is also a much-improved safety provision for ammunition and hazardous cargo in transit by rail or road.

Nostalgia

I spent one half of my forty-year army life in and around Marchwood and the LSL fleet. I even wrote some of the army bits for the LSL Handbook. I always thought McIver Roberts' design was a superb compromise between so many conflicting requirements and constraints. I think those of us who served together in the LSL world and at Marchwood did come to share a common bond. It is dangerous to mention too many names; it rapidly becomes unfair. But I cannot look back on those years without remembering in particular three captains who I count as friends. Captain Christopher Purtcher-Wydenbruck of *Sir Percivale* from the BI days. Always calm and courteous. The outrageously extrovert Captain Barry Rutterford – on one exercise he had a combined operations logo painted on two round cargo boards and had them fixed to the funnel, one either side. He let it be known that he should be known as Captain (L). Finally, Captain Phil Roberts who coped so well with the horrors of *Sir Galahad*. I could go on, but I sense that this is a good time for a brown job to stop.

References

General and ships

Adams, Thomas A, and James R Smith, *The Royal Fleet Auxiliary: A century of service* (London: Chatham, 2005).

Hannan, W, *Fifty Years of Naval Tugs* (Liskeard: Maritime Press, 1985).

James, Tony, *The Royal Fleet Auxiliary* (Liskeard: Maritime Press, 1985).

Kennedy, Greg (ed), *British Naval Strategy East of Suez 1900–2000: Influences and actions* (London: Frank Cass, 2003).

Puddefoot, Geoff, *No Sea Too Rough: The Royal Fleet auxiliary in the Falklands War: The untold story* (London: Chatham, 2007).

Sigwart E E, *Royal Fleet Auxiliary* (London: Adlard Coles, 1969).

Personnel

Force 4, newsletter of the Royal Fleet Auxiliary 1978–85.

Gunline, newsletter of the Royal Fleet Auxiliary 1986–2009.

National Archive, Kew:

Files consulted included those with the following department or series codes:

ADM – Admiralty papers	DEFE – Ministry of Defence
AIR – Air Ministry	FO – Foreign Office papers
BT – Board of Trade	T – Treasury papers
CAB – Cabinet papers	

Further information is available at the National Archive website at: www.nationalarchives.gov.uk

Deployments

Britain's small wars web site: www.britains-smallwars.com

Newspapers

The Times archive.

Various international, national and local newspaper archives.

Websites

www.royalnavy.mod.uk	www.toysoutofthepram.com
www.navy-matters.beedall.com	www.navaltankermen.com

Index